INTERIORS
A Black Woman's
Healing...
in Progress

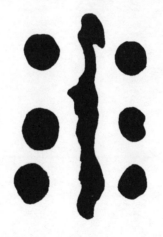

INTERIORS

A Black Woman's
Healing...
in Progress

Iyanla
Vanzant

Writers and Readers

Published for **Harlem River Press** by:
Writers and Readers Publishing, Inc.
P.O. Box 461, Village Station
New York, New York 10014

Cover and Book Design: Terrie Dunkelberger

ISBN 0-86316-321-1

0 9 8 7 6 5 4 3 2 1

Manufactured in the United States of America

This book is dedicated to

God, "the Divine Mother,"
manifesting in me and through me as
Yemoja, Oshun, and Oya,
who never asked me for credentials I did not have

and
in loving memory of
Sarah Jefferson, my mother
Lynnette May Brown Harris, my "Mommy" and best friend
Nancy McCullum, my aunt
Ruth Carlos, my first real sister

and to
Elvia "Omi Relekun" Myrie
Wilhelmina and Alfonso Myrie
Roseanne Logan
Melba Ramsey
Marjorie Battle
Stephanie Weaver
Denise "Ola" DeJean
Tulani Jordan–Kinard
Linda Green Beatty
Gemmia Lynnette Vanzant
Nisa Camille Vanzant
who saw my insanity and loved me anyway

and to
Susan L. Taylor,
who opened the door

Bebe Moore Campbell, who turned the key

Marie Brown,
who was the tool God used to point my feet
in the right direction.

TABLE OF CONTENTS

PART 3
Then There Was...
159

PART 4
Let There Be...
269

ACKNOWLEDGMENTS

Glenn Thompson, publisher of Writers and Readers Press, who bought the idea of this book without ever having seen one word on paper;

Debra Dyson, Beth, Wilhemina, and the rest of the staff at Writers and Readers, who continue to put up with me, and who, in my most insane moments, know exactly what to say to me;

Oluwo Oshun Kunle Erindele, who never stops affirming me and reminding me how beautiful I am, and who continues to teach me and show me the magnificent way of "spirit";

Gemmia Lynnette Vanzant, my daughter, who lent me her poems, "And One Day My Soul Opened Up," "Nobody Ever Asks," and "There Are Times," which are presented in the journal pages of this work. Thank you for being there when there was no one else to listen, to hear, or to care.

Alex Morgan, who, in concert with my daughter Gemmia, created my brand new grandchild and let me pick the name;

Yusef Harris, who, in my hour of need, brought me a brand new laser printer that really worked;

All African American women, Latin American women, Native American women, and Caribbean women who continue to muster up the strength, courage, and resources to heal themselves and the rest of the world.

I salute you all.

INTRODUCTION

I was born in Brooklyn, New York, in a taxicab, beneath the tracks of an elevated train. I am convinced that the circumstances of my birth have caused the many fluctuations in my life. Like traffic, I have been jammed. Like a car, I have broken down at the most inopportune moments. At times, I have been like a train, moving along with great speed despite the fact that I was carrying a heavy burden. At other times, I have crawled along, barely moving. There were times when I had a full tank of gas, but there were also many times I ran on "E." When I reflect on the sum of my experiences, I must admit that I have truly been "driven."

I have not had an easy life. What I have had is a series of empowering experiences that made no sense to me at the time they occurred. Taken all together, however, I would not change them one bit. The pain, abuse, confusion, and stagnation in my life have brought me to a sacred place within myself. It is in that place that I have found the peace, wealth, and love I have been searching for in this world.

What my life's experiences have taught me is that no matter what one sees, there is always more. There is so much we cannot physically see, touch, or comprehend because we are so much more than a physical body. Our bodies are the tools, the instruments through which we interpret our experiences, but unless we find another way of looking at the things we experience, we will lose the most sacred part of the self.

There is a power within each of us that defies all obstacles and laws of humankind. Had I known and accepted this principle long ago, I would have been spared a great deal of wear and tear on my "bumpers." The power I am referring to comes from the Creator. Each of us acquired it with the first breath of life. This power stays with us throughout our lives. It can guide us through individual growth and universal evolution. It is our life-preserver when we are drowning and our light when we are in darkness. We must simply turn the power on, follow its shining guidance, and give thanks for its presence. The power is "Spirit." In today's society, which each day makes less sense to the conscious mind, we must draw upon the power of spirit in order to grow and evolve.

Among all of the jewels stripped from Africans during their enslavement, the loss of spiritual culture and practices may have been the most devastating. Stripped from their land, our ancestors lost contact with Nature, which had provided them with resources and strength. Forbidden to practice their traditional culture, they lost the cohesiveness that had been maintained through tradition. Forced to abandon their native languages, they lost the medium for the translation of their experiences and the salvation of their knowledge. Trapped by a dehumanizing system of oppression, they lost contact with one another. They did not, however, lose their faith or the strength they found within themselves. They held on to their spirit. Like them, in my darkest moments, I have found it necessary to do the same.

Understanding the spirit of our ancestors is critical to the survival of the Black woman in America and beyond. Through the knowledge of the history, traditions, and cultures of Africa, Black women of today can rediscover a depth of identity that supports their innate psyches. African tradition and culture can support Black women in developing an appreciation for who they are now. By contrast, American tradition and culture teaches Black women to play a role that is often offensive, oppressive, and restrictive when measured against their God-given talents, gifts, and abilities. More often than not, the roles Black women play in Western society are determined according to their physical characteristics and material possessions. This is contrasted to precolonial African culture, which teaches that every individual is born to serve a purpose ordained by God. Moreover, that purpose cannot, must not, be altered by human or physical means.

Traditionally, African children are named according to their purpose and mission in life. Thus, each time the child's name is called, his or her spirit, that unconscious psyche, is reminded of what it has come to earth to do. The family and community have a vested interest in helping the child not to stray away from his or her God-appointed purpose.

In earlier times, it was considered the responsibility of African parents and the community to provide their children with images and encouragement to which the young could relate in pursuit of their life purpose. Parents served as models and examples for their children. Parenting was a task African parents took very seriously, for they knew the success of their children would ensure them the honor of the community and the blessings of God. They understood that it was their duty and responsibility to work together to raise their children, and they were willing to put aside their personal differences rather than allow them to taint the images they presented to these impressionable ones. Many modern parents of African descent born and raised in America do not have this understanding, for they themselves have been raised to play roles without a connection to purpose.

The images and environments in which many African American women are raised are not consistent with living a life of purpose; rather, they support role playing. Women must be dainty, delicate, subservient, and silent, we are told. Women must be followers, not leaders. Women should not have needs, desires, or ambitions that stretch beyond their prescribed roles. If the woman happens to be of the darker hue, the stakes are even higher. If she is not docile, she is dangerous. If she is outspoken, she is not respected. If she cannot be controlled, if she does not play the role, she must be destroyed. During my childhood in the 1950s, the public images of women were white domesticated servants or brazen, foul-mouthed harlots. Women of that era of any hue were offered few images that supported their yearning and searching for or—heaven forbid—finding purpose. In this scenario, Black women were all but totally ignored.

As a descendant of Africans born in America, I was not taught or supported in leading a purposeful life. My family considered and treated me as a burden following the death of my mother. As a result, my childhood bounced between having and not having, needing and not needing. The many adult conversations I overheard during my youth, along with the treatment I received, led me to conclude that something was wrong with me. My birth name, "Rhonda," which means "one who is loved and adored," was not supported by the actions of my caregivers. Early programming, which led me to believe that I was "bad," "not good enough," and incapable of doing anything "right," fueled my feelings of unworthiness and undeservedness.

As a child, I blamed myself for my misfortunes. As an young adult, I blamed others. For years I suffered from the BYHAW ("Beating Your Head Against the Wall") Syndrome. I could not figure out why I was not getting ahead, why my relationships were not working, why I experienced so much lack and restriction in my life. Why was I so unhappy deep down inside?

I was blessed one day to discover that I was the obstacle in my own way. I was the wall I had to tear down. I had lost touch with myself. I was mentally and emotionally separated from my spirit. I had many lessons to learn. I had to become reacquainted with the part of myself that held the secrets I needed to flourish in life.

These lessons were very difficult to accept, and the connection was often difficult to make. I had to be persistent, disciplined, and, most of all, ready. However, when I thought I was ready, I was not. When I thought I was not, I was. The mysteries of spirit are not always logical and rational.

The universe is so wonderful about answering our questions and providing us with guidance. My guidance came through exposure to the Yoruba culture, which provided me with a philosophy and principles around which I could structure my life. The learning materials came in the form of guidance from many wise and loving people and relationships that helped me to alter my self-perception. Through them, I learned that the most difficult lessons in life are oftentimes not the hard and painful ones but the simple ones, the ones right in front of our faces. The ones that seem so insignificant we often ignore them, and consequently ignore ourselves and the quiet voice that speaks from within, loving us, guiding us, protecting us.

Most, if not all, of my lessons in life have come through relationships. Family relationships, friendships, and, of course, relationships with men. Relationships are our training ground. They bring to us, through the body of another person, the secret thoughts and feelings we do not take the time to explore on our own. Most of us have bad relationships because we harbor bad thoughts and feelings. In this book I will share with you some of the more, shall I say, "memorable" relationships in my life because they have taught me the most powerful lessons. However, I must confess at the outset that I do not blame any of the men who have passed through my life for anything that has happened to me. It was not their fault. No matter what it looked like or what they did, my life was the reflection of the dark, secret thoughts I harbored in the depths of my own being. All of the men, indeed all of the people, in my life were merely a reflection of one thing: the relationship I was having with myself. That is all there is in life—the relationship you have with you, and the relationship you have with God. I now realize that I was blessed to have had someone come along and bring these truths to the surface. As I learned to look within, to live an internal life, my external life flourished.

As we grow, whatever is inside us must come out. If something in your life is not God-like, peaceful, loving, joyous, powerful, honest, and developmental, it is not God. It is you. Until you move beyond appearances to the essence of who you are, which is spirit, you will see and experience some pretty ugly things. When it comes out, it may look horrible. Like cleaning out a closet, a mess must be made before order can prevail.

This work is about my journey within and the empowerment I received from connecting with and healing that part of myself that was wounded, ugly, horrible. On this journey, I have discovered that the quest toward spiritual enlightenment must not be seen as a task or chore. It should be, must be, a conscious process and choice to revitalize the parts of your mind, body, and spirit from which you have been separated. The primary and most basic principle you must accept is that there is one Creator whose spirit and energy lives within each and every one of us. It does not matter what you call it, you must simply acknowledge its presence. As a priestess initiated into the Yoruba culture, I recognize the Creator as Olodumare. You may choose to call this life force by another name. I will leave that to you. What is important is that you take control of your life by developing a loving, healing process of connection to the spirit of the power within you.

When I was twelve years old, I had a vision. A beautiful woman appeared before me. She spoke to me, saying, "Look within, that is where your power is. That is where your beauty is. Before you can feel powerful and look beautiful, you must be powerful and know you are beautiful." In a flash, she was gone. At twelve, I had no idea what she meant or how I was to go about doing what she instructed me to do. Besides that, I had no idea who the woman was or why she was in the bathroom mirror talking to me. I thought I had lost my mind. I had not. Not yet, anyway. It took twenty years, two suicide attempts, several unhealthy relationships, an abusive marriage, three children, and a flaming inferiority complex before I understood what that woman meant.

The day that I stood face-to-face with insanity, the woman appeared again. This time she explained to me quite simply how to rebuild my life: "Begin within," she said. This is the story of my trip to personal insanity and back. It is the story of a journey that produced a healing that is still in progress.

I consider it a blessing that I have not only survived but flourished through my experiences. When I think of the millions of Black women who did not make it and of the other millions who fail to realize, no matter what is going on, that they are making it, I truly understand how blessed I am.

I once learned in a seminar never to ask the question, "Why me?" In asking that question, one is challenging the wisdom of the universe, the creative ability of the Divine Mind. A better question to ask is, "What can I learn from this?" or "How can I use this?" When I began to ask those questions, I realized I could use my experiences as a road map to support other people in healing themselves and regaining their spiritual power. As a writer, speaker, and teacher, I could use my experiences as tools of empowerment. I could use my own experience as the basis for healing the hearts, minds, and spirits of others.

The question then arose: "Who shall I focus my time, energy, and attention upon?" Of course, like draws like, so Black women became the most likely candidates. Yet, pain and suffering are not racially based; they are based universally on a lack of knowledge of self. Therefore, anyone who can use this information should feel free to do so.

Once I was clear about what, how, why, and who, I had to develop a mission and a method. Europeans call it a goal. Africans call it a mission. In putting these words on paper, I had to have a mission. It was not enough to simply write a book and make money. Something more had to take place, needed to be accomplished. I prayed about this and meditated on it. The answer came to me at 4 o'clock one afternoon as I was driving in my car. My daughter wrote what I said on a napkin. I now share it with you.

I write this book for every young, Black girl who has ever felt ugly, unloved, and unwanted. For every woman who loved her daddy, missed her daddy, and is still looking for him in the arms and beds of men who also love and miss their daddies. I write this book for every young girl who knows there is something she must do that no one else can do except her, so that she can remember these words when everyone tells her what she wants is impossible to do. I write this book for every Black woman who is struggling, suffering, jumping over hurdles, and moving through obstacles, so that she may realize she is "a king's kid"—born to inherit the kingdom. My mission in writing this book is to convey one simple message: God loves you, Black woman, and God is depending on you to spread that love to everyone else in the world.

In the 40-plus years of my journey, I have encountered many Black women who are lost or losing themselves. This book is for them and their journey.

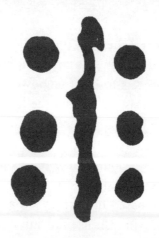

If she be a wall,
We will build upon her a battlement of
silver;
If she is a door,
We will enclose her with boards of cedar.
I am a wall, and my breasts like towers;
Then, I became His eyes,
As one who found peace.

Song of Solomon, 8:9-10

PART I

In the
Beginning...

THE Journal

When we are born, we are like blocks of stone, rough and unhewn, ready to be sculpted. Like an empty canvas, we stand ready to be filled with the colors of life. As we live, we are shaped by our experiences. Dark experiences, difficult lessons, all are etched into our consciousnesses to form the habits and behavior patterns we drag through life and obstacles we must overcome. The images we see are pictures in which we live consciously and unconsciously. The people with whom we have contact are the chisels and hammers that craft what we will become. Our life's journey is an ever-unfolding work of art that tells the story of where we have been and with whom we have traveled.

The creations we become bring to life the issues of the people who work on us. In some cases, these individuals are skilled and talented life artists, who, with careful commitment and loving attention to detail, are capable of creating masterpieces of grace, power, and beauty. When the artists are blocked, careless, inattentive, or uncommitted, the images of life they create become the kinds of work others must squint at in order to figure out what is going on. These misdirected artists create with bold strokes, slashing marks, or dripping dabs, resulting in a distorted picture of the self. The impressionable forms that careless sculptors create with careless chiseling and unmindful hammering become misshapen, chipped figurines.

The colors bleed rather than blend. The quarried stone becomes contorted. The portrait, worthless.

My life canvas was splashed early with dark experiences, all bleeding together to create images of senseless pain and uncreative misery. My life portrait was dark, distant, and hopeless, shaped by guilt and shame, pieced together with fear and anger, galvanized by dishonesty and delusion. I did not know that, like stone, I could be reshaped, molded into a new image. It took quite a while for me to realize I could erase the dark images by using brighter colors; that I could repair the rips in the canvas with loving care and paint a new picture merely by understanding who I was. I had no idea that all I had to do was take the brush from the hands of the neglectful artists and say ENOUGH!

First, I had to admit that the old picture existed, that the old figure was misshapen. That was the hard part. It was an ugly picture, a grotesque form. It was a painful experience.

All the images floating in my mind convinced me that I was not worth saving, that I was a waste of time and energy. Better people than I had tried to "fix" me and had given up in despair. Yet, something deep inside me did not allow me to believe that I was worthless. I could examine. I could erase. I could create a new tapestry, picture, form. And even if I failed, I was willing to try.

CHAPTER 1

The Blank Canvas

GRANDMA...

I remember all the excitement about finding something new for me to wear. I remember getting a gray coat with a matching hat and a muff from May's Department Store. I remember the steady stream of people in and out of the house. I remember the armloads of food they brought and how Grandma spread it out on the kitchen table. I remember them saying how sad "it" was. I remember them asking what was going to happen to "you know, the children." I remember Grandma waking me up, washing me, dressing me, putting me in a chair, and ordering me to sit still until it was time to go. I remember walking down the eight flights of stairs and getting into the big black car. I remember getting slapped on my hand for playing with the handle that opened the windows of the limousine. I know I was almost three years old, but I cannot for the life of me remember anything else about my mother's funeral.

I do not remember anyone ever explaining to me that my mother had died. I am not saying they did not explain, I just do not remember. I do not remember anyone rocking me, holding me, or telling me everything would be alright. Perhaps they did. Maybe they did not. I do not remember seeing my mother in the casket, although they tell me I did. I do not remember picking a flower from the wreath, even though I still have the flower. I do not remember crying or hurting or missing my mother. In fact, I do not remember her at all. The one thing I remember is all the food that people brought to the house. I also remember the only thing that stood between me and

4

the food was Grandma.

My paternal grandmother was a big woman, about five feet-ten inches tall. She was thick, not fat. She had a full head of salt-and-pepper hair, one of her most outstanding features. Her Cherokee heritage gave her broadly chiseled cheekbones and tiny, inset eyes. "Sister Harris," as she was called, was the backbone of any group because she worked harder and talked faster than anybody else. Everyone came to her for guidance and consolation because she knew what to do.

The main thing I remember about Grandma was her demeanor. She was always cool, until you crossed her. And when you did, she would bang one of her large hands on the table, squint her already tiny eyes at you, and begin a tirade that would last for hours, or days if it was a matter of her being corrected about anything. Nobody ever wanted to cross Grandma, and they did not.

Grandma was my primary caretaker after my mother's death. Unfortunately, no one ever told me that my mother had died. I have a vague recollection of a tall, thin, brown-skinned woman who spent a great deal of time in the bed. Once she was gone, I buried those memories because I had Grandma. Grandma swung between being incredibly loving and nurturing, although somewhat distant, and being incredibly cruel and abusive. She would lovingly prepare a wonderful meal and then slap me for eating too fast or slow. She would patiently and in great detail instruct me in how to perform a task, like cleaning the bathroom or ironing a shirt, then she would scream and curse at me if I made a mistake. I never told anyone I was afraid of Grandma. I did not have to. Everyone in the family, from the distant cousins to the cat, knew it. But they were afraid of her too.

Grandma had a sharp mind although she had never been formally educated. She was also highly spiritual. She saw spirits. She talked to them. She could hear spirits talk to her. Most of the spirits Grandma knew seemed to come from the darker side. I guess they were drawn to her for a reason. Today, Grandma would be considered a psychic, a clairvoyant.

When I was growing up I thought she was a witch. Grandma

could make people do what she wanted them to do merely by looking at them. I thought it was a special power she had. Eventually I realized that people were just plain-old afraid of her. I would not go so far as to say she was evil, but she certainly hung out with evil's first cousin.

Grandma was angry. She was angry at the world and everyone in it. She did not need a reason to be angry. She *was* the reason. And, for some reason, with all of the other people around, Grandma decided to take out most of her anger on me.

My grandmother's typical assessment of me was, "You ain't shit! You ain't never gonna be shit! You are just like your daddy!" Between the ages of two and twenty-one, I heard that negative affirmation at least once a day when I was in Grandma's company. She did not think too highly of my father—her son—whom I thought was a pretty decent guy. That is, until Grandma gave me the real scoop. She constantly complained about him to me and me to him. Compared to my brother, my father and I simply did not measure up, but, for the life of me, I could not figure out what I was doing so wrong to rate so low in Grandma's eyes. No matter what I did, it was not right or good enough.

Grandma taught me how to pray, and she prayed for me. When she was not praying, Grandma was pinching me, poking me, or backhanding me upside my face for one thing or another I had or had not done. She would often preface these assaults with, "God knows you deserve it," and I believed her. In my prayers I asked Grandma's God to help me do right. As I grew older, I came to believe that God had given Grandma a certain deep, spiritual understanding about me. I also learned that she had developed even deeper character flaws.

Grandma insisted that I bathe with homemade soap and oil my body with olive oil. Grandma's soap was brown, odorless, and contained lots of little sticks and leaves that pricked my skin. I hated it. It made me smell so "clean." I wanted to use Camay soap and Pond's cold cream like all my friends. You could smell the sweetly perfumed scent of these products on their bodies if the wind was blowing or if they were sweating. Grandma would not hear of it. Olive oil, she claimed, was holy oil. Moreover, she said, "There's a lot of things you can't see that you've got to be protected against." I never understood the significance of what she was saying until much later in life.

Grandma always got up before dawn. Some days, if I got up to make a potty run, I would see her sitting by the kitchen window with her Bible in her lap and a small candle burning. She would sit there, staring at the sky without blinking. I could walk right up to her and she would not move.

I remember days when it was barely light out and Grandma would come into my room and rub my body down with a thick yellow substance. She called it "waterproofing." It was actually lamb's mutton. She would tell me, "It's going to rain today and we don't want a cold," and without fail, before the day was over, the rain would come. I thought my grandmother knew everything. She was weird, but she knew everything.

Grandma had a small mahogany night table where she kept jars of colorful little pebbles. She burned those pebbles in a small black frying pan. I could tell by the scent what the day would bring. If the smell was sweet and lingering, we were having company. If it was a mixture of sweet and pungent, we were going out. If the smell was heavy, almost overpowering, Grandma didn't feel well. Grandma never spoke about the purpose or meaning of those scents, and I never questioned her. As an adult, I spent a great deal of money buying incense before I understood the true meaning of the different aromas.

One morning when I woke up, Grandma was in her usual place at the window, but something was different. Grandma was rocking and moaning. I walked up to her and saw tears rolling down her face. I panicked. I began crying and screaming at her, "Grandma, wake up! Please don't cry!" She cried, rocking and moaning, for what seemed like hours. Suddenly, she stopped, opened her eyes, and said to me, "What are you doing walking on the floor without your slippers?" I couldn't believe it. She never wiped her face. Her tears dried instantly. My eyes and nose were running profusely. Grandma wiped my face with her apron and said, "Hurry, now. Run to the potty and then get dressed. We've got to go to Virginia."

Uncle Jimmy, my grandmother's older brother, lived in Smithfield, Virginia, with his wife, Aunt Mattie. Uncle Jimmy was a bootlegger, and Aunt Mattie was, in my opinion, the best cook ever to walk the face of the earth. I could hardly wait to wrap my lips around one of her hot, honey-dipped biscuits. Grandma didn't say a word during the entire eight-hour bus ride. I chatted on and on endlessly about the trees, the birds, and the blue water in the toilet on the bus. I could hardly wait to see Uncle Jimmy and the chickens. I wondered if the swing he had made for me was still in the tree. I ate the cold chicken sandwiches Grandma had prepared for our trip and wondered what Aunt Mattie was cooking for dinner. When we arrived in Smithfield, Grandma hailed a taxi. It was then I realized that something was terribly wrong. When Uncle Jimmy opened the door, he wasn't surprised to see us. He said, "She's not going to make it. She's in a coma." Grandma responded brusquely, "Hush your mouth and take my bag." They both went into the house and left me standing on the porch. Over the course of the next hour I learned that Aunt Mattie had suffered a stroke. She was a diabetic and refused to stay on her diet. Uncle Jimmy showed us a little blue box containing a hypodermic needle. He told Grandma that he had paid twenty dollars for it, yet Aunt Mattie refused to use it. He also told her, in vivid detail, about Aunt Mattie's convulsions, her refusal to go to the hospital, and her ultimate collapse while feeding the chickens. She was in the "white folks's" hospital, he claimed, because the doctor insisted that she be taken there. Uncle Jimmy could visit her on Saturday the doctor said. It was Tuesday.

Within a matter of hours and over the course of the next few days, the house was filled with the smell of Grandma's little pebbles. It was a new scent I was not familiar with. I didn't like it. I remember vividly that it made me anxious and nervous. I could not keep still, so, to stay out of trouble, I spent a great deal of time in the yard with Fred and Rosie, the pigs. Uncle Jimmy spent the four days until Saturday in the rocking chair on the porch, holding the little blue box. Grandma spent the days washing, starching, and ironing Aunt Mattie's clothes.

In the evenings, we ate dinner in total silence. After dinner,

Grandma and I went into the woods to pick herbs. I was terrified of being in the dark, woody hills. Grandma talking to the bushes did not help matters any. I clung tightly to her skirt because she acted as if I wasn't there. Grandma collected bundles of herbs, which we took back to the porch. There, she picked the leaves off the branches and pounded them in a large washtub. She then took Aunt Mattie's clothes and swished them around in the slimy green herbal concoction. The next morning, she washed these clothes in the wringer washer and hung them on the line to dry. By noon, she was sprinkling and ironing the very same clothes she had washed and ironed the day before.

Between the silence, the smell of the pebbles, the washing and rewashing, and the amount of time I was spending with Fred and Rosie, I was convinced that Grandma had "lost it." However, I knew better than to ask or say anything.

Saturday finally came. We all awoke very early to a bright Virginia sun. To my surprise and delight, Grandma let me wash up with Aunt Mattie's Camay soap and lotion myself with Jergen's. I was literally smelling myself as we drove to town in Uncle Jimmy's big blue Cadillac. When we arrived at the hospital, Uncle Jimmy went upstairs to visit his wife. Grandma and I went to the ice cream parlor. I was totally ecstatic at the sight of the checkered tablecloths and soda fountains. Grandma gave me a dollar. She told me to get myself some ice cream and get her a Coke. The man behind the counter gave me a tray and a big pile of napkins. I think he gave me a little extra ice cream because I told him I was from New York.

I was about to enjoy myself for the first time in four days, but before I could get my lips around the first spoonful of coffee ice cream, Uncle Jimmy came back—with Aunt Mattie.

This could not have been the same woman who had almost fallen dead amidst the chickens, I thought. She strutted ahead of Uncle Jimmy, walked right up to Grandma, and greeted her as if she was the next-door neighbor. We sat around in the ice cream parlor for at least an hour. For the first time, Uncle Jimmy acknowledged my presence. He kept shoving dollar bills into my patent-leather purse, telling me, "A girl always needs to have her own to walk straight in life." Grandma kept giving me the "don't-mess-up-your-clothes" look. Aunt Mattie told us about sleeping in the hospital hallway without a blanket, about not being allowed to brush her teeth, and about how the nurses kept telling her she was as good as dead. I ignored everything except my ice cream and my bulging pocketbook.

Grandma and I left Smithfield on the six o'clock bus Sunday morning. Aunt Mattie gave me a small jar of Lady Esther cold cream. Uncle Jimmy gave me two rolls of quarters, one for myself, one for my brother. Aunt Mattie died, twenty-three years later at the age of seventy-four. She never had another stroke, and, according to Grandma, she never used that needle.

I did not talk much on the trip home. Grandma thought it was because she had let Uncle Jimmy fill me up with junk. That had nothing to do with it. I was simply disappointed that I had spent four days in Virginia and never had a single biscuit.

ᐱᐱᐱ

My grandmother, like many Black women her age, led a very simple life. Simplicity in approaching life and understanding nature are key elements of spirituality. Grandma never went to school, yet she could read the Bible and the newspaper, and she could count money. She believed that wasting time was wasting life, so she never did it. Her days were tightly scheduled as she put her considerable energies toward several useful endeavors.

Grandma was extremely self-reliant. Her experience of being raised on a farm where she picked cotton and peas taught her the value and meaning of work. At age ten, she went to work as a wash girl and cook. At thirteen, she married my grandfather, Lester Harris, a mulatto five years older than she. Grandma told me her mother-in-law hated her because she was a "squaw," but my grandfather did not seem to mind. When she was fourteen, she gave birth to my father, Horace Lester Harris, who was an only child. She was widowed at age sixteen, when my grandfather drowned while fishing. At twenty, she came to New York City with my father and went to work as a domestic and cook.

Grandma lived in the same place for thirty-two years: a

10

fourth-floor walk-up, seven-room apartment in Brooklyn. She was grounded and familiar with her environment, and knew everyone within a ten-mile radius of the place.

Grandma never called herself a spiritualist. She simply claimed she was blessed. She had a little black book—she called her prayer book—that seemed to contain the answers to all of life's problems. When someone was deeply troubled, they came to see my grandmother. The two of them would sit by the kitchen window and discuss the problem. Grandma never allowed me in the kitchen during these private talks; I had to peek around the door to see what was going on. After the talk, Grandma would open the black book, mumble a few words, and then scribble something on a piece of paper. I had no idea what she told the people who came to see her, but they were always thanking her and bringing her gifts afterwards.

Grandma introduced me to spiritual rituals at the age of four. Every Sunday morning, she would scrub me down with her homemade soap, grease my body with olive oil, dress me in my Sunday-go-to-meeting clothes, and pin a small white hankie to the top of my head. We never missed the 8:02 "A" train out of Brooklyn because we had to be at 135th Street by 8:40. Sunday school at the holiness church we attended began promptly at nine o'clock. I would go to class while Grandma and the other "saints" prepared the after-service dinner. At eleven o'clock, the fireworks began.

For many years, I thought church was a woman's club. The handful of men who were around performed menial duties like opening the door and collecting the money. The women, including my grandmother, did the big jobs: the cooking, the caring for the minister, the singing, and the shouting. The shouting was really important because it made the minister smile, and one thing I learned real early about church was that it was important to keep the minister smiling. Like Grandma said, "When the Reverend smiles on you, God smiles on you."

I had no idea what shouting meant, but I knew it changed your status in the church when you did it. Once the spirit "touched" you and made you shout, it became mandatory that you wore white every Sunday. There were at least fifty women in our church who wore white. I thought they were nurses. Once you shouted, it also meant you had to sit in the front row, right near the pulpit.

When I was about five, I got to sit up in the front with Grandma because the spirit touched her. It was a normal Sunday service. As usual, the Reverend began his sermon in a very soft voice. It was hard to hear him, but I remember that he began by telling the congregation what the Lord had said to him. It seemed that the Reverend heard the Lord all the time. I remember wondering how the Lord could speak to so many people without ever coming to church.

The church began to get very noisy. Moment by moment, the Reverend's voice was rising, and people began rocking and humming. The fat ladies began waving their hankies in the air. The skinny ones were crying and moaning "Amen." As the Reverend's voice got louder, the momentum in the room changed. People began shaking their legs, clapping their hands, and jumping up and down. The Reverend started to sweat, which also seemed strange because it felt to me as if the room was getting cooler. The hairs on my arms were standing straight up, and I was getting goose bumps all over. Sooner or later, I knew somebody would let loose the loud wail that would cause a domino effect throughout the congregation.

In every corner of the chapel, people were screaming and crying. The Reverend was sweating profusely and had to open up his jacket. The people in their seats were swaying in rhythm. Someone in the back screamed, "Thank you, Lord" and everybody started clapping simultaneously. The organist began accenting every ten words the Reverend would say with powerful bass chords. The Reverend got down on his knees, moaning and crying. Hankies began flying everywhere. Feet were stamping, hands were clapping, and people were popping up out of their seats in every row of the sanctuary. The ladies in white were running around frantically, trying to catch the fainters and the shouters. As always, I was amazed by these activities, trying to take everything in. This time, however, as my head was turned to watch a man who was shouting over on one side of the room, the spirit touched my grandmother, who, just seconds before, had been sitting next to me in her usual, cool way.

The next thing I knew, Grandma was racing down the aisle, hopping on one foot, waving her hands in the air, and screaming at the top of her lungs, "Save me, Lord, save me!" The white hankie she had pinned to her head flew off. Three nurses were hovering around her. The organ, guitar, and drums were playing loudly, and the Reverend was swinging his tie over his head, smiling benevolently up at the ceiling. I buried my face in my hands and cried. I thought Grandma was going to die.

Church was never the same for me after that day. Each Sunday, I would sit stiffly next to Grandma, fearful that the spirit would try to get me next, and vowing that if it did, I would fight it off. I also vowed to stop coming to church as soon as I was old enough, probably once I got married. I had no use for spirits or for being attacked by them. I had no intentions of embarrassing myself by jumping around to the rhythm of an unheard beat. And there was no way I was going to surrender myself to one of those nurses, who would sometimes get the spirit themselves and drop their "patients" to the floor.

I figured out much later that the problem with me and church was that no one ever explained the purpose. I went because I was told to go. I read the Bible because I learned that the more you read and memorized, the more stars you got on the Sunday School board—and that made Grandma happy. Because of Grandma, I believed that God was a cruel God who meted out punishment according to one's deeds—especially mine, it seemed. Grandma's God watched and recorded every move I made and used that information against me. According to Grandma, God never gave a person more burdens than he or she could bear, and I was her burden. Thus, she vowed to God and the community to use every breath in her body to break me down, and she prefaced her efforts to do so with, "I know what she needs because God told me."

I was 25 years old when I realized I had no idea what religion or church meant or how it fit into my life. Grandma's holiness church scared me to death. The Methodist church I sometimes attended with my cousin was so boring, I usually slept through the service. I went to a Baptist church on my own until a young minister bought me an ice cream cone and put his hand down my blouse. Grandma said I had to go to church because I was a sinner. We are all sinners, she claimed, wretched and born in sin. But no one bothered to explain to me what sin was. They only said church was the way to clean it from your soul. Still, I couldn't figure out how somebody could go to church like Grandma did, talk to the Lord and hang with the spirits, and still be so mean to me. None of it made sense.

⁘⌄⁘⌄⁘

Experiences like these made me wonder why the adults in my life believed they were not required to explain things to children. They seem to think children would pick up the understanding as they went along. That's why no one ever told me how or why my mother died. Nor did anyone ever explain to me that my brother had asthma and that was why he was treated more delicately and humanely than me. No one ever explained to me the things a little girl needs to know about life, about men, or herself. Nobody told me that there was a spiritual aspect to life or that the spirit of goodness resided in everyone. It would have been nice to have known as a child what I know now: that how people act and their spiritual worth are two completely different issues.

With this understanding, I have come to the realization that although my grandmother never told me she loved me, she tried to show me some love in the only way she knew how: by feeding me, by keeping me clean, by disciplining me. She did all that, but she never nurtured me. She believed in ruling with an iron fist, a switch, an ironing cord, a belt, and a razor-sharp tongue. Her theory was that if a child was frightened enough, he or she would not do the wrong thing. She never explained to me what exactly the wrong things were, she just forbade me to do them.

On the darker side, everyone in the family knew Grandma was mean to me and a little "off." They also knew that she, in her own words, "couldn't stand the sight of me," and that she favored my brother. That she was cruel and abusive to me did not seem to matter. They would simply pat me on the head or give me a reassuring hug when she wasn't looking, but they left me with her because they did not want to accept the responsibility of raising me. I was too "bad." I was a "burden."

Thus, very early in my life, the colors of my life canvas were muddied, the unformed stone of my budding consciousness disfigured and marred. I learned young that it does not matter if people who say they love you treat you bad. What happened to me was unimportant because "I" did not matter. "I" was broken and needed to be fixed. "I" was bad. Even God knew it.

However, God must have changed His mind because one day, many years and tears later, He showed me and everyone else a totally different picture.

THE
Journal

Nobody knows how you feel unless you tell them. Unfortunately, you
don't always know how to say what you feel. Even when you
do, the other person does not—no, cannot—hear what you
are saying. People have an uncanny ability to hear what they
think you are saying when you say what you feel. It is as if
they know that what you are feeling is so awful they do not
want to be polluted by it. To protect themselves, people will
listen to what they want to hear rather than what you are
actually saying.

I believe if people really knew and understood that they were
stomping on your heart, they would not do it. People who
really love and care about you never realize how deeply they
can invade your heart. It is their own fear, anger, guilt,
shame, and blame that they are trying to ignore, rationalize,
or avenge. People do what they have to do to save
themselves, and their actions have absolutely nothing to do
with your being hurt. It's nothing personal. It is survival.

Everyone must learn how to survive. Everyone must know exactly
what it takes for them to survive. Everyone requires
something different at different times, depending on who they
are and how much or how badly they want to survive.
Survival is different from "getting over" or "making it."
Survival is doing whatever is necessary, at any given time, in
order to stay alive. Survival is not always pretty; in fact, it can
be pretty ugly and awful. But people who are about survival
know that if they can just survive another minute, hour, or

16

day, they will undoubtedly meet up with the opportunity to survive some more.

There is one shortfall to the survivalist mentality: you can become so accustomed to it, you forget there is another way to live, that life can also be about growing, blossoming, flourishing, evolving, and thriving. Once you forget that there is more to life than just survival, something inside of you dies. When it does, the dead part takes over, making it easier for you to do to others whatever is required to ensure your own survival.

CHAPTER 2

The Vital Images

D ADDY...

My daddy was drop-dead gorgeous. He truly demonstrated the veracity of the saying, "It's not what you have, it's what you do with what you have that counts." He had an average face, which he highlighted with an impeccably shaven mustache. He had an average build, which he covered with expertly tailored clothing and expensive jewelry. He had a high school diploma, which he augmented by being an avid reader. He had a deep, rumbling voice, which he used to demonstrate his abilities as a great conversationalist and joke teller. He was suave and debonair. He was a numbers runner, a street hustler, a gambler. He was also emotionally unavailable to me.

As far back as I can remember, Daddy had two cars. One he drove during the week and the other, a Cadillac, he drove on Sundays. As a child, I do not remember Daddy ever sleeping at home. He usually came home around lunchtime to calculate his numbers and change his clothes. When he hit the door, Grandma would give him the laundry list of my misdeeds and needs. He would listen silently, then he would call me into the kitchen. Sometimes, he would instruct me on what not to do. At other times, he would scold and threaten me. If he had not hit the number in a while and was in a foul mood, Grandma could press him into taking off his belt and whacking me once or twice. These beatings never hurt my body, but they always hurt my feelings. I would sulk and cry for hours after Daddy spanked me, stopping only after Grandma threatened to beat me herself. If Daddy had hit the number, no amount of complaining from Grandma could make him hit me. He would give her some money and she would shut up.

I must have been about four years old when I started having very vivid dreams. Although I rarely remembered the details of the dreams, I remembered that they all ended the same way: a tall, thin woman would hand me a piece of paper, instructing me to give it to my father. There were always two or three numbers on the paper. When Daddy came home the next day, I would get my wooden number blocks and show him the numbers that were on the paper in my dream. Like clockwork, within a day or two, the number would come out.

Daddy bought two or three new cars with the money from my dreams. If he ever needed money, he would tell me, "Now you dream something nice for Daddy tonight." I always did. I became more valuable to him than Grandma. She hated the fact that he would no longer listen to her damning stories about me. Plus, I loved to dream about the pretty lady who gave me numbers. It always meant that Daddy would give me a quick peck on my cheek.

If Grandma was particularly agitated about some aspect of my behavior, Daddy would take me out with him for the afternoon. His friends Mr. Johnny and Rootman were always glad to see me. Few of my father's friends had real names, but I had to call them all "Mister" or "Miss" all the same. There was Mr. Can Man, Mr. Fish, Mr. Bubba, and Miss Itsy Bitsy. They all made a big deal about me because I was "Horace's daughter." I think Daddy must have told them about the numbers I received in my dreams because they always told me how nice I looked and they would fight to buy me ice cream and candy.

When I went out with Daddy, I got to go to bars, to women's houses, and to a variety of smoky haunts filled with loud, funny-acting people. If there was some place I could not go, Daddy would buy me gum, candy, or a popsicle and leave me in the car. I would entertain myself with the buttons and handles in the car. If I got dirty or dropped anything on my clothes, Daddy would have one of his lady friends buy me something to wear. He would not dare take me back to Grandma dirty.

My father was his mother's only child, so I guess he knew her better than anyone else. He knew that Grandma was an equal opportunity abuser, that she would scream and curse at him the same as she did me. Yet he never talked back to her. When she started ranting and raving at him about something or another, usually me, he would just sit there and take it. He'd cross his legs, twiddle his thumbs, and stare down at his shoes until she was through.

Where had he been? she would screech. How could he take me to those filthy places he went? And where the hell were my clothes? Every time he took me out I came back looking like a 125th Street whore! Who in their right mind would dress a five-year-old child in red?

I thought I looked pretty nice. Grandma always said I looked like a "floozie."

When Daddy had money, he would drop me off at the door, shove some money into Grandma's hand, and make his exit swiftly. If he did not leave her any money, he got the lecture, but before he would leave, he would look at me knowingly and ask, "You'll be alright until I get back, right?" I would shake my head sadly because I knew he knew Grandma would take out her frustrations on me.

And she would. The minute the front door closed, Grandma would do to me what she could not do to my father. First, she would drag me by the hair or the arm to the window where she would pray over me. She would ask her God to save my soul. She would ask that Satan be removed from my mind and my body. Sometimes she would shake me, spin me around, and scream, "Loose! Loose! Satan, loose this child!" After the shaking and spinning, she would stare into my eyes. I always thought she was looking for the Satan thing. Then she would tell me, "Every time you go out with your father, you come back smelling like a dog!" Before the words were out of her mouth, she would rip my clothes off, right there in the kitchen, even if they were new. She would then take me into the bathroom, plunk me down in the bathtub, and rush off to get the brush. That is when I would really start to cry.

The brush was a boar's head scrub brush, similar to the ones Grandma used to scrub the floors. She would lather my body with her foul-smelling, homemade brown soap that was filled with twigs and sticks. Then she would scrub me down roughly with the brush. She would scrub my head, face, and back. She would always tell me to open my legs so she could scrub my private parts. Depending on the length of time since the last bath and if there were still unhealed scratches from the last scrubbing, sometimes I would bleed. To Grandma, however, the blood was a sign that I was clean. She would not stop scrubbing until she saw blood, and when she did, she would mutter over and over, "The blood of Jesus will set you free! The blood of Jesus will heal your soul!" Afterwards, she would dry me off and rub me down with olive oil; then she would make me sleep on the floor beside her bed.

The next day, when Daddy saw the scars he would whisper in my ear, "Grandma gave you another bath, huh?" I would shake my head guiltily. "Don't worry," he would say, "you're tough like your daddy. You can take it." Then he would smile conspiratorially at me and ask, "What did you dream last night?" Somehow he knew that whenever I suffered through one of Grandma's bath attacks, I had a dream. The tall, thin lady always came into my dreams on the nights after I got a bath. I would run and get my blocks and show Daddy the numbers. He would pat my head, peck me on the cheek, give me some change, and leave. Those were the most loving moments I ever remember spending with my father.

ᗩᐧᗩᐧᗩ

As a child, my father spent a great deal of time alone. Grandma used to tell me how she had to leave him at home by himself, often for three or four days at a time, while she went to work as a domestic. Unlike me, however, he never got into trouble or broke things around the house, she said. Grandma taught Daddy how to cook when he was very young because he had to know how to feed himself. She also taught him how to wash and iron, that way, if she got a big job in a big kitchen, he could go to work with her and help her out. When they moved up North to New York City, Grandma sent Daddy away to school because she wanted him to have a better life. I think he went just to get away from her.

Daddy never knew his father, who died when his son was only two. The unofficial family legend is that because my grandfather was half black and half white, one or the other group had him drowned in the river. Some say Grandma had him drowned for beating her. My father never said anything at all about the subject.

Daddy went into the Army when he was 19 years old. He said he went to learn more about cooking. He was a first-ranked chef in the Army. I think he went to get even further away from Grandma. Daddy used to try to tell my brother and me what it was like to be a black man in the Army during the Korean War. He never told us the full story, but what he did tell was quite intriguing. Being from New York, he said, everyone in his barracks thought he was slick. That is how he became involved with the Black Market, bootlegging cigarettes, until he got caught and was sentenced to 25 years in Fort Leavenworth.

After 16 months in prison, the Army offered my daddy a way out of prison: if he would agree to go on a secret mission to destroy a communications center, the Army said it would set him free. He agreed to go. Many of the men who went on the mission were Black; all of them came from prison. Many of them died, but the mission was successful. Daddy said he always knew he would come back from the mission. He had prayed for a way out of the Army prison, and the mission was the answer to that prayer. What he had not done, he often lamented, was to have been more specific about *how* he wanted God to get him out. I always remembered that: when you pray for something, be specific.

Afterwards, Daddy was released from prison as promised, but he received a dishonorable discharge from the Army. Many years later, a movie was made about the mission. It was a box-office success called "The Dirty Dozen." My father never received any compensation from Hollywood for the telling of his story. He felt betrayed. He held on to that bitterness until the end of his life. That bitterness, like his aloofness, became part of my daddy's persona. Yet beneath his cool exterior lurked a seething rage. You never knew when he would blow, and when he did, it seemed for no apparent reason. I know he got that from Grandma. I also know that he was in pain, that he was angry. He had no identity as a man, a Black man, or as a father. He passed all of that on to my brother. I got whatever was left.

A daddy is supposed to protect you. Mine did not. A daddy should be there to tuck you in at night. My daddy did not sleep at home. A daddy is supposed to listen to you talk and always have something brilliant to say. My daddy gave me money and allowed his mother to abuse me. As I grew, I got the message: if a man buys you things, gives you money, and passes through now and then, you should not ask for more. A man will listen to you only if you yell; however, when a man gives you money, you should shut up and not bother him about anything else. Further, a man will not care what happens to you unless you *make* yourself valuable to him. Most importantly, my daddy taught me that when things get bad, do not deal with them, get away from them—fast.

THE Journal

People value, honor, and protect beautiful things. They show them off in public. They keep them clean and dusted, protect them from harm. If you are not valued, honored, and protected as a child, you come to believe you are not beautiful. When you are beaten, ignored, neglected, and abused as a child, you actually get ugly. This ugliness has nothing to do with the way you look. It has everything to do with the way you feel. You believe your ugliness is your fault. You believe there is something you can do or not do to make yourself a little less ugly. You see yourself as a blemish.

When you believe you are ugly, your ugliness feels as if it goes down to the bone, tainting everything you are and do. You have ugly looks. You say ugly things. You act in such an ugly way, eventually everyone begins to treat you the way an ugly person should be treated. The question is, however: Which comes first, being ugly or being treated as if you are ugly?

How can you make an ugly child feel beautiful? By holding that child, by rocking him or her in your arms. By caring for, supporting, and protecting that child because you know deep down they do not want to be or feel ugly. You could, if you had a mind to, teach that child that he or she is beautiful by treating the child in a beautiful way. By saying and doing beautiful things to that child. You could do all that and more if you wanted to, but who the hell wants to be bothered with an ugly kid?

CHAPTER 3

The Stone

THE MOTHER...

Lynnette was the most beautiful woman I had ever seen. She was fair-complexioned with straight black hair. I learned later that she colored her hair with henna. It did not matter to me, I still thought she was beautiful. She had small, narrow feet that complimented her small, delicate frame. She wore nail polish on her toes and she shaved her legs. She was so soft-spoken she seemed fragile. She bought her clothes at Macy's and Abraham & Straus, two very expensive stores in my youth. She smoked L&M cigarettes and drank Cutty Sark scotch. She was a very classy lady.

One of the things that first fascinated me about Lynnette was that she made her pancakes from scratch. Whenever Daddy took me to her house, she would hug me, kiss me, sit me on her kitchen stool, and bring out the pancake bowl. Spell-bound, I would watch her sift the floor, measure the baking powder, beat the eggs, and make a fresh batch of pancakes, just for me. If I ate my pancakes quietly while she and Daddy were in the other room, Lynnette would let me polish my fingernails. She had lovely red polish that made my fingers look long and elegant.

Everything Lynnette did for me made me look better and feel better. I think it was because she genuinely loved to do things with me and for me. She was my stepmother, my guardian angel, who eventually became my best friend. I called her "Nett."

My father married Nett two years after he started living with my mother, whom he never married. He tucked Nett away until a reasonable amount of time after my mother's death. Then, when it became evident that Grandma was going to either maim or kill me if I stayed with her any longer, Daddy introduced my brother and me to his "wife." I can imagine Nett was as shocked to discover that her husband had two children as we were to find out he had another wife. She never said a word to us about it though. Anyone else would have thrown Daddy and his children out the door. Nett did not. She, above all people, had a reason and the rationale to abuse me, but she never did. In fact, had it not been for Nett, I might never have made it to become a teenager.

After my mother died, Daddy was busted and could not write numbers for awhile, so Grandma went back to work as a domestic. This meant that my brother Ray and I had to be left in the house alone until Daddy came home around noon. Money was very scarce and Grandma refused to do anything for me. As a result, Nett told me much later, the first time she saw me I was dirty. I had dirt in my hair, scratches all over my face and back, holes in my sneakers, and the most beautiful but sad eyes she had ever seen, which I never raised from the floor. I remember her placing her hand under my chin and lifting my face until our eyes met. When they did, she asked me if she could have a smile. From that day on, she always got one, in exchange for a kiss and a hug.

Nett lived in a small one-bedroom apartment. Before we all lived together, my father, brother, and I would visit her in the evenings. When we did, she would let me take a bubble bath. She would fill the tub up to the brim with bubbles, but I would not let her take my clothes off. As soon as she left the bathroom, I would strip and jump into the tub.

I remember once, when she came into the bathroom to see if I was alright, I jumped out of the tub, fell on the tile floor, and split my lip. She said I looked as though I had seen a ghost. She did not know, but I had.

After a nice, long bubble bath, Nett would feed Ray and me, usually homemade split pea soup and tuna fish sandwiches. While we were in the kitchen eating, she would take my father into the living room. I never knew what she said to him, but after we ate, Daddy,

Ray, and I would go back to Grandma's house.

I saw Nett off and on many times during the year before we all lived together. Usually, she took me shopping. Before we went out, she always put a dab of White Shoulders cologne on me and lotioned my body with a sweet-smelling creme. She also played games with me and read stories to me. She talked to me and she let me talk to her.

Nett explained things to me. She told me there was not enough room for all of us to live together in her apartment. Until my father could afford to get us a bigger place, she said, we had to stay with my grandmother. Upon hearing this, I began to badger my father about moving, but he always told me there was no money. I told him I would ask the tall, thin lady of my dreams for a number, but she never came when I asked her to. I cried every time I left Nett's, but she would call me two or three times a day, so I wouldn't feel so bad.

Nett was the one person Grandma seemed to dislike more than me. She scrutinized and complained about everything Nett did for my brother and me. She complained that Nett's cologne smelled whorish, and that only whores painted their fingernails like Nett did. Whenever we returned from Nett's house, Grandma would ask what she had given me to eat. After I told her, she would force me to swallow a spoonful of castor oil to "clean that yellow bitch's poison out of my system." If Grandma answered the phone when Nett called for me, she would tell her I was asleep. She repeatedly griped that Nett thought she was better than us because she was lighter and of Caribbean ancestry. Nett probably thought of me as "her pet monkey," Grandma claimed; all West Indians kept pet monkeys, she said. But I did not care what Grandma said. I would rather be a monkey in Nett's house than a child in her house.

One day toward the end of the summer, shortly after Grandma had left for work, the doorbell rang. My brother warned me not to answer it. I told him it might be Daddy and pressed the buzzer to let the person in the front door of the building. We pulled a chair over to the door so we could who it was through the peephole. It was Mr. Cummings, the insurance man. After some debate with my brother, I decided to open the door. Mr. Cummings did not come in. Instead, he gave me a note to give to Grandma and stood in the hallway until I had locked the door. When Grandma came home, I proudly handed her the note.

Grandma lost it that day. She went into a rage about me opening the door. She shook me. She screamed at me. She back-handed me across the room. Did I understand what I had done? she shouted. Someone could have come into the house and killed your brother and you! To get her point across, Grandma got the ironing cord from behind the bathroom door and proceeded to beat me senseless.

I don't remember the pain. I don't remember bleeding. I just know it must have been pretty bad because Ray had to beg her to stop. Later, after dinner, she made me take off all my clothes and she beat me again.

I remember Grandma prayed real loud that night. I remember my brother told her he did not want to sleep with her, he wanted to sleep with me. I also remember Grandma's specific instructions: "If you ever tell anybody I beat you, I will kill you and throw your body out the window to the dogs." That was enough to shut my mouth for life. I was six years old and on my way to the first grade.

A few weeks later, Nett came home with Daddy while Grandma was out. She was going to take me to a big department store to go school shopping. Despite the pain I was still experiencing as a result of Grandma's raging onslaught, I was excited about going out to get new school clothes. First, however, I had to take a bath because Nett thought I had a funny odor. I knew I could bathe safely around Nett, so I went eagerly with her into the bathroom. As she ran the bath water, I took off my shoes and shorts. I refused to take off my shirt, though, and jumped into the tub with it on. Nett tried to get me to take the shirt off, but I told her no, I could wash with it on. When she threatened to call my father, I gave in. Reluctantly, I raised my arms up in the air. Nett pulled my polo shirt over my head, and with it, all the skin off my back.

I did not start first grade that fall. Instead, I spent ten days in the hospital. Nett came to see me every day. She helped me eat my asparagus soup and we made little jello men that jiggled in the bowl. Nett would stay until I went to sleep because she knew I cried when she left. One day, she brought Ray to the window outside my room. The nurse let me stand in the chair so I could see him. I really cried then. I thought: if I did not get out of this place soon, Nett would love Ray better than me. Just like Grandma did.

That night, the tall, thin lady came and stood beside my bed. I remember staring at her for a long time. She was stroking my face and hair. I asked her name. She said very clearly, "Sarah. I am your mother." At the time it did not make sense to me, Nett was the only mother I had known. Sarah said, "Tell your daddy not to forget your birthday, his birthday, and my birthday." I promised to tell him. Sarah said she would stay with me until I went to sleep. When the nurse woke me for my morning medication, Sarah was gone.

My birthday is 9/13. My father's is 5/10. My mother's birthday was 3/7. My father told me afterwards those numbers played once a day, every day, for seven days. He made a bundle. When I was released from the hospital, he took me straight to Nett's apartment. There was so much to do. We had to buy furniture, food, and clothes. When everything was ready, we went to Grandma's house to get Ray.

For the first time in my life I heard my father talk back to his mother. He actually screamed at her. I stayed very close to Nett. I don't remember what Daddy said to Grandma, but she started crying. I thought I had died and gone to heaven! Ding-Dong, the wicked old witch is crying! I sang to myself.

It got ugly. Pushing. Shoving. Pulling on the suitcases. Nett squeezed my hand and winked at me. As we got to the door, Grandma cried out, "Ray! Ray! Please don't leave me!" I thought Grandma was crying because Daddy yelled at her. I found out later that she was crying because he was taking my brother away from her.

THE *Journal*

Sometimes, I feel like a motherless child. And so does everyone else I know! On those really bad days, when the feeling of loneliness takes over, I just want to lay down and die. I can't breathe, I can't think, I can't feel—so I might as well be dead. But that is not going to solve anything because I know that when you die, you must answer for everything you have done. Now, won't that be special! Everything that makes you want to die is waiting for you when you die! So don't die, just dream.

I once had a dream. In this dream, I was in a big, empty house. It was my house, but it was empty. I was in a room that had two windows. Across the bottom portion of both windows were cafe curtains made of white fabric with pink and blue flowers. Not my taste at all. I remember thinking, they would definitely have to go.

I left one room and walked into another, which was also empty. In the middle of this room was a large wooden structure. It looked like an empty sandbox or a flower bed. It was made of white wood. I asked myself: Why would I buy a house with a flower bed in the middle of the floor? Then I realized someone else was in the house with me. I could not see who it was, but I could feel their presence. Suddenly, a raging fire broke out in the middle of the flower bed. Somehow I knew the fire would not leave the flower bed and spread to the rest of the house, so I just stood there staring at it. I did not try to

30

put it out because it seemed as though it should be there. I watched the fire until I woke up.

The empty house, that was me. Two windows, my eyes. Blue and pink curtains, I still haven't figured that one out. Fire. Fire on the floor. Fire on the floor in a flower bed. I wonder if flowers and bushes mean the same thing? When Moses did not know what to do, God appeared to him as a burning bush.

Maybe God is trying to tell me something. It would really be nice if I could figure out what S/He wants me to know while I'm still living. No matter. In a minute, any of us could be dead and we will hear it all, know it all, loud and clear.

CHAPTER 4

The Easel

R ay...

There were days when he was like a breath of fresh air, right there to protect, support, and nurture me. At other times, he was a cloud of doom—silent, sullen, and detached. I loved my brother. It always made me feel better just knowing he was around. He never said much. He never did much. Ray had an admirable quality that I clearly lacked: he was obedient. He always did what he was told to do. I, on the other hand, did exactly the opposite.

My early memories of my older brother are vague. I remember our playing together because I usually got scolded or beat for taking or breaking his toys. I remember that we ate together, and that Ray liked chicken wings. I remember being forced to eat the legs or thighs, which I hated, because Ray always had first dibs on the wings. I remember his brown teddy bear with the brown corduroy overalls and the one eye. I plucked the other one out and lied about it. I also remember that it was because of the things I did or said to my brother that Grandma deemed me "mean," "hateful," and "bad." In her eyes, Ray was none of those things.

Grandma loved my brother and she was not afraid to show it. I watched her hug and kiss him often. If ever Ray woke up in the middle of the night, he was welcome to crawl into Grandma's high-off-the-floor bed. The closest I ever got to sleep with her was the floor beside the bed on those nights I was forcefully bathed to cleanse my soul. Grandma would let Ray pick whatever color sourballs he wanted from the candy dish—since he was the oldest, Grandma claimed, but I always knew there was more to it than that. Ray got to pick first, consequently he always got the more-preferred red sourballs or the treasured pineapple-flavored ones that only occasionally showed up in the batch. Grandma would not let me pick out my own candy; instead, she would pick out a yellow or green candy for me, never failing to suggest snidely that I only wanted the red ones because Ray wanted them.

Eventually, I came to understand that the reason why Ray was treated so special by Grandma and others was because he had asthma. Somehow, this made him special, more loveable. Me, I was simply bad.

If Ray ate the wrong thing, he would have an asthma attack. If he ran too hard or played too much, he would get deathly ill. If he got upset with me for cheating at Candy Land or breaking one of his toys, his chest would swell, his eyes would run, and he would soon be gasping for his every breath. Whenever that happened, everyone would stop whatever they were doing to rush him to the hospital.

I don't remember how old Ray was when his asthma attacks began, but I remember the fear that gripped my heart each time he had one. It is a frightening thing to watch your brother fighting to breathe, to hold on to his life. Grandma would make him sit quietly at first, hoping to avoid the trip to King's County Hospital in Brooklyn. She would put the vaporizer near him, fill the tiny compartment with Vick's Vaporub, and soothingly plead with him to breathe the cool mist that soon filled the room.

I loved the smell of eucalyptus, so I would sit with Ray to keep him company while he sat trying to catch his breath. I tried my best not to be bad or bother him, but I always had a million questions to ask him, and these quiet, intimate moments seemed the most appropriate time to pose them. Inevitably, his attempts to respond would result in loud, gasping noises that alerted Grandma to shout at me, "Shut up! Leave your brother alone!"

Sometimes Ray would get better in a matter of hours. Other times, no amount of Vick's or restricted silence on my part seemed to

33

help. Those are the times I remember most vividly. Ray's chest would swell to twice its normal size. His words escaped his mouth in spurts that were barely audible. He seemed stiff, barely able to move as Grandma, Daddy, or Nett tried to help him put his sweater or jacket on. If no car was available, a taxi would have to be hailed on the street, and off to the hospital we would go.

I became an afterthought when Ray got sick. At some point in the frenzy to save Ray's life, they would remember me, order me to get my coat, and stick me in the back seat next to what I feared was my dying brother. In his weakest moments, Ray would lay his head on my lap and hold my hand.

King's County Hospital was a large, dismal, God-awful place. I loved it! Whenever we arrived, there were sure to be lots of people, noise, blood, confusion, and those great big candy machines. I became very familiar with the pictures of the little white children on the emergency room walls. I also knew which candy machines had the Tootsie Rolls in them.

The series of events was always the same. We would rush in with Ray, who would be barely able to walk, much less breathe. We would take a number from the guard and scan the room for a seat amongst the drunk and bleeding people who were either sitting, laying, or lounging on the brick-hard wooden benches. We would wait sometimes hours for our number to be called. When it was, one of the adults would walk up to the desk and give all the personal information needed so that we could wait some more. During the wait, Ray would sit, stand, lay down, or pace the floor sweating and crying and gasping for air. His suffering was a painful thing to watch.

Once, when Ray must have been about eight years old, Nett and I had to take him to "The County" emergency room. We had waited a little too long to bring him in. Not that the waiting room would have been any less packed had we come earlier. Nett half-carried Ray in herself. She did not take a number. She went straight to the desk, leaving Ray and me in the waiting room, Ray with his head laying in a stranger's lap and me sitting nearby holding Ray's cup of water. Desperately, Nett tried to explain to the receiving clerk that Ray was barely conscious. Soon she was screaming at the top of her lungs, "He's dying! Look at him! He can't breathe!" As if planned, the moment Nett finished her sentence, Ray slid off the woman's lap onto the floor. I screamed and dropped the cup of water on his head.

People came from everywhere. Doctor's, nurses, people in green uniforms, and Nett. The other waiting patients were not particularly alarmed. They knew this meant their wait would be longer. Somebody picked Ray up from the floor, placed him on a stretcher, and rolled him away. I could see one of his arms dangling lifelessly over the side of the stretcher. Nett ran behind him.

I started screaming my head off. Somebody, a stranger, picked me up. I thought my brother was dead. I wanted Nett. Everyone was staring at me. I could not stop crying. Somebody offered me some soda in a paper cup. I did not want it. A nurse tried to assure me that my brother was alright. I did not believe her. I was whimpering and sniffling when I looked up and saw my daddy rushing into the emergency room. He saw me. I called him, jumped from whoever's arms I was in to run to him. He walked right pass me through the swinging doors before I could get to him.

That was it for me. I went totally berserk. Didn't anyone realize I was scared to death? Why didn't someone tell me what the hell was going on? What I did in the emergency room that night became a family joke. I bit people. I screamed. I howled, as my grandmother said, "like a stuck pig." I do not remember running through the swinging doors of the room where the doctors were attending to Ray, but they said I did. I continued screaming, spitting, and biting like a lunatic until Nett took me in her arms and carted me back to the waiting room. She held me and rocked me until I calmed down. She told me Ray would be fine, but he would have to stay in the hospital for a while. They had given him several shots, she said, and while he was breathing easier, he could not come home.

What a disaster! There I was, totally exhausted, my throat seriously inflamed, and now I would have to go home without my brother! I could not imagine living without Ray. I needed him. He was the only constant in my life. He didn't serve much of a purpose, but I wanted him to be there.

Daddy eventually came out to the waiting room and we left.

It was nice having the back seat of the car to myself, I remember thinking. I could pick either window I wanted. But it wasn't any fun without Ray.

For the next three days, I had to sleep alone in my room, eat alone, and play alone. Nett and I went shopping and watched television together, but I still felt alone. I missed my brother. I promised God that if He let Ray come home, I would stop being bad. I would never take or break his toys again, and I would most certainly never stand in front of the vaporizer. I lied. Ray had several bad attacks after that one. Somehow I got used to them. I guess I just shut down the part of myself that was connected to his asthma.

After we moved, whenever Ray was recuperating from a particularly bad attack, he got to stay home and drink ginger ale and 7-Up. So did I. Since he could not move around too much, Nett would let him lay on the sofa and watch television all day, and she would let me stay home to keep him company. Best of all, wherever Ray went, so did the vaporizer, and, despite my vow, I continued to sit with him and play in the mist until it kinked my hair. Ray did not seem to mind. I guess he was glad to have my company.

Those were some of the best times I had as a child. I could bring Ray his water, so I was useful. I could turn the television to whatever channel he wanted, so I was helpful. I could put his dishes in the sink and wash them, so I was good. For the first time in my life, I felt I was good. Unfortunately, my goodness hinged on my brother's near-death experiences.

THE Journal

They are like a poison that seizes control of your entire life. They invade your thoughts, transforming everything you do to a dark shade of grey. They take over your environment, turning friends into crutches, strangers into challenges, fun into a chore. They deplete your body, turning your head into a pounding board; your heart into a simmering sore; your arms, legs, and feet into lead boulders. They bring you down, hold you back, cut you off. They are toxic relationships.

Why do we stay in relationships after they cease to be supportive, fulfilling, productive? Fear. Fear of being alone. Fear of letting go. Fear of feeling the pain. We have a misconception of the true meaning of relationships. Somewhere we got the idea that relationships can fix what ails us, that they can make us happy or fill the void in our lives. We believe it is our duty to make relationships work. It is not. A relationship should be a place of support and nurturing. A relationship should be a place of purpose.

We attract and are attracted to someone who is our complete opposite because we have an unconscious need to learn. Our goal in relationships is to support the learning process. Family relationships, love relationships, friendships—they're all the same, they're all about people coming together to learn and grow. If that is not happening, the relationship becomes toxic.

It is one thing to be in a toxic relationship. It is another thing to watch one. Parents participate. Children watch. In the end, toxic relationships poison both the participants and the observers.

CHAPTER 5

The Background Colors

The Family...

For the first time in my life, I had a family. A father, a mother, a brother, and me—all living under the same roof. Daddy had found a beautiful apartment in a pretty nice neighborhood. Ray and I shared a room, but that did not matter. We had a kitchen table and living room furniture, and there were no nick-nacks around for me to worry about breaking. Things were really looking up. I felt secure and, for the first time, wanted and loved. Some things did not change, however.

Daddy was still writing numbers, so there were good times and bad times. In the good times, we got to ride in his car, buy new clothes, and eat whatever we wanted. In the bad times, Nett cried and I felt helpless.

In the good times, I got to meet Nett's family. She had a sister who was a nurse, another sister who worked for the government, a younger sister who had children about my age, and a brother who was in the Army. My favorite was Aunt Nita. Aunt Nita was a carbon copy of Nett, just a little older. She was sweet, gentle, loving, and she took an immediate liking to me. It was great to have a family. In the bad times, the family argued about who should leave who, who should mind their own business, and who didn't know what they were talking about. Bad times were hard, but you could deal with them.

Then, disaster struck. One evening, Ray and I were sitting in the living room. Nett was in the bedroom. Daddy and Mr. Johnny were sitting at the kitchen table writing out their numbers. There was a knock at the door. Daddy went to look out the peep hole. I heard him whisper, "Oh, shit!" The next few moments became a tornado of activity. Daddy ran back into the kitchen. The knock at the door got louder. Nett called out, "Answer the door." Daddy and Mr. Johnny were scooping up papers from the kitchen table. The knocking became a banging. Nett came up the hall as Daddy and Mr. Johnny were racing down the hall. They knocked her down in their hurry to rush past her. The banging became a crashing as the apartment door was shattered, and planks of wood and pieces of metal flew wildly across the living room. Seven or eight huge, white policemen barged through the demolished doorway. The telephone rang. Nett tried to get up, but the charging policemen knocked her down again. More police came in. White men were in my family's kitchen. Mr. Johnny was half in, half out of the bathroom window. Daddy was on the floor, straddled by three policemen.

Then the unspeakable happened. One of the white police officers grabbed Nett by the hair and threw her against the wall. That's when I lost my mind.

I ran over to the officer, grabbed him around the legs, and bit him. He howled and tried to shake me off, and in doing so accidentally kicked Nett. I bit him again. Somebody grabbed me from behind. I could hear myself screaming. I was kicking, screaming, and biting like a mad dog. Somebody—a white man— began shaking me. Oh, my God! I had never been touched by a white man. I think he was trying to calm me down, but I bit him too.

The strange white man carried me out into the hallway. I was frantic. Where's my brother? My father? My mother? What in the world is going on? All the neighbors were staring at me. A next-door neighbor took Ray and me into her apartment. We put our heads down on the kitchen table and cried.

It seemed like hours before we saw Nett again. Her face was swollen. Her nightgown was torn. She was struggling to hold back her tears. Daddy and Mr. Johnny were in jail, Nett explained to us, but we could go back home.

What did it mean that Daddy was in jail? Somebody would have to go to court to pay his bail, but he should be home in a day or two. A day or two! Daddy in jail with white people beating him for a day or two! Nobody was going to beat him, she assured us. He would be fine. Meanwhile, we have to clean up the apartment. Why? We didn't have a door. Who cared what the apartment looked like? Everybody in the neighborhood knew Daddy was a numbers runner. We had nothing to be ashamed of.

Our neighbors were really great. The people from across the hall helped us pick up the broken furniture. Another neighbor started mopping, and another sweeping. Somebody else brought sandwiches and sodas. The super came up to put the door back on. In a matter of hours, the place looked as good as new. A few people came by. Each shoved some money into Nett's hand. She refused. They insisted, saying, "How many times has he helped me out by carrying my numbers?" Everybody gave Nett a reassuring nod, and everybody asked the same question: "Who told?"

When the apartment was empty, Nett lit a cigarette and began to make the calls to the family.

"Horace is in jail."

"His bail is a thousand dollars."

"The kids are here with me."

"We're fine."

"Can you bring it? You know I can't drive, and my face is all banged up."

"I don't know! I swear I can't figure out who did it!"

I would not leave Nett's side. When she went to the bathroom, I stood outside the door. She noticed some scratches on my face. We went to the bathroom together and she put some witch hazel on them. Nett put witch hazel on everything. She was sitting on the toilet seat with me standing between her legs while she nursed my wounds when we heard a knock on the door.

We froze. Nett stood up slowly, ordering Ray and I to go hide in the bedroom closet. Ray turned to run, but I refused to move. Exasperated, Nett pushed us both into the bathroom and slammed the door. The second knock came.

Neither one of us moved. We heard the door open and close. Then silence. We heard voices. My legs started trembling. Footsteps were coming down the hall. We jumped into the bathtub. Nett opened the door. She peeked in to find us cowering in a corner of the tub. It was Mr. Rootman. We all breathed a sigh of relief.

Mr. Rootman had heard the news downtown. The word on the street was that Grandma had ratted on Daddy. Nobody wanted to believe it, but it all made sense.

Nett started cursing. She never cursed. Mr. Rootman counted out some money. He tossed Ray and I several bags of potato chips and gave Nett a big hug, assuring her he'd be back in a few hours.

Nett made us go to bed. When I woke up the next morning, I saw something I never seen before: my father sleeping in bed next to his wife.

The bad times got progressively worse. I stopped dreaming about the tall, thin lady. Daddy could no longer write numbers from the house, so he was gone most of the time. Nett had to look for work. My brother and I had to take the bus to school way across town. The only time we all got together was on Saturday, and that was housework day. Daddy and Nett started arguing a lot. Ray became more and more stingy. I became more and more difficult to control.

Something had to be done. I don't know whose decision it was, but one day I came home from school to find Grandma in the kitchen cooking.

Nett had taken a night job in addition to her day job in order to make ends meet. Somebody had to be in the house to make sure Ray and I had something to eat, did our homework, and got to bed, she explained. Grandma had volunteered to do the job. I could not believe my eyes! If I had not been so addicted to food, I would have vomited on the floor. I thought she had ridden her broom off into the sunset. Now she was back.

This time, however, I was a lot older and wiser. I would not fall into her trap. I would not get in her way. I would not even look at her. For the first few weeks she was there, I only spoke to her when I had to. If she even looked at me the wrong way, I told Nett.

Unfortunately, there was nothing Nett could do. She needed Grandma.

After Grandma started coming around, things really changed. Nett started getting sick. Every week, something else was wrong with her. She had to quit her night job. Grandma still came over to help out. Daddy was rarely around, we saw him maybe two or three times a week, and when he was, he was always arguing with somebody—Nett, Grandma, my brother, or me. If he hit the number or ran across a nice number book, he would bring Nett some money. That seemed to quiet things down for awhile. Eventually, Grandma stopped coming around.

Friday nights were the best. On Friday, Nett got paid. Every Friday night, she would bring home a pint of Schraff's coffee ice cream and a bottle of 7-Up. She would make us ice cream sodas in those tall Tupperware tumblers, and we would all sit around watching television. One year, Halloween fell on a Friday. We were not allowed to go out to trick-or-treat, but Nett dressed us up and let us walk around the building. This particular year, Nett dressed me up like a lady. She made-up my face and let me wear one of her dresses and a pair of her high-heeled shoes. I was gorgeous. I had a ball falling off my heels as I paraded throughout the building gathering loot. When we were done, Nett rationed all the candy into little sandwich bags. She said we could have a bag a day until it was all gone. We were having a great time. Then Daddy came home for his weekly visit.

Things had been going so bad for Daddy, he could take the snap, crackle, and pop out of a Rice Krispies. He took the fun out of Halloween that year by announcing loudly and angrily that I "looked like a whore" in my costume. He ordered Nett to wash my face and put me to bed immediately. As always, she did what he told her to do. During the clean-up, I noticed that Nett had left her lipstick on the sink. I made a note of that fact in my mental computer. Later, when all was quiet and I was supposed to be asleep, I crept into the bathroom, got the lipstick, and took it back to bed with me.

How do you put lipstick on, in the dark, in the bed, when you are nine years old? You get your brother's flashlight, get under the sheets, and start practicing, that's what. What's missing? A mirror.

Of course. So, you creep back into the bathroom, stand on the toilet seat, and peep into the mirror. All is well until you knock the Listerine off the sink, which brings your Daddy down the hall in a rage.

I had lived through many of Daddy's rages. Nothing I had ever seen or experienced topped this one, however. This one was different, and, for the life of me, I still cannot figure out why. Perhaps he thought my affinity for lipstick would really make me a whore. Perhaps he had gingivitis and could not bear to be without Listerine. Or maybe, just maybe, the thought of my stepmother scrubbing the sheets on a scrub board to remove the lipstick drove him wild. Whatever the reason, he was in rare form that night.

Daddy caught me by the neck of my nightgown somewhere between the door to my bedroom and my bed. He demanded to know what I was doing. Foolishly I responded, "Nothing!" Wrong answer. Especially when the hem of my nightgown was dripping mouthwash and my face was covered with lipstick. As he unbuckled his belt with his free hand, I tried to think of a better answer, but he was choking me. As he maneuvered his pants to free his belt, I got away. I ran straight to the bed and dove under the covers. Wrong again.

My father began to beat me with all the rage and fury he had mustered in his 34 years. He beat me because his father died when he was two. He beat me because his mother left him home alone while she went out to work in the "Madam's house." He beat me because he was a numbers runner and a street hustler. He beat me because my mother had died of cancer and left him strapped with two children. He beat me because he was a Black man in America with a dishonorable discharge. He beat me because he had had another woman and another set of children his wife did not know about. He beat me because I was chubby. He beat me because I was a girl. He beat me until his pants fell off and the neighbors called the police.

Nett tried to rescue me about two minutes into the beating. She begged and pleaded with Daddy to stop. She tried to get me out of the bed, but whenever she got close enough to touch me, he hit her, too. Although Ray and I shared the room and his twin bed was only three feet apart from mine, I had no idea where he was or if he got any of the beating. I have a vague memory of him standing in the closet, crying. I wonder if he felt sorry for me or if he had gotten hit? Daddy eventually became so exhausted, he slowed down. It was then that Nett dragged my unconscious body from the bed and into the bathroom where she locked the door.

My eyes were beaten shut. My lips were beaten swollen. My arms, legs, and back bore huge welts as a result of all the blows they had taken. I woke up in a tub of cool water. Nett was on her knees beside me, holding a wash cloth over my eyes. Somebody was knocking on the bathroom door. She went out. I heard mumbling and silence as she slipped back in the door. Kneeling at my side, she kissed me, wiped my face, and whispered, "Why don't you listen? You've got to listen. Your daddy loves you, but you've got to listen."

Thank goodness he loved me, I thought. Had my father not loved me, I suspect he would have killed me for putting lipstick on the sheets and breaking a bottle of Listerine.

Things were still pretty tight around the house. Money was scarce and Daddy was ever scarcer. Nett's family had decided to let her suffer since she insisted on staying with my father, whose vocation they did not approve of. Nett did the best she could, really, but it was just too much for her. I remember there were times when we had absolutely no food but because we were always clean, no one knew we were hungry.

When Nett could scrape together enough money, seventy or eighty cents, she would buy a half-dozen eggs and a small loaf of bread. For the next few days then, she would make herself and Ray fried-egg sandwiches. One day she would eat the white and Ray would eat the yellow of the egg. The next day, they would switch. Since I did not eat eggs, I would have toast and tea every day. The tea bags Nett snuck home from her job. Each of us would take turns dunking the same bag for a few minutes until our hot water got some color. We each got a pack of sugar, also from Nett's job. That would be our dinner. We would live on the egg-and-tea diet for two or three days at a stretch or until Daddy came by with some money. It really wasn't as bad as it sounds because Nett had a way of making everything seem alright. While she and Ray ate their egg sandwiches and I was eating my toast, she would talk excitedly about what we would eat when she got paid on Friday.

One week was particularly hard. There were no eggs and no tea. Nett bought potatoes and made potato soup. We each had a little every night and every morning. All week, however, the plan was that when Friday came, Nett would bring knockwurst from the kosher deli near her job, Ray and I would meet her at the subway station on Fulton Street and Ralph Avenue, and we would all go to the Safeway and buy the rest of our dinner. We would get frozen french fries, pork-and-beans, and sauerkraut. We would pig out, have ice cream sodas, and watch television until midnight, just like Nett promised. It always seemed that Friday took forever to come.

Everything went according to the plan. Nett got the knockwurst. We went to Safeway and almost ran home. While Nett fixed the food, Ray and I paced hungrily in the living room. Nett wanted this Friday dinner to be really special, so she set the table with napkins and made the ice cream sodas in glasses rather than the Tupperware cups we usually drank out of.

We had just sat down to the table and said the grace when Daddy stuck his key in the door. We were glad to see him, but that night he took second place to the food we were getting ready to eat. He was in a particularly foul mood. He walked into the kitchen, stared at us, and shouted at Nett, "What is that shit on their plates?" he demanded. We were all puzzled. Nett explained that she had promised us we could have anything we wanted for being so good all week. Daddy went off. He started raving that his children did not have to eat this kind of crap as long as he was alive and breathing. Then Nett got into it. She informed him that this crap was better than the crap he had left for us, which was nothing. Increasingly harsh words were exchanged, and, in a frenzy, Daddy picked up my plate and Ray's plate and threw them, food and all, against the kitchen wall.

The sight of the beans and sauerkraut dripping down the wall was devastating. I was starving. My knockwurst had fallen behind the stove. Ray's was laying on the table. I swear I was tempted to

45

pick it up, bite it, and run into the bathroom with whatever else I could scrape up. I didn't. I didn't have time. I had to get out of the way because Daddy had Nett by the hair and was getting ready to slap her.

She was screaming. He was screaming. Ray and I were crying, first because our dinner was on the wall, secondly because Daddy had no reason to be mean to Nett. Much to my surprise, Ray told him so. "Leave her alone!" he yelled, grabbing at Daddy's legs. Nett pulled Ray loose and ran with him down the hall into the bedroom, locking the door behind them. For once, I was cool, still plotting on the knockwurst on Nett's plate. I made sure I stayed out of Daddy's way, however.

Daddy stomped around for awhile, then put on his hat and coat and left. I started cleaning up the floor and the walls. On my hands and knees I picked up the splattered food, bean by bean, off the floor. Nett and Ray came out of hiding to help. What the hell were we supposed to eat now, I wondered tearfully. I put Nett's plate in the refrigerator. Maybe she could heat it up in the morning.

A few minutes later, Daddy came back with two armloads of groceries. Nett looked at him coldly but did not say a word. Daddy made Ray and me sit in the living room and ordered us to watch television while he finished cleaning the kitchen and began cooking. Nett remained in the bedroom. Every now and then, Daddy would walk back into the bedroom and say a few words to her. He took her a beer. She did not want it. He asked her for a cigarette. She gave him one. Where was the flour? On the shelf. Why did she use Crisco oil? Mazola was better. Had his mother called this week? Did she know Mr. Johnny's wife had another baby? He made all sorts of small talk while Ray and I waited to eat.

By the time he finished, it was eleven o'clock. Nett suggested that it was much too late for Ray and me to eat a heavy meal, and that we should just be given some cereal and sent to bed. But Daddy was insistent. Everything was done, he said. Come on and sit down.

The plate was overwhelming. Pork chops with gravy. Mashed potatoes. Corn on the cob. Fresh string beans. Hot rolls. I looked at it, took two forkfuls, put my head on the table, and fell fast asleep.

THE
Journal

What was I born to be? There must be something I came here to do. What is it? Where is it? I know I was born to be something. I have heard that the thing that I am is buried inside of me. Why would God give me, no, **make** me, a jewel and then hide the essence of me from me? Everything I have seen thus far has so etched negativity into my mind that I cannot believe, not even for a moment, that God has chosen me to do anything. As a matter of fact, the more I think about it, the less I believe God has anything to do with me. I am bad. I am wrong. I ain't shit.

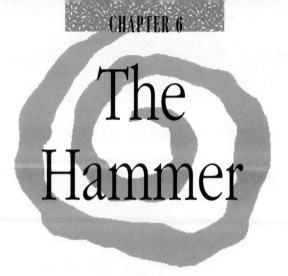

Aunt Nancy...

Things had really gotten bad. Daddy rarely came home. Nett couldn't pay the rent. We were going to be evicted. We packed everything in boxes so it could go into storage. The moving men pulled off with our household furnishings and the marshall pulled up. The super, the landlord, the marshall, and two white police officers knocked on the door. They instructed us to vacate the premises. The landlord seemed pretty pissed off because the apartment was empty. Nett told us he wanted to sell the furniture for the value of the back rent, but she had out-smarted him. There was only one thing left for us to do: leave. Nett had done the best she could for us. Now, she was taking Ray and me to live with Aunt Nancy and Uncle Lee in Crown Heights.

Aunt Nancy held herself out to be my mother's sister. I had become so confused by that point. I no longer knew who my mother was or who she was supposed to be. I had met Aunt Nancy when I was young. Ray and I had spent many afternoons at her house because she lived a few blocks away from the elementary school we attended. She seemed nice enough, but not nice enough to be an aunt, and certainly not nice enough for me to live with. I could not figure out how she was my mother's sister. The only mother I had known was Nett, and I had met all of her sisters. I wanted to know who this woman really was, and who this Sarah was that everyone alluded to, but I never seemed able to get the words out of my mouth to ask the question. So I listened to the adult conversations and drew my own conclusions. What choice did I have?

Aunt Nancy was four feet-eleven inches short. She was round like a pumpkin and had a very warm and friendly face. She wore eyeglasses like Nett did. She also wore a wig. I had never seen anyone take their hair off until I went to live with Aunt Nancy. She was a housewife, and she took in children during the day to make extra money. The day we went to live with her the children were not around, so Aunt Nancy had time to reassure Nett that we would be alright. It would not be for long, Nett told us. As soon as things were better, we could come home. We would have a new home where Ray and I would each have our own rooms. It was a temporary arrangement that lasted five long years.

I had never lived in a house before. Everyone I knew lived in an apartment. Aunt Nancy's house was huge. It had two stories and a furnished basement. There was even a backyard, so I did not have to go out on the street if I did not want to. But I usually did because there were so many other children to play with. We each had our own room. My room was on the first floor between Aunt Nancy's room and her daughter—our first cousin—Bunny's room. Ray's room was on the second floor with the family who rented from Aunt Nancy and Uncle Lee.

Aunt Nancy kept her house immaculate. The dark green floors shone from regular applications of Beacon Wax. Every piece of furniture had a hardwood sheen. There was no dust anywhere, not even on the nick-nacks. Even the basement was clean, with its built-in bar and comfortable family-room furniture. Aunt Nancy said we could play and watch television down there whenever we wanted to.

The neighborhood we lived in was very friendly and family-oriented, unlike the apartment buildings where I had lived with Grandma and Nett. This was very unusual because both Black and white families lived on the same block. The electrician and his family were white. Our neighbors on both sides were Black. The family that owned the candy store was Jewish. The family that owned the shoe repair shop was Italian. The Jewish deli on the corner was across the street from the Puerto Rican grocery store. There was a dress factory right on our block where ladies of all ethnic backgrounds came to sew every day. Every family knew every other family on the block. Every family also knew the most intimate details of every other family. The entire neighborhood knew that we were Nancy's sister's kids who had been abandoned by their father and his good-for-nothing woman.

For the first time in my life I had other children to play with besides Ray. I had never had any real friends until I went to live with Aunt Nancy. There were children in every house on our block. They all had mothers and fathers. All the parents loved all the children. We ate together. Played together. Went on outings together.

It took Ray and me a few weeks to get settled in. Aunt Nancy talked to us about our mother's side of the family and about family matters. We got to meet our relatives. They all seemed nice, but they always gave Ray and I that "oh, you poor things" look I hated.

Nett called us every day for awhile, but the more we settled in, the less she called. Daddy drove by the house every now and then, usually with Mr. Johnny or some strange woman in the seat beside him, but most times he would not stop. Sometimes he would drop by and give us some money. Most times, though, he would pass me by while I was outside playing or walking home from school. At first, I figured he had simply not seen me. Then, I began to wonder why he had not looked for me. Eventually, when I saw him in the car, I would turn my head in the other direction.

In the first months I lived with Aunt Nancy I got to know the routine. All week she watched children while Bunny, Ray, and I went to school. We came home, did our homework, helped her with the children, and did household chores. On Friday evenings, we went to the laundromat. I had never seen a washing machine before. Nett had taught me how to wash clothes on a scrub board, and having a machine do the work for me was a wonderful experience. On Saturday morning, everyone had to get up early to do the major housekeeping: dusting, moping, waxing floors, washing windows, cleaning the refrigerator, washing the front steps, and cleaning the basement. It was a lot of work to complete by noon, but it had to be done by noon because that was when Uncle Lee came home from work and the good times rolled.

Every Saturday, Aunt Nancy, Uncle Lee, and a host of friends and relatives would get together in the basement to drink and party. They drank Fighting Cock whiskey and Gordon's gin. They smoked Camel and Pall Mall cigarettes. They played Gene Chandler and Jackie Wilson records on the Victrola. They laughed, hooted, and howled way until midnight. If this gang of merry people were not at our house, we went to their houses. There was Aunt Dora and Uncle Lowell's house, Aunt Lizzie's house, Aunt Alma's house, Uncle Eli's house. There was an entire group of relatives I had never seen or heard of before who all knew everything about me and my life. They knew Grandma. They knew Daddy. They knew Nett. That is how I began to hear the stories.

"It's a damn shame!"

"That yellow bitch never wanted those kids!"

"That S.O.B. should be ashamed of himself."

"You know that other woman just had another baby! Yes, she did. Bold as the day is long!"

"Sarah is probably turning over in her grave."

"I wonder if they know about him."

"Somebody has to tell it sooner or later."

"It won't be me!"

"It damn sure won't be me."

The most interesting thing about Saturday nights were the fights. Inevitably, every Saturday night somebody would get drunk enough and bold enough to say something that insulted one of the other drunk people. That would start the fighting. Before you knew it, everyone was involved. Sisters fighting the other sister's husband. Husbands fighting the wife's brother. Husbands fighting wives. Wives fighting each other. The best fights took place between Aunt Nancy and Uncle Lee.

Together, this pair was a clone of Mutt and Jeff—one tall and thin, the other short and round. Uncle Lee was usually the drunkest one in the crowd. Aunt Nancy would get what she called "tipsy." In their fights, she was always the aggressor. At the slightest provocation, she would slap him or throw something at him. Once, she hit him on the head with a whiskey bottle. Poor Uncle Lee never fought back, he was usually too drunk. He would stagger around threatening her while she slapped him. It was a scene straight out of a comedy show.

On Sunday mornings, Aunt Nancy would crawl up from the basement to make sure we children went to church. When we returned, dinner would be cooked and ready and all would be well between her and Uncle Lee.

⋏⋎⋏

Aunt Nancy was the strong, silent type. She did not say much when she was angry, but when she did, it was usually followed by a pinch, slap, or a full-fledged whipping. Aunt Nancy whipped you. She would pick up anything within her reach and hit you with it. One time, she beat my brother Ray with the cat.

It went like this: Ray wanted to go out. Aunt Nancy told him no. He asked for a reason. She refused to give him one. As he walked out of the kitchen and up the stairs to his room, he mumbled something under his breath. Aunt Nancy hated mumbling. By the time he got to the top of the stairs, Ray had a little chant going:

"Going to Uncle Eli's, you can't go!"

"Going downtown, you can't go!"

"Going to the park, you can't go!"

Aunt Nancy heard him. Hell, everybody heard him he was shouting so loud. I was kind of proud of him. Ray had never talked back to anyone before, no matter what they did to him. This time was different, though. As he stomped up the stairs singing to himself, Aunt Nancy called him. He didn't hear her. She thought he was ignoring her. Baby, the cat, was lounging on the kitchen counter. Furious, Aunt Nancy grabbed Baby and went after Ray. Holding the cat by its feet, she swung it at him. Ray tried to ward of the blow, but both paws and all of Baby's claws caught him across the back. The cat squealed like a stuck pig. Ray screamed. I fell on the floor laughing. Needless to say, I got popped in the chops for being disrespectful.

Aunt Nancy was not fond of my father. Whenever Daddy

called to say he was coming, I would get all dressed and wait for him on the front steps of the house. He rarely showed up. If I cried about it, Aunt Nancy promptly told me to shut my mouth. At some point I got the message that she did not like Nett, either. Perhaps it was when I overheard some of the conversations between Aunt Nancy and Grandma. Maybe it was the things Aunt Nancy said to me while dressing me to go out with Nett on a Saturday afternoon. According to Aunt Nancy, Nett was a "lying witch" who no longer wanted anything to do with me. True, Nett's calls and visits were down to about once a month. Aunt Nancy also told me that Nett took me and Ray in because it was the only way she could get my father. Nett had been after Daddy for years, Aunt Nancy claimed, but he had ignored her. It was not until she took some interest in his children that Daddy even gave Nett the time of day. The final blow came when Aunt Nancy informed me that if she had her way, Nett would never see me or my brother again. I was devastated. I was crushed. I was lost.

Aunt Nancy and Uncle Lee had told Ray and me to call them "Mommy" and "Daddy" if we wanted to. I wanted to, but I couldn't. I simply did not want a mother who kept her hair in the dresser drawer and a father who only spoke when he was drunk. The most profound thing I ever heard Uncle Lee say was "Great Googa Mooga." Beside that, it just didn't seem right to have a mother and a father who did not have the same last name as I did.

⚞⚟⚞

Gradually, things began to change for the worse at Aunt Nancy's house. The fighting between her and Uncle Lee became more frequent. Aunt Nancy began taking in more children because Uncle Lee was increasingly absent on Friday nights after he got paid. Sometimes he would disappear for days at a time. Aunt Nancy started having trouble with her blood pressure. There were days she could not even get out of bed. On those days, I would stay home from school to help her with the children.

Aunt Nancy got word that Uncle Lee had another woman. She also got word about where the woman lived. If Uncle Lee had been gone for a few days, Aunt Nancy would call a taxi and have the cabbie drive through the block where the woman lived to see if she could spot Uncle Lee's car. I went along for the ride on many of these taxi missions. If she spotted the car, Aunt Nancy would have the driver take us home. Then she would get on the telephone and call the woman's house. She would call and hang up so many times, it must have made Uncle Lee's visit unbearable.

Shortly after Aunt Nancy started her calling, Uncle Lee would come home. As soon as he hit the door, the fighting would begin. If Uncle Lee was drunk, the fights were funny. If he was sober, the fighting was vicious and bloody. When I got tired of watching these fights, I would go upstairs and watch television with Ray. He always seemed oblivious to what was going on outside of his room.

Aunt Nancy gave me my first lesson in how to tame a man's wild oats. After having been gone for a few days, Uncle Lee came home, sober as a judge, bright and early one Saturday morning. Aunt Nancy didn't say a word to him as she breezed past him with a hammer as he came in the door. Silently, she walked outside to the car and, with two quick taps, broke its windshield out. Just as silently, she walked back into the house and went back to cleaning the greens. Uncle Lee broke down on the spot and cried like a baby.

Aunt Nancy's actions, and Uncle Lee's reaction to them, became the talk of the neighborhood. Everybody knew. The adults laughed. The children marveled. Because Uncle Lee couldn't drive to work with the windshield out, Aunt Nancy took in three more children to make the money to get the car window fixed. I learned then that the way to get a man to do what you want him to do is to destroy something he loves.

The car incident took the wind out of everyone's sails. The house became quiet, almost dismal. Uncle Lee came home every night and usually stayed home all weekend. Ray tried out for and made the football team, which meant he was gone most of the time. I stayed in the house with Baby the cat and ate everything I could get my hands on. Aunt Nancy started playing Bingo three or four nights a week and all day on Saturdays.

The more Aunt Nancy played Bingo, the drunker Uncle Lee got. When she came home late on Saturday nights, they would sit around in the basement and drink, and then they would start to fight. I always seemed to be around for the fights and for the clean up afterwards. I was the youngest one in the house, so I guess that made me the easiest to order around. Get the ice. Bring me the broom. Get the mop. Get the alcohol. Aunt Nancy used alcohol the way Nett used witch hazel.

It occurred to me that it would be much easier to try to get them not to fight than to clean up the mess afterwards, so whenever Aunt Nancy came home from Bingo, I tried everything in my power to keep her from going down to the basement, where I knew Uncle Lee would for sure be drinking, laying in wait, and itching for a fight. I would ask her a thousand questions, try to get her to help me bake a cake. Sometimes, I would even break something just so she would be mad at me and stay upstairs, anything to distract her. One time, I even cut my finger with a razor blade. Desperate times called for desperate measures. But Aunt Nancy would patiently answer my questions, mend whatever wounds or breakages I had caused, and then head straight for the basement to tangle with drunk old Uncle Lee.

THE

Journal

When things are happening in your life that you do not want, you simply have to say NO! When people are imposing things upon you that you do not want, you must say NO! When events and circumstances are occurring that you do not want to participate in, you have the right to say NO! This is called denial, not to be confused with the psycho-therapeutic term that means refusing to admit that something is happening. Spiritual denial is refusing to accept something that you do not want, that you believe is not good for you. When you deny a thing the right to exist, you dismiss it from your life.

By refusing to accept nonproductive, abusive, or destructive situations, attitudes, habits, or relationships, you can take control of your life. That is, if you are not a child. If you are a child who says no to certain adults who are in charge, you will either be ignored or chastised for being disrespectful. If you are a child who knows that what is going on in your life is not good for you, you become a danger to the adults in charge. And when children become dangerous, they must be silenced, by any means necessary.

CHAPTER 7

The Chisel

Uncle Lee...

   During the five years I lived with Aunt Nancy and Uncle Lee, I cannot remember Uncle Lee saying anything to me other than the obligatory greetings when he was sober. He never asked me about school, never spoke to my friends. If I asked him a question, he would ask me what "Mommy" had said, meaning Aunt Nancy. He called her "Mommy." She called him "Daddy." He refused to answer the telephone when it rang. He ate dinner in silence. I think I remember him reading the newspaper every now and then. I do not know if he had an education. When I think about it, I knew absolutely nothing about the man who fed and clothed me for five years and told me to call him Daddy too. That is, I knew nothing about the sober man. I knew a great deal about the drunk man.

   When Uncle Lee was drunk, he was a riot. He would tell jokes. He would wrestle you to the floor. He would dance and make believe he was singing a Jackie Wilson song. When Uncle Lee was drunk, he could do anything. He loved to paint when he was drunk. He did a pretty good job too, but in the process, he would paint his face, his hands, and anything that wasn't covered.

   When Uncle Lee was drunk, he would stagger up to me and ask, "What you doin'?" It was useless to try to explain, so I usually said, "Nothing." Most times, that would satisfy him and he would just stumble away. Other times, he would push, pull, or drag me around playfully. If I got annoyed with him, he would give me a sad, puppy dog face and offer money as consolation. He never counted what he gave. He would simply take the wad of bills from his pocket and shove it at me, weaving and reeling the whole time. Being conservative, I would only take a dollar or two. If he was very drunk, or if he had been particularly offensive, I could get as much as five dollars from him.

"You know I love you, don't you?" he would ask with that sad, drunk look on his face.

"Yes, Daddy, I know you love me, but you are squeezing my arm!"

"Oh, I ain't gonna hurt you, girl. I love you. Don't you know you are Daddy's little baby?"

"Yes, Daddy, I'm your little baby. Can I have some money, please?"

I should have seen it coming, but I did not. Even if I had seen it, I would not have known what it was. I had never seen it before. At age 11, with short kinky hair, straight skinny legs, no breasts, and no figure to talk about. I was bored, I was sad, I was lonely, and on my way out of my mind.

It was about two o'clock on a rainy Saturday afternoon, on a day not unlike many others I had come to know. My mother, who was really my aunt, had gone to Philadelphia to play Bingo. My sister, who was really my cousin, was out dancing and being marvelous. My brother, who was in fact my brother, was on another planet upstairs in his room. My father, who was really my uncle, was out cold, drunk on the sofa in the basement.

Money was the only way out of my chronic state of depression. With enough money, I figured, I could buy some comic books, a Pepsi in a long-necked bottle, and a few candy bars. If there was enough left over, I could get some purple bubble bath from Woolworth's. I knew Uncle Lee would give me some money, if only I could wake him up.

2:10. No one was around. No one was due back for awhile.

I crept downstairs to the basement where Uncle Lee lay sleeping on the sofa. The stench of liquor hung like a cloud over the room. As luck would have it, Uncle Lee had emptied his pockets on the coffee table. I was faced with a dilemma: Do I take the money and run, or wait until he wakes up? Another dilemma: there were only five- and ten-dollar bills on the table. All the coins had fallen on the floor too close to Uncle Lee, who lay asleep on the sofa.

Holding my breath, I carefully slid a five-dollar bill out of the pile. Very quietly, I crawled around the coffee table, crept noiselessly back up the stairs, left the house, and dashed up the block to Woolworth's.

3:25. I was back in my room with my loot spread over my bed, trying to figure out how I would explain this stuff. I had about three hours to devour the candy and soda. The comic books could be hidden. The bubble bath, that was another dilemma. I decided to worry about it later.

4:00. Uncle Lee stumbled up from the basement, calling up the stairs for Aunt Nancy. Quickly, I hid my new comic books under the bed and threw the sheets over the candy. Uncle Lee poked his head into my room. I reminded him, "She's at Bingo." Where's Ray? "He's upstairs, in his room." What you doin'? "I'm reading comics." Uncle Lee staggered away and went back downstairs.

4:02. Relieved, I went back to reading and drinking and eating candy.

4:10. I was enjoying a mouthful of Almond Joy when Uncle Lee called again. By the time I reached the top step leading to the basement, he gave me my marching orders.

"Fix me something to eat, please."

"Okay, I'll get it." I figured it was the least I could do. After all, I had stolen his money.

I went through the routine: get the ingredients out of the refrigerator. Bread, mayonnaise, sandwich meat. Slice the salami thin, picking those little black things out. Put the sandwich on a plate. Get a napkin. Check the kitchen, making sure everything is put away in case somebody else comes in.

I took the sandwich down to the basement, holding my breath

as I approached Uncle Lee. The smell of salami and stale liquor can make you sick to your stomach.

4:16. I could not tell if Uncle Lee was asleep or not. He was half-sitting on the sofa, half-kneeling on the floor. All his money was on the floor. That made me a little nervous.

"Here's your sandwich, Daddy." I put the sandwich on the coffee table and stepped back. God, I hated that smell.

"Thank you, baby. You want some?"

"No, thank you."

"Come on and eat some with me," he mumbled, his eyes still closed.

The guilt forced me to be nice to him. Moving closer to the sofa, I reached out to take a piece of sandwich from the plate. Besides, it looked like he had fallen asleep again.

Suddenly, Uncle Lee grabbed my wrist and pulled me to him. Half sliding, half falling, my heart leapt. He knows!

4:21. Sliding on the coins on the floor, I tripped over the coffee table. We bumped heads.

"Be careful, baby. Don't fall." He grabbed me tighter.

My heart was racing. He knew I had taken his money.

"I'm sorry. I'm sorry."

Uncle Lee looked even more confused. He didn't know why I was apologizing.

His voice was soothing, hoarse. "It's okay, baby. Be careful. Sit down and eat with me, please." He was pulling me down to the couch.

I sat. I wanted to cry.

Uncle Lee asked me if I wanted to have some fun. Oh, God! Cops and robbers! He knows!

"I can show you how to have some fun."

What the heck was he talking about? I wondered. I felt trapped. Mechanically, I picked up the sandwich. Fumbling with it, I stared at the floor. When he pulled me closer to him, groping at my shoulders, my brain went blank.

"I love you, and I want to show you how to have some fun."

My mind was trying to process what he was saying and doing.

It did not make sense. Bending me back on the couch, he took my face in his hands, turned it toward his face, and, in one swift move, he kissed me, plunging his tongue deep into my mouth. The smell of stale liquor filled my head. I squeezed the sandwich I was holding so hard the meat oozed out and slid through my fingers to the floor.

4:27. I was gagging. Uncle Lee was crawling, leaning, laying on top of me, mumbling about love and fun, pushing his tongue into my ear, licking my face. It finally dawned on me to drop the damn sandwich and push him off, but I realized I had mayonnaise all over my hands and that I had gotten it all over the sides of the sofa. All I could think was "Aunt Nancy is going to kill me."

Uncle Lee's hands were groping and fumbling wildly over my body. His knee was between my legs. He was pulling at my blouse. Pulling up my skirt. Yanking and tearing at my panties. They tore. He tore my blouse. This was not fun.

4:33. Where does your mind go when it leaves you? How do you breathe with someone's tongue in your mouth? How can you hold your breath and scream at the same time? How do you cry when something is ripping your insides apart? How do you fight your uncle who has been your father for the last three years? You don't. You lay mindlessly on the sofa and "have fun."

5:07. The stench of liquor will not make you sick when you know your mother is dead, your stepmother does not want you, and your father does not have time for you. The pain of a grown man's penis tearing at your vagina will not kill you when you know you are a thief. Your body has no meaning at the moment you are being raped because your mind has left you.

5:12. Parts of your body are numb. Other parts are hot. Parts are cold. Other parts bleed. Parts of you ache. Other parts are numb.

My ears were hot. My soul was cold. My heart was sore from pounding. My eyes were running water. Everything below my waist was dead.

5:20. There is nothing more soothing than a violet bubble bath after you have been raped. Thirty-two ounces of cheap bubble bath in a #4 bathtub will wash away the stench of liquor, sweat, and mayonnaise. It brings life back into your body. It revives your heart and the other parts of you that have died. It washes away the guilt of stealing money from your uncle who wants to be your father, who wants to be something else you have no name for. What violet bubble bath will not, cannot, do is bring your mind back from wherever it went during the unspeakable ordeal.

6:05. I think I went to bed. No, I went upstairs to tell Ray. No, I went to the telephone to call Nett. No, I went back to the bathroom to check my panties for blood. No, I went into the kitchen, crawled under the table, put my head on my knees, and cried.

I prayed: "Dear God, I am sorry I took the money and I will put it back. I won't eat any more candy. I will not read another comic book, just please help me not hurt. God, I'm sorry I put mayonnaise on the sofa. Please don't let Aunt Nancy be mad at me. I'm so sorry for everything, please help me. I don't have anywhere else to go. I spent all the money and I hid the comic books under the bed. I just want to throw up."

So I did, right in the kitchen chair.

6:45. I must have passed out. I woke up under the kitchen table, with my face in a chairful of vomit, after what seemed like hours. Baby, the cat, scratching at the back door brought me back to awareness of where I was and what I had done. I knew I had to clean up the mess before Aunt Nancy came home. I knew she would have no sympathy, no compassion, for me if she saw my regurgitated candy bars dripping off the side of her nice chair. I heard the sound of Uncle Lee's loud snoring coming from downstairs. As quietly as I could, I cleaned up my mess and washed my face. I let Baby in and swooped him up in my arms. I had to hold on to something, and I did not want anything moving in the house that could possibly wake up Uncle Lee.

I told Aunt Nancy the minute she walked in the door. She immediately went downstairs to the basement and confronted Uncle Lee. I sat stark still in the kitchen chair clutching Baby until Aunt Nancy called me to come downstairs. Uncle Lee was lounging on the sofa. I couldn't look at him. I stared at the floor. Aunt Nancy asked me to repeat what I had said happened. Somehow, I found the words to recount the incident in his presence. Uncle Lee lied, "I didn't hurt her. I didn't penetrate her." I did not even know what penetration was, but I knew he had hurt me, and I told him so. Aunt Nancy told me to go upstairs.

Everything was too quiet. The entire house was still. There was no fight that Saturday night. I sat on the edge of my bed with Baby in my arms, trying to hear what, if anything, was going on in the basement, not really wanting to know. I woke up Sunday morning in my clothes, with more blood in my panties.

I never heard another word about it. Shortly after that, however, Bunny started taking me everywhere she went.

⋋⋏⋋

I lost my mind to guilt and shame on a rainy Saturday afternoon. I stayed crazy for nineteen years. I went to school guilty and crazy. I won awards while I was guilty and crazy. I had my first child when I was guilty and crazy. I got married to ease my guilt when I was crazy. I had two other children by two different men, because I was guilty and crazy. I spent eleven years feeling guilty about being on public assistance when I was crazy. I went in and out of relationships with men who had absolutely no idea that I was guilty and crazy. I got a bachelor's degree, summa cum laude, even though I was guilty and crazy. When I was 32 years old, a gentle man told me he loved me, that I was beautiful, and he held my hand. That was when I totally lost my mind.

THE Journal

Splashing, frantic, broad strokes. Changing brushes, carelessly bleeding colors. Black. Grey. Brown. Dark blue hues thrown together, reflecting back to you the images of a dark soul, creating darker souls, reflecting all the pain. Bleeding pain. Crushing pain. Bone-chilling pain. You scream, but nobody can hear you because everybody is screaming. You run, howling hysterically through the night, into the morning. Why does morning take all night to come? During the night the colors dry, the pain intensifies.

Oh, Lord! Rock my soul in the bosom of light. The bosom of love. The bosom of peace. Wait! No rocking here! There is more painting to be done. Oh, Lord! My soul looks back and wonders... Please, please, rock my soul. In somebody's bosom. Anybody's bosom.

There seem to be no bosoms available. All bosoms are painting. Now, pick up your brush and let's get busy!

CHAPTER 8

The Model

Bunny...

She didn't say much. I can imagine that after being an only child for sixteen years, having your home invaded by two waifs would be a traumatic experience. But Bunny never showed any signs of resentment. She was nice enough, but basically she ignored us. She was our cousin, about to become our "sister."

Bunny was all Aunt Nancy lived for. Small and dainty like her mother, she was cuter than cute. She wore the best clothes, ate the best food, went to the best schools, and had the best of two worlds: her mother's heart and her father's wallet.

Bunny had a lot of stuff, and I was told very early on not to bother any of it. She had clothes, dolls, records, shoes, perfumes, money, and everything else I had never had to call my own. She had her own room. Her own bed. Her own television. Her own telephone. She had lots of friends and they loved her almost as much as her parents. It was quite sickening to watch.

Being a teenager, Bunny went out a lot. When she wasn't out, her friends came over to see her. Most of her friends were quite thrilled to learn that Bunny had inherited a little sister and brother. They did not seem to mind me hanging around, but Bunny did. She would shoo me away. If Aunt Nancy heard Bunny fussing at me, she would scold me for being a pest. That's what I became: a pest.

The worst thing about Bunny was not her fault. It was that

Aunt Nancy compared everything I did to what Bunny did.

"Why can't you be neat like Bunny?"

"Why can't you be quiet like Bunny?"

"Why don't you learn how to sew like Bunny?"

"You better stop eating so much, you are bigger than Bunny and she is older than you."

Everything Bunny did was right, which made everything I did wrong. But how was I ever to become a Bunny clone if I could not go in her room, borrow her stuff, or hang around her? Of course, I went in Bunny's room when she was out, and, of course, I rummaged through her things. That's what little sisters do. Of course, I always got caught and got in trouble for it. That was also part of the process.

As Bunny got older and started going out more, I found a way to turn the tides in my favor: I decided to become totally indispensable to Aunt Nancy. Anytime she needed something, I ran to get it. If she wanted something done, I would do it. When Bunny was not there, I helped with the children, cleaned the house, ran the errands, and did all the things Bunny did not want to do anyway. Bunny never went with Aunt Nancy on the taxi missions. Bunny was never there to clean up the basement after the Saturday night fights between Aunt Nancy and Uncle Lee. Bunny did not organize Aunt Nancy's Bingo chips by color and put them in plastic baggies. That's what I did. This made Aunt Nancy pretty happy and helped ease the tension between me and Bunny.

Still, I was totally fascinated with the person called Bunny. I wanted desperately to be like her. She was somebody. I was a nobody. I had no home. I had nothing. Bunny had a mother, a father, friends, clothes, and a pretty decent body. Plus, she was a dancer. An African dancer. The minute I showed an interest in her interest, things got much better between us. She even let me hang out with her.

Bunny knew every dancing haunt in New York City. We went to classes in Manhattan, Queens, and the Bronx. The best classes were the ones Bunny taught herself, in the projects in Red Hook. There were live drummers at those classes. I loved to hear those drums. I met some of the best drummers in the world at those classes.

Scoby Stroman. Chief Bey. Sunny Morgan. And a host of others too numerous to name. I met some pretty famous dancers too. Chuck Davis. Charles Moore. Alfred Perryman. Alvin Ailey.

But the biggest thrill of my life was when I met Michael Babatunde Olatunji. Not only was he a drummer, he was an African. Bunny was really into African culture, but to know that she knew a real African made her special. Meeting "Baba" dispelled all the myths I had learned about Africa. He did not have a bone in his nose, he did not swing from the trees, and he was not naked. He was a real person, and he treated me very well.

Bunny was one of Olatunji's dancers at the 1964 World's Fair. That made us celebrities in the neighborhood. Everybody was talking about it. My "sister" was a dancer at the World's Fair. They didn't even mind that she was doing African dance, and this was well before the days of "Black is Beautiful." Most folks figured that if Bunny was into it, it had to be alright.

On the weekends, I got to dress up in African clothes and go with Bunny to the World's Fair. I spent most of the time sitting backstage, which was just fine with me. I was one of Olatunji's dancer's little sister, so everybody took special care of me. It also got me out of the house and away from the Saturday night fights and Uncle Lee. I often wondered if that was the reason Bunny started taking me with her. I also wondered if Aunt Nancy ever told Bunny about what Uncle Lee had done to me. I did not ask. She never said.

⋀⋎⋀

Bunny also took me with her when she went to work for Mr. François. He was an elderly white man, a Frenchman. He was a pattern maker, Bunny said. He made patterns for bathing suits. His studio was housed in a dingy apartment building on Eighth Avenue in Manhattan. The first couple of times I went, I sat in a little room outside the studio and waited for Bunny to come out. On about my third visit, Bunny peeked in on me and asked if I would let Mr. François take some pictures of me.

Me? I looked around dumbly. What the hell did he want pictures of *me* in a bathing suit for? Mr. François came into the room and told me I would be just fine. He handed me a few bathing suits to try on. None of them fit. He said I would be a good model for a size 14 suit, but he would have to measure me for it. Since he had a dressmaker's model, a long table full of fabric and sewing items, floodlights, and a camera in the studio, I thought everything was legitimate, so I agreed. Besides, Bunny did it, so I knew it had to be okay.

Bunny waited for me in the other room. I stood stiffly in my underwear while Mr. François busied himself pinning and tucking pieces of material to me. It was a little weird, but at the end of the session, he gave me twenty dollars.

I went wild. Twenty dollars! This was absolutely the greatest thing to ever happen to me, I thought. All I had to do was stand in front of some white man in my underwear, get stuck by a few straight pins, and I could make twenty bucks? Stick me, baby, stick me!

It didn't take long before I learned what was really going on. One day, Mr. François called for Bunny, but she was not at home. He asked me if I could come to work the next day. I said sure. I liked the fact that I had a "job" at 13. I took the train into Manhattan alone, arriving at the studio right on time. Mr. François buzzed me in. I climbed the stairs to his apartment and began what had become the routine. Into the bathroom. Strip down to the underwear. Into the studio. Assume the position. Arms outstretched. Legs apart. We worked for about an hour before Mr. François matter-of-factly told me to take off my panties.

I didn't move. He asked me what was wrong. I couldn't think fast enough. No, I couldn't think at all. I had earlier gotten over the shock of having Mr. François see me in my underwear, but to even consider having him see me without my panties on shut my brain completely down.

Mr. François explained to me that he needed to make a tight-fitting bottom for a bathing suit. I would have to take my panties off so he could get the measurements just right. He said he would not hurt me. I didn't believe him, but the thought of the twenty dollars he always paid me gave me courage. I went into the bathroom and sat there for a long time. "Why can't you be like Bunny?" was ringing in my head. "Why can't you do what Bunny does?" Slowly, I took my panties off.

I wondered if this was why Mr. François always closed the door when he and Bunny were working. I wondered if he was taking advantage of me because Bunny was not there. I wondered if he was going to do to me the same thing Uncle Lee had done. The thought made me nauseous. Was I being like Bunny or not? She had brought me to this place. She had to know what was going on. I wanted to call home. I wanted to get out of there.

Mr. François knocked on the door. I jumped to attention. Slowly I opened the door, walked across the room, and stood in front of a white man stark naked. I walked across the room trying to ignore my nudity. Mr. François turned on the floodlights, went to the table and cut a piece of fabric, and approached me. He gently draped the cloth around my body.

"Open your legs," he said, patting my inner thighs. I froze.

"What's the matter? What's wrong? I won't hurt you."

I had heard that before. Open legs meant we were "having fun." Fun hurt. I closed my eyes, took a deep breath, and spread my legs apart, while Mr. François tucked the fabric into my vagina with his third finger.

I soon figured out that Mr. François was a bootleg pornographer and generally a "dirty old man." But after I posed naked, my salary rose to fifty dollars a visit, so I kept on going. Our pattern making eventually graduated into regular nude posing and a lot of touching and feeling on his part of my parts. He never tried to do it to me. One day, while Mr. François was "working" with Bunny, I found a bag of pictures. There were pictures of me, of Bunny, of people I did not know. There were other pictures too, of women and children, black and white, nude, making sexual gestures and having sex. My head started pounding. I felt sick. I took all my pictures out of the pile and stuffed them down in my socks. I had no idea what Mr. François planned to do with the pictures, but I knew he would never take another one of me.

By the time Bunny finished her session, I had turned green. I told Bunny I had an upset stomach and we left together. I knew I would never see Mr. François again. Bunny kept going. If she mentioned him to me, I got sick to my stomach. She knew what was going on. She also knew I knew she knew.

⋏⋎⋏⋎⋏

The accumulated traumas of my life began taking their toll on me. My hair started falling out. Soon I had no hair at my temples and a big bald spot on the back of my head. Bunny would massage Sulfur-8 into my scalp every night. When that didn't help, she tried a black hair grease called Dax. It had tar oil in it. My head smelled so bad, folks could smell me coming into the room. Nothing seemed to help. My hair continued to fall out by the handful.

It got so bad, Aunt Nancy bought me a wig to wear to school. Bunny cut and styled it for me, but the first day I went to school with it on, all the other kids laughed at me. Some threatened to pull it off. When I got home, I told Bunny. The next day she made sure to pin the wig to the few sprigs of hair left on my head.

In addition to going bald, I was getting fatter and fatter. Food made me feel better. It did not yell at me or hit me or hurt me. I loved food. It was my best friend, next to Nett, who hardly came around anymore, a fact that made me eat even more. Aunt Nancy complained that it was hard buying clothes for a fat kid. The only person who did not mind shopping for me was Nett. Whenever I needed clothes, she would come for me and take me shopping. We had to go to the chubby shop because nothing else seemed to fit.

Nett was good about shopping for me. She always knew just what to buy so I wouldn't look frumpy. She thought I looked good in white, so she always bought me white blouses and jumpers with a yoke to cover my bulging belly and butt. Sometimes, she would also tell me what not to eat so that I could lose weight. "Put mayonnaise on just one side of the bread when you make a sandwich," she would advise. I would agree to try, but when no one was looking, I would make not one but two sandwiches, with lots of mayonnaise. I'd eat one and hide the other one under the bed for later.

Then again, even though I was fat, I could dance. I went to dance classes with Bunny and to any other dance class I could find.

70

By the time I reached puberty, some of my fat had turned to muscle and I started to get a shape. It was a big shape, but it was a shape.

One day, I grew breasts. I had no idea where they came from, they just seemed to pop up overnight. Bunny took me to the store to buy some training bras. I bought one white one and one pink one. My breasts grew as I got bigger and fatter, but not in proportion to my body. Soon, training bras could no longer fit around my body, so I had to get regular bras. Bunny brought me a Playtex Cross-Your-Heart bra, you know, the kind with the stiff, pointy cups. Unfortunately, my cups were only half filled, so the cups crumpled under my blouses, and it looked as if I had two wads of newspaper stuck on my chest.

I quickly found a solution. I put one sock in each cup. That smoothed the picture right out. The day I put those socks in that bra, boys began to notice me. They no longer minded that I wore a wig. They did not care that I was chubby, or that my legs were thin. I had breasts. Nothing else mattered. It took a minute, but I soon made the connection between the socks in my bra and my new popularity with the boys. I started getting love letters. I had two brothers fighting over me. One boy asked me to "go with him." Even my brother's football friends began taking an interest in me. I took a chance and put an entire pair of socks in each cup. The boys went wild. The teacher sent a note home. In a matter of minutes after Aunt Nancy read the note, I was beaten, grounded, and reduced once more to the crumpled newspaper look.

⚶⚶⚶

One day, when Bunny and I were in Red Hook dancing, we got a call that Aunt Nancy had been rushed to the hospital. The ride home seemed like the longest train ride I had ever taken. When we got to the house, nobody was there. We caught a taxi and headed to the hospital. I couldn't go upstairs because I was too young, so I sat in the lobby for hours until Uncle Lee and Bunny finally came downstairs. We rode home in silence.

Days went by. Weeks went by. Aunt Nancy did not come home. I had no idea what was wrong with her and nobody told me a thing. Nobody even talked.

The house was still. The children kept coming for awhile. Bunny tried to take care of them, but she had to go to work in the evening and I had to keep up with my homework. Soon the children stopped coming. The silence really became unbearable then.

Finally, one Sunday, Ray and I were allowed to go up and see Aunt Nancy. She had lost so much weight I hardly recognized her. She could barely talk and her skin looked gray. Someone explained to us that she had gout, and that her circulation had been cut off. There were lots of people in her room, but Aunt Nancy focused all of her attention on us. She wanted me to sit on the bed with her. I did for awhile, but she smelled funny so I got up. We visited for about two hours until Aunt Nancy fell asleep. I kissed her on the forehead before I left. The moment I did, I knew I would never see her again.

Aunt Nancy died about three weeks later. By then, however, she had been gone so long, I didn't miss her anymore, but we had to go to the funeral. The day she died, the house filled up with people. Everybody brought food. There was lots of talking, laughing, and drinking as the family gathered to say good-bye to Aunt Nancy. Daddy came. Grandma came. Nett came. All the aunts, uncles, and cousins came.

My cousin Junior came with Aunt Dora and Uncle Lowell. I couldn't believe how much this kid looked like me. He was a year younger than me, but we had the same eyes, the same nose, the same shape face. He was even chubby like I was.

There was so much going on. People were really giving me the "you poor thing, you" look. I started having flashbacks. I didn't know what was happening. I saw the people. I saw the food. I saw my father and grandmother. I saw a big black car. Then I saw the casket with the thin lady named Sarah I had come to know in my dreams. Her eyes flew open and I screamed.

I was screaming and shaking my head. Bunny started crying. Somebody, I think it was Grandma, was holding my shoulders telling me to calm down. They thought it was my grief over Aunt Nancy. I didn't know what was happening. I was trying to clear my head, but there was too much going on. Nett told me to go upstairs to Ray's room.

I crept up the stairs. The room was full of boys. All of Ray's friends had come over and they were watching football. I crawled behind my brother and laid down on his pillow. I must have been there for an hour, listening to those boys talk about girls and football. My head was spinning, I had such a headache.

I was about to scream at them to shut up when Junior came into the room. He did a high five to all the guys and sat down on the bed next to Ray. Without any warning whatsoever, in front of all of those people, Ray said to me, "Hey Ronnie, guess what? Did you know that Junior is our younger brother?"

My head exploded! Jesus Lord, just let me die! I am only 13 years old. I just lost my "mother" for the second time. My wig is killing me and now you want me to deal with this! Just let me die! Please!

Ray tried to explain. I tried not to listen. Junior was born two months before our mother died, Ray told me. She "gave" him to Aunt Dora and Uncle Lowell to raise because she knew she was dying and she also knew Daddy didn't want him.

"Shit, Daddy didn't want any of us," Ray said angrily. "The least he could have done was kept us all together to give us all away!"

I looked at Ray as if he was out of his mind. "You are so stupid! He *did* give us all away!"

Ray thought about what I'd said a minute, then he went back to watching the game. "You got that right, Ronnie."

Junior just sat there, looking "like" me, without saying a word.

I don't remember the funeral. I don't remember the cemetery. I have a vague recollection of the people coming to the house afterwards, and of everything getting still again. The house was still. Uncle Lee was still. Bunny was still. Ray was always off playing football. I was crazy.

Not long after Aunt Nancy died, Bunny decided I should take off my wig and start wearing my hair in a natural. She and her boyfriend John gave me a nice haircut. The next day, I went to school with a quarter-inch of hair covering my head. The kids howled. They figured it was just some more of that "crazy African stuff" Bunny and I were into.

"Ugga, Ugga, Boo-Boo."

"Hey, Rhonda, have you seen Tarzan lately?"

I didn't even care. I was crazy. On the days I wasn't crazy, I was dead. The only reason I kept an ounce of life in my body was to dance. I continued to do my African dancing at all the local talent shows. Dancing helped develop the structure of my body. I was no longer fat; I was big and muscular. I may not have had any hair, but my breasts filled out the cups of my bra. After awhile, the kids in school just left me alone.

Something good had to happen for me, it just had to. Nobody, not even a big, ugly kid like me deserved to live this way, I thought. It took about three weeks after Aunt Nancy's death, but it did happen.

One Saturday, Bunny called me into her room. She said that Nett, she called her "Aunt Lynnette," had called and wanted to know if I wanted to come and live with her. By that time, however, Aunt Nancy had completely brainwashed me. I no longer trusted Nett. I believed what Aunt Nancy had told me about her just being after my father. She didn't want me.

Absolutely not! I replied. This pleased Bunny. You know Mommy would have wanted us all to stay together, she said. That was just fine with me.

In any event, Nett began to call and come around more often. At first, I was subdued about her visits. I wasn't going to be tricked again. But she persisted in being kind and attentive. We went to the movies every Saturday. One Saturday, we were in the Horn & Hardart automat. Nett asked me if she was my friend. I lied. "Yes." She explained to me that friends did not keep secrets from each other. Friends could tell each other anything and still be friends.

"I know that," I said coolly. I didn't.

Then she lowered the boom. Calmly, slowly, she asked, "Has your Uncle Lee ever, you know, touched you?"

I couldn't get my eyes off the plate of macaroni and cheese.

"You can tell me, you know. I've seen the way he looks at you, and I don't like it."

I began crying uncontrollably. No one had ever asked me about that. I had convinced myself that it didn't matter because I didn't think I mattered. Nett got out of her seat, came around the table, and put her arms around me. By now, I was wailing. People were staring at us.

"Come on, let's go to the ladies' room."

I couldn't move. I couldn't walk. Half dragging me, half carrying me, Nett took me into the bathroom, where I collapsed. We sat in the corner on the floor of the ladies' room in the automat and cried together.

The next day, I packed my clothes and went to live with Nett. Ray came a few months later after Bunny admitted she could not take care of him.

I was in such conflict. I did not understand why Nett wanted me after all the things everyone had told me about her. I was angry. I was in pain. Daddy was still writing numbers and making very little money. Nett was still working long hours. Ray was sulking and having more and more asthma attacks. Everybody was trying to capture the spirit of family we once knew, but it was too late. Too much had happened. The best we could do was be civil to one another and stay out of each another's way. But even that was hard.

PART II

It Came to Pass...

THE Journal

Nobody ever asks
> how I feel
> what I think
> what I want
> what I know

Or even if I know who I am.
Therefore,
> how can anybody know
> that I am not as okay
> as they all assume I am.

Or what I think about the fact
> that I am not one who particularly wants,
> but needs

Or that I don't know
> what they think I know

Or if I do know what they think
> I don't know.

I wonder if anybody knows
> who I am today or
> who I will be tomorrow

Or what it feels like for nobody to know
> what I feel
> what I think
> what I want
> what I need
> what I know.

If only somebody would ask anybody what nobody dares ask me,
maybe somebody, possibly anybody, would know,
how I feel
what I think
what I want
what I need
and what I know and/or if I know
who I am today or who I will be tomorrow.
Now, if nobody asks somebody
what anybody could ask me,
who will ever know?

CHAPTER 9

A Chipped Figurine

Ronald...

I really tried to like Nett again, but too many people had told me too many things. She had changed too. She wasn't as mellow and kind as she had been when I was younger. We now had differing opinions on almost everything, from how I wore my hair to what I wore to school. I was still chubby, but I knew how to dress myself. Nett seemed to be very critical of me and everything I did. She kept warning me about boys and men. She said I was "too naive." She did not like my best friend Debbie, who lived in the building across from us, because she said Debbie was "too grown for her age."

I stopped going to dance classes with Bunny, but dancing was in my blood. I studied ballet, modern dance, and, when I could find it, African dance. Nett liked the fact that I was dancing, but it wasn't enough. I was looking for a way to get away from her when I found out about a local drum-and-bugle corps called the Bluejackets.

Recruiters from the Bluejackets came to my school. They brought a troop of kids who did a drill routine. I had never seen anything like it. I was one of the first to sign up. The corps met every Tuesday and Thursday night. We wore uniforms that looked like those worn by enlisted men in the Navy. We learned most of the things you would learn in the Navy: the different kinds of boats, how to tie knots, how to tell military time, how to survive at sea. I had no plans to go to sea, but I was convinced the information would surely come in handy one day.

You earned rank in the Bluejackets by taking tests. When you got to a certain rank, you could join the color guard. If you were in the color guard, you could march with the band. The band was where all the top-ranking boys were. Black boys of all ages and shapes. Sharp black boys who could march and play instruments. Fine black boys who were laying bets on who would be the first one to get to me. I tested my little butt off and joined the color guard.

Nett did not mind that I was in the Bluejackets, but joining the color guard got to be a little sticky because it meant I had to add Friday night to the other two nights and to the Saturday daytimes when I was out at dance classes. When Mr. Holiday, the band coordinator, called to assure her I would get escorted home every night after the meetings, that cooled her out.

I had to stay on top of my school work and keep the house clean. It was a lot, but it was worth every moment of hard work. I was a good student, with a B-average even when I only studied a little bit, so school was not a problem. My biggest problem was deciding which boy I was going to go with. The ones I wanted were taken, and the ones that wanted me I did not want. By default, I ended up with Ronald.

Ronald wasn't bad, but he was about four inches shorter than I was. He was also very round. But he was nice. He had two younger brothers who were also in the Bluejackets, and he couldn't go anywhere without them, so he was a pretty safe pick. When the corps went on a bus trip, his brothers always sat between us. Mr. Holiday and Mrs. Mack, his co-coordinator, were also an obstacle. They were like watchdogs, watching to make sure the boyfriend-girlfriend thing between corps members did not get out of hand. Still, Ronald and I went unnoticed for a long time, partly because of his brothers, and partly because we looked so damn innocent.

One of the older members of the Bluejackets, actually it was Mr. Holiday's son Jackie, figured out that if the boys and girls in the group couldn't get together and socialize on trips, we should get together at some other time. So, he began to organize hooky parties. Once a week during the day, when we were supposed to be in school and when Mr. and Mrs. Holiday were both at work, we all went to the Holidays' house to hang out and get loose. We had the best hooky parties in town. Everyone would contribute their lunch money to buy food for the day. Jackie, who played football for the Boys High team and weighed about two hundred pounds, loved to eat and usually did all of the cooking.

For the first hour or so we were wild, listening to records and dancing, screaming, and hollering to the fast ones. By eleven o'clock, somebody would put on a slow record. That's when the fun started. People would retreat to their corners to kiss and make out. Thank God, the Holiday's house only had one bedroom! And that was usually reserved for Jackie and whatever girl he was seeing that week. For the rest of us, the living room chairs and sofa worked just as well. The newcomers got the kitchen. Ronald and I were sofa kissers. We were playing it safe.

Soon, Jackie began to hold the parties more frequently, three or four times a week, and before long, everybody started failing in school. After I failed a biology test, I figured I had to cool out for awhile. The first hooky party I missed, Ronald took advantage of.

Beverly was new to the Bluejackets, but she was not new to playing hooky or to boys. We became friends because she was also a dancer. I did not know it, but she also liked Ronald. On the days I did not go to the hooky parties, she and Ronald paired up. Eventually, they got a crack at the bedroom.

A few weeks later, we were on a trip with the Bluejackets. Every time I turned around, Beverly was in Ronald's face. Actually, he was in her face. He sat with me, but he talked to her. When he bought me a soda, he bought her one too. I became suspicious. I asked a friend in the band what was up, and he told me that Beverly had given up the goods. My heart sank. I sat next to somebody else on the way home. I wouldn't even look at Ronald.

At the next hooky party I went to, I went into the bedroom

with the same guy who told me about Beverly and Ronald. When I came out, Beverly was gone and Ronald was clearly disturbed.

Ronald and I had talked about him being the first boy I would have sex with. I had just taken that away from him. It was an exhilarating feeling. I did not consider what I had done a sexual experience. It was an act of defiance, of revenge.

Ronald dumped Beverly immediately. He stopped sitting with me on the Bluejackets bus, and he stopped coming to the hooky parties. We did not speak.

Eventually, Nett asked me what had happened between Ronald and me. I told her, at least I told her the part about Ronald and Beverly. I did not tell her the part about my having sex or about the hooky parties. She asked me if I was sexually active. I lied. Relieved, she gave me the "don't trust other girls around your boyfriend" speech and asked me if I still liked Ronald. I told her I did. She explained to me that men sometimes did things like that. She said it did not mean they didn't like you, it's just that men can't seem to help themselves around women. Ronald was a nice boy, she said, and maybe he had sex with Beverly because I would not have sex with him.

Nett told me I should forgive Ronald because he had been so nice to me. I thought about it for awhile, and at the next Bluejackets meeting, I spoke to him. I think he grew two inches.

So, Ronald and I were on again. We also resumed going to the hooky parties at Jackie's house. Then something happened that made that impossible. One day during one of the parties, the telephone rang. Everybody froze. Jackie told us not to answer it, but we convinced him it might be one of the other kids calling to say they wanted to come over. He picked up the phone. It was a neighbor from around the corner. She told him that she had been watching us, that she had called his father at work, and that we had all better get out of that house immediately. Kids started running around like crazy, some naked, others half-dressed, grabbing books, coats, and shoes. It took three-and-a-half minutes for all of us to clear out. The problem was, it was eleven-thirty in the morning. We couldn't go to back to school, and if we stayed in the streets, the truant officers would pick us up. Ronald and I decided that we should go to his house.

Being alone in the house with Ronald, with four empty beds, was not a safe thing to do. We resisted the temptation for about fifteen minutes, then it was on. We had our own private hooky party, complete with lunch and an afternoon of cartoons. When it was time for me to leave, Ronald walked me to the bus stop. He kissed me goodbye and told me he would call me later, which he did.

Ronald and I started meeting at his house twice a week. Nett knew something was going on but she couldn't quite figure out what it was. I was still dancing, still getting good grades, and the house was in pretty good shape. I told Ronald she was suspicious, so we decided to put some time between our visits.

Everything was fine until Mr. Holiday called a parents' meeting at Bluejackets headquarters. Nett had never gone to any of the meetings before, but this time she decided to go because Mr. Holiday offered to pick her up and bring her home. At the meeting, Mr. Holiday informed the parents that he had conducted several weeks of investigation. He had tracked down all the kids who had been playing hooky at his house, and he had called the parents together to inform them of who the culprits were. That was the good part. He went on to tell them that he had found a Trojan floating in his toilet. That was a disaster.

The band was disbanded. Every member of the corps was busted down in rank. Everyone lied. Nobody copped to knowing anything about anything. Everyone was grounded or put on some type of punishment.

Nett went berserk! She didn't beat me, but I sure wished she had. No beating in the world could have been worse than what she put me through. Every day for two weeks I heard the same lecture. I had violated her trust. I had lied. I had cut school. I was a sneak. I was a sneak and a liar. Thank God, she did not tell Daddy.

What she did was even worse, though, because after a while, for two weeks straight, she stopped speaking to me. Period. She would not say "good morning." She would not say "good night." She never asked me anything. If I said anything to her, she ignored me. I could live without television. I could live without dancing and the Bluejackets. But I could not bear the thought of Nett never speaking to me again.

After two weeks, Mr. Holiday called and asked Nett if I could come back to the Bluejackets. She agreed to let me go one night a week.

Everything was different. Nobody talked to each other. Nobody looked at anyone else. We all marched, tied our knots, did our drills, and studied for the tests to get our ranks back. I didn't even look at Ronald, or at anyone else, for that matter. We got the violation of trust speech there too. Mrs. Mack pulled me off to the side to tell me how hurt and disappointed she was in me. She warned me about pregnancy and disease and told me I had a bright future ahead of me. She made me promise never to do anything like that ever again as long as I lived. I promised never to look at another boy until I finished high school. I lied.

I guess the Bluejackets fiasco was not enough for me. I took up being friends with Beverly again. She was in my dance class, so we saw each other regularly. One day she walked right up to me and apologized. She said she was sorry about what she had done with Ronald. She knew it was wrong but she couldn't help it, she said. She asked me if we could be friends and if I wanted to go to a beach party with her and her sister Sonia so quick I never had time to think. When I finally got a chance to speak, I explained to her that I wanted to go to the party but I didn't have a bathing suit. Beverly told me she would help me get one. I never asked her how.

A few days later, Beverly and I went to Gimbel's Department Store in Manhattan, where she explained to me that if I went into the dressing room, put on a bathing suit, and put my clothes on over the suit, no one would know. She had gotten most of her clothes that way, she said, and it was safe.

I followed her instructions explicitly. After a few hours of trying on suits, I found a beautiful green-and-blue one-piece job with a nice little skirt to cover my very round bottom. Leaving the dressing room with our suits on under our clothes, Beverly and I casually shopped around for a while. We left the store without being suspected of any wrongdoing. My only problem was getting the suit by Nett.

When Nett came home that evening, I told her about the beach party and showed her the swimsuit. I assured her I would be watched carefully by Beverly's older sister. I went on to explain that Beverly wanted so much for me to go, she had given the suit to me. The story was that Sonia worked at Gimbel's and could get things very cheaply. She had several extra bathing suits and the blue-and-green one just happened to fit me. Nett told me she would think about it and let me know. I called Beverly and gave her a full report. We thought we were home-free.

The next afternoon, I was doing my homework when I heard the key turn in the door. I was shocked to see Nett coming through the door at five-thirty. She never got home before eight o'clock. Her nose was red and her eyes were swollen. I could not imagine what had happened, but I knew it was awful. Without taking off her coat, she walked into the kitchen and stared at me. I do not remember if I said anything at all before Nett began to speak to me.

"I am so ashamed. I am so hurt. I know I am not your mother, but I have done the best I could for you. I cannot give you everything, but that is no reason to steal."

It turned out that on her lunch hour, Nett had gone to Gimbel's in search of Beverly's sister. Discovering that no such person worked there, she put two and two together. Nett told me that she had grown up poor but never poor enough to steal. She told me how she had walked to school because her mother did not have a nickel for her to ride the bus. But she did not steal. She told me that she felt so ashamed that I wanted or needed something so bad that I had to go out and steal it.

Crying, she quickly turned and left the kitchen. She went into her bedroom and slammed the door, leaving me at the kitchen table, dumbfounded.

There is no way to describe the way you feel about yourself when you make your mother cry. Of course, mothers cry for their children all the time, in fear and from joy, but that is different. Even if Nett was not my real mother, to me, she was the only real mother I had ever had. And I had made her cry, not for me but because of me.

The shame was unbearable. I knocked on Nett's bedroom door and asked if I could come in. She ignored me. From the hallway, I told her I was sorry. I sat on the floor outside her room for what seemed like hours. I could hear her sniffing and moaning, moving around on the bed, walking around. Then she would stop. If it got too quiet, I would call her. She would not answer.

When Ray came home and saw me in the hallway, I told him what had happened. I know I'm stupid, I said. I know I'm crazy, but Nett is crying and she won't come out of her room. Ray just looked at me like I really was crazy and shook his head. Then he walked right past me, shrugging his shoulders, and flopped down in front of the television. Fifteen-year-old boys can be very insensitive.

I tried to make sense of what was going on. Was stealing a bathing suit that bad? I didn't even *want* the thing. I would burn it or cut it up, but there was no way I would ever put it on. I had a sinking feeling in my chest that this was about the worst thing I had ever done. This was even worse than the Bluejackets mess.

Then I heard her. She came to the door and opened it. She saw me sitting on the floor. She looked at me, through me, past me—as if I were invisible—and stepped around me, without saying a word, on her way into the bathroom. When she came out, she did the same thing. When she went into her room, she slammed the door in my face.

I started crying. It was a sickening, noiseless cry. I went to my room. I went back to the hallway. I went into the bathroom. I felt as if I had died. It was then that I decided that I no longer deserved to live. I was only thirteen years old.

Nett had high blood pressure. Ray had asthma. There were all kinds of pills in the bathroom. I lined them all up on the sink. I took a Dixie Cup from the dispenser, filled it with water, and contemplated my fate.

This had been coming for a long time. It was not just about Nett. It was about everything. It was about how I always broke things. I broke so many dishes and glasses, Daddy bought plastic ones just for me. So I took all of the Excedrin.

It was because I was fat. If I had not been so fat, Nett would have bought me a bathing suit. Because I was fat, I had to steal one like a common criminal and break my mother's heart. So I took all of the Anacin.

It was because I was an ugly child who would probably grow up to be an ugly adult. I had short nappy hair, a big nose, big fat juicy lips my brother called "soup coolers." Besides that, my mind was ugly. My mind was so ugly I lied about my life. I lied to other people about other people. I made up stories about my father, my mother, and told people how wonderful my life was. Ugliness needs powerful medicine. So I took a handful of some pills I didn't even recognize.

I felt dirty. I felt alone. Confused. I had betrayed and been betrayed. I was being abandoned because I was dirty. It was the dirt that made me ugly. No matter what I wore, where I was, or what I was doing, I knew everyone could see my dirt. Not only was I dirty, I was defiant, rebellious, and disruptive. I was a thief, a sneak, and a liar. Grandma was right. I was bad.

I did not have to be bad anymore, I reasoned, downing a mouthful of something else. I could be dead and it would save everyone a great deal of trouble. I took the rest of what I could find in the medicine cabinet, washed it down, and went to bed.

I could not hear Nett crying anymore. I was not crying anymore. The last thing I remember hearing was the faint mumbling of the television. I tried to make out the program Ray was watching. I could not tell. It seemed so far away.

Then it hit me: I am getting ready to die. I tried to sit up. My head was throbbing. I tried to get my mouth open. It was numb. I thought about all the pretty white ladies I had seen on television who took sleeping pills. When they laid their pretty white heads down to die, their hair flowed across the pillow. I had no hair. I wore no make-up. No handsome man was going to burst in the door to save me. I would be fat, ugly, dirty, and dead. That would be it.

The Journal

Dear God,

It's me again. I am really sorry to bother You but I've got to know, when is it going to get better? God, You know that I have been trying really hard to do the right thing. I have been trying to do good and be good, but no matter what I do, every time I turn around, some new disaster is upon me. I cannot seem to get this life thing right. I really don't think I can take much more of this. I am asking You, just one more time, to please help me.

I'm tired, God. I'm just so tired. I know in the past I have done some pretty awful things. I know I have told lies. I know I have been careless. I will admit I have said some pretty awful things. But You said You would forgive me. Please forgive me, God. Please don't punish me. I am sorry. I am so sorry if I have offended You. God, You must know I didn't mean it. You are God. You are supposed to know everything. You know I act a little crazy sometimes. It's not because I don't love you or trust You. I guess I really am stupid, but right now, God, I'm just tired and I need Your help.

God, I just want to do better, feel better, be better. I really am trying, but I think this is too much for me. If I could just have a break. If I could have a few days, maybe a week when I could be totally and completely at peace. If, for just a little while, I could just feel happy, feel good, and have a few good things happen to me and for me, I am sure I could

90

get back on my feet.

You know what, God? I don't even know what to ask You for. I mean, it's not money. It's not a house or anything like that. This thing that I need from You cannot be seen or touched. It is not a thing at all. I really think it's a feeling, a thought, a way of life. I guess You know what I'm talking about. I hope You do.

God, if You can't help me, would You please just tell me what to do to get it for myself? Where do You get it, God? Where do You get that good feeling about yourself? You don't get it at home, where people call you fat and ugly and stupid and lazy—then you do bad things so you can't go home anymore. You don't get it from school, where your hair is so short people point and stare at you or laugh at you because your body is so big. You don't get it from people, who hurt you and leave you. Or, from people who are too busy, too tired, too everything to be bothered with you. Where do You get that thing that makes You feel good? That softness, that gentleness, the happy thoughts and words that bubble around your heart? The singing and the joyous jumping around, the laughing and whirling that seems to be easy when you feel good about yourself? What do you do to get that thing that makes you feel worthwhile when Daddy and Mommy won't hold you or talk to you?

I have no idea what it is or what to do to find it. That is why I am so tired. I have been searching everywhere.

God, if You can, if You would, just help me out for a little while. If You help me, I promise to stay on the right path. Once I find it, I will never let it go. I promise to do things the right way. I promise to say the right things. I promise to be good all the time. Please help me, God. Please. Please. Please. If You help me this time, I promise never to bother You again. And this time, I really mean it!

Love,

Me

CHAPTER 10

A Solid-Line Drawing

Tommy...

I had seen him and his friends standing around outside in front of our apartment building. No one knew when he moved in, but he lived on the top floor with his mother, his brother, and his mother's boyfriend. Nett said he was a man, but he was a boy, nineteen years old. His name was Tommy.

He usually just smiled at me, but one day he actually spoke.

"I hope you're feeling better. I saw when they put you in the ambulance. Are you feeling better?"

Immediately, I sucked my stomach in to hide my pot gut.

"Yes, thank you. I'm fine."

I tried to walk past him but he was walking in my direction toward the corner. How could I hold my stomach in and still talk, I wondered.

"When are you going to go back to school?" he asked. "I mean, I used to see you and your brother leaving for school. I haven't seen you go in a while."

I figured that if he had been watching me, he probably knew I was fat, so I might as well let it hang out. I relaxed my stomach muscles.

"I don't have to go back until Monday."

"Where you off to now? Can I come?"

Damn! How was I going to tell him I was on my way to

the shrink? The only way Nett could keep them from putting me in the looney bin after my attempted suicide was to promise I would get psychiatric counselling.

"I'm going to my grandmother's house," I lied. "You cannot come."

"Well, I'll be here when you get back. See ya."

Before I could respond, he turned and ran back up the block. That was how it all began.

My psychiatrist, Dr. Feldman, was a short, blond woman with the most annoying nasal voice imaginable. She always sounded as if she was whining. She asked me hundreds of questions, mostly about Daddy and Nett. She asked me why did I think I wanted to die. I told her because I had made my mother cry. She asked me if that was any reason to stop living. I told her yes.

After three or four visits, Dr. Feldman told me Nett would have to come to a session with me. She asked me if that was alright. I didn't know I had any other choice. The following week, Nett went in to see Dr. Feldman while I waited outside. When they called me into the room, it was apparent that Nett had been crying. The doctor said the entire family would have to come to the next session. Again, she asked my permission. It was fine with me. Nett just nodded her head.

No way! My father said there was no way he was going to see a psychiatrist. If I insisted on acting like a fool, he would knock my head off. That way I could not be crazy. Discuss what problems? He did not have any problems. He was a Negro in America, that was his biggest problem.

Ray felt very much the same way. He had not done anything. He had no plans to do anything. *I* was crazy, not him, he said.

Nett and Daddy eventually took the conversation into the bedroom where Ray and I could not hear. By the time we went to bed, Daddy was gone.

I went to the doctor alone for the next few sessions. When I came home, Nett would ask me what we talked about. I tried to remember all the questions, but sometimes they were so far out, I could not make sense of them.

I remember once, I was playing with my mitten. Dr. Feldman asked me what did I like about the mitten. I said it was soft. She held the mitten in her hand so that only the rounded top portion was showing. She asked me what it looked like? I stared at it for a moment before responding. I told her it looked like the top of a penis. Nett had to come to the next session.

Dr. Feldman told Nett that I was emotionally disturbed. She said I was probably not a danger to others, but I was definitely a danger to myself. According to the tests and her assessment, certain trauma experienced in my early childhood was manifesting as self-destructive attitudes and behaviors. I was extremely guilt-ridden and suffering from a deep inferiority complex. She went on to explain that I also had a latent preoccupation with sex, which probably resulted from a traumatic rejection by one or more of my parents. Nett could not believe that the doctor had drawn such drastic conclusions simply from asking questions about mittens and when we ate dinner.

Dr. Feldman asked for permission to medicate me. Nett refused. In lieu of that, she recommended that I increase my visits to twice a week with a monthly family consultation. Nett explained that my father flatly refused to come and that she did not have the authority to make my brother come.

On my next visit, the doctor attempted to ask me some questions about my mother. I had no idea what she was talking about. She had seen my mother last week. Did I believe that Lynnette Harris was my mother, she asked. Of course! Why shouldn't I believe it? Who's crazy here, I wondered.

I told Nett what had happened. She told me I did not have to go for any more sessions.

Spring was blooming. The afternoons were warm and beginning to get very busy. By the time I got home from school, all the big boys would be hanging out in front of our building or in the park. I was not allowed to go to the park because Nett said the kids from the projects played there and they were bad. I thought they must be really horrible if they were too bad for me to play with.

Nett had begun to let me go out of the house again. I could stand in front of the building. That is how I got to see and speak to Tommy.

He was from Mississippi, where he had lived with his grandmother. He had finished high school down South and had come to New York to find a job. He was very dark, with a very firmly built body. Tommy was the nicest boy I had ever met. He was very gentle. He held the door for me. He always asked me about school. He called Nett "Mrs. Harris."

Nett seemed to hate him. If she saw me standing near him or talking to him, she would call me upstairs. In a back-handed kind of way, this worked to my favor because, to keep me from being around Tommy, Nett gave me permission to go back to the Bluejackets.

I soon found out that when you have almost died from trying to kill yourself, a drum-and-bugle corps is not the place you want to be. The people who were once your friends act very different. Everyone whispered when they talked to me, as if they thought talking too loud would upset me. They kept asking me how I felt, if I was okay, or if I needed or wanted anything. The only person who continued to treat me as if I had not totally lost my mind was Ronald.

One night on the bus ride home from a Bluejackets meeting, some of the guys started teasing Ronald. They told me that when he heard what I had done, he broke down and cried in front of everyone. They thought that was absolutely hysterical. I found it hard to believe that anyone would cry for me rather than because of me. Ronald told me he thought I was going to die. I think that confession, along with my rebellious spirit, led me to resume my visits to Ronald's house. I felt close to him in a very strange way. I think Ronald really loved me, but since we were just kids, everyone said we did not know what love was really about.

Maybe Ronald and I did not know, but Tommy sure did.

One morning when I left the house to go to school, Tommy was waiting for me in the hallway. He asked if he could walk me to the bus stop. I said sure. He carried my books, and when I got ready to get on the bus, he kissed me. I almost fell onto the bus. When I got home, Tommy was waiting in front of the house. He walked me to my door. Before I could get the key in the door, he kissed me again. This time, he really kissed me, full on the mouth, tongue and all. It was disgusting. It was great.

He asked me if he could come inside with me. Absolutely not. I was not that crazy. Curious, yes. Crazy, no. Would I come to his house? No. He pleaded with me. Finally, I put my books on the kitchen table and walked with him to the fourth floor.

Tommy's house was a lot different than mine. His living room was full with great big furniture. Everything was red and black. Black sofa, red chairs. Black lamps, red curtains. There were lots of dirty dishes in the sink. There were clothes on the floor in the bedroom and the bathtub had a dirt ring around it. We went into his bedroom. Tommy tossed the clothes off his bed onto the other bed in the room.

Then, right before my eyes, this gentle, soft-spoken guy became an octopus. Grabbing, pulling, touching me everywhere. Before I knew it, I was naked. I was standing in the middle of the floor, buck-naked, with a boy, no, a man, who had his hands all over me. Ronald and I never got fully naked. We only saw the necessity to remove the bottom portion of our clothes. This was a totally new experience.

When we laid down, Tommy began to do things I had no idea people were allowed to do. He kissed me everywhere, from my face to my feet. He fondled and caressed me. He asked me if I liked it. If this or that felt good. I never opened my mouth or my eyes. This was not rape. This was not "doing it." At fourteen-and-a-half, I had gone from sneaking around and having sex with Ronald to making love with a man. It was not uncomfortable. It was not painful. It was the most intimate experience I had ever known in my life. Besides that, everything he did felt good.

He told me to tell him I loved him. I never said a word. He said he loved me. I believed him. For seven-and-a-half minutes, a very handsome man loved me. I was beside myself with joy.

I began to spend one day a week with Ronald and two days a week with Tommy. It got to the point that I would even go to Tommy's house when his mother was home. She would smile at me and tell me he was in his room. I would go back there and he would close the door. His mother never said a word. Tommy knew better than to even look in my direction when Nett was around.

We met in secret. We kissed in secret. We made love in secret. He told me I was his girlfriend. I told him about Ronald. He asked me if Ronald and I had sex. "Of course not!" I lied. We must have been three months into our relationship when Tommy asked me exactly how old I was. I said I was sixteen. He told me never to tell anyone about us because he could go to jail.

Jail!? Why? I was petrified. He said I was "jail bait" because girls weren't allowed to have sex until they were eighteen. He said my father could have him arrested. The thought of that, combined with the fact that I knew I was actually much younger than I had told Tommy, made me shudder. What happened next made me throw up.

I knew from hygiene class that the only reason a woman stopped having her period was if she was pregnant. I was very pregnant. I knew it and I was scared to death. The only person I could think of who would know what to do was Beverly, so I told her. She freaked out!

We went to Sonia, Beverly's sister, who, I was told, had been pregnant quite a few times. Sonia asked me how late I was. I had no idea. She took me to a doctor she knew, who examined me. The doctor said I was four months along, much too late to do anything to help me. He gave me a note to take to the hospital. I took the note to Ronald. He freaked out too. Then, all hell broke loose.

It started out quite calmly. I was sitting in my usual spot at the kitchen table. Nett was standing at the stove. Suddenly, she turned and looked at me and asked, "Are you pregnant?"

I almost choked. "No," I said.

"Well, you look mighty pregnant to me. Besides that, I have been counting the sanitary napkins. When was the last time you used one?"

I could not think fast enough to respond. This was horrible! This was beyond a disaster. This was a nightmare. For the first time in my life, I shut up, completely. I would not open my mouth to say a word. Nett said that she was going to make an appointment with Dr. Griffin. He was a dermatologist, but he was the closest thing we had to a family doctor. I was to meet her at Dr. Griffin's office after school the next day.

I did not sleep. I could not eat. It seemed as if five years had passed from the time Nett had asked me if I were pregnant and the moment I rang Dr. Griffin's bell.

I knew the routine. Take off the bottom half of my clothes. Lay on the table. Put the legs in the stirrups. Instruments in. Instruments out. Verdict, guilty.

Nett and I were both silent all the way home.

"You know I have to tell your father," she finally said.

Just shake the head, I told myself. Do not under any circumstances open your mouth.

She told Daddy that night. Everything was quiet. It was eerie. Daddy just looked at me. I went to bed like normal. When I woke up the next morning, he was gone, as usual.

It was Nett's big idea to tell Ronald's parents.

Ronald's mother hit the ceiling. "Oh, my God! Oh, my God! Ronald, how could you?" she screamed at the top of her lungs.

Ronald's father was the voice of reason, "I think they are too young to get married," was all he said.

I never took my eyes off the floor. I never opened my mouth. Ronald opened his and told them I had already showed him the note. What note? Nett asked. Ronald told her about the note I had shown him from the doctor Beverly's sister had taken me to. This made Nett even more upset because I had made her waste her money to go to another doctor when I already knew I was pregnant. How ungrateful could I be?

Without so much as a word on my part, the adults decided I would have the baby and put it up for adoption. Ronald's mother said she would take the baby and raise it. Nett disagreed. The baby needed to be gone. Away. Out of my sight so I could get on with what was left of my life. Adoption it would be then. Everyone agreed.

In that moment, I realized for the first time that not only was I pregnant, I was going to have a baby. Holy Mother of God! This was really turning out to be a mess!

The next few weeks was a flurry of activity. We had to find a clinic. At four months, I had had no prenatal care. The doctors seemed alarmed that I was not showing. We had to find a school. In 1967, pregnant girls were not allowed to attend regular classes. We had to find an adoption agency to take the baby. We had to find some bigger clothes that would not make me look pregnant. I had so many appointments in so many places, I never got to see Tommy and I did not want to see Ronald.

The word got around the Bluejackets pretty quick. People were stunned. Not Ronald. Not Rhonda. This could not be true. It was very true.

There was one school for pregnant girls in Brooklyn. I was lucky, they had one seat left. I got it. When I walked in and saw all those other girls with their big bellies, I wanted to die. How had I gotten myself into this mess? I groaned. More importantly, how was I going to get out of it?

I learned things at that school I had never heard of before. I learned about my body, about sex, about babies. Most importantly, I learned that I was no longer a little girl. At age fourteen, I had become a woman. My body, the same body I knew absolutely nothing about, was going to change, the teachers told me. Some of the changes would be good, others would be quite uncomfortable. Swollen feet. Swollen breasts. Stretch marks. The swelling I could handle. I had seen Nett's feet swell, and I knew that if you soaked them or put them up, they would go down. But the stretch marks were a different issue. That was my punishment. With stretch marks all over my body, everyone would know what I had done: I had gotten pregnant. Jesus! What a mess!

We attended classes every day, and all of the teachers were Black. I had never seen a Black teacher before. I had heard they existed, but I had never seen one.

It was there, in the school for pregnant girls housed in a Brownstone in Brooklyn, that I learned how smart I was. The other girls had been out of school for quite some time. I was a year ahead of myself academically, so I had no problems with the math, reading, or spelling. I quickly moved to the top of the class.

Mrs. Devore, the school's director, told me I should never let anything come between me and school. She told me I had a bright future and that I shouldn't let one mistake stop me. She also told Nett about a foster home. She said it would be a good place for me to go so that I would not have to be around in the neighborhood while I was pregnant. She gave Nett all of the information, and before I knew it, I was assigned to live in a Mrs. Harris's house in Jamaica, Queens, with two other pregnant fourteen-year-old girls. Overnight, it seemed, I became a ward of the state, a foster child.

Everything was happening so fast, I didn't have time to think. I didn't have time to feel. For the first time in my life, I did exactly what I was told, when I was told. This thing was too big for me. I could not figure it out.

When it came time for me to leave for Mrs. Harris's house, Ray just stared at me, without saying a word. I think he felt sorry for me, but he never said it. Daddy said nothing. He would not even look at me. Nett was the only person who made any attempt to have an intelligent conversation with me. She dealt with the business at hand. When is your next appointment? Did you take your vitamins? Do you feel okay?

It was not until I was deposited at the foster home that I had time to think, to feel. It was the next-to-the-worst day of my life.

Mrs. Harris was a short, dark-skinned woman who wore glasses, a wig, and false teeth. She kept her wig on the dresser and her teeth in a jar. It was worse than Aunt Nancy's. The house was small and cluttered with furniture. Though there were windows everywhere, it always seemed dark inside.

My room was on the second floor. I shared it with Debbie, another girl from Brooklyn. Debbie was very pregnant, very big, and very street smart. She smoked a lot, and she did not like me. Come to think about it, Debbie did not like anybody. She did not want to be in a foster home. Her boyfriend was nineteen and she claimed he was going to marry her as soon as he got out of jail. Her mother had made her come to this place, she said, and she was going to stay until her baby was born, but after that, she was leaving and taking her baby home.

That first day, after I was all settled in, I laid on my bed and cried, very silently, very soulfully. My entire being was racked with pain and fear. I had never been away from some sort of family. I had never been away from my brother. Now here I was in some stranger's home, in the middle of nowhere, pregnant.

We, all the girls, that is, had chores to do around the house that had to be done by 9 a.m. because the in-home teacher, Mrs. Taylor, came at 10 o'clock. Mrs. Taylor was a tall, thin, dark-skinned woman whose teeth clicked when she talked. My God, I thought, did everyone in Jamaica have false teeth? Mrs. Taylor gave us math sheets to complete, and she taught us English and science at the dining room table.

I was in the tenth grade. Debbie was in the ninth grade. I could read and write. Debbie could not. It didn't matter. Debbie hated the lessons and the teacher, and she told her so. One day, they had an argument, and Debbie called Mrs. Taylor a "false-teeth bitch." My mouth flew open like a broken toilet. I had never heard a child swear at an adult. Before Mrs. Taylor could respond, Debbie hoisted her swollen body up from the sofa and waddled up the stairs, slamming the door to our room behind her.

Mrs. Harris came flying into the room. Mrs. Taylor tried to explain what happened, but she was so upset her teeth kept slipping out. She was slobbering all over herself. Mrs. Harris screamed up the stairs for Debbie to come back down. No response.

Mrs. Taylor gathered her things up and slobbered that she was going to report these events to the main office. She would not return until this matter was settled, she stuttered. As she left, she snatched my math sheets from me and huffed out the door.

The next few days were intense. Social workers came. Program directors came. Debbie's mother came. Mrs. Taylor's supervisor came. No one said a word to me except Debbie, and she busied herself with cursing and threatening people. She mocked what they said and vowed to "kick ass" if they did not leave her alone.

I had never witnessed anything like it. A pregnant fourteen-year-old who defied adults. And not only did she defy them, she was getting away with it. I watched and listened. The verdict: Debbie did not have to leave Mrs. Harris's house. She did not have to go to class if she didn't want to. She would still have to do her chores, but she would have to go outside on the porch to smoke. No more television and radio for Debbie, and no more collect phone calls from her boyfriend on Riker's Island.

ᐱᐧᐱᐧᐱ

Mrs. Harris's kitchen was in the basement. That was where her daughter Vy lived with her two daughters—Ramona, the model, and Charlotte, the singer. Vy was very fat, very nice, and very funny. Every morning when I went downstairs for breakfast, I got to see her.

Vy called me "Pumpkin," and she always made me laugh. She never asked me intrusive questions, and she told me things I needed to know about being pregnant. It was Vy who bought me some Mother's Friend to put on my belly to ward off the stretch marks, and who taught me how I would have to breathe when I went into labor. It was Vy who told me not to worry about what people said or thought. She told me I was pretty and that everything would be fine.

102

Whenever I was upset or lonely, Vy would let me sit on the sofa in the basement with her and watch the soaps. If I needed to cry, she would rock me and kiss my face. Vy was more than a mother, she was a mommy, a nurturer, something I had been missing most of my life.

Nett came to visit me every Saturday. Every Saturday for five months we went through the same ritual. I would meet her on Jamaica Avenue and we would go to the movies. After the movies, we would go out to eat. She would bring me something new to wear, a nice blouse or a pair of maternity pants with the stretch panel in the front. She brought me magazines, spending money, and stories about the rest of the family. Ray was fine. Daddy was fine. Grandma was the same. She would walk me to the bus stop. I would start crying. She would start crying. I would get on the bus and mash my face against the window for the ten-minute ride to Mrs. Harris's. Nett would take the "el" train back to Brooklyn. I would walk back to the house, go downstairs to see Vy, and she would rock me to sleep.

⋎⋎⋎

May came. There were lots of trees and lots of birds in Jamaica, but I couldn't see any of them at three o'clock in the morning when Debbie went into labor. She woke up screaming her head off. Mrs. Harris tried to calm her down. Vy tried to get her to breathe. Mrs. Harris told Debbie to get up and walk around. Debbie refused to get out of the bed and started cursing, "Oh, shit! Oh, shit! This shit is killing me!"

I sat in the corner of my bed and watched. Debbie could not, would not sit up. Mrs. Harris went out to start the car. Ramona and Charlotte were trying to help Debbie get dressed. Debbie was fighting them, screaming and cursing. Suddenly, out of nowhere, Mrs. Harris came back inside, walked over to her, and backhanded Debbie in the face. Everyone froze.

"You are not dying! You have not lost your mind! You are having a baby!" she shouted. "It happens every day! Now, shut your mouth, put your clothes on, and let's get out of here!"

Obediently, Debbie stood up. That's when her water broke.

By noon, Debbie had a baby girl. Seven pounds, four ounces. The next day, when I went to the hospital for my weekly check-up, I went to visit Debbie. She could barely walk. Her stomach was bloated as if she was still pregnant. She was still cursing, still smoking. The baby was beautiful. Debbie told me the whole, horrible story in vivid detail. The enema. The shaving of her pubic hair. The lights. The pain. The cutting and the stitching.

It sounded gross, and disgusting. Just wait, she said, I would see. Three days later, I found out exactly what she was talking about.

I had no idea that anything could hurt that bad. The contractions racked my body and took my breath away. My mouth went dry. Vy gave me ice chips and told me to keep on breathing like she had taught me. The longer we waited, she said, the less time I would have to spend in the hospital. Between pains, she told me jokes and teased me about "doing the nasty." She tickled my feet and sang funny songs.

By the time the pains were five minutes apart, I did not find Vy amusing. I couldn't bear it any longer. Where had Debbie found the strength to curse and fight, I wondered. I was exhausted. My brain was shut down. The only thing I could do was cry, which I did, all the way to the hospital.

We got there just in time. My water broke during the first pelvic exam. Quickly, the nurse shaved me. There was no time for an enema. In minutes, I was up on the table. Legs up. Push. Don't push. Breathe. Now push. Don't push. Snip. Snip. Breathe. Push. There's the head. Here it comes. Push. Push! Push!! It's a girl. A nice, healthy girl. What's her name, mother? Tracey. Well, that's a nice name. Stitch. Stitch. What a nice baby. 5 pounds, 13 ounces. Can I see her? Are you sure you want to do that? The records say she is not going home with you. I know, but I would still like to see her. Let me clean her up. Just a minute. Here we come. Here she is, mother.

The minute I looked into Tracey's face, I knew. My heart sank. My eyes filled up. This was not Ronald's baby. This baby looked exactly like Tommy.

Tracey had a few problems. She had a hairlip, which needed to be surgically repaired. She also had a slight heart murmur that the doctors said she would probably outgrow. There were no adoptive parents available, so Tracey would have to go to a foster home until parents could be found.

Nett came to visit me on the day Tracey was born. She would not go to the nursery to see the baby. She told me she had spoken to the social worker, who had suggested that I leave Tracey in the foster home for at least six months before we actively sought to have her adopted. She asked me if I had changed my mind. I told her no, I did not want to keep the baby, but I was afraid no one would take her because of her lip. My fears were put to rest when I met the social worker from the adoption agency. She had a hairlip too.

In those days, going home to your old neighborhood after having a baby as a teenage mother was like taking a trip to the Twilight Zone. People would seem happy to see you, but they would give you "the look," you know, the "I know you've been 'down South'" look. In the 1960s, most pregnant girls were shipped down South to country relatives until after their babies were born. Any girl who had a noticeably long absence from the block was presumed to have been down South. I was not one of those girls, I said defiantly. I had a different story. I had been to my aunt's house in Queens because it was easier for me to get to my new school from there. Then I would get the "sure, right" look. I had lost so much weight, what I said did not matter. People drew their own conclusions.

I had been home just a few days when I saw Tommy again. He walked right up to me and asked, "Was it a boy or a girl?" I told him a girl. He smiled and told me his mother was right. She told him I was pregnant. She also told him I was going to have a girl. He never asked me what happened to the baby.

It felt very awkward being around him. When he said, "See ya," and ran across the street into the park, I was relieved.

I went to the adoption agency on 86th Street in Manhattan once a month to see Tracey. On my first visit, Ronald and his mother went with me. Ronald held her and stared at her. His mother had to struggle with him to get the baby out of his arms. When she finally had Tracey all to herself, she looked at her and said, "She looks just like Ronald's father."

I couldn't believe it. Neither of them suspected that this was not Ronald's child. They did not know, but I knew. I never considered that when you are having sex with more than one person, the identity of the child would come into question. I thought because I had been having sex with Ronald longer, the baby had to be his. But when I looked at Tracey, I knew for sure she was Tommy's. Fortunately, Ronald did not know about Tommy, and fortunately, Ronald's father was as dark as the baby because Ronald sure wasn't and neither was I.

Ronald's mother tried to convince Nett to let her take the baby and raise her. She told her that she would not ask for or expect anything from me. She simply did not feel right about having her grandbaby raised by strangers. Nett was dead set against it. If I knew where the baby was, she said, it would be a constant reminder and a constant temptation. If the baby were around, it would be a reason for me to see Ronald again. Chances were that if I did that, I would get pregnant again. I needed to get back to school and put this behind me, Nett insisted.

When they asked me, I agreed with Nett. What else was I going to say? Nett had been the only person who had stuck by me. She had supported me and seen that I was taken care of. I was not about to turn my back on her or make her look like a fool again.

Ronald's mother kept insisting, but Nett would not budge. For six months, the conversation went back and forth. It ended abruptly one Tuesday morning.

Ray had gone to school. Nett was working. I was home alone, depressed, with all of the shades drawn and the windows closed. I was getting dressed to make my monthly trek to Manhattan to see Tracey, when the telephone rang. I thought it was my father checking to see if anybody had called their numbers in to the house, so I answered the phone quickly. It was the social worker from the adoption agency. She was sorry to tell me, but Tracey was dead. She had died in her sleep during the night. They suspected it was Sudden Infant Death Syndrome. She had not been sick. It was not her lip or her heart. Could I please come to the agency? They needed me to sign papers to have the body released to the funeral home. Could I please come quickly?

The usual twenty-minute train ride seemed to have taken several hours. I wailed all the way. People on the subway stared at me. Women came over to ask me what was wrong. I told them what had happened. They were obviously shaken. They sympathized with me. They gave me tissues and cough drops. What do you say to an unwed teenaged mother, a fifteen-year-old, wearing Keds and a ski jacket, who is on the A-train crying because her baby has died in a foster home? There wasn't much anyone could say. There was nothing anyone could do.

Nett, Daddy, and Ray refused to go to the funeral with me. Ronald and his entire family came. The foster parents came. The social worker came. The undertaker had lain Tracey out in a tiny white dress in a tiny white coffin. I have no idea how the funeral service went. My mind went blank. I sat there thinking, "I do not even know this dead person. This was not my child. She was not a part of me or my life. She was a baby I had given birth to and given away. I was in no way attached to her."

I didn't feel anything, not sadness or grief or loss or anything. I guess I was supposed to feel bad, but quite honestly, I did not. I was actually relieved that the ordeal of getting pregnant and having a baby was over.

It was as if I were watching the whole scene on television. Ronald cried. His mother cried. The social worker and the foster mother cried. Ronald's father took pictures of Tracey laying in her casket. I just sat there, numb. When the service was over, they put the tiny white casket in the trunk of the car for the trip to the cemetery. I have no idea what cemetery we went to. I have no idea who went to the cemetery. The only thing I remember was standing in the cold, looking down into the hole where she was buried. When they lowered the casket down into the ground, I looked up and saw the lady named Sarah standing on the other side of the grave. At that moment, I knew everything would be just fine.

THE

Journal

It just hit me. I am never going to be like Penny on the "Sky King" show. My daddy is never going to own a ranch or a plane. Men are not going to run to save me from wild animals or bushwackers. Okay! That's done.

But am I ever going to be beautiful? Hell, I would settle for just being pretty. I know I will never be Donna Reid pretty or Debbie Reynolds pretty, but there has got to be a pretty I can look like.

I see pretty women on the street all the time. Not only that, they are not "white pretty." They are "Black pretty." Some of them are very Black but they have straight hair. They have little bodies and nice clothes, all the things I don't have. I wonder what it's like to be pretty, to have someone tell you you are pretty? People used to tell me I was fat. Not anymore. Thank God, I am not fat anymore. Now, I'm just big.

People tell me that I am smart, but that's not something you are, that's something you do. God, why did you make me smart instead of pretty? That really wasn't fair, you know! I want to do whatever it takes to be pretty. No one has ever said that to me, except Vy. The only person who will even discuss the topic with me is my brother Ray, and he always says I'm "oogly," or a cross between a disaster and an accident. Maybe he's just teasing me. Maybe he's not.

I can't be all that ugly because guys still want to do it with me. But when they do, they close their eyes. They don't know what

I look like. They probably don't even like me.

I know what I'll do, I'll go on a diet. I bet if I lose weight, if I get really small and petite, I'll be pretty. I won't eat any more sandwiches or cake. I won't eat any more candy or drink any more soda. I'll save all my money and buy one of those nice dresses from the Joyce Leslie Shop. Then I'll be pretty.

I can do it, I know I can. I will start my diet tomorrow. No, I'll start it on Sunday, right after dinner.

CHAPTER 11

Quick Dabs with a Brush

Wayne...

I was sixteen going on forty-five. There were parts of me, pieces of my life, I could not remember. Other pieces were dead and decaying. I could not think. I could not feel. I moved from place to place, activity to activity, trying to do what was expected of me. Most of the time, I hit the mark.

I had made such a mess of my short life, I had to make an attempt to redeem myself. It was true. I was not a little girl anymore. I was a woman, with a woman's problems. At least, that was what I thought. That was what I felt.

After Tracey's funeral, everyone treated me different. In one way, they left me alone. In another way, they watched me more closely than ever.

I told Nett I wanted to get a job to help out around the house. She said fine. I went to work as a checker in a supermarket after school, but Daddy came to pick me up every night when I got off at 9 p.m. I stopped going to Bluejackets meetings and started dancing again.

When I was dancing, I felt beautiful and peaceful. Dancing also helped my body. I had finally developed a body. It was a big body, but it was firm, thanks to three dance classes a week.

I started going to Erasmus Hall High School, where Ray was the star tight end on the football team. I had to work my butt off to keep up with the lessons, but I did very well because I really was very smart. I did even better because everyone knew who Ray was and people went out of their way to be nice to me.

Still, I mostly kept to myself except for the girls I danced with. I did not trust myself to have an idle moment. I kept myself busy and preoccupied. I went to school until two o'clock, then I worked from three until nine every other day after school. When I was not working, I was dancing. I also danced on Saturday mornings from nine until noon and worked from one until nine at night. Tommy and Ronald were completely out of the picture. Nett was happy that I seemed to have settled down. I was happy that she was happy.

There were six of us in my new set of girlfriends. This new group knew nothing about my past, about my baby. To them, I was simply sweet, hard-working Rhonda. Smart, well-behaved Rhonda. I was the only one who did not have a boyfriend, and they figured it was because I worked so hard. Actually, the boys I met I dropped because it seemed they only wanted one thing, and I had had enough of that, or at least, I had had enough of the consequences of it.

Still, I had to find a boyfriend to keep up with the crowd. When my girlfriends and I got together, I told them made-up stories about guys I had met, or told them that so-and-so had called me and that I was supposed to meet X, Y, or Z guy at this place or that. When they pressed me to bring my mystery man by to meet them, I would claim that I had dropped him and then I would drop some new name in the hat for the sake of conversation.

My friends were all rooting for me to hook up with a steady, yet, while they did not think I was ugly, I knew that was really the number-one problem and the reason I did not have a boyfriend.

One day, I suggested that a little make-up or perfume might help. They agreed that we all could use a little lift, so off we went to Macy's to shoplift our goodies. Some of the girls were better at it than others, and those of us who were not so good, or who, like me, knew better than to even try, were allowed to share in the big loot. In any event, few of us got to wear make-up at all because most of our parents, single or not, were just plain ol' old-fashioned.

I did not have to shoplift because I had money from my job at the supermarket—plus, I knew Nett would kill me if I did. I usually had about fifteen to twenty dollars just to play with, so I bought what I needed. I made enough that I even helped Nett and Daddy with the rent and bought my own food. My friends thought that was the most amazing thing they had ever heard. Most of them received an allowance for doing chores at home.

Things were so tight at my house, Ray had to go to work too. He got a job as a salesman in a shoe store, which was helpful to me because I got a big discount when I shopped there. Ray was not as generous as I was though, and he did not feel it was right for him to pay rent. One evening, he and Daddy had a big fight about it. Daddy told Ray he should give Nett fifteen dollars a week. Ray refused. Daddy got angry. One thing led to another, and Daddy told Ray he was going to "knock his fucking head off." Much to everyone's surprise, Ray responded, "Not if I get to you first!" Daddy jumped him. Nett stepped in the middle to break them up. Daddy stormed out of the house. When Nett and I woke up the next morning, Ray was gone. He left a note saying he had gone to "find himself." Nett cried. By that point, I didn't even care.

I continued to fantasize with the girls about guys. I made up stories about what my fictitious boyfriends said to me, what they bought for me, what we were doing and not doing. Sex was out, I always told the girls. I was not giving it up to anyone until I at least got a ring. We all agreed that was the way to go. I did not realize it at the time, but those little lies began my history of fantasizing about relationships. By the time I was thirty, I had told so many lies to friends about my relationships, trying to make them better than they actually were, I could not distinguish what was real from what was not. At sixteen, it was fine. I did not know any better. At thirty, I knew better, yet I did it anyway.

As luck would have it, I did meet a guy. Dennis was a gorgeous track star from Boys High School. Now, if I had to have a boyfriend, a Boys High boy is exactly what I wanted. Dennis was hot. Every girl with two eyes wanted him. I couldn't figure out why, but he wanted me. Big me. Ugly me. It was a dream come true. Dennis and I would skip school, meet at his house, and go directly to bed. This time, however, I was very careful. I had learned about the dangers of unprotected sex at the school for pregnant girls. I never let him touch me without a "raincoat." I'd stay at Dennis's until noon, then I would go to school to get my assignments, and from there go to work. This went on for about two months.

One day I decided to surprise Dennis and meet him at track practice. I called in sick at work and went down to the field. There were a bunch of half-naked guys running around everywhere and, of course, a bunch of very hot young girls standing around watching them. At first, I couldn't find him, but when I did, he was standing at the door to the locker room, in his track shorts, kissing another girl.

This was straight out of the soaps, I thought. I stood there in total shock. I had just gotten out of Dennis's bed a few hours ago, and there he was, kissing somebody else. And look at her: light-skinned, straight hair, and wearing a Catholic school uniform. But she was big like me. Thank You, Jesus! At least he was not two-timing me for some petite little dip.

Catching my boyfriend kissing another girl was bad enough, but the way Dennis handled it was absolutely despicable. He saw me standing there. Half-smiling, he turned his back to me, grabbed the girl, and kissed her again. Then he took her by the hand and walked right past me onto the field.

It was at least ten minutes before I could move. It was only when Dennis's brother Trevor called my name and waved to me that I remembered who or where I was. I ignored him and left the field the back way, behind the bleachers, walking through mountains of garbage. I went straight home and called all my dancer friends to tell them what had happened. Dennis was a dead man, I told them. In reality, it was another piece of myself that had died.

With Ray gone and Daddy home only sporadically, Nett and I were basically living alone. We both continued to work. We shopped together and ate together, but basically we lived separate lives. I became sort of a ward of the community. My best friend Elvia and her family adopted me, and I spent most of my time at their house. Elvia's older brother James, who treated me like a sister, became the manager of sorts for the African dance group Elvia and I and the other girls had formed.

Our group was called "Omo Egbe Simba" or "Children of the King." All the training I had received during my days dancing with Bunny was paying off. The group was becoming very popular, and we began making an increasing number of public appearances. We danced at parks, and sometimes we were hired to perform at clubs. We all wore African clothes and changed our names to African names. We all wore our hair in short Afros. In the late 1960s, this made us celebrities in the community because Africa and things African were *en vogue.*

For the first time in my life, I was beautiful. My short hair was a cultural plus. My broad nose and thick lips were "ethnic." My large hips and breasts were viewed as attractive. I was no longer an ugly "Negro," I was a beautiful African woman. There really was a God, I believed, and He at last knew where I lived.

Unfortunately, I didn't live there very long. Nett informed me that she just couldn't afford to take care of me anymore. I would have to go live with Ray, who had gone to live with Bunny after he and Daddy had their falling out. Bunny had a small apartment in Brownsville. She also had a little girl. We worked it out so I would share a bedroom with Bunny. Ray had his own room.

This arrangement was just fine with me since I spent most of my time at Elvia's house anyway. When I wasn't at Elvia's, I was working. When I wasn't working, I was dancing. When I wasn't dancing, I was too numb to care.

In my heart, however, I wished I had a family like Elvia's. She had a mother, a father, and older brothers who treated her like she was a princess, and lots of uncles, aunts and cousins. They had

114

family dinners. They went on family outings. They had a great big house and they did not seem to notice or care that I was not related by blood.

When I moved to Bunny's house, I had to change schools again. My new school, Thomas Jefferson High, was a huge, ugly, run-down dump in Brownsville. At Thomas Jefferson, I met Wayne and began to destroy my life again.

⚬⚬⚬

Wayne was a track star, a long-distance runner. He was tall, very dark, and drop-dead gorgeous. It took me years to realize that Wayne was a younger, darker version of my father. They had the same features. The same body structure. The same attitude toward women. Wayne was also a lady's man, but I did not know that then.

I don't know how I met Wayne. I do know that when he first smiled at me in the hallway at school, my heart actually stopped. Really. I almost passed out. One day, I was hanging around the track while he was running and he asked me to hold his towel. I almost went into shock. When he asked me my name, I knew I was in love.

It was quick. It was painful. Whenever I called him, he was not at home. When I saw him in school, he would ask me if I was coming to practice. When I did, he ignored me. Wayne and I had sex together three times, once at his house, once at my house—or rather, Bunny's house—and once on the wall in the hallway at a party.

One Saturday morning, a few friends and I decided to go to a track meet. When we arrived, the first person I saw was Wayne. He gave me a peck on the cheek and told me to hold his towel and stopwatch. My friends and I were ecstatic. They were as happy for me as I was for myself.

I was in seventh heaven, sitting with my friends at a high school track meet, watching my boyfriend warm up. I knew he was my boyfriend because I had his towel and stopwatch. When he came off the field, I would be the first one he would look for.

He would come to get me with all that sweat pouring from his body. I would wipe his face. He would kiss me. We would leave together. Maybe, if I put on a little perfume, he would kiss me right there in public. The fact that Dennis and "Bertha Butt" were also at the meet did not faze me in the least. I greeted all of the other guys from Boys High and made a point of ignoring Dennis. I did not need him, I figured. I had Wayne. Right? Wrong!

Wayne was running in the 1,500-meter dash. It was the final lap. He was in third place. Everyone was on their feet, screaming and hollering. Wayne moved up to second place. The Jefferson crowd was frantic.

I was so excited I did not realize someone was tapping me on the shoulder. I thought it was the people behind me jumping up and down. The tapping became a push. I turned around, and there she was.

She was very fair with long, straight hair. She was not big, she was fat. She had on lipstick, eyeliner, and a tight little black skirt. She had big legs, big breasts, and a mean look in her eye. I knew this girl. I had seen her before. I thought, didn't she used to go with my brother? She did! Her name was Tonya. She went to Wingate High and ran with a very fast crowd. She pointed at Wayne's towel and extended her hand.

"Is that Wayne's?"

I was stunned. No, I was paralyzed. I did not respond. All my friends were watching.

"I'll take it," she said, matter-of-factly, grabbing the towel from me with one quick jerk.

I stared at her, speechless. It felt like everyone in the stadium was looking at us.

"The watch," she demanded coolly. "I'll take it too."

My lips would not part. My hand would not move. One of my friends took the watch out of my hand and put it in her outstretched paw. Tonya turned on her heels and walked away. When she sat down, two rows in front of us, she and all her friends sitting there with her howled.

I turned to my friends, who had all turned green. We all

knew we needed to get out of there but I couldn't move. I felt dead. I know there is justice in life because Wayne lost the race. It was his losing that gave me the strength and the courage to leave the stadium and go home.

She who knows does not die like she who does not know! When she is sixteen, pregnant by a boy who has a fat yellow girlfriend, she just dies, slowly and painfully.

Wayne would not return my calls. I could not stand the smell of the lunchroom. My already round body was getting rounder. I could not figure out which was worse: being pregnant again or being pregnant by a boy who would not speak to me.

My friends labeled Wayne a dog. I defended him by making up stories about him having an overly strict father. I kept telling myself Wayne would come back to me if it were not for Tonya.

I told Elvia and James about my condition. They were both furious but supportive. When I told Nett, she hit the ceiling again.

It was different this time, but it was the same. I cried myself to sleep at night, just like before. But this time, I had the support of my friends. I was the first in the group to "get caught," so everyone was both guarded and excited. Their attitude was like, "what the hell, we will all survive it." The group threw me a baby shower. They bought me maternity clothes and things for the baby-to-be.

I danced throughout my entire pregnancy. People were amazed that I could even move, but I jumped and leaped around just like everyone else. I went to school and work, just like normal. This was 1970. Teenage pregnancy was no longer a disease. Yet, while I was not publicly disgraced, I was privately ashamed. Going through another pregnancy, and going through it alone, was not painful, it was torture.

This time, however, I was not afraid. I was hurt. I was deeply, deeply hurt that this boy I really thought I loved would do this to me. I still had absolutely no idea how the boyfriend/girlfriend thing was supposed to work. Why would a boy have sex with me if he did not care about me?

I continued to see Wayne in school. When he was with his friends, he ignored me. When I was with my friends, who made a point of pointing him out to me, he ignored me. One day, I was walking alone in the hallway at school. Wayne walked up to me, said hello, smiled, and put his hand on my stomach. I spit at him. He looked totally surprised, so I did it again. He actually had the audacity to tell me it was rude to spit before he turned and walked off!

Nett eventually called Wayne's father, Mr. Watley. He had no idea who I was. Wayne was not allowed to have girlfriends, he said. Well, he has one, Nett told him, and he has knocked her up! Now, what was he going to do?

Mr. Watley, a middle-aged Caribbean man who himself had three sons by three different women, called Wayne to the telephone. He asked him if he knew I was pregnant. Nett heard Wayne's voice in the background saying yes. Mr. Watley asked Wayne if he knew it was his baby. Again, Wayne said yes. He may have been a dog, but he was not a lying dog. Mr. Watley asked Nett if he could meet me. She told him to tell his son to bring him to her house. We don't want to go to court, she added, we simply wanted to know whether Wayne intended to support his child. Mr. Watley said he most certainly would. Nett said thank you and slammed the telephone down. I was five months pregnant.

⋏⋎⋏⋎⋏

I moved back in with Nett. I was standing at the kitchen sink washing dishes when my water broke. Nett called Daddy at wherever he was. He said he'd be right over. We waited about an hour, but he never showed up. Nett called a taxi to take us to the hospital.

I wasn't in any pain, but the cab driver acted as if he was having a nervous breakdown when he realized I was about to deliver. We were going sixty miles an hour down a one-lane street when he screeched to a halt for a red light. Looking out the window, I saw my father walking across the street. The cabbie was about to take off.

"It's Daddy!" I screamed. I waved to him. He ran over to the car. "What's up? I just called and..."

He almost had to jump into the cab, which never actually stopped moving. Once inside, he told us how his car had broken down up the street. He was walking down to Atlantic Avenue to see if any of the repair shops were open.

What great timing, Daddy said. If the car had not broken down, he would not have known where we were. He asked me how I felt. Was I going to give him a grandson this time? It was all so nice. It was strange.

I had a very long, very hard labor. Eventually, I gave birth to a five-pound, three-ounce baby boy. I named him Damon Keith. He was perfect, absolutely perfect. He was not wrinkled. He had a perfectly shaped head and the softest, curliest, most beautiful hair I had ever seen or touched. He even had a neck. When Nett saw him, she was awe-struck. She had never seen such a beautiful baby in her life, she said. Even Daddy seemed pleased with his new grandson.

After several hours of alternately attending to me and casting adoring eyes on Damon, Nett told me she had to leave to go to work. It only occurred to me later to ask how she and Daddy got home that night. Nett replied quickly that they had taken a taxi to the car and from there Daddy had driven her home. That seemed strange to me. Daddy had told us the car had broken down. I asked Nett how he drove the car home if it was not running? Nett had no answer.

Wayne came to the hospital three days after Damon was born. His visit was not at all like I had fantasized it would be. He did not kiss me. He did not fall on his knees and beg for forgiveness. He did not have an engagement ring to slip on my finger. Instead, he looked at me, told me I had gotten too fat and asked why the baby had such a big nose. I had to fight back the urge to spit on him again.

He made small talk for a few minutes. He told me he was

going into the Army so he would be able to make some money to give the baby. I listened without listening. He asked me what was wrong. I asked him why he had not called me for four months. His face fell. He told me he had wanted to call me, to see me, but he did not know what to say. Plus, his father had strictly forbidden him against having anything to do with me. I had really ruined his life, he said.

I asked him about Tonya. He simply shrugged his shoulders. I was just about to spit in his face when Nett walked in the room.

When a woman feels unloved and unlovable, when she has never been listened to or spoken kindly to before or in a long time, she often will fall in love with any man who takes the time to say even a few words to her. When something comes along that even vaguely resembles the thing she thinks love is, she will jump at the chance to experience it. Any display of kindness on his part she will see as a sign of his love for her. The tiniest bit of attention will cause her to fantasize about what it is like to be loved. For some women, sex is the only kind of love they know.

Every woman wants to be loved, to be special to someone. Some crave love. Others long for it. But a woman who truly knows love, and who knows what love truly means, knows that it does not require the debasement of her *self*. A woman who knows a man does not love her must admit it to herself. She must also realize that his denial of her does not mean there is anything wrong with her. It simply means he is not the one for her.

I was thinking again. I wasn't feeling, but I was thinking. I *had* to think. I had a beautiful son to take care of and provide for. I had no time for foolishness. I had no time to feel bad or sorry for myself.

I felt bad for Nett though. She had been jarred by what I pointed out to her about Daddy and his broken-down car story the night Damon was born. She believed my father had lied to her. She wanted to know the truth about where he had been that night and all the others before it.

Soon after I came home from the hospital, I got the brilliant idea to check the telephone book. I knew I had seen my father a number of times on Lincoln Place, so I checked the listings for any Harrises in that area of town. Bingo! There was an Alberta Harris listed at 1474 Lincoln Place.

I called the number. A woman answered. I asked for my father by name. The woman said he was not in. Did I want to leave a message? Yes, I told her, tell him to call home. This is his daughter, Ronnie.

He called back within the hour.

"What's the matter?" He seemed annoyed.

"Nothing," I said, trying to sound as grownup as possible. "I just wanted to know where you were."

His voice turned angry. "What the hell do you mean? Who the hell do you think you are?"

I struggled to maintain my composure, but I lost it. My voice went up several decibels.

"I am your daughter, and I am sick and tired of what you are doing to my mother!"

"Have you lost your mind?" he sputtered. "You can't tell me what to do. I pay the rent!"

"Maybe you pay the rent there, but you do not pay it here!" I hung up the phone. Hard. I turned around to see Nett standing in the hallway with a look of shock and disbelief on her face. She had overheard my conversation.

Without saying a word, she went into her room and closed the door. She cried all night long. She cried all day the next day. I took care of the baby, and she cried.

Nett had been married to my father for eighteen years. She had raised his children for fourteen of those years. She had been faithful to him. She loved him. To discover that he had a woman and four other children on the side was more than a slap in the face. It was salt in a very old, very open wound.

It was three or four days later before Daddy dared to show his face at our house. I had changed the locks, so he did not have a key and had to be let in. He came in with an attitude.

"You have some explaining to do, Miss!"

I was uncharacteristically defiant. "You need to get your clothes out of my mother's closet, Mister!"

Incredulous, he started sputtering again. "Just who the hell do you think you are?"

I imagined I was talking to Dennis or Wayne. Or to Uncle Lee. Or to some man I did not know. Certainly not to my father.

"I have no idea who I am, thanks to you. But I can tell you who I am not! I am not some dumb bitch who is going to continue to be treated badly by you!"

Nett watched the whole scene. When Daddy and I had finished exchanging verbal blows, she simply left us standing there and went into her bedroom. He followed her. They were in there for quite a while before he left quietly.

Nett stayed in her room for three days, coming out only to go to the bathroom. She did not speak to me. She did not eat. She didn't even cry. I guess, like me, she was thinking.

THE *Journal*

I never liked him much, anyway.
He had beady little eyes.
Momma said,
"You can't trust a man with beady eyes!"
But
I did.
Not because I liked him that much.
I mean, he was nice and all,
And
He always brought me flowers and sent me cards signed, "Love."
And
One day, he sent me a singing telegram, right to my office.
The girls almost died.
But
He never gave me his home telephone number.

Momma said,
"If you can't call him, don't let him call you!"
But
I did.
Not because I really liked him or
anything like that.
But
He would call me two, three, sometimes four times a day.
And
He had one of those deep, deep voices,

The kind that would oil you in the rusty places.
He always knew what to say, and how to say it.
And
I couldn't help but believe him.
But
He always broke our dates.

Momma said,
"A man who breaks a date will break your heart!"
"Let him go, girl!"
And
I did.
But
I took him back.
Once. Twice. Too many times to count in five years.

Not because I liked him that much.
But, Lord, He was nice to have around!
On a cold winter night, or
When the bills were a little overdue.
To contribute those few extra dollars
To that new dress or shoes.
But,
He didn't like to talk about marriage.

Momma said,
"A man who won't marry you after two years is taking a free
        ride!"
"He can get off any time he chooses!"
And
He did.
He's gone.
And
I can't say a word because, everybody knows,
I never liked him that much anyway!

Momma said,
"If you didn't really like him,
How come your heart is bleeding all over my kitchen floor?"
And
It did.

CHAPTER 12

More Rough Sketches

Kirk...

The sun shining in my face woke me up. It was seven-thirty in the morning. I leapt out of bed and ran to the crib. Damon had slept all night. That was very unusual. He was a good baby who never really fussed about anything, but he never missed a meal. I leaned over the edge of the crib to see if he was alright. He was laying in a large pool of saliva.

Oh, God! He must have been crying and I had not heard him. I picked him up. His skin was clammy. The were tiny beads of sweat on his forehead. He was breathing, but something was not right.

Oh, God, please! Not another dead baby! Not today!

I ran with Damon in my arms into Nett's bedroom. She wasn't there. I ran into the kitchen. Nett saw the panic in my eyes. She jumped up from the kitchen table.

"What's wrong?"

"I don't know. He feels funny. Take him." I almost tossed Damon into Nett's outstretched arms.

We both stood there, staring at him. Then it started. He took a long gasp of air and started to shiver.

I screamed and ran out of the kitchen. Nett yelled after me, "Call an ambulance! Call the police!"

I was in the bedroom screaming my head off. "Ronnie, stop that and call an ambulance! Oh, God! He's choking!"

I didn't want to see it. I couldn't hear it! I could not stop crying.

Then, just as quickly as it started, it stopped.

"Wait a minute," Nett called back to me. "I think he's okay. Come here, fool! Come and get your baby!" Slowly I crept back into the kitchen as Nett was walking toward me.

"See, he's alright. Maybe he has a cold or something. Take him to the hospital."

I took Damon into my arms and fell to my knees. I was crying and praying at the same time.

"Dear God, I beg you, please don't take my baby. I couldn't go through that again. Not with this one. Not this time. Please, God! Please."

Nett just stood there for a moment before she came and helped me off the floor.

"Nothing is going to happen to your baby. You've got to believe that. You've got to know it! Now get dressed and take him to the hospital. I'll call the ambulance."

I changed Damon's diaper and got dressed. The ambulance arrived in five minutes. The attendants were very reassuring. Sometimes babies look like they are choking and sometimes they sweat, they said. Your baby looks fine, but let's just take him in to have the doctors check him out.

The emergency room waiting area at Brookdale Hospital looked a great deal better than the one at King's County, but it smelled the same. Sitting there, I had flashbacks of Ray's asthma attacks. I remembered going to the morgue to claim Tracey's body. I was holding Damon so tight I could have crushed him.

The doctors checked Damon from head to toe. He was fine, they said, smiling. "Some mothers would kill for a full night's sleep with a three-month-old baby. Go home. Don't worry. If he has any more trouble bring him back."

I went home. Damon didn't give me a single problem for eighteen years.

I got a job working in a day care center so I could take Damon to work with me. I made a hundred dollars a week. I worked from seven o'clock in the morning until six at night, five days a week. Wayne had gone off to the Army. He and Tonya were engaged. Bright one Saturday morning, Tonya called to tell me that, even though she and Wayne were getting married, she did not want to come between him and his son. She realized that I was entitled to certain benefits and I should get them. I thanked her for her kindness and wished her good luck.

Two days before the wedding, Wayne called. He said he didn't want to get married but Tonya had already planned the wedding. He would be home that weekend. Was it possible for him to see the baby? I told him to drop dead.

Anyone who thinks being a teenage mother is fun is out of their mind. Anyone who thinks young girls know what they are doing when they get pregnant is insane. I was seventeen years old. I had a job, a baby, a mother who did not babysit, and a hole in the middle of my heart. I loved my son, but I realized I had screwed up, big time. Walking the floor with him at night, getting up at five in the morning to be on a train at six, to be at a job by seven was no fun. I did it because I had no choice. I had fallen, but I was not down. I had to drop out of school with less than a year to go. I could not buy clothes because the baby needed so much. I could not go party and hang out because I had a baby.

At five feet-five inches tall, I weighed 109 pounds. I had wanted to be thin all of my life, but now that I was, I looked horrible. I felt worse. I was tired all of the time. I had so much to do. I began to fantasize again. I thought about some wonderful, rich man coming to take me away. He would love me. Put me in a big house. Give me everything I wanted. I thought about being rich. I thought about being famous. I dreamt about being beautiful, having beautiful clothes, and living in luxury. That's when I decided that I wanted to get married.

The only way I was going to get my life together, I figured, was to be married. If I had a husband, someone to help me raise my son, someone to look out for me, I would be just fine. I could go back to school. Go to nursing school and finally make a life for myself.

I remember now what Grandma always said: "Be careful of

what you ask for!" I had asked for a husband, and I got one. But he was a stark, raving lunatic.

Kirk was Bunny's baby's father's cousin. True to my form, he was gorgeous. Knock-kneed but gorgeous, and on his way to Viet Nam. I met him the day before he left. He promised to write and he did, weekly, sometimes twice a week, for five months. When he stopped writing, I started fantasizing again. Kirk wanted to marry me, I said. He loved me. He didn't care that I had a baby. He was going to buy me a house. I lied to everyone about Kirk for fourteen months.

One Saturday morning, the doorbell rang. I went to the door. I saw a strange man. Then I saw the uniform. Then I saw the face. It was Kirk. He had come home with an engagement ring. He wanted to marry me. We got married a month later over everyone's objections. The big lie had become the truth. It was amazing.

Kirk, Damon, and I moved to Fort Benning, Georgia, which was, at that time, in the heart of Klan territory. I did not know that then, and I did not care. I was an Army wife. We moved into a complex where many servicemen lived with their families. We rented some furniture and set up housekeeping.

Kirk went to work every morning. I stayed home and kept the house. I hung clothes out in the backyard. I baked fresh bread at least once a week. I took Damon to the park with the other children. I had coffee with the other Army wives. I did not lower my eyes when I spoke to the white men in the Piggly Wiggly supermarket. I did not flinch when the rednecks pulled their guns on me and called me an "uppity nigger bitch." I did not accept the white police officers' invitations to "have a real good time" in the back of the patrol car in the woods "down the road a piece." I called Nett once a week. I wore hot pants to the Army PX. And I began to notice something very strange about my husband.

I noticed Kirk's eyes were always red. He said it was an allergy he picked up in 'Nam. I noticed he was always scratching.

He said I used too much soap in the laundry. I noticed he rarely wanted to make love. He said he was too tired. I noticed he would scream at me for little things. Once he slapped me in the face for talking back to him. I noticed he never had any money. As an Army private with no specialization, he got paid once a month. Every month, by mid-month, we were calling home for money. His mother was always good for at least a hundred.

Nett always asked me if everything was alright. I was married, I told her. I was on my own. Things were fine by me, I lied. Before the words had time to settle in the air, Kirk was arrested for burglary. That was how I discovered my husband was a heroin addict.

When a Black man in Georgia is convicted of stealing a black-and-white television from the home of an elderly white woman whose son plays poker with the sheriff, he is going to go to jail for a long time. Kirk got three years. When that same Black man has a wife who is living in subsidized housing because her husband is in the Army but is now in jail, about to be dishonorable discharged, she is going to be evicted. I was.

I had no income, no money, a two-year-old son, and we were out on the street. Nett sent enough money to have our furniture shipped back to New York and for me to buy a plane ticket home. Damon and I arrived back in New York, seven months after we left. I was tired, emotionally stressed out, and three months pregnant.

Nett told me I could stay with her until I found my own place. She also told me there was no way I could bring another baby into her house. I decided to have an abortion. Nett told me I was crazy. Perhaps I was. God knows I had enough reason to be crazy, but I was not insane enough to try to raise two children by myself. I went to King's County Hospital to discover I was not three months pregnant but four-and-a-half months. It didn't matter, I still had time. I was told I could have an injection of saline solution shot into my womb. That would cause the baby to die. Once it died, I would go into labor. I was not to come back to the hospital until the pains were five to seven minutes apart. I would deliver a dead fetus, vaginally. It would take about three days.

Nett was horrified. She told me I could not come back to the house if I had the shot. In addition, she would not speak to me ever again in life, she said. By that point, however, I did not care. I made arrangements with a friend to stay with her.

I got up early the next morning, took Damon to my friend's house, and caught the bus to the hospital. As I stepped off the bus I felt a strange sensation. It was a fluttering in my stomach. The baby was moving and it would not stop. I walked to the door of the hospital, turned around, went back across the street, and took the bus back home. I was going to have another baby.

Of course, Nett changed her mind and let me bring the baby home. Kirk was going to be paroled in three months. We could stay until he got home to help me find a place. My daughter Gemmia was born in an intra-uterine position. That is, instead of her legs bending downward, they bent up. No one had the decency to tell me. After all, I was just the mother.

The nurse brought me my baby to feed. I looked at Gemmia in total disbelief. She was the ugliest child I had ever seen in my life! Her entire face was occupied by her eyes. Her lips were pursed tightly. Her nose was broad and flat. She was wrinkled and she did not have a neck. She was beyond ugly, even beyond "oogly," as Ray used to call me. She was hideous. That was not enough. Not only was she ugly, she was deformed.

Oh, my God, I thought. This was not my kid, I told the nurse. This is simply not my kid. There has been a mistake. There has been a switch. Do not bring that baby in here. I do not want it. I will not feed it. I want to see the hospital administrator. Someone has stolen my baby and is trying to pawn this creature off on me.

I was dead serious. For two days, I cried each time they brought Gemmia into my room. She was ugly, she was crippled, and she cried incessantly. The nurses became very concerned about me. Eventually, an administrator did come to see me. She put me in a wheelchair and walked me through the delivery room. She calmly showed me how the babies were tagged after birth in an effort to prove to me there had been no mistake. This was my child and I would have to take her home. Against my better judgment, I did.

Damon loved his little sister. He loved to watch her cry, which she did twenty out of twenty-four hours. She never shut up. She cried when I fed her. She cried when I changed her. She cried when I held her. The kid had serious problems.

Damon tried to help. He would spin Gemmia's bassinet around in the middle of the floor. She would be stunned silent for the moment it took me to get to her and save her from her big brother's attentions. Then she would start screaming all over again. Nett joked that Gemmia was going to be a singer one day, that she was just strengthening her lungs. I thought, this baby is trying to drive me crazy for trying to abort her!

Damon figured out the problem and took drastic steps to correct it. One day, as Gemmia lay in her crib barking at the moon, her tongue wagging in the wind, Damon dropped a handful of pennies into her mouth. I heard her gagging. I walked over to the bassinet and saw that she had become a human piggy bank. Quickly, I grabbed her, turned her upside down, shook the pennies out of her mouth, and sent Damon to bed with a spanking. Gemmia was quiet for the rest of that day, the next day, and every other day after that.

When Kirk came home, Gemmia was five months old. He had never seen her. It was a touching reunion. Kirk, his mother, me, Nett, Damon, and the dog. We all stood there staring at each other.

Kirk looked terrible. He was fat. He was acting rather silly. He looked very weird to me. It was in that moment I realized that I did not want to have anything to do with him.

There is nothing harder than admitting something unpleasant about yourself. There is nothing worse than facing something ugly that you have done. Yet, when you fail to admit what you must face, the universe will reveal it publicly, right in front of the last person you ever wanted to know: yourself. If you continue to run, the thing will haunt you. It will rear its ugly head at the most inopportune moments and you will think to yourself, "Oh, my God! Everyone knows!"

My husband was home, and I did not want him. We had made a daughter together, and the mere thought of him touching me made me sick to my stomach. I never said a word. Instead, I played the role of loving, devoted, and welcoming wife.

What I thought was a terrible and cruel thing turned out to be a blessing. Nett announced that although Kirk was my husband, he could not sleep in my bed in her house. She went on to say that although I was her daughter, I had sixty days to move out of her house and take my children with me. Everyone was stunned. Kirk and I immediately began to make plans. He would go to work. I would continue to receive public assistance. His mother would help us out. We should be able to get this done in the appointed time, we thought.

Nett and I never had a discussion about it, but I suspected Nett wanted us out because she had started dating again. Daddy had stopped coming around long ago. She said it was time for her to get on with her life too. I was hurt but I understood. I was being blessed but I could not see it.

Sixty days is not a lot of time when you have no money and no desire to find a home to live in with your husband. Kirk came over almost every day. My living room became his employment agency. I cooked for him. I talked to him, but whenever he tried to touch me, I left the room. The tables had really turned. At first, he did not want me. Now, I did not want him. I knew I had to carry out the farce, but I had my limits. I was trying to find an apartment, hoping I did not find one. Kirk was looking for a job, hoping he would not find one. The children were getting bigger and more troublesome. Nett was dating heavily and becoming less tolerant of our presence. I was smoking more and eating less.

I could not figure out how to get out of the mess I was in. Then I remembered something Grandma had taught me. It was time for me to pray.

I had not prayed in a long time. At an early age, I had turned my back on God because I thought God had turned His back on me. At first I couldn't find the words. When I closed my eyes they began to flow from me with a force I had never experienced.

God!

You know who this is! I am truly pissed with You! I have been working my butt off, trying to do the right thing, and look what You've done to me! Look at the situation I am in now! And where are You? Where are You when I need You? Are You off on vacation or something? I've been asking, trusting, and look what it has gotten me—nothing! Absolutely nothing! What is going on with You? I asked You to help me. I asked You to guide me. You take me to a certain point, and then what? What are You doing up there, anyway? I'm the one who is doing all the work. I am trying to get myself and my family together. I've seen people who act like You don't exist, and they are doing just fine. They have money. They have a home. They travel around and spend money like water. All I am asking for is a little consideration. I promised You I would do the right thing. I did. I got married. It is not my fault that I married a junkie. It is not my fault that he went to jail. Here I am trying to do the right thing, and I get nothing in return. I thought You were supposed to be fair and kind. I thought You knew who was who and what was what. I see I was wrong. You pick and choose who You bless.

Maybe that's it: You've got favorites. You bless them and forget about the rest of us. Well, I've had it with You. I'm not waiting on You any longer. It appears only fools like me, who want to be right, wait on You and get nothing. I'm not asking You for anything else. All I want to do is stay alive long enough and be strong enough to get what I want. What I want is to be left alone. I want all of this to go away so I can take my children and be left alone. Thanks for nothing! Amen.

I also remembered Grandma saying, "God doesn't care what you say to Him. He only cares that you say something. If you say anything at all, He will take care of the rest." The very next day, I discovered that to be the absolute truth.

At nine the next morning, Kirk called to tell me that someone had robbed his mother's house. All of her jewelry, silverware, televisions, and stereo equipment had been stolen. At two that afternoon, Kirk was arrested for trying to pawn his mother's jewelry. At seven that evening, I got a call from a landlord. I had gotten an apartment I had applied for. At four o'clock the next afternoon, I received a check for a month's rent and security deposit from the department of social services. Three days later, I moved. Two weeks after that, I was offered a job as a female counselor in a drug rehabilitation center. A week later, I pawned my wedding rings and got Kirk out on bail. Two days after that, he was on a bus on his way to South Carolina. My father gave me a car and a washing machine. In twenty-one days, I had a job, my husband was gone, and I was sitting in the kitchen of my own home, alone with my children. Now ain't God something?

THE Journal

When I was ten years old, I was fat. I was fat, and everybody told me I was fat. My brother. My aunt. My father. Only my stepmother was nice about it. She called me "chubby" and told me I would outgrow it. Sometimes, people would look at me and say, "My, she's a big girl." I remember that so well.

Sometimes, I see myself as a little girl, sitting on the front steps of my house in a romper suit, very fat, with very short hair, and very alone. All my friends had long hair. Nice hair. They all wore a size six or eight. I wore a size sixteen. I hated them. No, I hated myself. So I made up stories about what size clothes I wore and how much I weighed. I told myself that I was thin and sometimes people would shake their heads in agreement and say, "Is that so?" But I could see it in their eyes. They were really saying, "She's crazy! She's fat!" Then, I would go in the house, steal some food from the refrigerator, and eat it.

Eating always took away my pain. It was painful to be fat. I was fat because I was in pain. I was in pain because I was fat. Food was my pain reliever. When you are fat, it feels like something is wrong with you. You learn to deal with it because you just can't live with feeling bad all the time. But you know deep down inside that you are different from everyone else. You feel different, you act different, and, most of all, people treat you different.

136

I've always been different. Not because I was always fat, but because there were things I could do that were different from other people. Things like seeing and hearing people who were not there. Nobody believed me. Everybody said I was lying. I wasn't lying. They just wouldn't listen to me because I was fat. For me, being fat meant I was wrong. I wasn't good enough. I couldn't do what other people did. I didn't want to draw attention to myself, but I always did. I think that's why the voices and the visions went away, because people were always looking at me.

I remember one time I was at a store with my friend. She needed something, and we asked the lady in the store to help us. That lady went to get another lady to help us. When the second lady asked who needed the help, the first one said, "Not the fat one, the other one." People are so stupid and mean. They say the first thing that pops into their head without even thinking about how it will make another person feel. I try never to be mean to people. I figure I can't be fat and ugly and mean. That would just be too much.

I wonder why nobody at home likes me? They're not skinny people. They're not fat, but they're not skinny either. They seem to put up with me because I am there, but they don't really want me to be there, and they show it. If somebody liked me, they would show it. I always feel left out—like a doll that needs to be fixed or straightened out so it will look better.

I never seem to look right. Partly because I'm fat, partly because I'm so clumsy and sloppy. At least that's what everybody tells me. I can never do anything right. I am always dropping, spilling, or breaking something. Sometimes I break things on purpose because I am so damn mad. Then I have to be sorry.

I am always sorry for something. I am tired of being sorry. I am tired of being fat. I am tired of being broken.

Today, just for today, I am not going to be sorry for anything. I am not going to be unwanted. I am not going to be broken. Today, I am not fat. I AM NOT FAT! I AM NOT FAT! HALLELUJAH! THANK YOU, GOD, I AM NOT FAT!

But you know what? I am still fat. I still don't fit in. I am just not good enough. But you know what? Just because everyone else wears a size six and I wear a size sixteen does not mean I am doing the wrong thing. It might mean I have something else to do. Something good. Something special. I just wonder what the hell it is!

CHAPTER 13

A Shaded Silhouette

Charlie....

It was hard to believe that I was only nineteen years old. So much had happened so fast, it seemed as though I had missed something. I had two children by two different men, which was something I found very difficult to live with. I had a job in a field I knew absolutely nothing about. Drugs and drug addiction were totally foreign to me. I had a father who presented me with three sisters and two brothers I had not known existed for eleven years. I also had a new stepmother in addition to the mother I had known and loved for most of my life. I had a grandmother who was literally taunting me, waiting for me to fall or fail. She'd take either one. I had a brother who was drinking himself into an early grave. I had a welfare caseworker who was trying to prove I was working so she could cut me off of public assistance. Since I had changed my name and social security number for employment purposes, she was chasing her tail. I lived right next door to my son's father's mother. I got the opportunity to watch my husband come and go at least once a week without so much as ringing my doorbell to ask how his child was doing.

One bright Saturday morning, I sat alone at my kitchen table, trying to figure out what was going on in my life. I felt tired and scattered. I wanted to do so much. I felt like things were moving faster than I could catch up with them. I felt very weighted down, almost oppressed. I was tired of worrying about money. I never seemed to have enough. Even with working and collecting a public assistance check, the children were eating and growing faster than the dollars were coming in. I tried to pay my bills on time so I would not have to constantly be looking over my shoulder. Rent. Gas. Light. Phone. Babysitter. Food. Clothes. The house was clean. My children were well. But there simply was not enough money to go around.

I wanted to go away for a few days, just to relax. I saw an ad in the paper: Puerto Rico for just ninety-nine dollars. Who would watch the children? Puerto Rico was out.

I had come a long way, but I still had pretty far to go. It seemed as though I was stuck. I couldn't go backward, but I was not moving ahead. I felt an incredible sadness welling up in me that seemed about to burst. I couldn't put my finger on the cause, but I knew something had to give sooner rather than later.

I was working in a twenty-four-hour therapeutic rehabilitation center for substance abusers. My work schedule included working at night, which meant that I had to board my children out by the week. Every Sunday night, I would pack their clothes and food, take them to Miss Alice's house and leave them there until Friday night. Miss Alice had been Uncle Lee's girlfriend for years. Bunny had introduced me to her. She was a great babysitter, a terrific cook, and a wonderful person who truly loved children. On the nights I was not working, I would visit the children and have dinner with them and Miss Alice. I often wondered if she knew that it was me who had been with Aunt Nancy, scoping out her house every Saturday night.

When I worked at night, I got to sit at the front desk, check in on the residents every hour, and write counseling reports. I did most of my counseling during the day. It was during the day that I learned about encounter groups.

An encounter group is a counselling session in which people are confronted about their so-called "dark side." When substance abuse is involved, encounters are designed to help people look at the reasons and causes behind their drug use. The theory is that if you can get a person to look at what they do and admit that they do it, then they can make a choice to change their behavior.

The counselors at the center watched their clients' every move to discover their negative tendencies and behavior patterns. Certain behaviors are thought to be classic of a "dope fiend" and detrimental to his or her rehabilitation. During the encounter session, it is the counselor's job to confront the clients about their behavior and push them into making an admission and hopefully a change. All of this is done very aggressively with loud, foul, sometimes abusive language. People scream, cry, fall on the floor. Sometimes, they "cop to their shit"—that is, admit to their guilt— sometimes they do not. If a person cops, they are rewarded with a weekend pass or some other perk.

As the newest staff member, I did not get to participate in the encounter sessions. I got to watch.

One day it was a client named Larry's turn to be in the hot seat. Larry had been a heroin addict on and off for nine years. He had been in and out of jail and treatment centers across the country for at least five of those nine years. Larry was a short, well-built man, twenty-seven years old. He was an only child who had been raised in an intact family. During his drug addiction, he had robbed his mother, stolen from his father, and beat up several neighbors. He was eventually jailed for impersonating a mailman and stealing public assistance checks. The theory was that Larry would cop to his shit if the counselors accused him of being a closet homosexual who could not come to grips with the fact that he liked men. And so it began:

"You like boys, don't you, Larry?"

"No!"

"Yes, you do! I've seen you! Every time a new young guy comes in the door, you break your neck coming downstairs to check out his booty!"

"No, I don't! You just makin' that up!"

"Oh, am I? Am I now? Am I making up the fact that you and Jose were down in the basement swapping spit the other day?"

"What?"

"You heard me, mothafucka! You were down in the basement kissing Jose, and everybody knows Jose is a faggot! Right, Jose?"

"Yeah. Ya'll know I'm a queer! Right, everybody? I don't make no bones about it either. Shit."

"You hear that, Larry? Your girlfriend done put your business in the street. Or is he the boyfriend? Maybe you the one that gets stuck? You like to get stuck, Larry? You like to get stuck in the butt? Maybe that's why you stay in jail so much! I ain't never seen a nigger get busted as much as you, Larry! You go to jail Friday, get out Saturday, and be right back in the mothafucka on Monday! You like jail, don't you, Larry? In jail, you can get stuck every day, two or three times a day. Right, Larry?

"I ain't got nothing to say! I ain't got shit to say to you!"

"Oh, you gonna say somethin', mothafucka! You gonna say something to me today, ain't you? You gonna tell me that you are a faggot! That you like sticking and getting stuck! You gonna tell me you was in the basement with Jose! Kissin'! Kissin' another man in the mouth! Holding his butt! Feeling his crotch! Getting a hard on! Sneaking around like a common criminal, right here in my house! This is my house, Larry! I let you in here to help you. I give you food to eat, a place to sleep, and how do you repay me? You kiss my mothafuckin' son. Jose is my son, and you kissed him! You stinkin' faggot, you kissed my son! I ought to knock your fuckin' head off."

"He kissed *me*! He kissed *me*! I was minding my own business, and he kissed me. He made me do it! I didn't want to, he made me."

"Who Larry? Who made you do it?"

"My father. My father made me do it."

By this time, Larry and half the group were crying. For the next two-and-a-half hours, Larry told the group about his childhood of molestation by his father. He did not know if his mother knew. He hated her anyway because she stayed with his father and let him beat her. He said drugs were the way he escaped his guilt and shame. He did not want to be a homosexual. He simply did not know any other way to live.

When the group was over and the clients were in bed, I sat at the front desk and cried. I cried for Larry, but I cried more for myself. I knew his pain. The pain of guilt and shame. The pain of being forced. The pain of not knowing how to escape. I cried because, while I was not a homosexual, I knew sex had another meaning for me. I had not yet figured out what it was, but it was not an act of love or intimacy for me. It was an escape for me just as it had been for Larry, so I cried for both of us.

"You'll get over it."

The voice surprised me. It was Charlie, the male counselor on duty.

"The first few are always the roughest, but you'll get over it. Don't get in it with them. It's their stuff, not yours. Besides that, he was lying through his teeth."

"What do you mean? His father didn't rape him?"

"Probably not. I know this guy's father. I did the intake on Larry. Plus, I talked to the counselors at his last treatment program. He told them the same story. If it was true, he wouldn't still be shooting dope."

"So why did he say that? Why did you buy it in the group?"

"It's a start. Now next week, when he doesn't think he's on the hot seat, I'll catch him in the lie. I'll bring his father in and ask Larry to tell his father what he told us. That's when he'll crack."

Charlie and I talked all night. He was an ex-addict who had been a counselor for six years. He had gone through this very program. He knew all the games and all the angles. He spent that night educating me.

The female drug culture was even more devious than the male, Charlie informed me. According to Charlie, once a woman sold her body, lost her kids, and lived the life of a junkie, she had lost a piece of her soul. Her rehabilitation was much more difficult than that of the males. She usually wanted it more than the men did, but society made it harder for her. He told me how hard my job was going to be. He did not, however, tell me how hard he would make my life.

143

Charlie and I started dating. First lunch, then dinner. He would go with me to visit the children. He went with me to pick them up. He sat with me during my first encounter session. He taught me about counseling and about monitoring clients. In three months, Charlie had become my third leg. Every other word out of my mouth was, "Charlie said...."

I did not know it then, but all the male counselors had been betting on who would get to me first. All ex-addicts, all street smart, they had all been watching me very closely. Charlie won the bet. On the fourth-month anniversary of starting my job, I gave Charlie a key to my house.

I don't know when it went bad. When I look back, it seems as if it happened overnight. I don't remember that we argued. I don't think we ever had a disagreement. Charlie was the man. *He* spoke. *I* was the woman. I kept my mouth shut and did what Charlie said. He was six foot-two and 200 pounds. I was five-five and 125 pounds. When Charlie said jump, I said, "How high?"

I do remember Mother's Day. Every Sunday, I took the children to Nett's house. She would make them pancakes, and she and I would talk, drink coffee, and smoke together while the kids were eating. On this particular Sunday, Mother's Day, Charlie wanted to go to his mother's house first. Absolutely not, I told him. I was going to my mother's house, with my children, like I did every Sunday. I was going to get in my car, which my father had given me, and go. Was he coming? He came.

As we were walking toward the front door of Nett's house, Charlie asked me for the keys to the car. "Why?"

"Don't ask me shit! Just give me the keys!"

"No!"

That's when it must have gone bad. I did not see his hand go up. I did not see it coming toward me. I felt the sting of it only after I had hit the pavement. The children were crying.

He snatched me up. I covered my face. He was trying to hold me, kissing my head, saying he was sorry. I was pushing away, running away, looking for the children, grabbing them, running again.

Nett opened the door. "What the hell happened to your face?"

"Charlie just slapped me."

My eye was swollen shut. My lip was twice its normal size. The children were eating their pancakes. Nett was ranting and raving.

"Put his ass out! Do it today! If they ever get away with hitting you once, they will never stop! I did not raise you to be beaten to death! Put his ass out!"

Through breakfast, lunch, and dinner, Nett tried to convince me to leave Charlie, who was calling every fifteen minutes. I would be home later, I told him. No, I was not going to go to his mother's house. Yes, I know you're sorry. I'll call you back.

Nett said Charlie could never set foot in her house again. She wanted me to call my father, my brother, and all of my brother's friends. She wanted me to call the police. She wanted me to poison him. Better yet, she suggested we walk around the corner to the police station, take out a warrant, and have him locked up immediately.

I had to leave Nett's that evening to get the children to Miss Alice's and get to work by midnight. Charlie also had to go to work at midnight. At midnight, Charlie and I went to work.

I wore a pair of sunglasses I had borrowed from Nett and kept an ice pack on my lip. The story was that I had been in a fender bender and had hit my face against the steering wheel.

At work, Charlie followed me around like a puppy. He was sorry. Did I know that? He loved me. Did I know that? That he would cut off his arm for me? Did I want him to do that? What did my mother say? Did I tell my father? Did I love him? Was I coming home?

Charlie said he would ask the director to give me a few days off. Did my face hurt? He was sorry. Did I know that? He loved me. Did I love him back? Did I want to get married? Did I have enough money to take a cab home? Leave the car with me. Take a cab. Go to bed. He would tell the director.

I finally got up enough nerve to ask him.

"Why did you hit me?"

"I don't know. I was mad. You made me mad when you yelled at me. I wasn't going to hit you. I didn't want to hit you. You *made* me hit you. Please go home. I don't want people to see your face like that. Take a cab. I'll see you in the morning. You'll be home when I get there, right? Maybe we'll go see the kids and take them to see my mother. Okay?"

"Okay."

It was two years later when I "made" Charlie hit me again. I was four months pregnant.

Charlie's mother simply did not like me. For that matter, most of his family did not like me. It was nothing I did, nothing I said. It was my very presence. We had gone by Charlie's mother's house to tell her I was pregnant. After we told her, she looked me dead in the face and said, "I guess you've really got him now. You've got him right where you want him. Trapped!"

Charlie asked her what she was talking about. She said I wanted him for his money. I had saddled him with two children that weren't his, now with me having his child, he would never get away from me. She started laughing at him, mocking him. "You trapped now! She really got you now!"

I stood up, grabbed the children, and left. I was at the car when Charlie came running down the block. I knew how his mother was, he said. She didn't mean nothing by it. I was crying and trying to get the kids in the car. Don't leave, he pleaded. Come on, let's all go out to dinner. I pulled away from him.

"Don't do that," Charlie was begging. "Come on, wait for me. I'll get my stuff."

When Charlie walked back to the house, I got in my car and drove home.

You know how you know something, but it's just too horrible to face, so you don't? I knew Charlie and I were not meant to be. I knew it, but I did not know what to do about it. We worked together. We lived together. Now I was going to have his child. He was trapped! I was trapped!

Charlie and I had been together for two-and-a-half years. I had discovered that he was functionally illiterate. He could barely read or write. He was very insecure about his abilities, so he covered it up with a very macho image and presence. He also had a breast. As a result of some glandular problem, one of his breasts protruded like a woman's. When he was dressed, you could not see it, but Charlie didn't believe that. He always thought people were looking at it.

I also discovered that Charlie was an incredible liar. He lied about things when it was totally unnecessary to lie. He liked to impress people with what he knew, where he had been, and what he had, which was clothes, money, and me. I was the thing Charlie most liked to impress people with. This made him very possessive and very jealous. Charlie would not let me out of his sight for more than an hour. The only place I could go without him was to Nett's or to my father's house, and they both hated him. He was not fond of them either.

I had never had a man, or anyone else for that matter, pay as much attention to me as Charlie did. At first I thought it was fine. It showed that he loved me and did not want to lose me. But throughout the relationship, I felt like a prisoner. Charlie told me what to wear and what not to wear, how to wear my hair and when to wear make-up. If I did or said anything other than what he told me to do, he accused me of being with another man. He was constantly accusing me of having another man. I always responded with "When? Where? We live, work, eat, and sleep together, Charlie. Where I am supposed to be meeting this man? In the frozen food section of the supermarket? There is no other man!"

We argued most of the time about men, money, his mother, and my "dead-beat" family. We never once talked about the other women Charlie had, and he had several.

Charlie got home from work at about three in the morning. I was usually in bed, sleeping. One night when he came in, he stormed into the bedroom and snatched the covers off me.

"Where the fuck have you been?"

I had been home all day.

"You are a lying bitch whore! I've been calling here all day, and you have not been home!"

"Charlie, I shut the ringer off the phone. Check it out. It's still off."

"You don't want to talk to me?" He was hysterical. "I've been worried sick about you, and you don't want to talk to me?"

"Charlie, I'm tired. Leave me alone."

That's when it started. I think he slapped me first. Then he picked me up off the bed and threw me across the room. As I was crawling away he slapped me again. He grabbed me by the hair on my head, pulled me to my feet, and slapped me again. He slapped me for screaming, so I stopped. Then he slapped me for not answering his questions.

Who had I been with? Where had I been?

Nobody! Nowhere!

It seemed like he beat me for hours. Damon came running into the bedroom. Gemmia was crying.

When the children were quieted down, I crawled back into bed and had sex with the man who had just beaten the mess out of me. I was twenty-one years old. I was all grown up.

᠅᠅᠅

I was sitting at the kitchen table the first time it happened. I saw a shadow out of the corner of my eye. When I turned, it was gone. The next time, I was standing in the bathroom. I saw a woman standing behind me. I jumped and turned around. She wasn't there. The next time I saw the woman, it was in a dream. I was walking near a body of water. She walked up to me and told me her name. Carmen. She was my friend, she said. She was always with me and would always be with me, she said. She had come to tell me to leave the place where I was living. To leave the man I was living with. He would hurt me if I didn't leave him, she said.

148

Carmen said she would tell me what to do and where to go, but I would have to trust her. She told me I was going to have a little girl. She told me she would help me raise my children, but I had to leave the man alone. I do not remember what I said to her in response, but I do remember she told me she would show me proof that the man I was with was no good for me.

Charlie was staying out two or three nights a week. Once, he went to the store to buy bread and did not come home for twelve days. I was six months pregnant and very weak. I stayed home more than I worked. I had been transferred to another facility, so I did not see Charlie at work anymore. Even when I did, I did not dare ask him where he had been. We were fighting most of the time now. Actually, we were not fighting. He was beating me up. I was quite sure that the moment I had the baby, I was going to leave him. To go where, I did not know.

I was hanging clothes on the line outside the bedroom window one day. The children were playing in their room when the doorbell rang. I found two women standing at the door. One was about forty, the other I later discovered was nineteen. They introduced themselves as mother and daughter. The older woman spoke. She said they had come to ask me why I would not divorce Charlie so that he and her daughter could marry. She had helped them get an apartment together. According to the mother, Charlie said he wanted to marry her daughter but I would not divorce him. He knew the baby I was carrying was not his, but he could not prove it. She had come to ask me to please let him go. She feared her daughter would lose her mind if she and my husband did not make some definite plans soon.

I asked the women to come in and wait a few minutes. I got three garbage bags. I put all of Charlie's clothes in the bags. I went to the window, pulled his wet clothes and underwear in from off the clothesline, and packed them in the bags. I presented the bags to the women. They said thank you and turned to leave. I asked them to wait a minute. I went down to the basement, out to the backyard, and got Charlie's dog. I put the dog on her leash, brought her upstairs, and gave her to the women. Then I spoke to them as calmly as I could.

"I can understand your daughter, a nineteen-year-old girl being stupid enough and disrespectful enough to come to my house. I cannot for the life of me understand you, her mother, coming along with her."

They both smirked. The daughter then turned to her mother and said, "He said she was a bitch!"

Everyone knew Charlie was beating me even though I denied it. I never told anyone except Nett, and she was helpless to do anything about it. She could not understand why I stayed with him. I could not figure out how to get away from him. I did not want to be with Charlie, but I wanted to be with somebody. I was about to have another child. That meant I would have three children by three different men. Who in the world would want me after that? Even though I had lost weight, even though I had grown hair, I still believed I was ugly. No man would want an ugly woman with three children. I had some other problems, too. I had no high school diploma. I did not know what I wanted to do with my life. I had a terrible inferiority complex. I had spent most of my life having sex and children. I did not know what else I could do. I could sew and I could dance, but I doubted whether I was good enough at either of those things to make a living.

Most of all, I believed Charlie loved me. When he was not beating me, I thought he took good care of me. I was never hungry. I had clothes. My children were well provided for between his salary, my salary, and my public assistance. We lived very well, relatively speaking. All I had to do was figure out how to make Charlie stop beating me. And I had to do it very quickly, because when he came home and found out I had given two strange women all of his clothes, he would beat the mess out of me for sure. And he did.

I never fought Charlie back. He was too big, and I was too

scared. He never punched me, he always slapped me. That was enough. He liked to choke me too. He would choke me until I passed out. Afterwards, he took great pride and care in patching up my wounds. He would put cold water on my face. He would rub my bruises with witch hazel. He would fix me tea or coffee and serve it to me in bed. While I laid there, he would feed the children, bathe them, and put them to bed. If it was daylight, he would play with them and insist I go for a ride in the car with them. The children loved the car. I was too pregnant and too tired to care.

When Charlie saw my wounds he would cry. He would cry and tell me how sorry he was. After he cried, he would lay me down and have sex with me. I would close my eyes and leave my body.

It was over a hundred degrees outside. Everybody was miserable. For pregnant people like me, the heat was unbearable. I was sitting on the front steps of the house watching the children play. Wayne's mother, my next-door neighbor, was just coming home from work. She hugged and kissed the children and sat down next to me on the steps.

"Why do you stay with him?" she asked. "Why do you stay with a man who beats you like that?"

My eyes filled up with water. I did not bother to deny it. This was not my neighbor. This was my son's grandmother. A woman who had always been pleasant to me.

She told me how she could hear the arguing and fighting. She had seen my bruises, she said. She had told Wayne he should help me get away. She told me she would help me get away. Staying with Charlie was not good for the children, she warned, and it was not good for the baby. She asked me if my father and brother knew what was going on. Her theory was that the only reason Charlie treated me so bad was because he knew I had nobody to turn to. If he thought he would have to answer to my father or brother, she said, he would never put his hands on me again. She invited us up for dinner. I said no thanks. I was already miserable. Food was the last thing on my mind. It was too hot to think, so I sat there crying. She took the children with her, fed them, and sent them back when she saw Charlie pull up in my car.

Charlie came in like a madman. He started by locking the children in their room. Then he started the inquisition. How many times had I gone to Alex's house? Alex was a co-worker. His girlfriend Freda and I had gone shopping together a few times, I explained. Where had I gone after I left my mother's house on Sunday? When did I go to the Bronx to pick up a new client? I could not answer most of the questions because he would not give me time. The others made no sense. I had no answer. I watched him become more and more agitated. I could not believe that with four weeks left in my pregnancy this man would put his hands on me. Actually, that did not make sense. Charlie had beat me more than ever while I was pregnant.

He finally got to the bottom line. He had been out with a few of the guys from work. They were making a big joke, actually taking bets on who my baby was going to look like. Rumor had it that the baby was not Charlie's but that of one of the men I worked with at the other facility.

"That's ridiculous, Charlie," I said. "I was already pregnant when I went to work there!" This was his baby, I swore it was. That was not good enough.

The emergency room was packed but the system had changed. Asthma patients and pregnant women had priority over everything except gunshot wounds and heart attacks. I was so beat up, I think they were looking for the bullet hole. They suspected that one of my ribs was cracked. They also thought my jaw was broken. I was too pregnant to be x-rayed. Where did it hurt, they asked. Everywhere! Where were my children?

A young Black doctor came into the examining room. He pulled the curtain and sat down next to me. He asked all the usual questions about my medical history. He examined my bruises. Then he held my hand, looked straight into my eyes, and said,

"You don't have to take this. If you don't have anywhere to go, you can stay at my house. I'm never there. I'm always here. If you don't want to come home with me, find somewhere else to go, but go. This man is going to kill you. You know that, don't you?"

I nodded my head and cried.

There were police and police reports. There were social workers and psychiatrists. I would not press charges. I was not crazy.

I couldn't remember the first blow or the last. Wayne's mother had called Nett. Nett had taken a taxi to my house. She found me bruised and unconscious on the bed. The children were crying, Charlie was gone. Nett had brought me to the hospital. Wayne's mother had taken the children. Nett went back to pick them up. She had told me I was to come to her house if and when I was released.

A sonogram let the doctors know the baby was fine. My ribs had to be wrapped. My jaw they said would heal on its own. I was free to go. The young doctor dangled the keys in front of me.

"Two bedrooms in an elevator-service, air-conditioned building right across the street...?"

I thanked him again and went to pick up my children.

Nett went to pieces when she saw me. She wailed from the pit of her soul. She begged and pleaded for me to report Charlie and have him locked up. I couldn't do it. I thought then that I was too scared to do it. I realized later that I just didn't want to. Something inside of me just couldn't let go. It just could not bear the thought of starting over. It could not face the idea of being alone.

This was about more than Charlie beating me, I thought. This was my last chance to make my life work. If this thing with Charlie did not work out, then it would mean I had failed, again. It would mean that I had done the wrong thing, again. It would mean that Grandma was right, that I wasn't shit! I was not ready to admit that. I could not admit that, and I could not be left alone with three children. Charlie would stop beating me. Once he saw what had happened this time, what he had done to me, he would stop. Of course, I didn't say any of this to Nett. I simply told her that I loved him. She said I was hopeless.

∧∙∧∙∧

The shadow of the woman in the mirror and in my dreams was replaced by the shadow of a man. A huge, Black man who wore no shirt. I saw him standing over my bed once. I saw him sitting in the room with the children. Whenever he was around, Charlie did not come near me.

I had not seen Charlie for three weeks. We talked on the telephone, but he said he would not come home until he got some counseling. That was great. I held out hope that he would get it together. Our telephone conversations reminded me of when we first got together. He was sweet and gentle. He listened to me. For the first time in quite some time, he let me speak without interrupting me or telling me I was stupid. We began a new friendship over the telephone, and I felt a lot better about our relationship.

Charlie had only been back in the house two days when I went into labor. Forty-six hours of labor produced Nisa, a five-pound, thirteen-ounce baby girl, born on the same date, at the same time, as her brother Damon. She looked exactly like Charlie. When I saw her I knew immediately I would never have another child.

∧∙∧∙∧

Charlie's family went ga-ga over Nisa. She soon had more clothes and toys than she would need in her entire life. I had to tolerate his relatives trooping in and out of my house for weeks. It didn't matter. I was so depressed and tired, I was glad to have anyone take care of the baby.

I had not been working, so we had big financial problems. We owed a few months' back rent, and a myriad of bills had accumulated since Charlie's departure. The lease had expired and the landlord wanted us to move. The people in the neighborhood had told him about "you know, the fighting," and he did not want any problems with the police.

Charlie assured me that he would take care of everything. He would get the money, find us a place, and we would move. The director of my facility said he could get me all of my vacation pay while I was on maternity leave. That was about twenty-five-hundred dollars. He submitted the papers for me. Charlie said he would get some money from his aunt, and we started looking for an apartment.

People are funny about accepting children into their apartments. They want to know your whole life history and your mother's pedigree. We had a real hard time finding a place in a decent neighborhood, near public transportation, for a rent we could afford. We finally came across a really good deal.

Charlie made all of the arrangements. I packed up everything and prepared to move. It was a bright Saturday morning. Charlie had to go to the office for a meeting, he said. He told me the moving van would be arriving at ten o'clock. He would be back by then.

By two o'clock, he was not back, and the van had not come. I started getting a little nervous. The telephone had been disconnected, so I could not call. But then, call who? I did not know which moving company Charlie had hired.

Somewhere in the back of my mind, I knew something was wrong. Why had Charlie not come back? How come the truck had not arrived? I knew Charlie was a liar, but this was too cruel, too horrible, even for him.

By six that evening, I was in a panic. The baby was crying. The sterilizer was packed. The children wanted their toys. I could not get the boxes open. My head was killing me. I could not breathe. I took the children to the corner pay phone. I knew the super's last name and the address of the apartment building. His number was not listed. There was a Winston somebody listed at that address. I called. A woman answered. Somehow, I told her bits and pieces of my story. Did she have the super's name and telephone number, I asked. She did. I called.

"Hello. My name is..."

"We are supposed to move in today..."

"My husband is working..."

"The truck has not come yet..."

"What should I do?"

"Lady, what are you talking about?"

"Don't you remember? I'm the one with the baby..."

"Your husband never came back. I rented that apartment last week."

"What...? Wait a minute... Hello...?"

It was too late. I was dead.

From somewhere, I kept hearing someone say, "Keep breathing. Just keep breathing." I couldn't breathe. I was dead. My entire body was numb. I have no idea how I got home. I remember sitting in the middle of the kitchen floor staring at the boxes. I do not remember what happened to the children or the baby. I was struggling to breathe. I saw the box marked "bathroom." I opened it with my hands and teeth. I removed all the pills I could find. One by one, I took everything I found. Tylenol. Aspirin. Phenobarbitol. Charlie's asthma pills. Vitamins. Water pills. Nightol. I washed them all down with Listerine.

I no longer wanted to breathe. I had failed, again. I had truly messed up my life and my children's lives. I did not want to breathe. I wanted to die.

A quiet sense of peace fell over me. At first, I saw brilliant colors. I heard beautiful music playing all around me. I saw a man walking toward me. It was Charlie. I lashed out at him, kicking, biting, screaming. He pushed me away. I could feel my chest heaving up and down. The voice was back. "Breathe. Just keep breathing."

I heard the baby crying, but I could not see her. Then it hit me: I was going to die. I panicked. "I'm not breathing! I can't breathe!" My entire body felt like lead. I wanted to get up, but I did not know where I was. "I want to breathe! Oh, God! Please, help me! I want to breathe!"

Then I saw her. The beautiful Black woman. The one I had seen in the bathroom mirror when I was twelve. That I had seen when my brother teased me and threatened to beat me up. I had seen her in my dreams. Her name was Mary, she told me. She was the Divine Mother. She reached out to me. I ran to her and fell into her open arms. At first, I screamed. Then I cried.

Mary stroked my head and kissed my face. I looked at her. I saw Vy and Nett and Wayne's mother and the lady named Sarah. I saw myself. When I woke up, I was in the hospital. I was crying. And I was still breathing.

PART III

Then There Was...

THE
Journal

Every day, pieces of me die. A piece of my mind. A piece of my heart. A piece of my life. This piecemeal death can be transformational when I take the time to participate in the process by consciously surrendering what I no longer need. If I allow myself to get still enough to think and feel, I will experience these deaths as a release that takes me to a new level of understanding. These deaths are lessons. Things I have done and experienced and hopefully learned from. These deaths are painfully painless when I accept them and embrace them. They are the demands of life waiting to be acknowledged, recognized, and accepted. However, when I allow the burden of responsibility or the fear of feeling or dying intervene and cut off the learning, these mini-deaths become murderously devastating and destructive.

Ignoring, resisting, and fighting death promotes the onset of rigor mortis—a stiffening and hardening of life. Pieces of the mind become stiff in the memories of past errors and choices. Pieces of the heart harden from feelings unexpressed and unrequited. Pieces of daily life lie dormant, unmotivated by the thoughts or emotions required to stay alive. When I avoid the necessary deaths required to fully appreciate life, I destroy my ability to move beyond the form to reach the essence.

Today, I feel the pain of death. My entire body is in pain. I feel heavy. I feel tired. My hair is heavy. My head is numb, but I feel it throbbing. Every hair on my body is standing on end. As I move, chills run through me. A million thoughts are running through my mind at once. I can't catch them. They make no sense. Every breath is an effort. I take long, deep breaths terminated with a deep sigh. Somebody is talking to me, pulling on me. I guess that's the reason I am still here. If it were not for this person, I would leave my body forever.

I need to be alone to die. I cannot die with other people around. I want to get into the process—the death—and feel it. I want to go within so I can come out again, whole and complete. I am dying today. It is a painful death. I am trying to die in peace, but I have to figure out who will watch the children. I have to make sure all of the laundry is washed and ironed. I have to sweep under all the beds and make sure the dog has food. Then I can die.

I am dying broke and depressed. I owe money everywhere, to everyone. I am so ashamed, humiliated, and frustrated. No, angry is a much better word. I am so angry that I have to live like this—waiting, wanting, not having the one thing I really want. I try to be positive, but in moments like this it is very hard. I know I should not focus on the negative, but right now, in this moment of death, I can't seem to help myself. I want to feel better fast. What I feel like is dying.

I'm going to die today, and it is alright. I'm going to die to every bad feeling, every bad experience and bad memory that seems to keep repeating in my life. I am going to die to making excuses for myself and others. I am not going to live like this anymore. I want to die to suffering and pain, and I want to take some people with me. My children. I want my children to die to the memory of a mother who always promises to do and then doesn't. I want them to die to not being able to depend on me, not being able to come to me, and not being able to get from me whatever they need for their security and survival. I want them to die to the memory of a mother who is always dragging them in and out of crises.

I am going to die today and it's okay. I want to die to the patterns of isolation, desperation, and starvation of my need to be whole. I am dying to be whole, to be complete, to be free of lack, fear, and doubt. I want to lay down, close my eyes, and wake up in another state of being. I want to be the wonderful, marvelous person I know I can be but do not believe I am. I want to feel the spirit of love moving so strongly in my body that when I talk it will spill forth.

I can laugh in the face of death because I know it is just a momentary condition of change. I need to pray, but I don't want to. I am ready to die right here and now. I am not making any plans or promises. I am simply dying to the old me and awakening to the divine Light that I am.

CHAPTER 14

A Collage of Pain and Confusion

For the first time in my life, I was in the right place at the right time: the psychiatric ward of Brookdale Hospital. It was a lovely place. There were lovely doctors and nurses who gave me lovely drugs, which helped me to feel like a lovely person. I had a lovely green room with a lovely window that did not have any bars. I had a lovely bed with a lovely green spread and lovely little black straps on my wrists and ankles. There were lots of lovely people with lovely distorted faces who came to poke me, stick me, and ask me lovely questions about my lovely state of being. It was great.

What day is this? Tuesday. You've been here since Saturday. Where am I? Snapper Five, the psychiatric ward. What happened? Do you remember what happened? I took some pills. What happened to make you take the pills? That's when the dam broke. I began to wail. I told them about the moving experience. I told about Charlie beating me up. I told about being fat when I was a kid. I told about Tommy and Ronald and the baby dying. I told about Grandma brushing me until I bled. I told about sleeping on the floor next to her bed and what happened when Bunny told Aunt Nancy, who told my daddy, who had a fit, and how mad Grandma got. I told about Grandma not letting me have any donuts until Ray had eaten all he wanted. Bunny told that too. I told about playing with the handle on the crab pot, and how all the crabs jumped out and bit us. Everybody had crabs hanging off their fingers and clothes. I told about how I got a beating for doing that.

I did not tell about Uncle Lee. I did not tell about Mr. François. I did not tell how the butcher on the corner used to feel my breasts under my shirt when Aunt Nancy sent me to buy meat on credit. I did not tell how the young preacher from the church right across the street from my house bought me an ice cream cone and then put his hand on my breast. I did not tell about going into the woods with the boys down South, laying on the ground, and letting them "do it to me." I did not tell how Daddy beat me until his pants fell off. I did not tell how I stole money from his pants pocket when they were laying on the floor. I did not tell how Daddy would pick me up from work on Thursday night and take my paycheck money and give me just enough to get back to work the next week. I did not tell about the time Ray found out that his football teammate Spider had made me "do it" in the hallway. I did not tell them that when Ray found out he chased Spider down the block with a hatchet.

I told about feeling ugly. I told about feeling useless and stupid, unwanted and unloved. I told about moving to so many places, living with so many people, I did not know where I belonged. I told about stealing the pennies from Bunny's bank and lying about it. I told about Aunt Nancy's funeral and finding out that my cousin was really my younger brother, but I couldn't figure out who my mother was and who my father was. I told about going to the psychiatrist when I was younger. Why? I don't remember why. I told about Nett's sister Evelyn and her five children and the time we were at their house. I told how we were all in the room playing jacks, and I told a dirty joke. I asked them if they had a dog would they suck his wee-wee. I told about how I got beat and punished for that. I told how I was never allowed to be alone with them again. I was only four years old. I had no idea what I was talking about. I told how I always talked too much and said all the wrong things, which was why I was always being told, "Shut up! You talk too much!" I told about hearing voices, having dreams, and seeing people in the flesh who no one else could see. I told about Sarah and Carmen and the man in the mirror. I must have talked for hours before I looked at the white man sitting next to my bed and asked him, "Who the hell are you?"

"Dr. Miller. I am afraid you will be staying with us for awhile."

He gave me another shot and took the straps off my ankles and wrists. When I woke up again it was Saturday.

For the first twenty-one years of my life, I lived in a constant fog with a dull ache. I ached to be wanted and appreciated. I ached to feel good about myself, to know that I was worthy of being treated with some semblance of decency and dignity. I ached to feel beautiful, to have beautiful things, to look beautiful and have someone mention it, even if just in passing. I lived in perpetual love poverty and material lack. For a while, I thought money would lift the fog and take away the ache. Not having the things I thought I wanted turned the dull ache into a gnawing pain.

I ached for my father's approval and for a man to treat me like I mattered. I ached for a mother. I wanted my own mother to hold me, rock me, and love me, even if just for a moment. I ached as a mother because I could not do the same for my children. I ached to know what I was supposed to be doing with my life. Nothing made me happy. Hell, I didn't even know what happiness felt like. I was easily bored and easily distracted. No amount of activity fulfilled my need to be needed. I was so confused about who I was, who I was not, where I was going, and how I was to find out the right way to find out what I did not know and could not figure out.

I was Black. No, I was an African. I was weak because I was a woman. No, I was strong because I was a Black African woman. People didn't like Africans. People didn't like me. I was a strong, Black, proud African woman—who had no idea what any of that meant. I needed to know. The fact that I did not know meant that the ache grew deeper and deeper until it had hit the core. The result was total, absolute confusion.

Charlie's beating me turned the dull ache into a throbbing pain. My mind and heart were alive with the pain of my life. Three children by three different men. No real family connection and support. No education to nurture and support my innate talents and abilities. No goals for my future. No money and no faith in my ability to do anything but survive in pain. In the beginning, Charlie was my dose of Tylenol. He came along at a time when the pain was about to consume me. He gave me strength, courage, and a reason to live. He said what I needed to hear. He did what I needed to have done, the way I wanted it to be done. Just when I was about to breathe a sigh of relief, he changed. No, he became real.

The thing about confusion and aching is, until you get to the cause of it, no amount of medication will cause it to go away. Food will not take it away. Sex will not take it away. Twenty years of aching will not go away when you enter a new relationship. The ache of a childhood of abuse and neglect will not go away with the purchase of a new dress. The ache of losing yourself will not go away when you move into a nice, new apartment. You must learn the cause of the ache, confront it, and stare it down. Once that is done, you can lift yourself beyond the fog of confusion.

Unfortunately for me, however, I had no idea I was aching or confused. I had no idea when it started or what caused it to continue. I thought I was fat because I ate too much. I believed I was ugly because I was dark, with short hair, and because I was fat and ate too much. I had no idea I had become delirious from the constant ache and the blinding confusion. I spent six weeks in a psychiatric ward trying to figure it out and stop the aching.

⋏⋏⋏

The minute I got my wits again, I called Wayne. He came to see me the same day. He was very sad to see me in such a place and such a state. I was very happy to see him. We engaged in small talk for about an hour. He could not believe Snapper Five was a mental ward. The people looked perfectly normal, he said. True, the patients wore street clothes, and there was a lot of "normal" activity going on. No one was making baskets. The doctors and nurses wore street clothes too. You could not tell the staff from the patients.

166

It took him a while, but Wayne eventually got around to talking to me about Charlie. He said he knew Charlie beat me and asked why I stayed with him. He told me that he and Tonya had broken up. He had a new job and he would try to give me some money to help me out. He told me to leave Charlie, and I promised I would. When he stood up to leave, he hugged me and kissed me on my forehead. He told me to stop acting crazy and get myself together. I was too smart and too beautiful to waste my life like this, he said. He left, and I did not see him again for several years.

Not knowing who you are is very confusing. I am not talking about knowing your name, your family heritage, or the circumstances of your life. I am talking about not knowing who you are as an expression of life. Your life's purpose is your "self." The self has desires, dreams, and goals. The self has fears, but it also has abilities. The self has meaning—a depth, a philosophy, values, and ideals of its own. I had none of that. I was so engrossed in living day-to-day, I had no self. I had moved from childhood to motherhood to adulthood with such speed and confusion that I missed several developmental steps along the way. I never had time to explore *me*, to feel *me*, to see and know what *I* looked like. I had never been taught how to like myself, nor had I ever taken the time to do so. I did not know who I was. What I did know about me, I did not like.

Not having a constant, consistent mother figure had contributed to my confusion. The mother images I had were inconsistent with one another. They represented an incongruent collage that made absolutely no sense to me. They were all so different. All so distant. All so in conflict with themselves, each other, and with me. I never knew what it was like to have a real mother. Nett was about as close as I got. I knew she wasn't my birth mother, but I could not accept that. Because no one else in the family liked her, it was difficult for me to express what I felt for her.

None of my "mothers" had ever talked to me about the "woman things" I needed to know. They did not teach me about the growth and development of my body. They did not tell me about menstrual periods or sex or having babies. So I watched. And I listened. And I drew my own conclusions. Before I could figure out what was going on, things had begun to happen to me.

My father was at the core of my heart's aching and my mind's confusion. Unwittingly, unknowingly, without malice or forethought, he had played the lead role in the near destruction of my life. He was the lead player in all of my dramas, but he never really showed up. He was never really there for me. He did not give. He could not do what I needed him to do. He did not have what I wanted him to have. My father never kissed me. He never held me or made me feel safe. He never said, "I love you." Instead, he beat me. He abandoned me emotionally and physically. Still, I believed that my father had the one thing I needed to make life worth living: love. The fact that he did not know how to give it to me almost destroyed me.

When your daddy can't love you, you look for someone who can. For me, it began with Uncle Lee. When you find a new daddy to love you and he rapes you, you become even more confused. The physical experience of being raped is not what caused the confusion. It was the betrayal. Uncle Lee betrayed my trust, my faith, my need to have a daddy who really, truly loved me. He betrayed my confidence in myself to pick a man who was worthy of being my father. He took me into his home when my own father did not want me. He promised to take care of me and protect me. He told me I was pretty. He said I was his "big, pretty baby." He made me feel wanted, and then he betrayed me. The rape was inconsequential. My hymen was gone and my body would mend, but the pain of betrayal he injected into my heart was nearly fatal.

During my six weeks in Brookdale, the images of my early life splashed haphazardly onto the canvas of my brain. The memories bled together to form a mutant decoupage of confusion—black and green surrounded by deep blues. My mind was scattered. My heart was pierced. My self had been formed on a pedestal of instability, dishonesty, abuse, and neglect. I longed to be cherished. I yearned to be valued. I needed to be honored.

Thinking back, it would not have taken much. An expression of genuine love or appreciation would have brought some brilliant color to my dreadful life canvas, would have smoothed out the rough edges of my developing personality. An occasional word of encouragement. A moment of nurturing here and there. When I did not get it, I sought it out. The closest thing to love and nurturing that I found was sex. As a result, sex became the most colorful activity of my life.

My father came to see me after I had been in the hospital for three weeks. I had lost a lot of weight, but I looked fine, he said. He and his "wife" had my children. Well, they had two of them. Charlie had Nisa, who was then about nine weeks old. Daddy told me he had asked Charlie to come by to see the children. He did, and he brought the baby with him so they could see her. She looked fine. She was getting fat. Nett was fine too, he said. She could not bring herself to come to the hospital, but she had sent me some clothes.

Daddy asked me when I thought I would be leaving the ward and going back to work. I told him I didn't think I was going to go back to work. I could not take another day of trying to help other people solve their problems. He told me that he had arranged for my public assistance checks to come to his house, and that he had brought two of them with him. If I signed them, he said, he knew how to get them cashed. I followed his orders.

I told him about the bag of money I had hidden in the closet of my hospital room. He looked at me as if I had really gone crazy for stashing money away in a mental ward until I went to the closet, pulled out a plastic bag, and gave it to my father. It was over three thousand dollars. My then-best friend and supervisor at work, Ruth Carlos, had brought me the checks for my vacation time. She had cashed them and brought me back the money. Daddy took the bag and left. I didn't see him again until I was released from the hospital six weeks later.

THE Journal

One day, my soul just opened up
and things started happenin'
Things I can't quite explain
I mean
I cried and cried like never before
I cried the tears of ten thousand mothers
I couldn't even feel anything because
I cried 'til I was numb

One day, my soul just opened up
I felt this overwhelming pride
What I was proud of
God only knows!
Like the pride of a hundred thousand fathers
basking in the glory of their sons
I was grinning from ear to ear

One day, my soul just opened up
I started laughing
and I laughed forever
Wasn't nothin' particularly funny goin' on
but I laughed anyhow
I laughed the joy of a million children playing in the mud
I laughed 'til my sides ached
Oh, God! It felt so good!

One day, my soul just opened up
There were revelations, annihilations, and resolutions
feelings of doubt and betrayal, vengeance and forgiveness
memories of things I'd seen and done before
of places I'd been, although I didn't know when
There were lives I'd lived
people I'd loved
battles I'd fought
victories I'd won
and wars I'd lost

One day, my soul just opened up
and out poured all the things
I'd been hiding
and denying
and living through
that had just happened moments before

One day my soul just opened up
and I decided
I was good
I was ready
I was good and ready to surrender
my life
to God.

So I sat down and wrote Her a note
and told Her so.

Dear God,

It's me again. I woke up this morning, and I couldn't think of anyone I would rather start my day with. There are so many things I want to tell You, but I'll start off with "I love You, God." I think You are absolutely wonderful! I love You with all my heart and soul. I am so glad, so grateful that all You ever do is love me back. You don't ask me for anything. You just love me 'cause you're God.

I just wanted to say thank You this morning. Thank You for loving me. I know you do because I woke up this morning, and everything in my body was still functioning. My blood is flowing. My lungs are expanding. My cells are reproducing. Even those parts of me that are a little rusty and squeaky are doing okay. I have died and gone to heaven because I know You love me in those places and because I haven't broken down yet.

Thank You, God, for all the opportunities that await me today, this week, this year, and throughout the rest of my life. I known I have a lot to learn. I also know You have many wonderful things in store for me because that's what You do for those You love. You give and give. I, for one, thank you. I thank You, God, that You are opening my mind, heart, and eyes to see the wonder of Your ways in all things. I am primed and ready to move forward because You have loved me healthy again.

I thank You, God, that no one and no thing has beaten me down. Yes, there have been some rough spots, dark days, and difficult times. But just like a knight in shining armor, an angel from the clouds, You have always arrived at just the right time. I didn't always know it was You, but You didn't mind. You helped me anyway. You came as people, as songs, as books. You came in the mail, through the telephone, and in my dreams. Sometimes, You were an expedience. At other times, you looked like a delay. I remember the time You looked like a horrible mistake. And remember the time You showed up as a downed *computer system. Boy! That was a close one! But there You were, loving me, helping me as much as I would let You. I remember it all now, and I just want to say thank You and tell you I love You for all You have done and given me.*

I thank You, God, for the peace and joy in my heart right now. In this moment, there is no one and nothing but You and I. I feel the warmth of your arms around me as life. I sense the strength of your hand upon me as breath. I know the comfort of your being as love. All around me and in me is peace. As I write this letter to You, giving You my full attention, I am at peace with the world.

Thank You, God, for being right here, with me, right now. As we move into this day together, let us show the world what the love of God looks like and what it can do. Thank You, God. I know I would not have made it without You, and I know I don't want to.

Love,

Me

CHAPTER 15

A Tinge of Rebellion

I wish there was a way I could tell you in ten words or less what is meant by spirit and spirituality. If there is a way, I have not figured it out, so I ask you to bear with me as I take you through one of the memorable experiences from which I have drawn the conclusion, "Spirit Is!"

The Snapper Five experience was the beginning of the end for me. It was the beginning of my spiritual innocence and the end of my spiritual ignorance. When I refused to take any more drugs, the doctors decided to leave me alone. Whereas the doctors would attempt to provide me with therapy every day while I was drugged, they came only once a week when I was in my normal state of mind. It turned out to be a good thing. I spent many hours over the course of that six weeks thinking about and feeling what was going on inside of me. I began to write, and I began to pray. "Be still and know" was my favorite passage. The stiller I got, the more I came to know about myself.

∧∨∧∨∧

As a child, I had learned to be afraid of people who were bigger than me, who had power over me, and who could determine what I did and had. I learned from Grandma, Aunt Nancy, Uncle Lee, and Daddy that people could hurt you. They could hurt your body and they could hurt your feelings. I learned that people lied.

They lied to you, on you, for you, and about you. They did not think you knew they were lying, but you knew. You were simply too afraid to say anything about it. I learned to be afraid of people who lied because you could not trust them. Lesson Number One: Don't trust people!

As a child, I learned to worry. I worried about where I was going to live, who was going to feed me, if they were going to beat me, and, most of all, if they were going to leave me. I learned to do whatever was necessary to keep people from leaving me. Lesson Number Two: You just don't know what is going to happen to you, and there is nothing you can do about it anyway.

I had grown into a worrying, distrustful woman who lied in the face of perceived danger. I grew up to be everything I hated about the people who took care of me as a child. I was irrational, irresponsible, unstable, inconsistent, self-abusive, and scared to death that at any moment I would do or say something—the wrong thing—and something awful would happen. Of course, I did not look like that on the outside. If you looked at me, I resembled a perfectly capable, normal, functioning mother and woman. I kept myself neat and clean. My children were well-fed and well-behaved. I had a job, a man, a house, and a car. I even had a dog. I could hold a normal conversation and spell my name while tying my shoes. From all appearances, I was completely normal. That is what made me so dangerous. I could go anywhere in the world and people treated me as though I was a normal human being, when all the while I was totally out of my mind.

All of this may sound dramatic. It is not. When I look back at the things I did, the things I said, the things I believed about myself and others, I know I was insane. Because I posed no danger to society or others, no one paid attention to the subtle hints of my madness.

In my madness, I had created a monster. The monster was the hardened encrustation of my negative thoughts, beliefs, and experiences. The monster chased me, taunted me, and tortured me using my own mind. All the things I never talked about created the monster's face. All the questions I had never asked shaped themselves into the monster's body. All the things I knew to be true but pushed to the back of my mind had formed the monster's legs and its great big feet. All the negative things that others had said to me became the monster's huge arms. All the lies, the ones that had been told to me over the years and the ones I had told myself, were the monster's claws. My fantasies gave the monster a very dramatic snarl. It growled and drooled at me any time I even thought about being or doing things in a different way.

The monster knew I was bad. The monster kept me in fear. It was particularly fond of ugly people. Fat people. The monster chased me in and through one drama after another.

The monster was a male monster. His name was Mr. Uncle Daddy Lee François, but his friends called him Ronald Tommy Dennis Wayne for short.

Somewhere, deep inside of me, I knew there was a brilliant, beautiful woman. I did not always feel that way, but I daydreamed about myself in the hospital. I had visions about myself and my life being a totally different way than what I had come to know. I realized I had brilliant ideas I had never acted on. I was intelligent and outgoing, but I always anticipated failure. I was talented and capable, yet I was inconsistent and unreliable. I was angry. I was angry at myself and the world. My anger had surfaced as lateness, arguments, conflict, and, most of all, lack of confidence in myself. Somehow, from somewhere deep inside myself, I knew I would have to be better and do better than I had done. I simply did not know how to make that happen.

That is when I began to pray. I did not pray like I had been taught, reciting memorized words from books or the Bible. I prayed from my heart, from the pit of my soul. It sounded like I was talking to myself. To the doctors and nurses on Snapper Five, it looked that way too.

I had been able to elude the monster for quite some time, but I now knew my "stuff" was not going to work anymore. The way I saw it, I was not in the hospital because I had *lost* my mind.

I was in the hospital to *find* my mind.

For some, there comes a time when you just have to say, "I cannot go on like this anymore!" For others, there is a point where everything just feels so bad, when the conditions in your life become so unbearable you just have to cry out, "Dear God, please help me!" That is when the phenomena called "spirit" steps in. That is when you leave your physical nature and move into your spiritual consciousness. In my case, it was not a conscious decision. It was a matter of survival.

I had cried out by my actions. I had cried out by ignoring all the warning and signs. I had cried out when I ignored or forgot what Carmen had said to me in the dream. I was fighting to believe that I was normal, when I knew all the while I was not. There was no medicine, no therapy that could have shown me what I saw during four-and-one-half weeks of silent contemplation with God. During that time, I was given a formula and a plan for slaying the monster. The question was, was I prepared to listen and follow through?

I arrived home from the hospital to find my house filthy. The dog was so weak from hunger she could not bark. Charlie and the children were gone. The telephone and lights were off. All of the packed boxes sat in the middle of the floor, still waiting to be moved. As I walked around the house, I saw my life pass before me. Every moment was a scene, a new horror that culminated in that very moment.

My mind and body felt weak. I could feel myself beginning to panic. I started to cry, but a voice from nowhere spoke to me and filled the room. It said:

> *When you panic, you do things in fear. The moment you think the thoughts, speak the words, commit the acts, you know you are out of balance and out of control. Yet, for some reason, you cannot stop yourself. When it is over, you go into remorse—berating yourself, feeling bad, being sorry. It is important to learn to stop yourself at the panic stage. When you sense fear, panic, and desperation welling up inside your head, you must get still and say, "STOP! I will*

not panic! I will not go into fear! I will be still! I will be shown what to do. I will be told what to say!" Until then, be still!

I froze. I had heard voices before, but never like that. I began to wonder if I had been released from the hospital too early. I did not move. A thought popped into my mind: "Feed the dog and go to Millie's." Millie was Charlie's mother.

I obeyed without question. I warmed some water in a pot, poured it over half a bag of Gravy Train in a bowl, and sat the bowl on the floor. I locked the door as I left.

Millie lived about ten miles across town. I have no idea how I got there, but I got there in record time. She seemed surprised to see me.

"When did you get out?"

I walked right past her through the opened doorway. I went straight into the bedroom. There was no sign of Charlie or the baby.

"He's not here," she said.

I still remember how calm I was that day. I wasn't frightened or angry. I was focused. I felt as if I had left my body. My mind and body had been taken over by a presence, a force, that was doing what needed to be done. When I heard the words come out of my mouth, I knew that something, someone, a force, was in control of my body and mind. My own mind was in a corner somewhere, cowering and crying, safely out of the way.

"Would you please call him and tell him I am here?"

Either I looked insane or Millie believed I was, but she knew better than to argue with me. She went to the telephone and quickly made the call.

For the thirty or so minutes it took Charlie to get to his mother's house, I sat perfectly still. While Millie sat across the room watching television and drinking beer, I watched various scenes of my life play out on a screen in my mind. I saw myself as a little girl, always in fear, always on guard, always poised for disaster and disruption. I saw myself as a teenager, emotionally fragile, in pain, creating more pain by my thoughts and actions. I saw myself doing and saying things to hurt myself.

I remember thinking as I sat there: Not today. Today I was growing up, I said to myself. Today, and over the past few weeks, I had been forced to admit some very painful things about myself. Things I had not done for the purpose of self-destruction, but that were self-destructive. Today, I thought, I had no time for guilt or shame or fear. I was reaching out for my life. There was no need to fight or struggle. My task was simple. All I had to do was reach out.

I saw my children as children and as adults. They looked fine. Healthy, prosperous, and well-adjusted. I took a deep breath for that one. Then I saw the pain. The pain of isolation, fear, and abandonment. I saw myself in relationships and out of relationships, looking for love, acceptance, and a sense of worth and completion. I saw myself crawling, then dragging, my body across the floor, moving toward a dark, hovering cloud of smoke. As I reached the smoke, I pulled myself into a standing position. My body was trembling. I walked toward the darkness, reaching out to grab something. I heard someone call my name. Slowly I turned around. Behind me was light. Above my head was light. Brilliant white light was streaming down into every corner of the room except one—the one in which I was standing.

A voice whispered, "Why have you left me for the darkness?" I stood trembling. In a barely audible whisper in my brain I said, "Help me turn around, please."

The light moved through me. I closed my eyes and gasped for breath. My body became stiff. There was a rumbling in my head. I felt as if I was falling from a cliff. The impact of a vision sent a jolt through my body. As my eyes flew open, the door bell rang.

Millie went to open the door. She was totally oblivious to the fact that the spirit of God had been in the room.

Charlie walked in cautiously. He was clutching Nisa to his chest. She was wrapped in the blanket Nett had crocheted for Damon some five years ago. I looked Charlie straight in the eye as he came into the room and backed his butt into the chair across from me. I diverted my eyes from his face. I could tell he sensed something different about me. Considering I had just spent six weeks in a psychiatric ward, he probably thought I had lost my mind. When I finally looked up at him, through him, I could hear him thinking, "Oh, shit! She's *really* crazy now!"

That was when I saw the woman. She was standing in the doorway of the living room with my daughter's pink baby bag slung across her shoulder, poised for a show-down. She was ready to attack and fight for her man. Instinctively, I knew she had already lost.

Charlie seemed extremely nervous. "How you doin'? When did you get out? How'd you get here?"

I never turned my eyes from him. I was so still, so calm, it seemed as though I was speaking without opening my mouth.

"Give me the baby, please."

Charlie clutched Nisa closer, trying to unwrap her blanket and hold on to her at the same time. The monster that I knew he could be reared its ugly head. He lowered his eyes from my gaze and began unwrapping the baby frantically.

"I ain't givin' you shit, you crazy bitch! You ain't gettin' shit from me! This is my baby too!"

I heard another voice from within, calming me, soothing me. *"Remember he beat you because somebody told him this was not his baby. Shhhhh."*

Charlie's words were so vile, so harsh, his mother and the woman simultaneously called his name. They, like me, could see that his hands and mouth were trembling. Nisa's blanket was finally open, however, and I saw my daughter for the first time in six weeks.

She was dressed in pink with little white lace booties. She was asleep. She was beautiful. Something welled up in my heart as the tears welled up in my eyes. I was back. The force was gone. I felt like a little girl again, sitting on the steps of Aunt Nancy's house, waiting for my father to pick me up, knowing full well he was not going to come.

I heard the voice again: *"Remember, when you sense panic,*

fear, and desperation welling up in your head, get still! You will be told what to say! Speak the words with dominion, power, and authority!"

I took a deep breath, exhaling as loudly as I could, "Give me the baby, please!" Millie and the woman were both talking at the same time, "Let her hold the baby, Charles! Don't be stupid, she's not going nowhere. Give her the baby! That's right."

The monster was adamant. "Shut the fuck up! Don't tell me shit! You don't know this crazy bitch! Don't tell me what to do!"

The room fell silent again.

The voice said: *"Be still and know!"*

I stared at Charlie. Suddenly, he lunged forward in his chair, "What the fuck you lookin' at, you crazy bitch?" It wasn't a question. It was an invitation to get my face smashed. My body remained totally still.

"Yea, though I walk through the valley of the shadow of death, I shall fear no evil..."

I took a deep breath and responded, "Nothing. Absolutely nothing." Charlie sat back in the chair having completely missed the point.

I had no idea I was having a spiritual experience. Everything seemed physical and tangible. Everything except my body, that is. I was aware that something inexplicable was going on inside me. Several things were going through my mind at once. One minute I was sitting across from Charlie, the next minute I was a little girl somewhere in my life. I was in the room, yet I was outside of my body looking into the room, directing everything that was going on.

The most amazing thing was the stillness, the absolute calm that prevailed in my being. I could hear every thought as it moved through my mind and ultimately poured out of my mouth. I knew the television was on, but I could not hear it. I knew cars were passing by, children were playing on the street. Things were happening in and out of the house that I was aware of, but all I could see was Charlie, the monster, holding my baby. I was focused on one thing: getting my child and walking out of that house in one piece. It did not happen.

Charlie and I became engaged in a reasonably sane conversation. Who did what? Who said what? Who was right? Who was wrong? Who was this woman? Charlie told me he was leaving me and taking the baby, his baby, with him. He told me I was crazy. I told him he was abusive. The more excited he became, the stiller I became. Somehow in our verbal exchange, Nisa was transferred from his arms to mine.

"I'm leaving," I said calmly, still sitting and holding Nisa.

"No, you're not." Charlie stood up, all six-foot-two of him. He began pacing back and forth, screaming at me, flailing his arms in the air. He cursed me. I stayed focused on the baby. I kissed her. Stroked her head. Sniffed her neck. She was so clean, so peaceful.

The voice spoke again. *"Children are God in work clothes."*

Of course, Nisa did not know her father was losing his mind or that her mother was saving her own. Several times Charlie lunged toward me with his fist drawn back, ready to strike, but I made no move to defend myself.

The voice soothed me, gave me strength. *"He will not hurt you unless you panic."*

The two other women in the room did all of the work for me. Shocked and frightened at seeing how close Charlie was to crushing my face, realizing that he would probably injure the baby in the process, they screamed his name over and over. Maybe Charlie's new woman did not know he had hit me before, that he had blackened my eye and fractured two of my ribs. Perhaps his mother had forgotten how Charlie had once dragged me by the hair from her kitchen and thrown me on top of her snow-covered garbage cans. The other woman may not have known, but Charlie's mother definitely knew. She had never seen the worst of it, but she knew.

I stayed focused on the baby.

Charlie eventually exhausted himself with his ranting and

raving and slumped back into his chair. Millie took his place, pacing, screaming, and swearing. She went on and on about how wrong I was and how stupid Charlie was to get involved with me. She had told him about me, but he wouldn't listen, she said. She had told him I was a bitch, now look at what I had done. Finally, she screamed that she was sick of all this mess and she could not take it anymore. With that, she pulled off her wig and threw it on the sofa. Then she threw it across the room, where it landed on the dog, who grabbed it in his mouth and began to wrestle with it.

Millie freaked and came back to her senses. She ordered Charlie to get her hair from the dog. She had to wear it to work the next day. Charlie struggled with the dog for the wig. When he got it, he threw it to Millie, who slapped it back on top of her head and ordered all of us to get the fuck out of her house. It is comical now. Then, it was sad.

Still calm through all the hysteria of the hair piece and the dog fight, I turned my attention to the woman and told her: "I want to thank you for taking care of my baby. She is clean. She looks healthy and well-fed. Have you taken her to the clinic? Thank you. No matter what happens, I have to thank you. But I need to know one thing: what could Charlie have possibly told you that would make you take in a man with a two-month-old baby? You must have seen that she had been well-cared for. Did you think he had done that alone? What did he tell you about the baby's mother?"

The room went still again. The monster reared its ugly head again, "Don't tell this crazy bitch nothing about your business!"

The woman squirmed in her chair, then she resumed her war stance.

"He told me you left him. Look, I've been with him for six months. We're in love. I love him and I love his baby, and I've got a five-year-old son who loves him too! You can't trap him with a baby! I'll take him and the baby! I don't care!"

I looked through her. "How old are you?"

"Twenty-one."

"Where do you live?"

Before Charlie could tell her to shut up, she replied, "In Bushwick." Places, faces, lies flashed in my brain.

I stood up, tenderly kissing Nisa's face. She had slept through all the noise and commotion. The others stood poised to attack. I knew that if I tried to get out of the door, either I or the baby would be ripped apart, so I said to the woman, "All I can do is thank you."

I walked over to her and placed my sleeping daughter in her arms. I kept moving toward the door. "I'm going home now to clean my house," I said with quiet confidence. "I expect to have my baby in her bed, asleep, by eight o'clock tonight."

I did not stop moving until I reached my front door. When I stuck the key in the lock, the dog barked. It was a weak, raspy bark, but it was a bark. The dog jumped on me playfully as I entered the house.

Without a word, I changed into my work clothes and rubber gloves. It was four-thirty when I started cleaning. I was cleaning the dog crap and the rest of the crap out of my life. At seven-fifteen, the doorbell rang. It was Charlie and the baby. As he walked through the door, the energy that had moved through me and with me throughout the day left my body, leaving me on my own to figure out what to do.

What we see and what we are taught, told, and experience as children is critical to how we perceive and experience ourselves and our lives as adults. Growing up in poverty, instability, and abuse causes a great deal of damage to a child's emotional and psychological development. Childhood is supposed to be our training ground. It is supposed to be the place where we develop our virtues and vices, based on the overt and covert messages we receive from adults and others. As children, we figure things out based on what we see and hear externally. We blend that information with what we see and hear internally. When the two sources of information conflict, we usually go with the dominant, most pervasive idea, the one that those who have power over us tell us to follow and demonstrate to us to follow. But the conflict continues in our minds.

All Black women do not grow up in poverty, instability, and abuse. Most, however, do receive conflicting messages. I believe an overwhelming majority of Black women are taught to want less for themselves and expect less from themselves than their white counterparts are taught. Many of our parents were taught to make do with what they got and not to make any waves. They taught us to do the same. Likewise, some of our parents were raised with archaic ideas about women's abilities and status in this society. Society still supports some of these ideas, which have become ingrained in most of our conscious and subconscious minds. In addition, a large number of Black women grew up in religious homes under the mandates of a religious philosophy that teaches the dirtiness, lowliness, and subjugation of women.

This is the kind of "stuff" we bring into our lives as adults. It is the root of the weakness, conflict, and fear we must struggle to overcome. It is the monster that chases us and keeps us in bad relationships. It is the demon that teaches us to believe we cannot have, cannot do, cannot be anything unless someone else tells us we can. It is the poison apple that pollutes our minds, strangles our lives, and perpetuates self-destructive attitudes and behaviors.

The messages I received as a child told me that I was no good, that I was weak, powerless, and unworthy. As a child, I soon figured out that I was not wanted and that the people who cared for me were doing me a favor. I grew up with violence, which made it easy for me to accept violence in my life as an adult. I witnessed dishonesty, which led me to believe it was okay to be dishonest at certain times with certain people, particularly men, and with myself. I was taught to accept whatever was done to me. It was my punishment for being bad. I was ashamed of myself. I was guilty—both about the things I had done and the things that had been done to me. Worst of all, because of what I had witnessed and experienced as a child, I believed that something was wrong, that something was not good about being a woman.

I brought all of that and more into my life as a woman and mother. I accepted violence because I thought I deserved it. I allowed people to lie to me because I had no confidence in myself. I settled for what I had because I thought it was the best I could get. I lived in constant fear of abandonment and rejection and did everything in my power to make people like me because I felt ugly and therefore worthless. I believed I was doomed to poverty of mind, body, and spirit.

However, there comes a time when the conditions and circumstances in your life become so physically and emotionally overwhelming, it seems as if there is nothing you can do. And when that time comes, you are one hundred-percent correct—you cannot do anything about anything. But the spirit within you can!

In her book, *A Return to Love*, Marianne Williamson states, "All nervous breakdowns are an opportunity for a spiritual breakthrough." Amen! I am here to testify to the truth of that statement. When the mind shuts down, there is a force, a power, an energy that will emerge through you. That energy is called *Spirit*. The energy of Spirit is pervasive and all encompassing. It engulfs you and takes control of every aspect of your being, your mind, and your body. If you do not resist—if you surrender—Spirit will move you. It will speak through you and to you. Spirit will do whatever needs to be done, not only for your well-being but for the well-being of everyone involved.

The process of surrender is simple: breathe deeply, shut your mouth, and listen. Spirit will tell you exactly what to do. Your job is to do it, without question, without doubt. The good news is, you do not have to be in crisis for Spirit to work. You can consciously call forth the energy at any time you choose. The process of calling Spirit forth is called meditation.

Spirit has no fear. It has no memory of the past or goals for the future. Spirit is the energy of now. Spirit knows that if what is required is done in the present, the future will respond accordingly. Spirit has no decisions to make or hurdles to overcome. It flows. As it flows, it brings with it the absolute power of the oneness of all things. When Spirit moves, it brings everyone and everything together. It does not ask how, when, or why. It knows. It knows that is connected to the One Mind, One Life, One Power of the universe. Spirit is not limited by anyone or anything.

As women, many of us are trained to doubt, question, and limit ourselves. We rely on our human abilities, fragile and unstable as they may be. Like Eve, we have been taught that we are dirty, naked, disobedient, and unworthy to be in the presence of the Most High. We live in perpetual fear, believing we are bad. We live with the pain of the past as if it were an albatross directing us into the future. How much we suffer in our hearts and minds, how many of us sacrifice our lives in ignorance because we do not know and have not been taught that "Spirit Is!"

Spirituality is a state of constant stillness, surrender, and listening. Spirituality focuses all of your attention on the oneness of now. Now is not a moment. It is the essence of everything coming into alignment and focusing the energy on what is. God is. Spirit is the energy of God, which brings with it all that God is: power, strength, understanding, peace, and love. Spirituality is a constant state of recognition that the Spirit of God is—there is absolutely nothing that is not God. Spirituality is having the ability and willingness to call the energy of Spirit to the fore at any given moment and allow it to work through you.

When our physical being is faced with conflict, our "stuff" comes up. All our fears and limitations, our helplessness and hopelessness, surfaces and invades our thinking, short-circuiting the brain. Everything starts happening at once. All that we have ever experienced happens over and over again. Add to this the stimuli of what is going on in the environment, the things that other people are saying and doing, and the mandates of each of our own secret agendas, and it is clear to see the scope of the conflict that begets the confusion. In those moments, we need to get still. We do not need to think, we need to *hear*.

We have all had experiences where, in the face of confusion or danger, we know exactly what to do. Chances are it was something we thought we could not do or say. Something we thought would upset or hurt somebody. However, if we do exactly as we are told to do by Spirit, we can move through any event safely. A dear friend of mine explains it by saying, "You don't have to do it. Let the Holy Spirit do it through you!" I could not have stood in my husband's face, with his mother and his other woman by his side, without the presence of Spirit. I know that now. Charlie had beaten me, and I was afraid of him. I was so frightened at the thought of losing him, I probably would have done anything to keep him. I knew he had other women, but I did not care. I was so ashamed of having children by different men that I made myself content with whatever I had. I suffered from the "Something-Is-Better-Than-Nothing Syndrome" that plagues so many Black women today. But on that day, straight out of the mental ward, I knew that I could not fix, change, or control any of what was going on at any moment in my life, and I promised myself that if I got through this, I would never put myself in this situation again. And this time, I told myself, I meant it. I had asked for help, and it came.

The nature of a woman is intuitive. It seeks from within. The power of a woman comes from knowing what to do from within herself. This power is not something a woman must acquire. She is born with it. It is grounded in the emotional nature of all human beings. However, the emotional intuitiveness of a woman is her source of divine power. Emotions are the energies that move the feminine spirit. In the quest for spirituality, it is imperative for women to cleanse and balance their emotions. When the emotional nature is out of balance or clogged with fear, anger, resentment, guilt, or shame, the intuitive flow of power is disrupted and disjointed. That was my downfall. I had had a spiritual experience, but I had not built a solid foundation upon which to sustain my spirituality. There were still many things I was not willing to accept or face. The universe—Spirit—was supporting me to a large degree, but I still had a lot of spiritual work to do. I probably would have been fine, but I started listening to other people. I started to doubt myself again. I had not yet come to grips with my own deep, dark secrets. Spirit and spirituality require total, complete, and honest surrender. Unfortunately, I was simply not ready.

THE Journal

Somewhere deep inside, I know it is meant for me to be happy. Why then do I ask for things, and expect to receive them, even when I know they will not promote my well-being? I guess it's because I want what I want. I want the old ways, old habits, old worn-out desires because they are what I know. I know that what I want is killing me, but I want it anyway. I have not come into the full understanding that the way to happiness is to kill off the old. I have not been taught that in order to die to the old stuff in my life, I must be reborn in my soul, with the soul's knowledge.

In the mirror of my soul, I see it all. It is all there, reflecting back to me the pain, the shame, the guilt, and the paralyzing fear. In the mirror of my soul, I recognize the truth. I sense the truth and fear it because I know it must be exposed. Oh, God! The thought of it is enough to drive me crazy! How can I speak the unspeakable, think the unthinkable, feel the unfeelable? How can I look at what I cannot bear to see? Maybe, if I am real quiet, it will all just go away. Maybe if I ignore it, it will leave me alone.

But who said the truth has to be bad? Why does it have to be painful? The truth is who I am and what I do, even when I do not realize it. The truth is the light to a pain-free, shame-free, guilt-free life of fearlessness. The truth will not restrict or limit me. It will expand and release me.

189

The truth is transparent. It allows more light in so I will be able to see more and see more clearly. Even when I do not face the truth, it shows up. It shows up as everything I do. I guess the time is right. I hope I am ready. Better now than never.

CHAPTER 16

A Study in Desperation

There was an empty apartment in the building where my father lived. A fourth-floor walk-up with two bedrooms for three hundred-fifty dollars per month. Public assistance gave me a monthly budget of two hundred-eighty-five dollars, which meant I would have to make up the difference. The landlord did not mind that I was on public assistance or that I had three children. I moved in the week after I got out of the hospital. I painted the kitchen lemon yellow and burnt orange. The children had their room, and I had my room. It was great.

In addition, Daddy and his family lived on the first floor. How lovely! I got to watch him cook for "his children," shop with "his wife," take "his family" for outings in "their car," and do all the things for these children he never did for my brother and me. Everyone on the block knew my father because apparently he had lived there for years. He was a model neighbor, and everyone called him "Mr. Harris." It made me sick to my stomach, but I was cool.

To my three new sisters and two new brothers, I was the "big sister." They showed me off to everyone in the block. The good thing was they loved the idea of baby sitting for their new little nieces and nephew.

Much to my surprise, everyone also knew my brother Ray. He had met this side of the family many years before I had. When I tried to talk to him about it and ask him how he could associate himself with "those people," knowing they were the reason Daddy had treated Nett so badly, he said, "Look, Ronnie, I ain't got nothing to do with that! Nett is not our mother. She did what anyone else would do for the money." That was the second time I had heard some allusion to money regarding my care. I wanted to pursue the matter, but I was too furious with Ray. I wanted to kick him, but I was at his job. I stormed out of the store, walked around the corner to my yellow-and-orange kitchen, and chain-smoked two packs of cigarettes.

I did not want to like my new family, but I had no choice. For the first time in my life, I did not live within walking distance of Nett. At best, I had to take a forty-five-minute bus ride or pay fifteen bucks for a cab to get to her place. We talked on the telephone every day, but I missed our Sunday morning coffee sessions. The kids missed her too. "When are we going to Nana's house?" they would ask. "Is Nana coming over today?"

Nett would not step foot in my house. To get to me, she would have to walk past the apartment door where her husband lived with his wife, and she would not, could not, do that. I told her I felt like a traitor. I had to be nice to Alberta, Daddy's new wife. I had to look at their children and call them my brothers and sisters. It made me angry. It made me sick. It made me ashamed. Nett said not to worry about it, but I did. I felt as though I had done something wrong by being the child my father had kept hidden away. I felt as if I posed a threat to the sanctity of his family. I saw myself as the oddball, the freak who had shown up on the doorstep fresh out of the loonie bin. I did not want to like them, but they were all so nice to me, so helpful and supportive, I had no choice. When I started working temporary jobs to make ends meet, Alberta and Daddy were always willing to keep the children. I always paid them, and that made them even more willing.

I hung in with keeping Charlie out of my life as long as I could. I went to work. I came home. I visited Nett. I came home. I went downstairs and visited with my father and his family, and I went home. It was all that time "home alone" that weakened me.

For the first time in my life, I was by myself. No man. No relationship. Charlie called almost every day. He came by once a week to give me money for the children. Each time he came, they begged him to stay.

"Daddy are you going to stay with us today?"

"No."

"Why Daddy? Why aren't you going to stay home today?"

"I don't know, ask your Mommy."

It was a set-up, pure and simple. When they started in like that, I would always find something to do that would take me out of the room. Charlie would get up to leave. The children would start crying. He would ask if he could stay until they went to bed. The first few times I said no. Eventually, I gave in.

After the children were asleep, Charlie would want to sit and talk. He'd tell me he was sorry. He wasn't with that woman anymore. He was staying at Millie's house. She was sorry too, he said. Then he'd really start pouring it on. He'd ask if I'd gone back to school yet? You should go back to school, he'd say. You're too smart, much too smart not to go back to school. I know, you could go at night. Yeah, you could go to school at night, and I'll stay here and watch the children. He said he wouldn't pressure me about getting back together or anything like that, he would just watch the children until I got home.

Yeah, sure, Charlie. Right.

I was letting him out the door one night, and he touched me. He grabbed me by my shoulders and kissed me. When he stopped kissing me, he held me in his arms. That was when I started crying. As I cried, he held me, rubbing my hair, kissing my face, telling me everything would be alright.

Why did I kiss him back? If I had not kissed him back, I would have been fine. But I kissed him and he kissed me. The next morning when the sun came up, we were still kissing. We both went to work and came back to the apartment and kissed some more. Three weeks of kissing. No talking. No planning. No structuring of our lives. We just kissed. And with each kiss, another piece of my brain shut down.

I did not tell anyone Charlie and I were back together. He would spend the night, go to work, and come back late at night when I thought everyone was asleep. I forgot my father lived on the first floor and that his window faced the street. I forgot that five-year-old and two-year-old children tell everything. First they told Nett. When she asked me about it, I lied. Then they told Grandpa, who already knew since he could see anyone who came and went in and out of the building. Eventually, everyone knew, but I was still denying it.

I told Charlie I did not want to see him anymore. He told me he wanted to marry me. I told him I couldn't marry him legally because I was still married to Kirk. So, we bought rings for each other, went to an empty church, knelt down in front of the crucifix, prayed, and exchanged vows. He vowed to love me, cherish me, provide for me, and never to treat me in an abusive way again. Then, he cried. I vowed to love him, honor him, provide him and our children a good home, and support him in becoming the wonderful man I knew he could be. Then I cried. We exchanged rings and embraced. We talked about how wonderful our life would be together. We both lied.

⋌•⋏•⋌

Trouble is what God uses to prepare you for better things. When you run from trouble, it follows you and begins to stink. The stink of trouble is desperation. Desperation is fed by confusion and panic. Desperation is wearing a hat when you do not have the strength or desire to comb your hair. It is smoking two packs of cigarettes a day because your nerves are shot, but you cannot, dare not, sit down and try to figure out what is bothering you. The stink of trouble is getting dressed in clothes that were in the dirty-clothes basket because you don't have money to do the laundry. It is eating Ring Dings and Cheese Doodles in order to justify giving them to your children for dinner and washing them down with Pepsi Cola.

The stink of trouble will follow you until you put your

hands on your hips, stomp your feet, and dig way down deep inside yourself to come up with a way to fight it. When I dug down deep inside myself, I came up with a lie: "I need him."

For a long time, I lied to everyone about everything. I lied about how I was doing because I was ashamed to tell the truth. I lied to bill collectors and the landlord because I did not know what else to do. The "check-is-in-the-mail" lie wasn't good enough for me. I had to create bigger, better lies to make my story more believable: I was robbed. My mother died and I had to bury her. My drug-addict brother stole my money. I lied to my friends to get them to help me. I lied to myself about why I was lying to everyone else. Unfortunately, one lie always leads to another, and you have to keep them all in order. You must always remember who you told what lie to in order not to get caught. In the end, however, the lies are always revealed, and you have to tell even more lies to explain away the first batch.

When you are at a low point in your life, desperation and dishonesty seem to go hand-in-hand. You lie to avoid trouble, to get out of trouble, and to explain away trouble. Because you are usually in a state of panic and confusion, you do not realize that lying only creates more trouble. Sometimes, the lies create more trouble than the original problem. That's when you know it is time to get it together.

There is no easy way, no short cut to getting it together. It is hard work. It is painful. It is lonely, and it is ugly. Getting it together means taking a long, hard look at yourself, at all you are and all you have ever done. It means telling the truth about where you are and how you got there, and admitting it is not where you want to be. You cannot blame anyone for where you are. You cannot ignore the role you have played in creating your circumstances. You cannot make excuses for yourself. To do that would be to tell another lie. To get it together, you must own up to your fears and weaknesses, to the compromises you have made and the lies you have told yourself and others. You cannot put the process off forever. Once you start it, you must complete it. Once you look at yourself, you must accept what you see. You do not have to like it, but you must accept it.

A very important step toward getting yourself and your life together involves knowing that what you have experienced in life, whatever you have done, and wherever you have been are of value. Who, what, and where you are at any given moment is a reflection of where you have been. The key is to remove the judgment, blame, emotionalism, and fear of admitting that you have seen some dark days, felt some real pain, and done some dumb things. The beautiful part of the process, which most of us miss, is that we do not have to tell anyone. We do not have to send a memo to the office manager or an editorial to the local newspaper. We do not have to wear a sign on a string around our necks telling the world how bad or dumb we have been. The only person who needs to know is you. Admit your failings to yourself, and the rest is gravy. The information will serve as the seeds of growth. As these seeds grow, you will learn what does not work for you, what areas you need to work on, and what areas you can depend on. The truth is a valuable resource.

On the way to getting it together, you will need to learn to accept your "I AM" self. I AM is the presence of God, the divine energy that lives at the level of the soul. When we surrender our I AM selves to trouble, we cut off the flow of divine energy. Statements like "I am confused," "I am lonely," "I am broke," "I am too fat," "I am ugly," and many other restrictive sentiments are prevalent among Black women. They are the troubles we claim as a result of our experiences. If you remove the "I am" from these statements, what you will find is that your mother said you were this or that, or your father, brother, or sister gave you the idea. The result is what Sondra Ray, in her book entitled *I Deserve Love*, calls a "personal lie." Personal lies manifest as negative thoughts: "There is something wrong with me!" "I can't do anything right!" "I can't have what I want!" Whether we realize it or not, these personal lies govern how we view ourselves and dictate the choices we make.

The process of getting it together and getting to know who the I AM is for yourself means creating a way for the truth to come forth. The truth being "I AM the flow of experiences—none good, none bad, all purposeful. I AM living now as a result of the choices I make or fail to make. No thing and no one has any power over me that I do not give them. I AM an expression of God. Right where I AM, God is."

✺✺✺

Two years after Charlie and I exchanged vows and rings, the trouble began—again. Charlie began staying out all night every other night. When he came home, we would argue and fight. Actually, we did not fight, I would get beat up—again. I still could not figure out how to get the best of someone who was almost a foot taller and a hundred pounds heavier than me. Most of our fights were about Charlie's infidelities and my spending habits. He liked women. I liked clothes. He slept with women. I bought clothes. The women he had, he had all for himself. I had to buy clothes for me and the children. I bought clothes before I paid the rent or bought food. I bought clothes, hid them, and lied about them. That really pissed Charlie off after a hard night with one of his girlfriends, so he would beat me. My father and everyone in the neighborhood knew it, but they never said a word. Even if they had, I would have denied it.

I had not had a temporary assignment in months. I had three growing children who were no longer fully satisfied with eating peanut-butter-and-jelly sandwiches at my house when they could go to Grandpa's and get a meal with three things on the plate. I had an order of protection that kept me separated from a husband who made thirty-five thousand dollars a year, and I was living with a man who beat me. I was depressed, broke, and desperately avoiding my troubles, which were piling up in the mailbox.

I knew my life had hit an all-time low when I developed a "mailbox phobia." It seemed as if all impending disasters came from the bowels of that tiny metal cubicle. Crammed within it would be a rainbow of doomsday announcements: Cut-off notices came in green envelopes. Overdue notices came in yellow envelopes. Welfare recertification notices came in pink envelopes. Enticing and colorful sales circulars promising "Drastic Reductions!" "Sales Galore!" and "The Last Chance to Snatch up a DEAL!" reminded me of all the things I wanted and needed but could not have. Everything I dreaded and wanted to avoid came through that wretched box. Each time I walked past it, my heart would pound, my breath would grow short, and a sharp pain would shoot to the top of my head. I made a habit of turning my face in the other direction when I passed the mailbox as I was coming into the building. All the way up eight flights of stairs to my fourth-floor apartment I cursed and swore my life would not be intruded upon by the contents of that foul device of torment.

Each month, when check day drew near, my hate for the mailbox intensified. I would leave the mail in the box for five or six days before I expected to receive my public assistance check. When I did finally retrieve my mail, I would wait another two or three days to open it. When things were real bad, I would leave the mail in the box for two weeks. During one period, it got so bad, the mailman thought I had died and brought the mail to my apartment door.

The only thing worse than a mailbox full of bills is a knock on the door at eleven o'clock in the morning when you've been sitting at home for days drinking beer, chain-smoking cigarettes, eating junk food, avoiding going to work, avoiding paying your bills, avoiding facing yourself, the world, everything. I was idly watching "The Price is Right" when I heard the knock. The sound made me light-headed. I panicked. Is it Charlie? The landlord? The electric or gas company? Oh, Jesus! What am I going to do? I turned the sound on the television way down. I closed the living room door, which led to the kitchen, which led to the front door. Quietly, I pressed my ear against the living room door. All I could hear was the sound of my heart, pounding wildly. Hot tears started streaming down my face and I had to pee real bad. By the time the second knock came, my knees were shaking, I felt faint, and I was nearly prancing up and down like a madwoman to hold the pee back.

Through the sounds of panic in my body I heard a small voice from behind the front door say, "It's the mailman."

I went into total shock and peed on the floor.

Breathing at a rate that was sure to cause me to hyperventilate, I opened the door, stepped over the puddle I had made, and walked through the kitchen. As I approached the door to my apartment, I could hear voices in the hallway. The mailman was talking to my neighbor.

"She's in there."

"She must be sick. Her mailbox is jammed."

"Well, I saw her yesterday."

I know I must have looked wild as I opened the door. They both jumped and stared at me. My neighbor asked me if everything was okay. I could not get my mouth open, so I just shook my head. The mailman explained that he had been worried. He had never seen me before, so he did not know if I was elderly or not. Sometimes, he said, the old people of his route would die and nobody would know it except the mailman because their mailboxes would get so full. He just wanted to know if I was okay. He handed me a stack of multicolored mail with my welfare check on top. As he walked away I heard him explaining to my neighbor that he had discovered over fifty dead people during his six years as a mailman.

I stood there for what seemed like an hour, waiting for my body to calm down. My son brought me back to reality when I heard him say, "Mommy, Mommy, the dog peed on the floor."

I looked at him and smiled, "Damon, we don't have a dog."

THE
Journal

What does it feel like to sleep with a man you know does not want anything from you but sex? The moment just before you must answer that question, you are in conflict. You feel so low, so bad about yourself, you will do anything to feel good. Then he touches you, and it feels good. In that split second, you forget how bad you are feeling in order to feel good. You forget he does not, cannot, look you in your eyes. You forget he does not tell his friends about you while you are making up lies to tell your friends about him. You forget that you feel ugly. In the split second when he touches you, your mind goes blank. You feel good. You surrender to his body. He enters you passionately. Your blankened mind tells you it is love. It is the love you need and want so desperately. You want to cling to him, but he is done. He gets up, pulls his pants up, never looking you in the eye. He tries to find something to say. He does, but your mind is blank, so you can't answer. By the time you figure out what would be the right thing, the smart thing, to say, he is gone. Always promising to call you later.

Suddenly, your mind is back, and you know he won't call. He's gone. Your mind is back reminding you how bad you are, how bad you feel. Your mind is wrong this time. You don't just feel bad. You feel like shit!

CHAPTER 17

A Stroke of Anger

I simply had to get away. I was losing it fast. I was smoking two, sometimes three, packs of cigarettes a day. My hair was falling out again, and I was gaining weight. With all that was going on, I had become a nervous wreck.

Alberta and Daddy were good to me. They helped a great deal with the children, but the conflict of seeing them together was getting the best of me. I knew I had to get away from Charlie. A friend of mine had an apartment in a beautiful neighborhood she wanted to sublet. I jumped at the chance. The fact that my apartment had been robbed twice in one month made the deal even more attractive. I needed a new environment, a new start.

I moved to Canarsie, a quiet, multiracial community in Brooklyn. I went back to night school to get my high school diploma. I also entered a beauty pageant.

The pageant was a riot. At twenty-five, I was not the oldest contestant, but I was the only one who was married with three children. It gave me something to do and something to look forward to. It also gave me a reason to dance again. Much to my surprise, my family and Charlie were very supportive. Grandma had my gowns made. Nett sent me to her beautician, who fixed my hair and a wig just alike so that you could not tell one from the other. Charlie picked me up every day, took me to rehearsal, and watched the children. I went on a diet and lost fifteen pounds. On the big day, I was a slim, trim one hundred-twenty pounds. Getting back into my dancing had flattened my stomach so much that no one believed I had given birth to three children.

The night of the pageant, I danced my heart out. I strutted the runway. I answered the judges' questions with intelligence and humor. And I won. Can you believe it?! I won a beauty pageant! Over thirty-five other single, beautiful women in the competition, and I was the one crowned "Miss Restoration Plaza." That's when the trouble began—again.

At first, some of the contestants said the contest was fixed and demanded a re-count. Others accused me of sleeping with the judges, one of whom was Don King, the fight promoter, and another of whom was then-Congresswoman Shirley Chisholm. Then, the losers began to call my house and threaten me. They threatened to go to the newspapers and tell what I had done. They threatened to hunt me down, cut my throat, and throw my body in the river. I was devastated. For the first time in my life, people had said I was beautiful and other women were saying they had lied.

I turned to the only person who I "knew" believed I had won fair and square: Charlie. He knew how hard I had worked. He knew I had not slept with anyone to get that crown. He knew, or at least I thought he knew, I deserved it.

Three weeks after the pageant, Charlie began to question me about why I was still friends with my dance coach, the woman who had helped me train for the pageant. She was encouraging me to keep dancing. She let me teach a children's dance class in return for free tap lessons. She had a car and she liked my children, and we would sometimes hang out together. There was nothing strange about that, was there? I was entitled to have friends wasn't I? Not according to Charlie. In his mind, my dance coach and I were lovers, and that was something he intended to beat out of me. His wife was not going to be a lesbian.

It got worse. If the telephone rang and I picked it up, Charlie would snatch it away from me and beat me if it was someone he didn't approve of. If I went to the supermarket and stayed longer than he thought was necessary, he would slap me the moment I walked into the house. If dinner was late, I got beat. If the children made too much noise, I got beat. If the sun came out or the moon was full, I got slapped, punched, knocked down, kicked, choked, and otherwise brutalized. Then, we had sex.

I was not totally passive throughout this ordeal. I did things to Charlie too. When he was asleep, I would search his pockets, looking for clues that would prove he had another woman. If I found a telephone number, I would call it and hang up. I also took money from his wallet. Charlie always said he didn't have any money when I asked him for some, so when he was asleep, I checked, just to make sure. When I found more than forty or fifty dollars, I would take it and hide it in the children's room until he left.

Once I found a love letter in Charlie's pocket that read:
Dear Charlie,
I want to thank you for loving me. You make me feel like a "natural woman." Whenever we are together, the entire world opens up for me and I feel "brand new." You have made life worth living..."
It went on to babble some other intimacies. When Charlie woke up from his nap, I was folding laundry. I confronted him.

"I want to ask you something. What is it that you do for other women that makes them feel so 'nat-u-ral'? I wash your drawers, cook your food, clean up after your children, and I feel like a damned fool!" At which point, I threw the letter in his face.

He beat me good for that one.

Eventually, I did the ultimate: I started seeing another man. His name was Charles. I guess it was the "ch" sound that helped me fall in lust with him. Charles was absolutely gorgeous. He also lived with another woman. He was an excellent writer, and I encouraged him in his efforts. He wrote poems for me. He did not make much money, so I had no problem lending him some of mine. Actually, I usually gave him the money I had stolen from Charlie.

Charles was a radio disc jockey, and he worked at night, so in the mornings I would take the children to the day care center and spend my days with him while Charlie was away at work. I'd leave Charles's place in time to pick up the kids and get back home before Charlie did.

We had been seeing each other for about three months and

things would have been fine, but one day it snowed.

I left the house around eleven o'clock, took the children to day care, and went to see Charles. We were in the house doing what you do if you are a married woman seeing a man who lived with another woman and she was not at home. Afterwards, we fell asleep. We woke up at three o'clock in the afternoon to find almost fourteen inches of snow on the ground, no buses running, and most businesses shut down. Before I could get out of the house to go home only God knew how, Charles's lady friend came home. Before she got to the bedroom door, Charles shoved me into the closet. I must have been in there for hours before she finally went to the bathroom. When she did, Charles pulled me out of the closet and frantically ushered me through the front door, naked, except for a sheet. A few seconds later, he threw my clothes, shoes, coat, and purse into the hallway.

I got dressed under the stairs by the garbage cans and went out to try to catch a cab. There were none. I was eight, maybe ten, miles from home. I called the house. Charlie answered.

"I'm downtown waiting for a bus," I lied. "I was out shopping when it started snowing. I can't get a bus home now. I'll try to find a cab." I hung up quickly.

Two hours later, I arrived home by taxi. Charlie and the children were so glad to see me. He never suspected a thing.

I was the treasurer of the day care center's Parent's Committee, which meant that I kept the group's checkbook. One day, I got a call at work from the president of the committee.

"We know about the checks," she said.

"What checks?"

"We have been to the bank and we know you forged our names."

"What the hell are you talking about?"

"We are going to meet tonight. Will you be there?"

"Of course."

I ran home to check the checkbook. Everything seemed in

order to me, so off I marched to the meeting, arrogantly demanding to know what was the problem. There before me were four checks, each bearing my forged signature and the forged signature of the group's president. The total came to five hundred-and-fifty dollars. Where had they come from? The back of the book. Obviously, somebody had taken the checks, signed them, and cashed them. How was I going to pay the money back? I had no idea.

I had to wait three days to confront Charlie, who had been away with one of his women. When I did, he went crazy. But this time when he slapped me, I went after him like a mad dog, biting, kicking, scratching—fighting for my life.

Charlie loved it. He grabbed me, punched me to the ground, and stood over me, waiting for me to get up. I couldn't see. My eyes were swollen shut, my head was aching, and blood was flowing from somewhere on my face. Still, I refused to give up. I lunged at him again and again, only to get hit harder each time.

We were rolling on the floor in a death-lock when it happened. Charlie started gasping for air. He could not catch his breath. He was having a violent asthma attack. I was pinned under him in the narrow hallway. He couldn't move, and I couldn't get him off of me. Somehow, I managed to squirm away by sliding down between his legs. He was trying to talk, but he couldn't get the words out. He was clutching his chest and reaching for me. I looked at him and saw my brother.

"Where's your medicine?" I asked, trying to turn him over on his side. "Where is your spray?"

I could barely hear him, but I figured out he was trying to say "coat." I ran to the closet to get his coat. I reached in the pocket and felt the inhaler. Suddenly, I stopped dead in my tracks, turning to see Charlie, the helpless monster, laying on the hallway floor, gasping for air, his whole body heaving in pain.

A voice within me was saying, "Let him die! Let him lay there and die!" If I let him die, I thought, all of my troubles would be over. The monster would be gone. I would never have to worry about him bothering me again.

I stood watching Charlie reaching for me, clutching his chest, trying to crawl toward me. I stood there watching him die, and I was quite willing to stand there and let him die. Until it hit me: Oh, my God! Am I losing my mind! Am I a monster too?

I rushed to Charlie's side. Damon came into the hallway. He saw Charlie laying on the floor. He ran over to him.

"Mommy, are you killing Daddy?"

"No, baby, I'm just helping him with his medicine."

Reluctantly, I gave Charlie the little green canister that saved his life. When the ambulance arrived, they said that his heart could not have taken much more.

⋏⋎⋏

In my willingness to let Charlie die, I recognized the dead parts of myself. My dreams were dead. My goals were dead. More importantly, each day I remained in our relationship, a piece of my spirit died. I blamed Charlie for disrupting and dismantling my life, when I knew that I had died long before he came on the scene. I had died in the midst of the many painfully negative experiences that had occurred in my life. I had died from motherlessness, fatherlessness, ugliness, fatness, and loneliness. The smell of my dead being had attracted buzzards. Charlie was simply a buzzard picking at the scraps of meat left on my carcass.

Charlie reaching for me to save him was a reflection of what was left of my life. I was reaching beyond death. I wanted to live. I wanted to survive. I simply did not know how to go about it. I was reaching out from a place of pain, confusion, and fear. I thought all I had to do was "be good" and everything would be alright. I was reaching out because I had opted for pleasure over my own good common sense. I was reaching out because I knew there was still a shred of hope, a glimmer of light, somewhere.

I was angry at Charlie. Angry enough to let him die. I was even angrier at myself for allowing death to capture me. I had made the same bad choices repeatedly. It seemed as if I was mesmerized by my ability to endure the pain of living death. How much more could I take, I asked. How much longer could I endure? I was playing with death, egging it on by not taking time to get clear, release fear, and move into a state of aliveness. Watching Charlie, I realized that I had not fully studied the rules of the game. I did not want to play anymore, but death would not give up or go away. As the drama in my life intensified, I became more and more frightened. That was when I got angry with death and myself.

Holding that little green can, I realized I held the key to my living. I realized that I had the answer, that I had the weapon to fight off the grip of death. What is it? Where is it? How can I gather up what is left of my life and live it? I did not have time for a long psychological discourse. I had to make a choice quickly. My life was dangling in the wind. One false move and I was a goner.

I realized it would take more than a squirt from a little green canister to save my life. I needed mouth-to-mouth resuscitation, electric shock treatments, and CPR. As I handed Charlie his medication, I knew I would have to trust that emergency treatment was available.

Charlie moved out shortly after his attack. This time for good, I hoped. He would call and come around to see the kids, but as far as I was concerned, he and I were through.

I went back to the welfare office to be recertified for public assistance. As I was sitting there, I overheard a case worker who had just had a very rough time with a client talking to another worker in the next cubicle.

"These welfare mothers are a menace to society. All of them should be taken out to a field somewhere, put on their knees, and shot like cows."

I saw a vision. Hundreds of Black women, out in the middle of Prospect Park, on their knees, naked, facing a firing squad. I was in the front row looking down the barrel of the gun. I jumped up from my seat behind my social worker's desk. Startled, she asked me what was wrong. I sat back down. She said

I looked ill. I was shaking, and one thought was playing over and over in my mind:

"I'm outta here!"

It was like a mantra, "I'm outta here. I'm outta here..."

I sat through the interview, answering the same questions with the same lies I had been using for seven years, thinking, "I'm outta here!"

All the way to the bus stop, "I'm outta here!" On the bus, "I'm outta here! I'm outta here! I'm outta here!"

I looked up and saw a sign that read, "If you want to do something good for yourself, come to Medgar Evers College." I looked around. I was three blocks from the college.

I got off the bus and walked to the admissions office. When the woman behind the counter asked me if she could help me, I said, "Yes, I'm outta here!"

She looked at me as if I were crazy.

I was working during the day and going to high school classes at Medgar Evers at night. Damon was in elementary school. The girls were still in day care. I was avoiding Charlie and seeing Charles on and off. I was dancing on the weekends and praying every day. I had found a baby sitter, Miss Pansy, who lived on the corner with her retarded son Harold. Miss Pansy would pick the children up from school and day care, take them back to the house, give them dinner, and stay with them until I got home.

One night, I was too exhausted to go to school, so I decided to go home early and get some rest. The children were happy to see me. I prepared a lovely dinner for us. I was just about to wash them up to eat when I overheard their conversation.

"So you do the nasty too?"

"Uh-uh! No, I don't!"

"You do, too! That's what ya'll be doin' in the bathroom!"

What were they talking about? Who did what nasty? When I confronted him, Damon spilled his guts. The baby sitter's son had tried to pull his pants down and do the nasty with him, he said, but he had refused, so Harold had taken Gemmia in the bathroom and tried to do it with her. Gemmia wouldn't let him do it, either, so he took Nisa, three-year-old Nisa, who didn't know anything, and was doing the nasty with her every day.

My mind went blank, except for the image of Uncle Lee's face. I could smell the stench of liquor and kosher salami in the air.

I grabbed Damon and shook him. "Why didn't you tell me?! Why didn't you tell Miss Pansy what Harold was doing?"

"I did tell you, Mommy. I told you. You were doing homework, and I told you."

I had established a rule that the children were not to bother me when I was doing homework. Damon must have tried to tell me about Harold while I was studying, and I had ignored him. I grabbed Nisa. I held her and kissed her.

"Did he hurt you?" I asked her.

"No," she replied, innocently. "He did the nasty to me."

Quickly, I put her down and ordered all three of them to go to bed. Once they were down, I ran out of the house, down to the corner to Miss Pansy's house, and back. I called Charlie's cousin Paul, who had always been like a brother to me. When he answered the telephone, I told him to get his gun and come to my house. What's wrong? he asked. Somebody raped Nisa, I said and hung up the phone. Then I ran out of the house again and back down to the corner.

When Miss Pansy opened the door, I pushed passed her. "Where is Harold?!" I demanded.

"What's wrong?"

"Where is that mothahfuckin' son of yours?!"

Dumbly, Harold came into the room, smiling like he always did. I did not ask him anything. I grabbed the nearest thing to me, which happened to be the iron, and began to hit him with it.

Miss Pansy started screaming, "What's wrong?! What happened?!"

I would not stop beating Harold. I was beating Grandma and Uncle Lee and Dennis and Wayne and Charlie. I was beating everyone who had ever looked at me the wrong way, said the

209

wrong thing to me, or done anything mean to me. Blood flew everywhere. I beat Harold until I couldn't raise my arm anymore. Exhausted, I staggered to my feet, over to the door where a traumatized, crying Miss Pansy, who was not too right in the head herself, cringed, whimpering, "What did he do? What did he do?"

"He did the nasty with my three-year-old daughter! That's what he did!" I left and went back to my house.

Paul came. Charlie came. Nett came. Daddy came. I was very tired, and very bruised. In beating Harold, I had beat myself too. I would not tell them what I had done. Nett dressed my wounds. She and I took Nisa to the hospital.

The doctors examined her. Her hymen was intact.

What?!

She still has her hymen, they said. She's still a virgin.

Oh, my God!!

When we got back to the house, I questioned Damon again. Apparently, the nasty consisted of Harold laying on top of Nisa, moving his butt, and feeling her butt.

That's it?

That's it.

I had just beaten a 14-year-old retarded boy to within an inch of his life for grinding with my daughter on the bathroom floor. Nett said it did not matter, that Harold deserved a whipping. I could not bring myself to tell the others, so I just went to bed. Nett told them.

Charlie and I had been separated about six months. He knew I had an order of protection against him, so he began stalking me. There were days when he would wait outside the house for me to leave and he'd follow me to the train station. He was careful to keep his distance. I was careful not to say or do the wrong thing, which could have been anything.

I prayed and asked God to give me a car so I could avoid Charlie and get around without having to ride the train. I saw a beat-up 1972 Buick with a "for sale" sign taped to the window right outside the train station. The children and I went to meet the owner.

He loved Damon. He practically gave me the car for a hundred dollars. When Charlie found out, he was furious. Whenever he came around, I would get in the car, lock the doors, drive off, and leave him standing at the curb.

Once, I lent my car to Charles overnight. He was to bring it back to me the next morning in time for me to get to work. The next day, just as the children and I were walking out the door to go to the car, Charlie walked up. I tried to avoid him, but he saw the car.

"Who is that nigger in your car?"

I kept walking, pushing the children ahead of me.

"Oh! So you got a nigger you let drive your car? I'm your husband and I can't drive it, but your nigger, he can drive your car?"

I started running, pulling the children along behind me.

Poor Charles had never seen Charlie, so he had no idea the man walking behind me, ranting and raving like a maniac, was about to kill him. He got out of the car to come to my defense. Charlie took off running toward him.

I screamed at Charles, "Get in the car! Get in! That's Charlie!" Six-foot, two-inch Charlie was about a yard away from five-foot, six-inch Charles before Charles realized what was happening. He turned and ran back toward the car, getting inside and slamming the door just as Charlie jumped across the hood.

I yelled, "Run him over! Run him over!"

Charles started the car in reverse and tried to take off. Somehow, Charlie managed to hang on. Charles finally got himself together and put the car in drive. It jerked forward, spilling Charlie to the ground, and Charles sped away.

That left me standing there with three frantic children and a very irate estranged husband to deal with. I tried to run back to the apartment building. I did not make it.

Right there, in the courtyard of my home, at 7:45 on a weekday morning, with all the neighbors and my children watching, Charlie beat me so bad he almost killed me.

Grandma always used to say, "Girl, it seems like every time you take two steps up, you take four steps back!" I used to think I was just plain-old dumb.

Why do we do things we know are not the things we should be doing? I knew better than to try to get a new man when I had a crazy ex-man lurking around and watching my every move. I knew it was impossible to move on to a new thing before I had achieved closure on the old thing. Closure is critical. You and everyone else involved must be clear about what has happened and what will happen next. You must sit down and discuss things. If that is not possible, you must write it out or talk about it over the telephone. By any means necessary, you must have closure. If not, the people involved will be operating under different criteria and different expectations.

It is difficult to come to closure when you are angry. When you are angry, you strike out. You want to put an end to things in the quickest, most convenient way. When you are angry, you cannot achieve closure until you figure out who you are angry at and what you are angry about. You must take the time, sort through all of the mess, and figure it out. This is not an easy task.

More often than not, you want to blame and find fault. That is the basis of your anger: you want to prove a point. You want to be right. You will never get anywhere like that. You will certainly not get to closure. Closure does not require anyone to be at fault or guilty or to blame. It's simple. Whatever happened before is not going to happen again because the matter is closed. You tell the other person or persons involved, "This is what I intend to do. This is what I expect you to do. If you do not comply, this is what I will do as a result. Now this, this, and this, we can negotiate. This, this, and this is non-negotiable. Let us move on." That is closure.

No matter how wonderful or traumatic our experiences are, we must bring them to closure in our minds. The mind is a computer that stores every experience we have and every word we hear. It stores this information, based not on its truth or relevance but on our perceptions and experiences. People live as much in fantasy about the past as they do in the pain of it. When we do not reach closure, our past thoughts, perceptions, and experiences establish the patterns of behavior that we will follow throughout our lives and re-create at every level of our lives. For many, childhood experiences of neglect, abuse, poverty, unworthiness, dishonesty, and violence become the monsters we face as adults. How we are treated, spoken to, and cared for as children defines how we treat, speak to, and care for ourselves and others as adults. If there has been no closure, those early experiences become who we believe we are and determine what we do.

Nothing in my life had ever been brought to closure. No story was complete. Events were patched together inconsistently, haphazardly. I was very angry about that. All the things I had seen as a child had become the things I did as adult. All the things that were not done for me or to me became the things I wanted to do as an adult but could not get done. I had a lot to be angry about, but I also wanted to lay blame. I wanted to blame everybody but me for what was happening to me. I blamed Grandma, Daddy, Uncle Lee, Wayne, Charlie—all the people with whom I was angry. All the people with whom I had not reached closure.

As a child, I received so many conflicting messages. I was told I was loved, but I was treated cruelly. I was told I was protected, yet I was exposed to and lived in situations that created fear. Demeaning criticism created self-doubt. Abusive chastisement created issues around my self-value and self-worth. Consequently, as an adult I had no sense of self, yet I was responsible for the lives of three other people. I wanted so much for myself and my children, but I had no idea how to accomplish any of my goals. I knew I had a problem with the sex thing, but I did not know how to deal with it. While all of this was going on inside of me, I was expected to work, take care of my family, and behave like a normal-functioning adult.

I was angry. I had a right to be angry. Most of all, I was angry with me. I was doing all the things I promised myself I would not do, yet I could not seem to help myself or stop. I was beating up on myself mentally while Charlie was beating up on me physically. I was debasing myself emotionally while Charles was debasing me in life. I was telling myself I wanted to get ahead while I was doing everything in my power to stay in exactly the same place. I would take small steps to get myself together, but I never took a positive stand on getting rid of some of the anger, fear, guilt, and shame I was carrying around. Instead of facing situations head on, I avoided them or lied to myself about them. I was always pissed off and I always wanted to fight. But each time the fight started, I would get beat up. And that would piss me off even more.

We are talking here about the 1970s, when this society did not take the issue of domestic violence very seriously. It did not matter if there was a policeman standing on the corner or at my front door, all the laws in the world could not have stopped Charlie from beating me, or me from sleeping with him. He was my husband. I believed, and society told me that it was my duty to serve him. He also served a very sick purpose in my life. I was prepared to sneak him in through the garbage alley if necessary. I told myself that Charlie loved me. When he was not beating me, he would have sex with me, and that made me feel good. It also made me angry. Why couldn't I find a man who loved me who did not want or have another woman? Why couldn't I have the kind of storybook romance in my life that I dreamed about? Why was I working so hard to get someplace and finding that the harder I tried, the less progress I made? It was simple. I had not had come to closure on my past. My life was like an unfinished portrait, marred and blotched with dried-up paint. Like an abandoned piece of sculpture, carelessly chiseled, partially demolished, and left to ruin.

Nett had given up all hope of me ever getting away from Charlie. It had been seven long, hard, perplexing years. Immediately after the last assault, Charlie expressed remorse, as usual. He took me back inside the house and nursed me back to health. He promised that he would not beat me again if I promised not to have him arrested. Everything was calm. It lasted for about six months. It would have lasted longer, but I stopped sleeping with him. I would not let him touch me. Eventually, the monster came back. Angrily, Charlie told me that if he didn't get "it" from me, he would get it from somebody else. I told him that was fine by me.

Charlie helped with the rent when he wanted to. He watched the children sometimes. He came and went as he pleased, and so did I. I wasn't seeing anyone, though. I was trying to get through school and get myself on a more positive course. I was trying to spend more time with the children. I realized that they, too, had been through a great deal. I wanted to provide them with a more stable home life. I simply did not know how.

It was just a few days before Thanksgiving and Charlie had not been home for days. I had no idea where I was going to get the money to make our holiday dinner. Ten inches of snow had fallen outside, so going out to the store was not something I had to worry about right then. I was in the kitchen frying fish and french fries, the children's favorite dinner, when Charlie came home. He had on a brand-new black cashmere coat and a hat to match. He stood at the entrance to the kitchen looking just like an undertaker. I had on a cotton nightgown and no shoes. He asked me where I had gotten the money to buy food. I told him he had not given it to me. He asked me if my "nigger" had given it to me. I did not bother to respond. I think that made him mad. He started toward me. I made up my mind I was not going to get beat up in my kitchen again.

I picked up the frying pan full of grease and Porgies and threw it at him. I missed, but some of the hot oil got on his coat. That infuriated him. He kept coming toward me, calling me a crazy bitch, and he would have grabbed me, but he slipped on the grease on the floor. While he was down, I picked up the pan of french fries and threw them at him. All of the grease that was not on the floor was running down the front of his coat. He was sitting on hot fish and potatoes. I grabbed a knife. He was so busy trying to get out of his coat, I was able to slip by him out of the kitchen. Now where was I going?

"I'm outta here!"

I ran right out of the apartment, in my nightgown, with no shoes on, out into the street. The snow came up to my knees, but I didn't feel the cold. I was angry and desperate. I saw the children at the window. They were crying. Charlie was right behind me. I made my way across the courtyard to my neighbor's house. I was screaming wildly, "Call the police! Somebody call the police!"

It is almost impossible to run in the snow in a nightgown with no shoes on. The best you can do is fall, which I did. Charlie was gaining on me. I had to get up. People were at their windows. Several called out to me, "Come over here! Come over here! He's right behind you!" One neighbor was standing just inside her building door, urging me to run faster. "Quick! You can hide in here," she cried.

I was diving through the snow, falling, getting up, and diving again. I found I covered more ground that way. I was almost to the door when I looked up and saw a police car pull up. I couldn't believe it! Ten inches of snow and they had arrived in three minutes! On a bright, sunshiny day, it took them three hours. What a blessing!

The cops grabbed Charlie. He fought them. I turned around and headed back toward my house. Only then did I feel the cold, but strangely enough, I felt as if my entire body was on fire.

I dragged myself up the stairs and went back inside, locking and chaining the door behind me. I turned out all the lights and stood watching the street scene below from the window. The police were hitting Charlie with their night sticks and he was still fighting. One cop got the best of him and he went down. They tossed him into the back of the police car like a piece of meat.

An officer came to the door and asked me if I wanted to press charges. I told him no. He said they would hold him overnight and he would be out the next morning. Maybe the snow would keep him away, he said. It didn't matter, I was numb. I had frost-bitten toes, arms, and legs, and snow in my vagina to deal with. I really didn't care what they did with him.

᠅᠕᠈᠕᠅

216

Just before things get better, they get worse. It must be a metaphysical principle that before you receive something really good, something bad must happen. The trick is to live through the bad part without giving up. You must keep in mind what the goal is, what you are aiming for, and, no matter what happens, you must hold on. It guess it's like having surgery for a life-threatening disease. During the process, there is much blood and pain. You have to be opened up so the doctors can get to the disease. Once it is removed, you are stitched up. Then you must endure the pain of the stitches. If you move slowly and take real good care of yourself, you will heal and all will be well—that is, if they have gotten all of the sickness out. There are times when the surgeons miss a little piece and you must go through the process all over again: the pain, the blood, the cutting, the stitches, and the healing. But once it is done, it is done, and you are on your way to a full recovery.

Over the years, I have worked in and for many major corporations, both as a temporary worker and in permanent positions. I was always told what a "good worker" I was. I had a great telephone manner, a keen eye for details, and I was exceptionally good with people. Still, I never stayed in any position for more than a year. Partly because it took just about that much time for my social security number to come up in a computer match at the public assistance office, and partly because it took about that long for the pattern to emerge.

The pattern was always the same: I would come in early and stay late. I would get to know my job and the jobs of others around me. I rarely got a raise, and I never got promoted. This, coupled with my disastrous relationship with Charlie, supported my suspicion that I was not "good enough" or that I could not do anything "right." I would start to suspect that something was wrong with me or with my clothes or my hair or, as I was often told, with my "attitude." I finally figured out what it was when I went to work for a major publishing company.

I had been in my position for about six months when they hired her. She was tall, beautiful, and white—a "friend" of one of the vice presidents. She was a teacher who eventually wanted to become an editor. She was the only one in the department with a college degree. I was told to train her. As the department grew, we would eventually share responsibility, I was told. I did exactly as I was told. We got along well, and I trained her well. I trained her so well that in three months I got a lousy evaluation, and she was promoted to become my supervisor! This was not the first time something like that had happened. It, too, was part of the pattern.

But the pattern took a different twist this time. The woman herself challenged the move, calling it racist and sexist. I was shocked. She encouraged me to challenge my evaluation and challenge my supervisors. I had never done that before in my life. I had never challenged a white man—or any other man, for that matter. She vowed to walk through the challenge with me, and she proved a powerful ally.

First, I wrote a letter contesting the information in my evaluation and requested a response to specific issues. I asked for a meeting and a detailed job description, which I had never received. The department head was stunned. The head of personnel and two vice presidents came in to meet with me. There were certain points I had to concede, they said, but the major points were up for grabs. Every time I mentioned racism and discrimination, they cringed.

I recall one vice president telling me that he was Greek, his wife was Italian, my department head was Jewish, and my supervisor was a WASP. He got along very well with them all, he said. How could I think I was being discriminated against? I reminded him that they were all white and I was not.

I was given a list of requirements I would be expected to fulfill and placed on probation for ninety days. Since the requirements were not much different from what I had been doing, I breezed through the probationary period. When I was called in for another evaluation, I got rave reviews. I was offered the new position and a raise. I was shocked.

I resigned.

There comes a time when you get to a point where you simply cannot allow other people to treat you any way they want to. There comes a time when you simply must stand up for yourself. You must speak your truth without fear, knowing that, no matter what happens, it will be better than what is going on. You can, however, only do this when you have healed your weaknesses. You will be successful only after you have resigned yourself to take control of what happens to you. If you move too soon, if you are not confident in your ability, you will end up worse off than when you started—not because the situation will be worse, but because you will feel worse.

If you are not working on self-empowerment and healing, you will not see bad experiences as stepping stones to better ones. You will be attacked by your old disease, whatever it is for you. My disease was "I deserve whatever happens to me. I deserve it because I am bad." In my case, it almost proved to be fatal.

⁂

The kids and I were getting into the car, on our way to school and work, when Charlie drove up. Damon and Gemmia ran to him. They had not seen him in several weeks. Before I knew what was happening, he scooped them up and ran back to his car with them. I ran after him. He pulled off. I stood there, in shock, holding Nisa by the hand. The monster had my children. He had taken my children off to his castle to eat them. I was still standing there when Charlie pulled up again. He got out of the car, walked right up to me, slapped my face, grabbed Nisa out of my arms, and sped off again. Now, they were all gone.

I ran back inside and called the police. Did I have a court order giving me custody, they asked. No, I told them, two of the children are not even his! How did I know he had not taken them for ice cream, they asked. At eight o'clock in the morning?! I would have to wait twenty-four hours to file a complaint. Chances are he would bring them back by then, they said. I hung up.

I called Nett. "Good!" she said. "Let him have them for awhile. You need a break. Maybe now you can get yourself together. Ronnie, he does not want those children. He is only using them to get to you. Don't fall for it! Don't let him back in your house! He'll bring them back. If he doesn't, good!"

I called my father. "Did you call his job?" No. "Did you call his mother?" No. "Well, call them and call me back."

I called my brother. "Look, Ronnie, you made your bed hard, now you have to lay in it. You got any money you can lend me?"

I called Dial-a-Prayer. "Suffer little children, for yours is the kingdom of heaven," the voice on the other end said. "God will take care of his children. They are not your children, they are God's children. He has not brought them into this world to abandon them or see them abused. They are safe. Know that right now. The power of God is wherever your children are. God never ignores the cries of a mother.

"Get a picture of your children. Sit it in front of you. Read Psalm 109 repeatedly. Within twenty-four hours, you will hear from your children. They will be fine. If you have not heard from them in that time, call the police."

It was ten in the morning. Charlie called at six o'clock that night. I had been reading the psalm for ten hours straight, stopping only long enough to go to the bathroom. All he wanted to do was come home and take care of his family, he said. He was tired of running around. He loved me. He loved his children. Could he please come home? He did not want sex or anything. He would be good to me, he promised. Could he please come home?

"Do not panic! Be still!" I told myself. The psalm reverberated in my brain: *"But do Thou for me, O God, the Lord, for Thy name's sake. Because Thy mercy is good, deliver Thou me..."*

Yes, I said, he could come home.

The children were fine. It was just another outing with Daddy as far as they were concerned. They had gone to see Grandma Millie. They had played with her dog. They had gone to McDonald's. Daddy had bought them some new toys and he was going to buy them all bicycles, they said. Good, now it's time to go to bed.

"Hold not thy peace, O God of my praise, for the mouth of

the wicked and the mouth of the deceitful are opened against me..."

Charlie seemed very calm. He helped me bathe the children and put them to bed.

"They compassed me about also with words of hatred, and fought against me without cause..."

We tried to make small talk, but we were both exhausted.

"For my love they are my adversaries, but I give myself unto prayer..."

Charlie said he was going to bed. I had some homework to do. I told him I would see him in the morning. We would talk then.

"And they rewarded me evil for good and hatred for my love..."

I sat at the kitchen table for hours trying to figure out what to do.

"Help me, O Lord my God, O save me according to thy mercy.."

I tried to think, but my mind was in a fog. I could not, would not, have this man in my life anymore, I decided. It was time to cut the cancer out. Enough was enough.

I knew that if I did not panic, if I did not go into fear, I would be shown what to do. I finally went to bed, carefully crawling in next to Charlie so as not to wake him.

"That they may know that this is thy hand, that thou Lord hast done it..."

I was sleeping. I felt someone shaking me. I opened my eyes and rolled over. Charlie was still asleep and none of the children were at the bed. I closed my eyes again. The minute I did, I was shaken again. This time I sat up. There was no one in the room but Charlie and me. Then, I heard the voice.

"Get up and get out of here. This man is going to kill you if you stay here. How much proof do you need? Leave now!"

Instinctively, I knew the voice. It was Carmen, the woman from the dream so many years ago. But there was such urgency in her voice. I thought to myself, I must be going crazy. The voice responded, *"You are not going crazy. I am here with you just as I promised. You must leave! Now!!"*

I eased out of the bed. Standing, I hesitated.

The voice answered another thought. *"Take only what you need."*

I gathered the bare necessities: underwear, socks, a few outfits for each of the children. I dressed them, one at a time. They were still asleep. I wondered, how am I going to carry three sleeping children out of this house at five-thirty in the morning?

"Don't give up five minutes before the miracle!" the voice said.

Damon stretched and sat up. "Are we going to school now?" he asked sleepily. "Shhhhh," I told him. "We have to go out, okay?" Gemmia woke up. With the two big ones up to carry the bags, I figured I could carry the little one. I gathered Nisa up into my arms and the four of us padded softly into the living room.

I had about three dollars in my pocketbook. I stared at Charlie's wallet on the coffee table. Again, the voice responded to my thoughts.

"Do not repay evil with evil. You have all that you need. Go!"

We were out the door, down the street, and standing in front of the train station when I realized I had no idea where to go!

THE Journal

Okay! I can do this. I know I can. I think I've got the hang of it now.

The things we do in life teach us lessons. Lessons are some sort of initiations I must go through that take me to deeper levels of understanding about who I am and what I do. Okay. Lessons are necessary in order for me to grow mentally and emotionally. Without them, I will not grow or really understand the depths of my mind and my ability to act under different circumstances. Uh, huh. I think these lessons are also the keys that unlock the doors to the secrets of who I am and what my mission is in life. The people who participate in my lessons are like the teaching instruments I need in order to fully understand all that I have been through. They show me certain things by the way they behave in my lessons. That makes perfectly good sense. Great. Continue.

I must face certain lessons as a result of my behavior. It is only my behavior that helps me to recognize and accept what I can do, what I cannot do, and how I will behave while doing or not doing. Lessons also come as a result of what I believe and what I do based on those beliefs. What I believe causes me to act in a particular way. Actually, my behavior and my beliefs create my lessons. I draw to me what I need in order to grow. When I see what I am doing, I am actually seeing what I believe. I see what I believe, then I act on it. If I want to change what I am seeing, I must change what I

223

am believing. Damn! That is really deep!

I guess I can accept my lessons, ignore my lessons, or totally miss the point. If I see something I do not want, I can accept that it comes from what I am believing and then do what is necessary to change. Or, I can act like what is going on has nothing to do with me. Like it is other people who are doing it, and I am just the victim. Or, I can continue to do what I am doing, try to figure out why it isn't working, and continue to chase my tail. Although in my wildest dreams I cannot imagine that lessons are designed to be painful, I guess pain is the only thing that really gets my attention. Pain makes me focus. It tells me that something is wrong, and that I need to pay attention to what I am believing and doing. If I do not pay attention, I could do things that will create new lessons and cause more pain.

Everything I do, then, is part of the learning process. If my theory is correct, once I accept my lessons, I will grow. I will achieve some new level of understanding. My mind will be cleared of the old beliefs, the old wounds will heal, and I will move on. However, if I insist on remaining ignorant, I will continue to miss the lessons, and I will keep right on doing the same thing over and over and over, like an idiot.

Hey! If I don't begin to focus on what I am doing, I could stunt my growth indefinitely. If I am not careful, I could be a mental and emotional midget!

CHAPTER 18

A Mound of Fear

I took Damon and Nisa to my father's house. Gemmia and I went to Ruth Carlos's house. Ruth was so glad to hear that I had left Charlie she downed two shots of vodka at seven-thirty in the morning. Ruth told me her home was my home and said she would help me figure out what I should do. Besides, she was Gemmia's godmother and was really glad to have her around. Gemmia called her "Missy Carlos."

"Girl, we were getting ready to take up a collection to send you to Siberia! I've been in love too, but I ain't never loved nobody enough to let him beat the shit out of me for breakfast!"

Ruth wanted to know all the details. When I told her about the voice, she howled with laughter.

"There you go with that spirit shit again! I wish you would tell one a them spirit mothahfuckahs to give me a number!"

I told her how I had given my father numbers when I was younger. She said that wasn't doin' shit for her today. She started calling the spirits, telling them if they wanted her to put me up they had better give her a number too.

Ruth was the director of the drug program facility in which I had worked. An ex-addict and ex-prostitute, she had a very colorful vocabulary and an even more colorful life. She smoked refer, drank vodka out of a coffee mug, used "mothahfuckah" as the basic adjective in her vocabulary, and could figure her way out of anything. When I worked at the center, Ruth had been there for me, plugging for me, teaching me the lessons of womanhood I had never learned. In the midst of all her craziness, though, she was great with children.

Ruth also knew a great deal about men, most of which she had learned from turning fifty to sixty tricks a day. She described Charlie as "your basic once-a-week trick."

"You know," she'd say, "the kind who comes around once a week and then has the nerve to try to bargain with you over your price. He gets his thing off in three to five minutes, and thinks he was so good you'll just be waiting around for him to come back next week, to do the same thing all over again."

I had never turned a trick in my life, but I knew that Ruth was basically right about Charlie. She was also right when she described me as "new to the corner" and as not being able to handle men.

Nett was a little upset that I had not come to her, but I explained that I did not want to take a chance on Charlie finding me at her place and breaking out her windows or both our necks. Charlie would never think of looking for me at Ruth's house. He couldn't stand Ruth because she had been a dope fiend and a whore.

I spent one night at Ruth's house before I got not one but two jobs. With that income and my public assistance check, I figured I would be able to get an apartment quickly. I worked from eight to four during the day doing keypunch work, and from eleven at night to seven in the morning at Ruth's rehabilitation facility. I did this for two whole weeks before I had another visit from Carmen.

I was on the subway on the way to my day job when I looked up and literally saw Carmen standing right in front of me. I have no idea how I knew who she was, but I knew. She bent over, placing her hands on my knees, and said, "Have you had enough yet?" I realized that nobody else could see her, so I shook my head rather than answer out loud. "Go home and change the locks," she said, smiling, then she rose and got off the train at the next stop.

I rode the train all the way to 168th Street when I should have gotten off at 14th Street. My mind was racing. How the hell was I going to change the locks? The answer came from somewhere inside me: "Go to the hardware store, buy a tumbler, and put it in the door." I was even more confused. What's a tumbler? "Go to the hardware store," came the voice within in response.

I rode the subway back to Brooklyn and went to the first hardware store I could find. Not only did the salesman know what a tumbler was, he showed me how to install it and only charged me five dollars, no tax.

I got back on the subway to make the trip to Canarsie. I wanted to smoke on the train, I was so nervous. By the time I reached Canarsie, sweat was rolling down my armpits under my clothes. I jumped off the train and stood outside the station smoking one cigarette after another and pacing back and forth.

Isn't it amazing that when you are in crisis, the thing you worry about most is what other people are thinking about you? Every time someone would pass me to go into the station, I felt as if they knew everything there was to know about me. I would smile at them and say "hello," as if, by speaking to them, they would change their minds. Actually, people do not care what you are doing when you are smoking in front of a subway station. I finally figured that out after about ten people asked me for a cigarette.

Finally, I started walking toward the house. There was nothing I could think of that was not answered instantly. I thought, "Suppose he's home?"

"He's not home," came the voice.

"Suppose he changed the locks?"

"He did not change the locks."

"Suppose he's waiting in the bushes for me?"

"Will you *stop* making excuses and go change the locks!?"

I was scared to death. I was one block from the house, but it seemed like a mile. Then it hit me: call him. Call him at work to make sure he's there. I ran to the pay phone and waited for Charlie to answer. When he did, I disguised my voice and said, "Hold, please." Then, leaving the receiver dangling, I ran up the block to the house. I let myself in, found the tools I needed, and started fumbling with the lock. My hands were shaking, my nose was running, and I kept burning myself with my cigarette. One of my neighbors saw me. I told her what I was doing. She called one of her maintenance-man friends. In less than three minutes, the tumbler was in. My neighbor volunteered to go pick up the children for me and let them stay at her house while I packed Charlie's clothes. I called my friends and family to give them the red alert. Within ninety minutes, the children and I were locked inside the house and ready for the show-down. At 6:30, the fireworks began.

Charlie came home, stuck his key in the door, and went crazy. The children and I were hiding in the bathroom. I kept telling them to be quiet, as if Charlie did not know we were in the house. He screamed and cursed. He went outside to the window and did the same thing. We stayed in the bathroom. When the telephone started ringing, I panicked.

The voice came back. *"As long as you do not panic, you will be told what to do! Answer the telephone."*

I crept to the telephone and answered it.

"Why are you doing this to me? Where am I supposed to go?"

The voice that answered him was not my voice. It was not me. Whoever it was, did not feel like being bothered.

"That is not my problem. You do the same thing I have been doing for the past seven years. Figure it out. If you keep calling me, I will have you arrested."

Then, whoever it was who was speaking for me hung up and unplugged the phone.

I was in the kitchen when Charlie came up behind me. Somehow, he had convinced Damon to throw him the key out through the window.

"You better teach the kids not to give the key to anyone."

I turned around to face him. He had a sinister smile on his face. The Lord's Prayer came immediately to my thoughts.

"The Lord is my shepherd! Yea, though I walk through the valley of the shadow of death..."

"How are you?"

I was calm as he walked over to me. It was my knees that were scared to death. He grabbed me by the shoulders.

"I will fear no evil for Thou art with me..."

"Don't you love me anymore? he asked, shaking me. "Why are you doing this to me? I love you! Don't you know I love you?"

"I shall not want! I shall not want!"

He started kissing me on my neck and face.

The words of a psalm came to my mind.

"...the mouth of the wicked and the mouth of the deceitful..."

"I love you, but you have to go now," I said. The voice was again that of the person who did not want to be bothered with any of this.

The monster was returning. "Why! Why do I have to leave my family? You got another man?"

"...that they may know that this is thy hand, that thou Lord hast done it!"

"No. I do not have another man. I just need time to think. I need to be alone."

"Help me, O Lord, my God. O, save me according to thy mercy."

Wilting, Charlie let me go and sat down at the kitchen table. The children came out of their bedroom and gathered around him. He played with them for a while. I watched him and prayed. After we put the children to bed, Charlie started crying. He cried for all the times he had beat me. He cried for all the times he had been unfaithful to me. He cried for the terrible things he had said to me and done to me. In the middle of crying, he got down on his knees and begged me to forgive him. I forgave him. He cried some more. He begged me to take him back. I told him I needed to think about it. I needed time to think. He cried some more. Then he started promising. He promised to go to counseling, to never hit me again, to bring all of his money home, and to never, as long as he lived, look at another woman.

"Do you believe me?"

I wanted to believe him, I told him, but I had been through so much. He said he was sorry about that, but he promised never to put me through it again. I made a deal with him. If he gave me a week to think about it, a week when he would not call me or follow me around, I would let him know what I wanted to do. Reluctantly, he agreed. Hesitantly, he left.

As I locked the door behind him, I heard the words of the psalm again. *"Behold, I stand at the door and knock. If anyone hears My voice and opens the door, I will come in to him and dine with him and he with Me."*

I knew he would be back, and that he still had the key to the door.

◢◣◢◣

The "shoulds," "should nots," "cannots," and "do nots" we live with daily etch fear into the very essence of our beings. For Black women, these "nots" are doubly disturbing because we are almost expected to break the rules. As a result, we are watched. We are watched by society. We are watched by each other. We are watched by our family and friends. They are all waiting to see what we will do next. Are we going to break the rules or "do the right thing?" We are watched by the fearful eyes of people who want us to make it, but who are afraid that if we do, we will take their place. We are watched by the knowing eyes of people who realize that if we make it, we will leave them behind.

As we are watched, we become afraid. We are afraid we will do or say the wrong thing. We are afraid we will get caught. We are afraid we will be hurt. We are afraid we will lose what we have.

Men, being logical, analytical beings, can figure out what not to do and not do it. Women, being instinctual, emotional beings, know what is logical, but they also know what things "feel" like. Most women will move with their feelings, breaking the rules, trying to make everyone happy, so they can feel good about themselves. However, there comes a time when a woman's feeling and thinking worlds must be brought into alignment. When she must slow her heart down enough to hear what is going on in her mind, or open up her mind enough to feel what is going on in her heart. This is difficult, for there are times when we, as women, know what we should be doing, but we feel that we cannot do it. At other times, we feel that there is something we should not do, but we do not know what else to do. In the worst-possible-case scenario, we know exactly what we should or should not do. But when we cannot figure out what else to do, we do not do anything at all.

Take, for example, any two creatures—dogs, birds, or crocodiles—and frighten them. Afterwards, they will be on guard, cautious. They will try to get away from the source of their fear. When they see one another, they forget that it was an outside source that created the fear. They forget that they are both targets. They become fearful of one another. Cautiously, they move around one another, each trying to see what the other is doing, both trying to get away from the attacker. In their individual escape attempts, every move the other one makes looks suspicious. Watching through fear-filled eyes, each is ready to pounce on the other in defense. If one moves too swiftly, the other will retreat in fear or attack. If one moves too slowly or deliberately, the other becomes suspicious. Being on guard, neither realizes the other is simply trying to get close enough to say, "I am here for you! Do not be afraid!"

Many Black men and women are like frightened animals. While they are desperately craving love, companionship, and the safety one of another, they suspiciously watch, criticize, and pull away from each other. This fear permeates all of their relationships—family, social, and intimate—on all levels—political, economic, and sexual. As the Black woman begins to untangle the web, she remembers that "he who looks like me is not the enemy!" Intuitively, she can feel her way through certain situations. When she feels her power moving up and through her, she hears the voices of the universe calling her. She is ready to move around, through, or over others, if necessary, to get away from the shoulds, should nots, cannots, and do nots that have created her fear. She may still be frightened, but she is willing to move. She may still be cautious, but she realizes she has no choice. If she does not move, her children will die. She wants to move—no, she has to move—from her state of stagnation. Unfortunately, someone who looks like her—oftentimes, her man or some other Black man—will remind her of what she should not do because she could get hurt. Once again, she is led to believe that she cannot move, so she does not dare to.

To some, the average Black woman appears arrogant, domineering, and ruthless. Others see Black women as lazy, slovenly, hostile, and ignorant. In reality, most Black women are desperately frightened, lonely, and confused. We feel and know we are powerful, but we have not been taught the source of that power. We become attached to conditions and emotions that make us feel powerless. The truth is, Black women, like all women, are co-creators with God. The force, power, and consciousness of God stirs in all women, and it is that source that can move Black women beyond their fears. We Black women must begin to call up the God force that is laying dormant in our spirits and take it to the streets!

After Charlie left, I leaned against the door for almost two hours trying to figure out what to do. I prayed. When I was done, my mind was filled with words:

But know this, that in the last days, perilous times will come. For men will be lovers of themselves, lovers of money, boasters, proud and blasphemous, disobedient to parents, unthankful, unholy...unloving, unforgiving, slanderers, without self-control, brutal, despisers of good....And from such people, turn away!...For of this sort are those who creep into households and make captives of gullible women, loaded down with sins, led away by various lusts...always learning and never able to come to the knowledge of the truth.

I knew Charlie would be coming back. I also knew that if I believed one word of what he had said to me, I would end up dead. I ran to my bedroom and got my pillow and blanket. Then I ran to the kitchen and got a butcher knife. I went back to the front door, spread the blanket out on the floor, and laid down. He returned about two in the morning.

I heard the downstairs door to the building open. I heard footsteps on the stairs. I heard the door at the top of the stairs open. I heard my heart pounding in my head.

The voice again: *"Fear not! For I am with you!"*

I heard Charlie stick the key in the lock and turn it slowly, quietly. Quickly, I turned it back. He turned it again. I turned it back. The only thing between me and Charlie was that lock and the chain on the door. He got quiet. I got quiet. This time, he turned the key and pushed the door at the same time. He reached his hand inside to try to open the chain lock. I swear he was growling, like an animal. I tried to push the door shut, but his foot was in the doorsill.

It was then that I grabbed the knife and began to hack through the small opening in the door. Four or five hacks later, I made contact with Charlie.

He screamed and backed away from the door. I immediately shut and locked it. I heard his cries through the door.

"I'm dying! I'm bleeding! Please! Please, let me in!"

I never opened my mouth.

"Please, help me! I'm bleeding bad!"

I heard him stumble down the stairs. He had gone back outside and was standing beneath my bedroom window, begging and pleading for help. From behind the curtains, I could see his hands were full of blood. I panicked. Oh, shit!

The voice came back. It was insistent: *"Do not panic!"*

I ran in the bathroom, grabbed a towel, and threw it to him from the window. He was on his knees, bleeding and whimpering. I heard the sirens before I saw the police cars. Oh, shit, I thought, I am going to jail! My children are going to be motherless and fatherless! I am going to jail.

"Yea, though I walk through the valley of the shadow of death... Be still! You will be told exactly what to do, what to say!"

The cops were standing over Charlie, examining his wounds. I dashed back to the door to get my knife. I ran with it to the kitchen and threw it into the sink. I squeezed some dishwashing liquid on a dishcloth and ran back to the door. I began scrubbing the blood off the wallpaper. I was sitting at the kitchen table, calmly smoking two cigarettes, when the police knocked on my door.

When I opened the door and saw all the blood on the hallway wall, I cringed and covered my mouth.

"What happened here?" the police officer asked.

"I don't know! My ex-husband was out here trying to get in, but I don't know where he is now."

"We have him downstairs in the car. He must have cut himself on the glass. You might want to clean this blood up so your neighbors won't see it. We'll get him to the hospital. If you have any more trouble, just give a call. We are car 913."

When they left, my neighbor and I washed the wall. When we were done, I went inside and called Ruth Carlos. She was the only person I knew who could appreciate hearing about what had happened at three o'clock in the morning.

Ruth was ecstatic. She could not believe I had "taken control of my corner." She had some good news for me too. She had had a dream the night before in which she dreamed a number. She had played it, and it had hit. She was twelve hundred dollars richer, she said, thanks to me and the spirits. What was the number? 913. My birthday.

THE Journal

I am free! Praise the Lord, I'm free. No more dark clouds, no more chains holding me. My soul is resting, it's just a blessing. Praise the Lord, Hallelujah! I'm free!

Today, I am grateful to be alive. Today, I am grateful I can see. Today, I am grateful for my health. Today, I am grateful for the lives of my children. Today, I am grateful I have a home. Today, I am grateful I have something to eat. Today, I am grateful that I am getting it together. Today, I love myself. Today, I forgive myself.
I forgive myself for being stupid.
I forgive myself for being impatient.
I forgive myself for feeling abandoned.
I forgive myself for feeling unloved.
I forgive myself for being cynical.
I forgive myself for telling lies.
I forgive myself for sleeping around.
I forgive myself for not paying attention to what I am doing.
I forgive myself for not saving money.
I forgive myself for smoking.
I forgive myself for playing with my life.
I forgive myself for neglecting myself.
I forgive myself for not taking care of myself.
I forgive myself for not being a good mother.
I forgive myself for not being forgiving.
I forgive my father.
I forgive my grandmother.

235

I forgive Bunny.
I forgive Aunt Nancy.
I am not ready to forgive Uncle Lee.
I forgive people all over the world for creating pain.
I forgive everybody for everything they have ever done to me.
I forgive myself totally, unconditionally, and completely.
I forgive God for leaving me when I needed Him most.

CHAPTER 19

A Profile of Loneliness

Charlie did not die. The doctors told him I had missed his heart by a half inch. That did not upset Charlie. What upset him was what my neighbor did while he was on his knees in front of my window, "dying." Apparently, my neighbor, Mr. Davies, a corrections officer, walked up to Charlie while he lay bleeding, put his gun to Charlie's temple, and said: "Look man, I don't know you, I don't know your wife. I do know that I see her coming and going. Her children are always clean and well-mannered. She is always pleasant. I do know that I see you beating her, harassing her, and bringing disgrace on every Black man in this neighborhood. I also know that if you do not die and I see you bothering that woman again, I will blow your brains out."

Charlie was upset about that. To him, it was indication that I was sleeping with Mr. Davies. I told Charlie I was not sleeping with him. He was simply God's ram in the bush.

So, there I was, twenty-six years old, with three children, no husband, a bag full of bills, a temporary job assignment to augment my bimonthly welfare allowance of two hundred-fifty-six dollars, and a fear of being alone. I did not want to be alone. Being alone meant that there was something wrong with you. It meant that nobody wanted you. To me, being alone meant that I was still ugly.

I was scared I would never find another man who would accept me and my children. Ruth told me I was crazy. She said

237

that all I had to do was go to any bar, on any Friday night, in a tight black dress, and I could have all the men I wanted. I could have one for every day of the week if I wanted, she said, so I would not have to worry about any one of them becoming attached. Ruth said men were like buses: if you waited long enough, one was sure to come along. She said I needed to get out, let my hair down, and have a few meaningless flings. I told her she was crazy and went to bed.

I stayed in bed for six weeks. I would not eat. I rarely talked to anyone on the telephone. Nett was sure I was having a nervous breakdown and encouraged my father to come and take the children. When he left with them, I went back to bed. I smoked and cried. I slept and cried. I walked the floor and cried. When I was not smoking, sleeping, crying, or walking, I was calling Charlie.

When I realized it was really over between us, I panicked. I began to realize that I had absolutely no idea what it meant to be an adult, to be on my own, to take care of myself. There were so many things I needed to know that my parents and caregivers had not and could not teach me. I knew the basics: cooking, cleaning, keeping the children clean and safe. I did not, however, know anything about budgeting, saving, planning, or building a future. Up to this point, everything I had done had been done out of necessity. Either I had been forced to do certain things, or my situation had forced me to do them. Now that I needed to feel safe and secure in my ability to survive, I had no idea what to do. So, I stayed in bed.

When Charlie got out of the hospital, he went to his mother's house. When I called him, if Millie answered the telephone, I would hang up. A few minutes later when I called back, he would answer. There were times when I found myself begging and pleading with him to come home. He refused and seemed to get great joy out of calling me names. At other times, he would call me and beg to come back. I would refuse and hang up on him. Sometime during the third or fourth week of this cat-and-mouse game, Charlie stopped calling. A few days later, he called to tell me he was moving in with another woman. That's when I really fell apart.

I realized that I did not want Charlie, but I wanted somebody, anybody, to make me feel better. My mind continuously showed me mental images of a long, lonely life. I kept praying, asking God to tell me what to do because I did not have a clue. I blamed myself for the mess I had made of my life and vowed to clean it up. When I thought about what that meant, I would start crying all over again. I felt as though I were being punished. I thought about killing myself, but I could not bear another stay in Snapper Five if I failed again.

I had no idea that solitude was what I needed. What should have been "down time" for me, a rest period, turned into a period of self-induced torture during which I beat myself up emotionally. I woke up each day berating myself, convinced that I had absolutely nothing to live for except my children. Then when I thought about them, I cried some more.

I don't know why I opened the door one day. I thought it was one of Damon's friends I could send to the store for cigarettes. It was my step-sister Keturah and her friend. They had come to take me out. They demanded I get out of bed, wash up, get dressed, and go with them on a boat ride. I refused. Keturah was insistent. She literally threw me into the shower, and while I was in there, she started digging around in my closet for something for me to wear. She found a dress, my wig, and one shoe. As she was dragging me out the door, I begged her to find my other shoe. She let me go back inside to find it only after her friend agreed to go with me to make sure I did not lock myself back in.

On the boat, there were lots of men. The music was very loud, the liquor flowed as if from a fountain, and the reefer was being passed around as if it were legal. I sat in a corner, sick to my stomach. Each time Keturah insisted that I get up and dance, I nearly gagged on the smoke. She laughed, telling me I was getting a "contact high," which to her was very funny.

I watched the party-goers bump and grind, eat and drink, hoot and howl, and generally enjoy themselves. The old men with the big, round bellies were a riot. They loved to dance with slim, petite, young women, who would roll their eyes in disgust as they danced with them. But the men did not seem to mind or notice. It was hilarious. After a while, things started to get wild. A fight broke out. Somebody threatened to throw somebody else overboard. A woman got drunk and threw up on a very fine, very well-dressed young man and his girlfriend. Two women started fighting over a man. A white woman was cornered by three Black women, who gave her up-and-down about being on the boat with a Black man. It was like a carnival—two hours up the Hudson River, and two hours back down.

When we got back to shore, I had a headache, an upset stomach, and a real contact high from all the marijuana smoke. I was walking to the deck to leave when I literally fell over a man. I collected myself and kept on walking. I didn't even look back. Shocked, Keturah told me I should have at least told the man "excuse me." I turned around and said, "Excuse me, man," and continued to walk off. He caught up with me. He promised he would forgive me if I let him take me home. To my surprise, Keturah explained to him that we were not going home, but he was welcome to come along. Despite my protests, we all left together and Keturah's friend drove us to a noisy, smoke-filled after-hours club in the basement of an abandoned building.

The place was so dark, you could not see your hand in front of your face. People groped for one another, feeling to see who was male and who was female. This was exactly the kind of place Ruth Carlos had told me about, and I had no intentions of staying. I told Keturah I was going home. She insisted I have one drink. We all sat down at the bar, waiting to be served. I was sitting, mindlessly eating the stale potato chips when the man from the boat asked me, "Why are you going to ruin your beautiful body with that junk? I know a place where you can get something really good to eat. Come on."

Anything was better than this rat hole, I thought. And before I knew it, and to Keturah's delight, I was leaving the club with him. Fifteen minutes later, I was sitting at the kitchen table in his apartment.

I was totally new to this. I had never really dated, and I don't think I had ever known a man who had his own apartment. He had a one-room studio apartment. It was nicely furnished and immaculately clean. He was very pleasant, very funny, and the more I focused my eyes on him, the more I realized he was also very handsome. We talked and laughed while he cooked: beef bacon, eggs, and Pillsbury biscuits. He served the food to me on a tray with a flower and a paper towel for a napkin. He was very disappointed when I told him I didn't eat eggs and insisted on making me three biscuit-and-bacon sandwiches. It tasted like steak. Somewhere between the biscuits and the orange juice, I decided I was going to have a one-night stand. Even that was a new experience for me. I was quite sober and quite ready when we went to bed.

I woke up first. I looked at the gorgeous man laying beside me and asked myself, "What in the world does this man want with me?" Then I remembered: it was a one-night stand. I got up, bathed, and dressed. When I came out of the bathroom, he was awake. He offered to take me to breakfast. I told him I had to go get my children. I gave him my telephone number, but he told me he couldn't call. He didn't have a phone, he explained. We kissed. As I was stepping out the door, I turned back to ask him, "By the way, what is your name?"

Much to my surprise, Ernie called me the night after the morning after. I actually never expected to hear from him. Meeting him and spending the night with him did wonders for me. I picked up the kids, went home, and began making preparations to go to college, which would begin in three weeks. I was excited. For the first time in a long time, I was happy.

Ernie was the sweetest, most gentle man I had ever known. He loved to read, and he was the first man who ever held a real conversation with me. He was three years younger than me, but he was so much fun to be with and he loved children. He called almost every day. He came by every time he called. He was always on time and he always brought the children and me something. I thought to myself: God really does answer prayer. He sent me Ernie.

⋎⋎⋎

There is a state of consciousness between sleeping and waking called the "twilight state." In this state, things seem so real you believe you are awake. Both your mental and physical experiences seem so real, you believe you are having a conscious participatory experience, but you are not. You are in a state of semi-sleep, coming into a state of consciousness. I have had many twilight experiences. In some, I have found myself laughing or crying. Once I awoke and found myself swatting at flies. On another occasion, I almost wet the bed.

Scientists describe the twilight state as a release of inhibitions. Spiritually, it is when your spirit re-enters your body after a period of "floating" or dreaming. The floating is not the important aspect. The spirit re-entering your body is.

There comes a time in your life when you are forced into a state of consciousness. For some, it may be political or economic consciousness. For others, like me, it is spiritual consciousness. With Charlie out of my life, at least for the time being, I was gradually becoming aware of myself and what was going on around me. I was becoming conscious of my motives and the motives of others. I began to hear things that were not being said and see things that were not being done. I could not, however, decipher what was real and what was not real, partly because I had no one to talk to about what I was experiencing, and partly because I was afraid. So, I shut down. When I saw or heard things that were difficult or unpleasant for me to comprehend or that were beyond my comprehension, I told myself it was all in my mind. And everyone knew you could not trust my mind. After all, I had spent time in the mental ward. My mind was not to be trusted!

I often wonder how many Black women who do not understand their spiritual heritage do the very same thing? How many women shut off their intuitive inclinations because of lack of support? How many Black women, who come from a long line of spiritually attuned ancestors, shut down the part of the brain that provides them with clues and hints about what is really going on— because of insecurity, fear, and the inability to distinguish between reality and nonreality? My own reality up to that point had been so harsh, so vividly demeaning, that I wanted to stay spiritually asleep, or at least stay at the twilight level, where everything was real but unreal. Unfortunately, my spirit was ready to enter, to come into being in my consciousness. It was time for me to wake up. I struggled to keep my eyes closed, but my spirit pushed me to open them. I had to make a choice: look and listen or get knocked down.

You guessed it, I chose to get knocked down. Again.

If you want to know how a thing will end, look at the beginning. I started Medgar Evers College with a lot of excitement, a lot of hope, and a great deal of confusion. The student body at the college was ninety-nine percent African and Caribbean American. The faculty was eighty-five percent African American. I registered for four classes and wound up with three European professors and one African American professor. But I was determined to make it, and Ernie was supporting me one hundred percent.

In one class, I had to write a position paper and a proposal. I had no idea what either of them were. I researched, asked questions, and found all that I needed to write about. I worked hard on that paper and turned it in on time. It was returned to me ungraded with a note from the professor, a European woman, suggesting that I had plagiarized it. The professor indicated that she had doubts as to whether or not a freshman student could have prepared such a document unaided. She wanted me to list all of my references in the back of the paper. I explained I had done that. Every book and newspaper I had used had been listed. Still, she refused to grade the paper.

Grandma had always said that I was too smart for my own

good. I was beginning to think she was right. I had only been in school a month, and already I was in trouble. I took the matter to the head of the department. He reviewed the paper, thought it was quite good, and demanded the professor re-read the paper. She refused. She was certain I had plagiarized it, and she said she could prove it. I took the matter to the dean of administration. She read the paper and ordered a hearing. The professor refused to attend the hearing, but said she would give me a grade if I wrote another paper on another topic. I did. I got an "A." It was my first victory in my new life. It was the first of many. Carrying twelve to fifteen credits a semester, working during the day, going to school at night, I stayed on the dean's list with straight A's for six semesters.

Most of the faculty and students at Medgar Evers were extremely supportive. When I did not have a baby sitter, I took the children to school with me. They would sit in the hall or in an empty classroom or go play in the gymnasium. They quickly got to know all the professors and deans.

Eventually, one of God's rams showed up. My brother Ray needed a place to stay. He had been living with a woman and the relationship had gone sour. Great! Ray stayed home in the evenings during the week, cooked dinner for the children, and helped them with their homework. He did the laundry and grocery shopping. He also required very little pay—a few dollars here and there, a pack of cigarettes now and then. But he wanted to be left alone on the weekends. For two-and-a-half years, this arrangement worked very well.

During that time, Ernie introduced me to his family. I met his mother, his stepfather, his younger brother and sisters, aunts, and cousins. His family did things together and supported one another. They had holiday dinners together, and even created activities and reasons to get together. As Ernie's girlfriend, I was welcomed among them.

Ernie's younger sister Dolly and I became very close. I encouraged her to go back to school and she enrolled at Medgar Evers along with me. Her daughter became a sister-friend for my older daughter. Dolly and I talked about everything. We hung out together and really supported one another.

Ernie, on the other hand, was everything else: brother, friend, surrogate father for my children, and lover. I don't think we ever had a fight or an argument. He never said a harsh word to me and he was there for me, most of the time. I say most of the time because there were times when Ernie liked to be alone, do things alone, and, when the mood hit him, to be with other women. It was never anything serious, but it supported my insecurity that I was not good enough. Whenever he and I talked about making ours a committed relationship, Ernie was real clear: he did not want to get married, he did not want to marry me, and he did not want a ready-made family. I heard what he said, but I did not listen. I believed that if we stayed together long enough, he would change his mind. I was not willing to let him go, yet when he would stay away for three or four days, I was miserable. I never said a word to him about it though. I did not want to upset him. I did not want him to leave me. He was good to me. He did not beat me. He was good to my children. Most of all, having Ernie meant that I was not alone.

⁂

Remember when I said that it always seems like just before something good happens, something seemingly bad always happens? Well, it happened to me again. This time, in college.

I was president of the student government at Medgar Evers during my senior year. That year, the college president attempted to fire the school's only female dean. The dean rallied support among the students, a large group of whom, in turn, took over the president's office and went on strike. There were police, lawyers, meetings, and eventually a court case. There were press conferences, meetings with administrators, strategy sessions, and a general atmosphere of anarchy prevailed. I was getting my first lesson in Radical Behavior 101. Everyone was wrong. Everyone was suspect. Everyone wanted something different from what everyone else wanted.

I was a student leader, but I had never taken on "the system" before. I simply wanted to finish school and get out of there. It was, however, my responsibility to see to it that the students' rights and demands were protected. A group of students, including myself and my children, practically lived in the president's office for more than two months. The case went to the state supreme court, and we won. The president resigned right before graduation. The students, along with supportive faculty members, planned to conduct the commencement ceremonies without him.

Prior to the controversy, I was a straight-A student and, on the basis of my 3.99 grade point average, had been selected class valedictorian. In the midst of all the student protest activity, however, I realized that I was failing math. This was my first bout with failure as a college student. I was desperate to find a way to avoid it and I eventually did. Rather than take a letter grade, I opted for a pass–fail grade. This meant that as long as I did enough work to get a "D" in the class, it would be reflected on my records as a "pass" and would not affect my grade point average. It was all very legitimate. I thought I was home safe. However, the same confusion with which I entered college soon came back to haunt me. It came in the form of a man.

I had quite a reputation at Medgar Evers. I was the first woman to complete her term as president of the student government, and the first student government president to be selected class valedictorian. I was also the first student government president to lead a student take-over. I was also a woman who, supported primarily by other women, had brought down the reign of a man. There were many male students at Medgar Evers who did not like that. There were many male professors who did not feel comfortable with the idea of women becoming so aggressive. They let me know exactly how they felt by challenging my right to be valedictorian.

There was a male student at the college with a GPA of 3.98. Somehow, he found out about the "passing" grade I had gotten in math and decided to challenge my right to be valedictorian. He took the matter up with school officials, who checked it out and determined that, even without the passing grade, my GPA was higher than his, or, at the very least, about the same. He was not satisfied. He took his grievance "to the streets," placing signs all over the school that insinuated I had slept with my professors to get my grades. When that did not work, he further insinuated that I was a lesbian and therefore should not be allowed to represent the students.

Whenever a man wants to disempower a woman, he need only to attack her morality. In my case, such an attack was extremely damaging. This man, who did not even know me, was single-handedly destroying both my character and my emotional well-being. Even though what he was accusing me of was not true, I was devastated. I felt as if everyone in the school knew about me, about my past, and what I had done. The old fears resurfaced. I worried once more that there was something "wrong" with me and that I was "bad."

I was still operating under the premise that I had to be a "good girl" in order to be liked. While I had little or no problem working for and leading a student movement, I was totally incapable of standing up for myself. I had not yet learned that what other people say about you does not matter. What matters is whether or not you believe it. I quickly began to fall apart.

My salvation came from the mouth of my dear friend and classmate, Ann Applewhite. As I sat in my car one day, crying my eyes out about the smear campaign that had been mounted against me, Anne very gently took my hand and said, "If you are a lesbian, I would be honored to sleep with you. Perhaps if we got together, some of your strength, kindness, and intelligence would rub off on me." I looked at her to see if she was serious. She was, and we both burst out laughing.

In the end, I won. I stood and spoke on behalf of the students and my class. Still, I had not quite yet learned the true meaning of the lesson.

My father did not come to my graduation. He did not have carfare, he said. None of my brothers, sisters, or grandmothers came. Nett could not come because she had been very ill for several months. My children came. Ernie and his entire family came. I went. I was so sad, I could barely fight back the tears. Everyone thought I was crying out of joy, but inside I was miserable. For the first time in my life, I was doing something good, and none of my family was present. For the first time, I could stand up before the world and say, "Hey, I'm okay," and the people I wanted to say it to were not there. People from all over the city were applauding me. I, a single mother with three children, had graduated at the top of my class and was on my way to law school. My story made the local papers, but my own family was not there to participate.

My children were great though. They walked across the stage with me to get my diploma. They took pictures and made such a fuss over me. So did Ernie and his family. But it simply was not enough. I wanted to prove to my family that all the things they had believed about me were wrong.

A month after graduation, Ernie took me to a Stevie Wonder concert. He was still warm and loving, but in my gut I knew something was wrong. When we got home, we sat down at the kitchen table to have one of our regular "after-the-event" discussions. Ernie told me he wanted out of the relationship. It was over. It was time for him to move on, he said. I thought he was kidding. He was not kidding. He left, and when I had not heard from him after about a week, it hit me: he was serious.

It made no sense. We had a wonderful relationship. We had a loving relationship. We were good together. His mother liked me. It was still over. Every night for weeks thereafter, I would panic before I went to bed. Some days, I would call him every hour on the hour. No answer. I would drive by his place late at night to see if the lights were on. No lights. I imagined him everywhere, with everyone, doing everything he should have been doing with me. The images were vivid. The images were horrifying. The images were painful.

I could not move. I could not breathe. Every time the telephone rang, I would run to see if it was Ernie. Maybe he had changed his mind, I hoped. Maybe he had come to his senses. He did not.

My school friends became very concerned about me. They had never seen me in such a state. To them, I was the strong one, the one who could handle anything. They were not accustomed to seeing me crying or breaking down or having a problem I could not figure a way out of. They were scared to death that this meant I was human. Some of them decided I was a victim of witchcraft. Someone, somewhere, they told me, had put something in Ernie's drink and turned him against me. Men just don't leave just like that, they said, there had to be a woman behind it. Some evil woman must have put a "fix" on Ernie. They suggested that I see a "root doctor" and get to the bottom of it. I didn't have the strength.

It was the longest summer in history. Four years of my life had come to a screeching halt after a Stevie Wonder concert. What had I said? What had I done? If Ernie would just give me the chance, I told myself, I would change. I wanted to tell him I was sorry. I wanted to ask him why, but he would not call. It just did not make sense! How could a man who had spent four years loving you, taking care of you, supporting you—just stop, just like that? There was definitely something wrong, I reasoned.

Every song I heard made me think of Ernie. Everywhere I went made me think of him. Every word he had ever said to me played over and over in my mind, all together, at the same time. I heard it all, day by day, minute by minute, word by word: *"I love you." "I don't want to marry you." "I love being with you." "I don't want a ready-made family." "You are special to me." "I like to be free."*

I felt as if I was being tortured. What could I have done different? Maybe if I did not have so many children? I did not know what had happened, but I just knew it was all my fault. I had to fix it. I just had to, but I did not know how. So I went to bed—again. I turned the telephone off, sent the children to camp, and went to bed.

When you are alone, if you listen, you can hear yourself think. That is the benefit of being alone. When you are alone and in pain, you cannot think. You cannot hear. If there is anything you need to hear, you resist. You want what you want and nothing else will do.

The energies that have been guiding, directing, and protecting you throughout your life have a very difficult job during such times. They must get you to listen and hear and act. *"The Lord is my...."* Wait a minute, I do not want to hear that! There is no "Lord," no "God" who could expect me to believe He or She loved me that would allow me to go through this, I thought. *"If you do not panic, you will be told...."* Shut the hell up! What are you going to tell me? Are you going to tell me Ernie is coming back? Are you going to tell me that everything will be like it was? If you are not going to tell me that, shut the hell up! *"The Lord is my light and my salvation...."* What do I need to be saved from? *"Witchcraft! There is witchcraft!"* What am I supposed to do about witchcraft? *"You need to see someone. You need to get to the bottom of it!"* I don't know where to go. *"You will be shown...."*

Thoughts and images flooded my mind. Voices called out, alternating between silence and revelations. It was over between Ernie and me—I knew it, but I could not let go. I wanted to, needed to, understand why. As long as I had that big question mark lingering in my mind, I could not, would not, let him get away. It was painful to hang on to the threads of hope, but it was devastating to think there was no hope. Maybe my friends were right. Maybe this really was a case of witchcraft. Could someone really do that, I wondered. Could someone really make another person change his mind and heart so drastically? If that were the case, Ernie could be in trouble or in danger. They were right! I needed to see someone. But who?

Eventually, I mustered up enough strength to call Ruth Carlos. She knew everything about everything. I was sure she would know what to do. Ruth was hysterical with laughter. I had really lost my mind this time, she said. The man was gone! Get over it! It's time to wait for another bus! However, when Ruth sensed how serious and desperate I was, she agreed to help me find a "reader," someone who could tell me what was going on and what to do.

That was at seven in the morning. Ruth told me to meet her at her place by noon. Her new boyfriend Po was coming by at nine, but he should be gone by noon, she said. We could go through the newspaper, make some calls, and find someone who could help. I loved Ruth Carlos. She was always there when I needed her.

I was dressed by seven-thirty. I sat at the table smoking and waiting to go to Ruth's the rest of the morning. I had not eaten in several days. I was weak and my head felt light, but I was going to get some help, so that gave me all the strength I needed.

I rang the bell several times, but Ruth did not answer. A man came out of the building, and I went in the door as he left. I took the elevator to Ruth's apartment and knocked on the door. No answer. Where the hell was she? I went to all her usual haunts. The bar down the street. Her friend Minnie's house. The numbers hole. Ruth was nowhere to be found.

I went back to her apartment. She was still not there. Finally, at two o'clock, I bought the paper myself and went back home. Ruth must have gone out with Po, I figured. I would have to go it alone and find a reader by myself. Oh, well, I thought, riding home on the subway, the voice said I would be shown what to do.

The paper was full of names and advertisements of people who guaranteed to do all sorts of things. They could save your marriage, get you the money you needed to get out of debt, and remove all kinds of jinxes, crosses, and hexes. I started thinking there really was something to this witchcraft stuff. I had heard Grandma talk about it, but I never paid any attention to her. Reading through the ads in the paper that day, I began to develop a healthy respect for the fact that people really could ruin your life through witchcraft. They could take your man, dry up your money supply, and make you lose your mind. I thought: I had not worked in months. I had no money, school was about to start, and Ernie was gone. This was witchcraft for sure! This was serious! I was in big trouble, and I needed help fast!

▲▼▲▼▲

The mind is such a wonderful instrument. It can create and destroy in a matter of seconds. Ernie's mind had destroyed our relationship. His mind told him it was done, over, finished. It was good while it lasted, but the time had come to move on. My mind created images of fear and failure. My mind told me I needed Ernie, that without him I was nothing. My mind told me that if I had to start all over again, I would die. No one would want me. There was something wrong with me. I was ugly. Ernie's mind told him that he was free to make choices and decisions in his own best interest, that no matter what, he had to look out for himself. My mind told me that people you love should love you back, no matter what. People you loved and wanted and needed should not leave you. They owed you. Ernie's mind told him there was something better out there for him and the time had come to seek it out. My mind said I wasn't good enough for him. Ernie's mind said that it was time for him to settle down, raise a family, and get on with life. He had to make a choice. He had made it. My mind said: if I cannot have him, no one will have him.

The mind will create what you need to see and hear. The mind will also play tricks on you.

I kept reading the ads. One said, *"If your loved one has left you, there is only ONE MAN who can help you!"* That sure seemed to fit my case, I thought. I read on. *"It takes a SPECIAL POWER to clear FINANCIAL BLOCKS! I've got it"* I really did need something special. The ad was for a "Dr. Bones." I decided he was the one who could help me. He could save me. I made the call. As soon as I walked in the door to his "office" apartment, however, I knew I had made a mistake. But I was desperate, so I sat down.

There were at least twenty people in the waiting room, a living room cluttered with old furniture, nick-nacks, newspapers, and dust. Everyone in the room was at least sixty years old, and most of them were nodding off. Old-time spirituals were playing on an ancient stereo. The record was scratched, so the same line would repeat three or four times before it jumped to the next song. That didn't bother me. What bothered me was that the room was so dark. It felt dark. It seemed as if a presence, a fog, was hanging over me and everyone else in it. No one else seemed to notice it. I noticed everything. The old newspaper clippings on the wall, the roaches playing tag on the mantlepiece, the smell of sickness that lingered over some of the people, and the smell of incense in the air. I was quite familiar with the latter smell. Grandma always burned incense when she was not feeling well.

When Dr. Bones called me, I jumped to my feet and almost knocked over the all-in-one table lamp. He smiled and led me into the kitchen. It was almost as cluttered as the living room. In fact, he had two living room-type chairs at the kitchen table. On the table was a white candle, several glasses of water, and an opened Bible. Around the room were hundreds of jars of stuff: sticks, twigs, powders, and pebbles. He began by turning the pages of the Bible and, without asking me my name, started to tell me about my life: my mother's death, my childhood of abuse and neglect, how many children I had, and the order of their birth. I never said a word. He went on to speak about my failed relationships and the present situation I was in and my financial devastation. He couldn't come up with Ernie's name, but he knew it began with the letter "E." I was shocked.

He told me not to worry about Ernie. He would be back to marry me. He put together a jar of stuff for me. I was to wash my hands with it, three times a day for ten days. I gave him fifty dollars. If things did not improve, he said, I was to come back in ten days. When I left, I was so excited I almost ran home to sit by the telephone to wait for Ernie's proposal.

The telephone rang three days later. It was Ruth's sister Fannie. Ruth was dead, she said. She had been shot in the head, in her apartment, three days ago. Her friend Minnie was found dead in the apartment with her. She had been beaten to death with a hammer. Ruth did not have any insurance. There was no money. What could I do? Could I come over? Once I stopped screaming and found my mind, I told Fannie I would do anything, everything, I could.

Ruth was dead. It could not be true. What in the world was I going to do without Ruth? How was I going to figure things out? Who was going to keep me in line, on track, and out of trouble?

I got dressed and took a taxi to Ruth's apartment building. Everything seemed normal. I took the elevator upstairs. There were two police officers standing in front of her door. A strip of yellow tape was across the entrance to the apartment. I walked right up to the door and started past the police. They grabbed me. I told them that this was my friend's apartment, that I was supposed to meet her three days ago and she never showed up. The police told me she had been killed three days ago at approximately ten in the morning. They started barraging me with questions. When had I last spoken to her? What had she said? What were her plans? Who was with her when I spoke to her? I told them everything I knew. As I was speaking, the face of the man who had left the building that day flashed before me. I told them that too.

Ruth's body looked horrible. Her face was bloated, her hair was straight, and she had on pink lipstick. That was strange. Ruth never straightened her hair and she never wore lipstick. I sat staring at her body for hours. The police said they believed Ruth had been involved in a drug deal that had gone bad. Someone must have thought she had drugs she did not have. Minnie must have been beaten and tortured as a way to get Ruth to talk. Minnie's son, who found the bodies, had said there were signs of her having been beaten in every room of the house. Her bleeding body had been dragged into the closet. That's where he found her. Ruth had been shot, in her nightgown, in her bedroom.

I told the police the killer had to be someone Ruth knew

because she never opened her door unless she knew you were coming. Then I thought: *I could have been there!* I could have been in that apartment with Ruth, looking through the newspaper like we'd planned, trying to find a reader to help save my failed romance. Minnie had five children. Now they had no mother. It could have been me!

I gave every dime I had to Fannie for Ruth's funeral. Ten days after my first visit to Dr. Bones, my best friend was dead, my telephone had been disconnected, I was two months behind in paying my rent, there was nothing in the refrigerator, and Ernie had not called to propose to me. I called Dr. Bones, who told me to come right over. This time, he let me in on the seriousness of my problem. Somebody had "fixed" my boyfriend so that he would either leave me or I would die, he said. Someone had brought an evil spirit into my house. That spirit had destroyed my relationship and had made Ernie think he did not love me. The spirit was what was creating problems for me financially and otherwise. When I told him about Ruth, how she had died, and how I could have been there, he slammed his hand on the table and shouted, "It's the spirit!" I was in great danger, he warned. The spirit meant for me to be killed too! This was serious! Then he started chanting: "Thank you, Jesus! Thank you, Jesus! Yes, yes! Thank you, Jesus!"

The spirit was in my stomach, he said. He could get it out. All I had to do was to take off my panties and let him put some "Run Devil Run" oil in my vagina. It would cost another seventy-five dollars, but it would fix everything.

That was when reality hit me. I was desperate. I was frightened. I was lonely. I was sure I needed help. What I was not, however, was crazy! What did Ruth's death, Ernie leaving me, my not having a telephone, and owing back rent have to do with my vagina? I asked.

He became very stern. "If you want to get your life together, stop acting foolish! I see hundreds of people a week. I help them all! What makes you think I want you?"

It was a good question, but then I remembered all the other women in the waiting room were at least fifty or sixty years old.

"I'll tell you what. Give me the oil and I'll put it where it should be." Reluctantly, he handed me the bottle of oil and pointed me to the bathroom.

My pants were down around my ankles, I was smelling the oil and reading the label, trying to figure out its contents, when the good doctor crept into the bathroom behind me. When I saw his face, I knew my telephone would not be coming on, Ernie would not be coming back, and I would probably be evicted. "Please, don't..." were the only words I could get out of my mouth. Scrambling away from him, I dropped the oil. Dr. Bones screamed, "Oh, shit!" and fell to his knees to try to save it. Pulling up my pants and stepping over him at the same time, I ran out of the bathroom. I grabbed my things from the living room chair in the kitchen and left. Three blocks away, I started crying. I cried all the way home.

ᐱᐱᐱ

What was I going to do now? Ruth was dead, and I had probably seen her murderer. He was sure to come after me. Ernie was gone. He had another woman who had put a spell on me. He would probably lose his mind, and I had an evil spirit in my stomach. I was broke, and my children were coming home in two days to a house with no food and no telephone. Dr. Bones was mad and would probably put a curse on me. I was desperate, and I panicked. I was alone, and I did not know what to do. I was ashamed of myself for all I had done, and I needed to find a way out.

That was the problem. I did not want to understand, I wanted out. I did not want to open my eyes. I wanted to stay in the twilight zone. Ernie was no longer the issue. I was the issue and I had to face it.

I could not. It was too horrible to think about. I spent the afternoon moping around the house. Every time I thought about

Ruth, Ernie, or Dr. Bones, I would start crying again. I sat on the edge of the bed for hours, just letting the thoughts run through my mind. Without thinking, I picked up the newspaper. A little below the advertisement for Dr. Bones I saw the words: "FREE CONSULTATION BY TELEPHONE."

How dumb could I be? Dumb enough to call. I went to the public telephone at the corner. The line was busy for fifteen minutes. Finally, a woman answered on the other end on the first ring. She began immediately by saying, "Let us pray."

For several minutes, a soft, melodic voice filled my mind. I was told how beautiful I was and how much God loved me. The woman said a prayer for my clarity and peace. She told me that everything I needed to know I already knew. Everything I wanted I already had, she said. All I needed to do was to ask for it and have faith. She instructed me to confess my heart to God. To tell God exactly what I felt, thought, wanted, and needed. She told me I needed to "get still" and listen to the voice of God speak in and to me. She told me not to eat or drink anything for the next six hours and the answers would come. People come into our lives for a reason or a season, she said. When their purpose was served or the season was over, they left. It was God's will. Lastly, she told me that in fourteen days I was to put twenty-five dollars in an envelope and send it to Post Office Box G.O.D. in Brooklyn.

I went home and followed all of the instructions I had been given. The day after the children returned from camp, I got called to work on a temporary assignment. I made arrangements with the landlord to pay my back rent. Wayne gave me the money to get the telephone turned back on and buy some food. When I received my first paycheck, I put one hundred dollars in an envelope and mailed it to the post office box. A few days later, I received a thank-you note from "Mother Mary." At the bottom of the card was a scripture: *"For the Lord thy God will hold thy right hand, saying unto thee: I will help thee. I will make thee a new, sharp threshing instrument having teeth."*

Three weeks later, Ernie's sister told me he was engaged to be married. Two weeks after that, I started law school.

THE Journal

Everything must change. In different ways, at different times.
That's what makes life so confusing. Me, I can't seem to
figure out when something is changing and when I am
simply getting jammed! I guess what turns change into a
nightmare for me is the insecurity of it all. I feel very
insecure whenever I am confronted with change, and that
insecurity creates so much confusion for me. Insecurity
makes me think I am always "the blame" or "at fault."
When I feel insecure, I get confused about the meaning and
purpose of what is going on. Insecurity, confusion, and
fear of change places me on a mental treadmill. I find
myself feeling insecure about myself, about being a woman,
about being a Black woman, about being a Black woman
who feels confused. Then I really get confused and
frightened. Then I think to myself, "Hey what's going on
here? Is this being done to me because I'm a woman? Is
this being done to me because I'm a Black woman?" Of
course, I never get an answer because I'm asking myself
and I'm already confused!

I must start thinking of myself as being a responsible participant in
the ever-constant changes of life. Change is not my
punishment. It is not evidence of my failure. Change is the
constant, consistent development of new ideas, beliefs, and
understandings. I know I am resisting change by
bemoaning the way things used to be. I know I am fighting

change by asking disempowering questions like, "Why is this happening to me again?" I know I am being suspicious of change by feeling as if I must always be on the alert so that I do not get jammed. Unfortunately, by the time I figure out what is really going on, I've already been jammed, and the change has taken place anyway. Eventually, because I have no choice, I often surrender to change. And when I do, I find that it actually takes place rather gradually and peacefully. I am not saying that it still does not confuse me though.

Some people try to support me in facing change. They tell me I can do "it," I should do "it," and that I am, in fact, doing "it." I, on the other hand, am so insecure and confused, I have no idea what "it" is, but I guess I keep on doing "it," anyway. I get confused when "it" works for me, and even more confused when "it" does not work. I finally realize that the "it" is life. Doing "it" means taking the time to figure out how to make my life work and bring me the things I want without getting jammed.

I have been so insecure, fearful, and confused that I believed I did not have the ability, the right, or the necessary support to make life work for me. I bought into the notion that I could have what I wanted and did not deserve better than I had. Insecurity told me that I was not good enough. Confusion made me believe that I did not know what to do. Fear held me grounded in the very place I did not want to be.

There is one simple way to get off this treadmill and stop jamming myself: I must tell the truth to myself about myself. If that does not work, I must ask someone else to tell it to me. When they speak to me, I must listen. The time has come for me to do "it." I have no more time to throw away running around trying to figure out what is going on. I am going on!

CHAPTER 20

The Picture of Guilt

When I got the letter, I almost fainted. The Department of Human Resources was investigating me for welfare fraud, punishable by five years in jail and a fine of a hundred thousand dollars. I was to report for a hearing in two weeks. Holy shit! I had finally gotten off welfare after eleven years, and now they wanted to ask me about fraud! I have just started law school, I thought. I am on my way to doing something with myself. I cannot go to jail!

Then I panicked. Who was going to take care of my children? How could I ever be a lawyer if I had a criminal record? I know, I thought: I'll pay the money back. I'll walk in there, admit everything, and pay them their stinking money back. Then I thought: Where am I going to get that kind of money? Holy shit! I am going to jail!

After I paced the floor for several hours, I called Bunny. I knew she would know exactly what to do.

Bunny asked me if I wanted to go get a reading done. I told her about my experiences with Dr. Bones and decided to pass. She insisted that she was going to take me to someone good, a priest, who would let me know exactly what to do. Reluctantly, I agreed. She took me to see Lolita Rodriguez, a priest and diviner in the culture of Santeria. Bunny explained that Santeria was really a form of the Yoruba culture I had learned about when I was younger and going to African dance classes with her. The Latin community practiced it differently, she said, but it all came from the same root: Africa. She also told me that Africans do not say "reader"—that is not part of their culture. Instead, they say "diviner."

Lolita was, at the time, Bunny's spiritual godmother. She was a beautiful, soft-spoken, genuinely caring woman, and an awesome diviner. She gave me a real clear idea about what had been happening in my life. She told me I had been sabotaging myself, that I had fallen off from my mission as a spiritual being. I was destined to be a priest and spiritual teacher, she said. However, because I had not been listening to my own inner voice, I had placed myself in situations that were designed to force me back on course. Regarding the situation at hand with the public assistance people, Lolita told me there were ceremonies I would have to go through and rituals I would have to perform. If I complied with the mandates, she said I would not go to jail, and all of my troubles would be over. She went on to say that if I chose not to comply with my obligations, I would not only not find satisfaction in my life or relationships, I would not realize my full potential, and I would lose something I treasured very much. I listened to her and decided she was out of her mind. I glanced at Bunny, who was taking copious notes as Lolita outlined everything that was entailed in her plan for my salvation.

When we left, I told Bunny she was crazy, and that what Lolita had said had frightened me. What mission did I have? How was I supposed to know what it was? I was getting ready to go to law school. What did that have to do with spirituality? I had a million questions, most of which Bunny tried to answer. She reminded me of things I had learned when I was younger. She asked, did I keep a candle and a glass of water for the ancestors? No. Did I remember to pour libations of thanksgiving to the earth? No. Did I pray for guidance every day? No. Those were my obligations to the spirit world, she said. If I did those things, confessed my heart of all wrongdoings, and believed in God, I would be just fine.

That seemed easy enough. I began as soon as I got home. I started praying. At first I prayed to be saved, but the frantic pleading and begging soon got on my own nerves, so I changed to the confession part. I confessed everything I had ever done in life, from stealing Uncle Lee's money to cheating on Charlie. I confessed the negative things I had thought as well as those I had done. I confessed feelings too. I confessed feelings of ugliness, insecurity, and fear of being alone. The more I prayed, the better I felt.

I remembered what Bunny had said about the ancestors. I went out and bought a candle and placed it, lit, next to a glass of water in my bedroom. Every day, sometimes two and three times a day, I would ask the ancestors for guidance. I asked them for forgiveness and strength. Mind you, this was no easy task. I felt absolutely ridiculous and embarrassed about the things I heard myself saying. The only thing that kept me going was my fear of going to jail. To avoid that, I was willing to hop on one foot and bark at the moon.

One day, a very strange thing happened. I had just come home from school and I went into my bedroom to pray. When I got to the door of the room, I saw that the entire room was glowing. It was not dark outside, but I could see the reflection of the candle beaming on every wall. It frightened me. I stepped into the room, thinking it was on fire. I could sense a presence, like a mist, all over my body. My heart was pounding and my mind was racing. Very quietly, I heard something move behind me. I could not turn around. Then I felt the touch and heard the voice in my ear whisper, "It is done. Stop asking and give thanks. It is done." I felt faint. I closed my eyes briefly. When I opened them again, the room was back to normal.

I was a total wreck. I did not want to believe what had just happened. I could not believe it. I was a rational, intelligent, educated person. I remembered having similar experiences in the past—the voices, the images, the dreams—but nothing like this. This was real. No, I told myself, it was not real. It was a figment of my imagination. I would have continued in that belief until

Damon walked into the room and asked me how I made myself glow like that.

In that moment, I understood that what had been creating most of the fear I had felt most of my life was guilt. I believed I was guilty about almost everything. I was guilty about not being good. I was guilty of being disobedient. I was guilty of lying and stealing, and even of being raped. My mind was so riddled with guilt, I believed I deserved to be punished. My punishment took the form of being abused and beaten by Charlie, being abandoned by the people I loved, and now, of being accused of fraud. Yes, I had worked while I received public assistance. Yes, I had failed to report the income. Yes, I had income from sources other than welfare. Yes, I had been married and lived with men while receiving support from the state. However, that was not what this hearing was about. This hearing was about me being punished for the guilt I harbored toward myself.

As I sat on the edge of the bed, my mind began to whirl. Scenes and memories of everything I felt guilty about began to play out in my mind. I came face to face with what I thought was the darkest, most negative side of my being. There were things I saw in the visions in my mind that I had completely forgotten.

I remembered a conversation I had with Ruth Carlos. She asked me why I stayed with Charlie. I told her he was the best I could do. Vividly, almost as if she was in the room with me, the conversation played back in my mind. I heard Ruth say to me:

"Shit, Rhonda, you are a good girl. You haven't done anything to deserve this! What have you done? Tell me! You slept around as a child when you didn't know what the hell you were doing. You had a few flings as an adult. You were raped! So what? What did he take from you? A ounce? A pound? A cup of pussy? You can't measure pussy. Once it's gone, it's gone. Hell, it's not yours to give away anyhow. It's here for the good of the world. That's why women have babies. They use what they have to make the world better. It's not yours, it's on loan to you.

"Look at me. Look at what I've done. I shot dope into my veins and sold my body on the street. That is why I can't, don't, pray and do that God stuff any more. I have to get myself together first. I am so ashamed about what I did that when I go back to God, I want to be clean and have something good to say. You don't have that problem. You can go to God any day of the week and be proud! You have done good for yourself. You have nothing to be ashamed of or guilty about."

As Ruth's words echoed inside my head, I realized that, in her own colorful way, she had given me the answer to my problems years ago. But I could not hear her then. I was too busy beating up on myself and feeling bad about myself.

I also realized that I had to come to grips with and understand that whatever a person does at any point in time is what he or she believes he or she needs to do. It is not right or wrong. It is what we believe will help us to survive. It was really not my intent to defraud the welfare system. They simply did not give me enough money to live on. There was no way I could raise my children and progress in life on a hundred-and-thirteen dollars per week. I had not always been careful with the money, but I did not live high off the hog. I bought good food. I bought my children what they needed, and I bought clothes for myself. I had taken my children to places they would never have seen otherwise. I kept my house clean and well-furnished. Above all, I had gone to school. I paid babysitters, I bought books, and I went to school. I realized that the welfare system had written me off as simply another Black female "baby machine." I was not expected to do anything other than have babies and survive in below-standard housing. But instead, I had used my welfare money as an opportunity to get ahead, to do something better for myself. The minute I had gotten on my own two feet and could see my own way clear, I left the welfare rolls.

I concluded that I did not deserve to be punished for what I had done. I was willing to pay the money back, I was willing to tell the truth, but I was not willing to go to jail. I made up my mind not to go. And I made up my mind not to be guilty anymore.

On the day of the hearing, I was nervous but not afraid. I had been waiting for four hours and was just about to inquire about my case when my name was called. I walked into a large room with a long table and seven or eight chairs. There was no one else in the room. Moments later, a very frenzied-looking woman came in and asked my name. She sat down and began looking through her files, shaking her head. My heart had begun to pound. After what seemed like an hour she said to me:

"I am sorry to have put you through this. It seems as if there has been some kind of mistake. All of the names in this file are different. All of the social security numbers are different. It also seems as if this case is closed. I hope this has not caused you any inconvenience. You are free to go."

I was dumb-founded. I had never imagined an outcome like this. I ran home to call Bunny. She agreed that it was great and reminded me that I was obligated to come to a ceremony with Lolita. I was so grateful, I agreed to attend one that weekend.

ᐱᐧᐱᐧᐱ

One of the most powerful forces of energy available to the living being is the mind. The mind, which harnesses the energy of thought and emotion, is the creator of every experience we have in life. The mind controls and sustains bodily functions. The mind expands through focus, training, and exposure to new ways of thinking. The mind will also shut down for lack of use. So much of our lives has become dependent on machines and predetermined scripts, we often forget we are thinking beings. We forget we are stimulated by what we see, hear, and touch. These experiences, all of which are processed through the mind, are translated to us based on our beliefs. Therefore, we are not what people tell us we are. We are what we think we are. As we focus and control our thoughts, we can change our beliefs and ultimately the conditions of our lives. Some call it magic. Others call it spiritualism. Whatever you choose to call it, it is a basic fact of life.

We are each also the embodiment of thousands and thousands of years of experiences. The energy of life that runs through our bloodstream is not new energy. It is energy that has been recycled over and over from the beginning of time. It is on loan to us for the physical experience we call life. At any given time, by focusing our thoughts, we have access to thousands of years of knowledge and information. This knowledge has been stored in our bloodstream and in the DNA molecules of our body. We are today the embodiment of every life in our bloodline. That is the nature of evolution: growing and expanding to new and better levels of existence.

The descendants of people who once communed with nature, we Africans in America have evolved in a community based on technology. Our individuality, our heritage, has brought us to this time and place. Throughout that history and evolution, we have remained spiritual. We continue to believe in the individual's connection to the one source of life called God. We have adapted and renamed our spirituality, and, in many instances, have been hindered by our ignorance of it. However, we must, each of us individually, recognize the spiritual essence of our existence before we can focus our minds and take control of our lives.

Each of us comes into the world a unique individual through the experiences of our spirit. We each have a mission or goal to fulfill. From the moment of our first breath, the energy and life force of the Creator's spirit—God's spirit—is the foundation of our being. No matter what we experience in the physical world, we are never separated from that spirit and never ignorant of our spiritual mission. Spirit is the essence of us that is immortal. It is totally unaffected by what happens in the physical world. Our minds can be affected, but our spirit remains pure and untouched.

Each spirit sent to life to fulfill a goal must evolve through learning. The experiences we face in life are the teaching tools required by the spirit. These experiences are not meant to hinder us. They are meant to make us stronger. Yet, we often get confused because our physical experiences seem painful and unnecessary, because we are not in touch with our spiritual essence. The goal of spiritual evolution is what we call "life." Our quest is to find our life's purpose and bring ourselves into alignment with that mission as a way of purifying the spirit. Whether we are aware of it or not, our spiritual mission will guide and direct the events of our lives in order for us to complete the tasks to which we are assigned.

When, as a result of crisis or choice, you learn to focus your mind and thoughts, you will tap into the awesome power of spirit. It happens to everyone at some time or another. Psychologists call it the "first thought," or intuition. For some, it comes as a conscious choice, such as through meditation. For others, crises push the mind to a state of silence and the messages of spirit come through. Prayer is another way of focusing the mind. When we pray, we focus our mental energy on a desired outcome and release that energy into the universe.

Prayer is the most creative form of thought available to the living being. The more earnest we are when we pray, the greater our belief in the desired outcome, the faster will we realize the results. Because prayer focuses the mind, it also taps the latent spiritual abilities inherent in everyone. For some, the ability is to "see," for others it is to "speak." Still others will "hear" the energy and voice of spirit. What we have not been taught and need to understand is that the alignment of the physical body and physical mind to the nature and energy of spirit is the key to the peace, happiness, and success we have been taught to seek in the world.

There were over a hundred people jammed into the tiny basement room. The drums were playing. People were laughing and talking. Some were trying to dance. I had forgotten how much I loved drumming and dancing as a kid. I took my place along the wall near the drummers and tried to keep my feet still. It was almost impossible. The music moved through me. I could feel my ears getting hot and my breath coming in short gasps. Something was going on in my body and my mind I could not explain. I closed my eyes. I was floating. Then I was flying. I was standing outside myself, looking at myself fly. I was not afraid, but I was not in control either. I watched myself fly around the room and eventually out of the building.

I could feel my body beginning to move. First rocking, then in slow, jerking movements. I wanted to open my eyes, but I could see with them closed. I saw the beautiful image of Mary I had seen so many times in my life. I saw images of other people moving very quickly. Someone called my name. I turned to see the preacher from Grandma's church. He was smiling at me. When I turned again, I saw myself standing before me, dressed in a beautiful white dress. I was wearing a crown and I was glowing.

That's when I was jolted back to reality. I was laying on the floor. People were fanning me and forcing water down my mouth. I felt fine, I told them. A little light-headed, but fine. As a matter of fact, I felt wonderful. I realized I had just had an out-of-body experience, and it had been wonderful. I also realized that I, who had been in and out of church all my life, had finally found religion and spirituality—in a crowded basement in the Bronx.

PART IV

Let There Be...

THE

Journal

I guess all of us are on a road to somewhere. For some, it may be a road to a fresh start, a new beginning, a better way. For others, it is a road of healing, recovery, and peace. A few people choose to take the spiritual road. Others choose the political road. Some take the easy road. Others cannot choose which road to take. But it really doesn't matter who you are or what road you are on, you get to your final destination by traveling along a particular path. The path is who you are, what you do, and what happens to you because of what you do.

I have taken many paths in my life. I have traveled many miles on the paths of anger, rebellion, and deceit. I tried to take a short-cut once and ended up jogging along the path of self-doubt. The paths of self-hatred and self-sabotage are well-beaten by my tracks. There is a memorial to me on the path of denial. I have been a co-op resident on the path of pain. I traveled all these paths in order to avoid the path I feared the most: the path of love. Most of the time, I traveled these paths because I did not realize that if I had enough courage to stay in one place, doing one thing to the best of my ability, the road of life would have opened up to me. Then and only then could I have understood that all the paths were leading me to the road of self.

I am finally beginning to understand what all of this traveling is about. It is the only way I could cut through all of the crap

270

people have inflicted upon me and find out who I really am. I consciously put myself on a path of self-awareness. I wanted to be better and live better. I was trekking fiercely down the path to becoming the best I could be. Still, the day I met my true self, I did what any self-respecting lost soul would do: I cried.

An amazing and frightening thing happened when I started to find me. It was as if a hot cattle prod had touched me at the core of my being. It was like trying to eat piping-hot food when you're real hungry. You know, you put the food in your mouth, knowing it is going to burn like hell. Frantically, you shift it from side to side, trying not to spit it out. You try to blow it. You prance in place. You start fanning away at your mouth, trying to do something to stop the burning, but the food is too good and you're too hungry to let go of it. That's when you have to make a decision: do you swallow the hot food and burn your throat as well as your mouth? Or do you spit it out and wait for it to cool off?

Me, I swallowed it.

I asked to know what I needed to know, see what I needed to see, and, before I knew what was happening, it happened. I was sitting in the public library, studying, when I had a vision. I saw a frightened little girl, cowering and crying. Suddenly, she became an angel floating on a cloud. I saw a confused adolescent. She was running, screaming and pounding her head as she ran. Then I saw a budding rose in a sacred garden, where a headstrong young woman sat pouting and moaning. As I looked at her, she was transformed into a diamond that was being chiseled and molded ever so gently. Next to her was a depressed and burdened adult, writhing in pain. As if by magic, she became an eagle, perched and ready for flight.

I felt a prick in my heart, a pinch on my behind, a slap on my face. One minute I felt a tearing sensation at the core of my

being, the next it felt as if someone was stroking my brow and gently rocking my body. A cool breeze swept by. As it passed through me, it took away all my pain.

I heard a crash of thunder, followed by an echoing blast. Then everything came to a screeching halt. Out of the silence, from a distance, I heard a melodic voice calling my name. I turned around to face what appeared to be a shadow. It beckoned. I moved closer until I was standing face-to-face with myself.

I saw a transparent me. Around my body was a yellow glow. I was draped in yards and yards of flowing white cloth trimmed in blue. I held my hand out to me. I looked down at my outstretched palms and saw a flaming red light. Immediately, the light turned green. The green glow spelled out the word "love." I looked at my face, then down at my palms, then up at my face again. When I smiled at me, I fell to my knees. That is when I started to cry. I'd had similar kinds of experiences before—visions, apparitions, and visitations—but nothing I had ever experienced prepared me for what I saw on that day when my soul opened up and took me straight to the road of my self.

I am love. That is all I that I am. My journeys along all the paths I have trod were mapped out for one purpose: to bring me to total, unconditional love of myself. When I can honestly say "I love me" to myself and to the world, I guess I will have no choice but to love everyone else. That does not mean they will not get on my bad side sometimes, but it does mean that I will know how to love them regardless. It is love that opens the soul and allows peace, light, and God to come in.

No matter what I do or what I think I want to do, the choice to swallow or spit out the truth about my self is mine alone to make. If I had chosen to spit it out, I'm certain I would have stayed on the path, searching and groping in some *kind of pain or another. Swallowing the truth whole like I did took me directly to the road where I became aware of my self. It took me directly to the point where I could accept all that I found out about myself and learn to love me anyway. It is my humble and heartfelt prayer that I can keep on swallowing the truth about myself while learning to take better care of myself, so that I can be in good enough shape to love me when I need it.*

CHAPTER 21

The Shaping of Strength and Courage

Each of us wants to do the right thing. Some of us become so obsessed with it, however, that we do nothing for fear of doing the wrong thing. Making matters even more difficult is our obsessive need to please everybody, to make everybody happy—except ourselves. In the process of trying to do the right thing and make everybody happy, we get lost in fear, doubt, worry, and the needs of other people. We lose our minds. We lose our dreams. We lose ourselves. Our lost minds are replaced by the minds of other people. We become walking, talking "right-aides" with no vision, no dreams, and no purpose other than doing what we think is right for the good of others.

Some of us stay stuck in this mode by convincing ourselves that it is our "responsibility." Others simply give up all hope of things ever being any other way. In the worst-case scenario, we convince ourselves that this is the way things have to be, or are supposed to be, simply because we are mothers, wives, daughters, or just plain, ol' *women*.

The strangest part of the whole phenomena of the need to be right is that somewhere, deep inside of ourselves, we know that what we are doing is absolutely not right. We know that there is something more, something else, something better for us, but we seem somehow powerless to get off the treadmill of rightness. So we become angry. We become so damn mad at everyone and everything that we act out our anger. Unfortunately, we are not aware that we are acting out, so we tell ourselves that we act this way because we have "so much to do."

How do we act out? We are late. We are argumentative. We work on jobs we hate. We cry. We smoke. We drink. We sleep around. We tell little lies about things we have no good reason to lie about. We forget things. We lose things. We have high blood pressure, diabetes, fibroid tumors, uterine and breast cancer, and we allow our hearts to attack us. We do these things so we will have an excuse for not being right, for not being able to do that which we are afraid to admit we do not want to do. We do these things rather than step out on a limb and say to everyone, "I do not want to do this anymore! I have a new idea, a better idea! If you don't like it, it is not my issue!"

Now that takes courage. That takes strength, which most of us do not believe we have. We believe we are bound to the minds of others. We believe we are bound by duty, by responsibility, or by the mistakes of our past. We believe that if for one minute we make someone unhappy, we are not doing the right thing. We believe that if we are not right, we are going to lose our teeth, develop cellulite lumps on our faces, and be banished to the woods to sleep with the wolves. Hey, I slept with a wolf once. It really wasn't that bad. I am also missing a tooth on the right side of my mouth, which no one seems to notice. And I am sure we have all developed an unsightly blemish on our forehead at one time or another. So what is the real problem? What is it that keeps Black women stuck on the need to be right and to please everyone? It is the core belief that we are wrong. It is the belief that if someone does not like us, is not pleased with us, or has something bad to say about us, then that someone proves the fact that we are wrong.

Where did this belief come from? It came from your mother's mother's grandmother, who was told she was an animal, thrown into a ship, sold from an auction block, and raped. It came from your sister's sister's mother, who got it from her grandmother, who got it from her grandmother, who was beaten for speaking her mind. She got it from her grandmother's father's mother, who got it from her grandmother's aunt, who was raped, and when it was over, she was thrown naked into the mud. As she lay there, bruised, battered, and crying, she thought to herself, "Something must be wrong with me! Why else would somebody do this to me?"

In other words, it is in your blood. There is an ancestral memory in the bloodstream of Black women. That memory, like the shape of your head, the structure of your body, the length of your hair, and the size of your breasts, has been passed through the bloodlines. It is an insidious memory, one that viciously attacks the very essence of our beings, reminding us that if we do not do "the right thing," something bad will happen to us. Like a pit viper, it preys on our minds, haunting and stalking us, causing us to run away from who we are by encouraging us to be somebody else— the somebody everybody else wants us to be. This latent ancestral energy keeps us in a place of powerlessness and servitude, for if we dare—even just once—to step beyond its boundaries, we are reminded that we will be beaten down. And we know that is not right.

So how do we capture this creature that is eating away at the fibers of our lives? How do we stop doing the things we are not doing and create the quality of life we want? Some of us need "soul surgery." We need to go down into the marrow of our memory and cut the sucker out! Ever so delicately, gently, and skillfully, we must tear its ugly head off with prayer, meditation, and an infusion of healing light. Others of us need to take more drastic steps. We need to brace ourselves by placing both feet squarely on the ground and both hands firmly on our hips while looking at our reflection in a mirror, through squinted eyes, and yelling at the top of our lungs: NO!

That's right, No! No, I am not going to listen to you anymore. No, I am not giving in to you anymore! I am not going to allow you to eat away at my life anymore. I am putting an end to this madness right now by releasing the need to be right! I don't want to be right. *I am all-right!* I don't want to make you happy!

I am happiness! I will no longer jump through hoops, swing at curve balls, or allow you to do your thing at my expense. *I am good and good and very good!* I know that because the One who made me told me so and then S/He rested, which is exactly what I am going to do. And if you don't like it, you can go somewhere else and do something else with somebody else!

For those who are chronically addicted to being right, if you just take a moment to do this, I *guarantee* it will be enough to get the creative juices flowing in your brain again.

⋀⋁⋀

At one time or another in my life, I have lacked many things. Intelligence was not among them. Then I went to law school. I have never been so intimidated in my life. You simply cannot take a goldfish, put it in a tank with sharks, and expect it to feel comfortable. I was among the super minds. The language they used. The books they expected me to read. The things they talked about: cases and judgments and trends. I had absolutely no idea what was going on. Out of pure frustration, I mentioned my distress to another African American student only to discover that he felt the same way, as did many others. Eventually, we all got together. We began to meet and study together to work our way through the fog.

Things were looking up and going pretty well until I got the telephone call: Nett was in the hospital. She had been suffering for quite a while from high blood pressure. Now she had a fever. The doctors thought it was pneumonia. They were going to run some tests. She should be out in a few days, they said.

The first week or so was fine. I would go to school in the morning, pick the children up from school, drop them off at my father's, and go visit Nett in the hospital. I tried to stay with her until she went to sleep at night, just like she used to do for me. Then I would go pick up the children, take them home, put them to bed, and hit the books.

I had ten, sometimes fifteen cases a night to read and brief. I did not understand the cases, and I did not know how to write a brief. I would sit in class trying to figure out where the professor had found all the stuff he knew about the cases. I sure had not seen it. Perhaps it was because I spent most of the time sleeping on my books rather than reading them.

By the time Nett had been in the hospital three weeks, the children were practically living with my father. Nett's sister Selma would spend the day with her, my law books and I would spend the night. Nett was not doing well. The doctors could not determine what was wrong with her. She was losing weight, they could not break her fever, and there was something "strange" showing up in her blood. Selma and I were getting very concerned. As she grew weaker, I was not comfortable leaving her with the nurses, who always seemed too busy to be bothered. By the fourth week, I was exhausted. I had no idea what was going on in school, and I desperately wanted to know what was going on with Nett.

It was about eight-thirty one night. I had just given Nett a bed-bath, and she was about to fall off to sleep. For some reason, my back was to her when I heard a strange sound. I turned around and saw that Nett was gasping for air. I leaned over and asked her what was wrong. Her eyes rolled up in her head, and she began to convulse or something. I freaked out. I ran to the nurses' station and told them what was going on. One nurse said she would be right there. I ran back to the room. Nett was still going at it, gasping for air and jerking uncontrollably. I rang the intercom for the nurse.

"Yes?"

"Can you please come and see what is going on with my mother?"

"Someone will be right there."

I waited, watching the only mother I had ever known struggling for breath.

Two minutes later, which seemed like two hours, no one had come. I went into the hallway and screamed at the top of my lungs, "Will somebody please come and see what is going on with my mother?!" Everybody stopped. Patients and their visitors came out into the hallway. The nurses came out of other rooms. The head nurse had the nerve to have an attitude as she approached me asking, "What seems to be the problem? You are disturbing the other patients!" I was babbling and pointing. She came into the room, took one look at Nett, and went to work. She pushed a bell somewhere and shouted, "Code Ten in Room 927!"

People came running from everywhere. They brought machines and tubes and needles. I stood there totally helpless, watching them twist and turn Nett, shake her, stick things in her mouth. From the pit of my soul came a scream, a plea, "Please, help her! Please! Please! Please!" Somebody ordered, "Get her out of here!" and backed me into the hallway, shutting the door in my face. I slid down the wall and sat on the floor for the next two hours.

When I walked back into that room, I had no idea who or what I was looking at. There were machines and tubes everywhere. One especially large coiled tube extended from a huge, noisy machine, which led to a bed and a body that I no longer recognized. This body was covered with black and blue bruises. It had two swollen eyes that were blackened around the edges. The great big tube led to a smaller tube that was protruding from the mouth of the body, which had only one tooth gripping at its lower lip. Another tube extended from the body's blotchy, swollen arm. This tube led to not one, not two, but three bottles hanging from a pole. Yet another tube extended from the body's nose, and another was hanging out the side of the bed. That tube came from under the sheets, was attached to the body at the vagina, and ran out into a bag hanging from the side of the bed.

"What the hell is this?" I screamed. "Who the hell is this? My God! My God! What have they done?"

I heard a noise behind me. It was a nurse. When she looked at me standing there, she must have seen the fear in my eyes. Turning her head from me, she asked, "Is this your mother?" My lips were sealed in shock, so I just shook my head to indicate it was.

"She's very sick, you know. She is very, verrrry sick."

I wanted to grab her by the throat and say, "Tell me

something I don't know, asshole!" I didn't. I fell to my knees, put my head down, and cried.

I cried silently all night as people came and went, checking the tubes and machines. I cried so long and so silently, my throat and eyes began to hurt. My heart hurt. Every time I raised my head to look at that body, I cried. I cried for Nett and with her. I knew that, wherever she was mentally, zoned out on all the drugs they had given her, she must have been crying too. Nett did not like needles, she did not like hospitals, and she would never have liked the fact that someone she did not even know had stuck a tube into her vagina.

What was I going to say to her if—no, when—she woke up, I thought? How was I going to make this okay? What was I going to tell her about her missing tooth and her swollen eyes? I had to think of something quick. Besides that, I had to get ready to go to school.

I needed to go to school, but I was afraid to leave her. I did not want her to wake up and no one be there. It was seven o'clock when I went out into the hallway to phone Selma and ask her if she could come over earlier than usual that morning. I explained how Nett had gone into respiratory arrest and was on a respirator. She said she'd be right over.

When I got back to the room, the very drugged but alert body was looking me dead in the face. I walked to the bed, began rubbing Nett's hair softly, and said, "Hi, sweetie. How do you feel?" A tear the size of a lemon bubbled out of one of the body's eyes and ran down the side of its face. It was followed by several others.

I cooed and hushed her. I dabbed at the tears with tissues, but they were too big, too wet, and coming too fast. With her eyes, Nett was asking me, demanding to know, what was going on. I explained as best I could about the gasping, the convulsions, the Code Ten thing. The respirator, the IV, and the little bag that was by then full of urine were somewhat harder to explain. I used up an entire box of those cheap tissues trying to get my point across. Everything was going to be fine, I told her. I would be right there. Selma was on her way.

When I went back to school two days later, I sat in class acting as if I knew what was going on. At lunch time, I called the hospital to let Selma know I would be there around three. By 1:30, I was standing at Nett's bedside. I had gotten so frustrated trying to play catch-up, I just left.

Nett could not speak with the respirator tube in her mouth, so I gave her a little pad to write on and a short pencil. Unfortunately, she was left-handed, and the IV tubes were in her left arm, which meant that she had to write with her right hand. Besides that, she could not see. There was no room on her face for her glasses, and she could not sit up. If it took me too long to figure out the awkward little scribblings she made on the paper, she would get frustrated and start to cry. This particular day, to cheer her up, I joked that if she was not careful, she would electrocute herself in all that equipment. Mimicking some of the speech and airs of my law professors, I warned her that the hospital tissues could not handle the "profound magnitude" of her tears. She laughed. After a bit more deciphering and joking, I figured out what she had written. She wanted to know how the children were and when they could come to see her.

I was twenty-nine years old. For all intents and purposes, I believed I had just about made a complete mess of my life. Here I had been on the road to what I thought was doing something with and for myself, and then this happened. Gnawing at the pit of my stomach was the fear that I could not continue going to law school, what with all the time I had missed tending to Nett in the hospital and all. Raging in the fibers of my brain, however, was the insistent idea that I could not stop going. I was not between a rock and a hard place—I was under the rock, falling into a bottomless pit.

The thought resounded in my brain: This is not fair! It is simply not fair! It was followed by: Not only is this unfair, but I am pissed off! How am I supposed to figure out what to do? I cannot keep running back and forth like this. I am exhausted. I am not taking care of my children. I have no idea what is going on in school. In the midst of it all, my best friend, my mother, may be dying. NO! I cannot think about that. She is not going to die! She is not going to die! I am *not* going to quit school! I am not going to quit school!

So, my dear, came the reply from inside, just what are you planning to do?

Beats the hell out of me!

Someone, I think Teddy Roosevelt, once said, "In the moment of decision, the best thing you can do is the right thing to do. The worst thing you can do is nothing." We always want to do the right thing, but not making a decision is the wrong thing. Decisions have power. Decisions have force. They usually take us to the exact place we need to be, exactly the way we need to get there. It is the wavering back and forth, the fear of seeing things they way the are and making a decision about what to do, that creates the pain associated with decision making. Only when we are in conflict about right and wrong do decisions become painful. The rightness of a decision is based on our ability to make the decision in the first place. Because time and opportunity wait for no one, our lives will not be our own until we decide to make them our own by deciding what to do. Fortunately, when we weigh what we want against what we will have to do to get it, the decision usually presents itself clearly.

We must take the time to figure out what we will do and what we will not do, what we can do and what we cannot do. We must work through our fears, through our self-imposed limitations, and make a choice. Rarely will the situation change in our heart and mind until we make a decision. That is when the freedom comes. That is when the resolve comes. That is when we begin to feel better and think more clearly. When we have a plan, a course of action, we know exactly what to do. That is where the power, the force, comes into play.

Decisions help us focus. With focus, we can do anything. The challenge for women is that there are times when we "think" we should do one thing and "feel" we should do another. When our heads and our hearts are in conflict. Behind all of this are the questions: If I do this, what will people think? If I do that, what will happen to me? When most women are involved in an emotionally charged situation, this conflict between the head and the heart make decision making virtually impossible.

Imagine yourself hanging from a very thin branch over the edge of a cliff leading to a drop so low you cannot see the bottom. You cannot move. The branch is too weak. If you make one move, even a small one, the branch will snap and you will fall. Your arms are getting weak. Pain is shooting through your body, and your hands are beginning to sweat. If only you could swing over to the cliff. However, if you miss, the branch will snap and you will fall. Your mind is racing. You are in pain. You know you cannot hang on much longer, but you do not know how far you will fall or if you will be killed in the process of swinging.

You can't swing. You can't hang. You can't fall. So what are you going to do? You know you must do something. You must make a decision. If you do not, the decision will be made for you. You will have no choice but to go along with the events, whatever they are. At that point, you might try asking yourself, Does falling mean I will die? You do not know what is at the bottom or how far down it is. It's possible you could land safely on a ledge or in a tree. The challenge is, you will not know until you let go. You might do yourself a favor by reminding yourself that even if you fall on rock-bottom, it will not matter because God made the rock. By the way, S/He also made the branch.

Nine weeks later, I was still going to law school, still spending my nights in the hospital. I was holding on. Then the branch snapped.

The alarm on the respirator went off. I jumped up and ran to the bed. Nett was laying stark still. I called her name, but she would not, could not answer. In they came again: the people, flying in from everywhere. Well, this time, I am not leaving! I left her alone with you people before and look what happened.

It did not matter. This time it was a Code Nine, which meant they had to take her out of the room. I ran along behind them, frantically asking questions, trying to find out what was the matter. Nobody bothered to answer. When we got to the elevator, someone tried to push me back, but I stood my ground. On the elevator, I learned Nett had gone into cardiac arrest and that we were on our way to the cardiac unit.

Five hours later, we ended up in the intensive care unit. The tube was gone from Nett's mouth. It now protruded from her neck and had been surgically implanted. Although the nurses in intensive care were a great deal more pleasant and attentive than those on the regular medical floor, I took one look at Nett and realized that I was about to drop out of law school. I also knew it was time to call Lolita and get another reading.

Lolita told me Nett's mother was calling her to the other side. She said Nett had been very unhappy and had suffered a great deal in her life. The spirit of her dead mother was trying to convince her to let go, but Nett was fighting her. But there was a bigger problem, she said: I had not fulfilled my spiritual obligations and was about to suffer some devastating losses—I was about to lose my home. Well, that made sense, I thought, I had not paid my rent. I was about to lose my job, Lolita said. I did not have a job, I thought. She must have meant school. I was about to lose my sanity. That was really strange, I thought it was already gone. She continued, telling me that I was in a state of spiritual crisis and needed to make some decisions.

Hold it right there, I told her. I can *not* decide! Don't you understand that? I cannot decide. I already feel like I am being selfish by staying in school. Nett is the only person in my life who has stuck by me through everything. She is the only person who never turned her back on me, no matter what I did. By the same token, if I drop out of school, what am I going to do? I cannot go on just working for people, barely making enough money to feed myself and my kids. I need help, and I need it *now*, I demanded.

Unfazed, Lolita told me that I needed to be initiated into the Yoruba priesthood, that if I did that, my life would change. If I did that, I asked her, will it save my mother's life? She had no idea, and neither did I.

Nett had been in intensive care for two weeks. I could not forget the things Lolita had told me. They did not make sense, but I could not get them out of my mind. What was this priesthood thing? What did it mean? How would it help me be a lawyer or take care of my mother? I had watched Nett disintegrate from a vibrant, loving human being into a tube-filled heap of rotting flesh, and I was expected to believe that dedicating my life to some priesthood would somehow make things better? I couldn't buy it.

As I packed the furniture in my apartment to go into storage, I still could not buy it. As I packed up the things from my desk at school, I still could not buy it. When I explained to my children that we could no longer live in our apartment and would have to go live in Nana's house, I was still refusing to buy it.

After I had been sleeping on Nett's living room sofa for three weeks, I began to give it some serious thought. Then again, I wondered, if I did this, if I allowed myself to be initiated as a priest, would I finally find a man to love me?

Two more respiratory arrests, a lung biopsy, and a doctor's candid admission that he did not expect Nett to live sent me back to Lolita. I had lost so much weight, my shoes were too big. I had no money. I was mentally drained. *And* I had not been laid in almost nine months. I was not a happy camper. Lolita reminded me of all the things she had told me in my earlier reading. She also agreed to have what she called a "spiritual reunion" for Nett, meaning that we would invoke the spirit of Nett's mother and find out what we should do for her.

I was reluctant, but I was also desperate. This reunion thing sounded like a seance to me—you know, people sitting around the table, burning candles, and talking to spirits. With a bachelor's degree and a half-year of law school under my belt, it was a lot to swallow. Even so, I showed up at Lolita's on time, ready to go.

Two people other than Lolita and myself, a woman and a man, were in the room. Neither one of them spoke any English.

The ceremony began with prayer, in Spanish. I sat there, quietly laughing to myself about what a fool I was.

The woman began to speak to Lolita in Spanish. Lolita translated for me. The woman said I had been very abused as a child. There was a woman who did not like me, she said, who cared for me in a very bad way. Is this true? Yes. I had a brother who had lived with me, but now he was gone. Is this true? Yes. I had been beaten by a man, a very big man, but he was gone too. Is this true? Yes. Then there was a man whom I had loved very much and all of a sudden he left too. Is this true? By then I was crying, but I couldn't figure out if I was sad or scared. I did not want to believe what was going on. I did not know this woman. I had not told Lolita what the woman was telling me. I could feel the pain and sadness rising in the room. My life was being laid out before me, by candlelight, in a kitchen, by people who did not know me. It was pretty frightening.

It was just about that time that the man began to hiss and shake. He began waving his arms in the air, jerking back and forth, hissing and writhing like a snake. He jumped up. He sat down. He slammed his hand on the table and began to scream. He began talking in Spanish. Lolita told me that he was saying the spirits had come to help. They had come to help me. They had come to help my mother. The spirits wanted me to know that they had always been with me, protecting me, guiding me, but that I had been stubborn. I always wanted to do things my way. My stubbornness, he said, had gotten me into a lot of trouble, which they had always fixed. Now the spirits wanted me to develop myself to work with them. They wanted me to do what I had been born to do. They wanted me to stop suffering and start living in their world. In the meantime, they would help my mother. He stopped talking and fell limp onto the table. Lolita and the woman started praying again. I watched in amazement.

Several minutes later, the man was up hissing again. His arms moved in a circular motion over his head. He was making a sound similar to the sound of the wind when it blows between two buildings. Abruptly, he stopped, moved his head from side to side, and said, "Good evening," in English. He said his name, or rather the name of the spirit who possessed him, was Ivy. I was the only person at the table who knew that Ivy was Nett's mother's name. She had come to take her daughter away, she said.

Everyone at the table screamed at her: "No! You cannot have her. She does not want to go with you!" The man, possessed by the spirit, started crying. "I do not want her to suffer. I do not want her to be unhappy. I want to love her, to take care of her."

Lolita asked the spirit to help us make Nett better and promised her we would see to it that Nett did not suffer. The spirit continued to cry. Then she began talking to me.

"I know you very well. You are my baby's baby. She loves you very much. Do you know she loves you very much?"

I was crying uncontrollably and could not answer.

"If you ask me to let her stay, I will, because I know she loves you."

Somehow I found the strength and courage to move my lips. "Please let her stay. I don't know what I will do if you take her."

The man, the spirit, told me to buy a purple candle and a piece of purple silk. I was to put the candle on a plate with a piece of bread and drape the purple cloth in front of it. If I did that, the doctors would find out what was wrong with Nett and she would live.

No one at that table except me knew that Ivy had been buried in a purple shroud. No one, not even the doctor who had given up hope on Nett, knew what was wrong with her.

∧∘∧∘∧

My grandmother always said, "Don't believe your lying eyes!" Her theory was that the eyes only told half of the truth. The eyes revealed what you would allow yourself to see, which was generally only one percent of what was really going on.

The way to know the truth is to feel it. There is an energy in your heart that will let you know what the truth is, and often it may have nothing to do with what you can see. The fact of the matter is, your heart, when it is pure, will not lie to you. Your heart is the door to God's dominion. The challenge is to keep the heart pure and to trust it when you know it is telling you the truth. The minute you try to reconcile the truth in your heart with the logic your eyes present, you are lost. The eyes are attached to the brain, and the brain can only "see" what it knows. The heart, on the other hand, like God, knows everything.

There is a level of existence beyond what the eyes can see. This level of existence is very real. There are forces, powers, and energies that impact upon our lives every day, and we have no idea what they look like or how to interact with them. Some call these forces "spirits." Others call them "angels." We do not like to talk about them because we do not want to risk someone challenging our beliefs or experiences, so we act as if they do not exist. It is only if and when these spirits or angels present themselves to us in an undeniable way or when someone else brings the subject up that we are willing to say, "Yes, I know what you are talking about. I have had an experience like that." In the meantime, these spirits move around us, with us, and through us every day, accomplishing their tasks, doing their work, which generally is of great benefit to our lives.

My eyes did not see the bodies of my children being formed inside my body. I did not give any instructions as to what was to go where, how this or that should be placed, or how I wanted them to look. In the end, however, I had three perfectly formed children, who were endowed with every organ, muscle, and tissue required to sustain their lives. I did not see it, yet somehow it happened.

There have been many times when I simply did not know what to do. A problem or situation would challenge me, and I could not see a way out. Yet, while my eyes were locked on the problem, somehow, from somewhere, the answer showed up. It showed up as a thought or an idea that led me to the solution, or it showed up as the money or the help I needed.

Grandma also said, "There is a place called 'Nowhere.' If you have a little faith and trust, what you need will come from Nowhere." Nowhere does not show up on any map. There are no signs directing us how to get there from the highway. I, like many people, want to know where things come from, how things happen, and how or why they work or do not work. I am very uncomfortable in situations that do not make sense to my logical, thinking mind. I become afraid when I find myself in situations that I cannot logically explain. I want to be in control—that way, I can determine the outcome. If I allow myself to think that a spirit or an angel, over which I have absolutely no control, can do things in and for my life—well, then, I am lost.

Besides that, people warn you against that kind of thinking. People tell you this is a "man's" world—owned, operated, and controlled by the human being. Well, if that is true, then how come some babies come perfectly formed and others do not? Does man pick and choose which babies will be physically or mentally challenged? If man is really in control, how come the alarm clock does not wake up anyone at the cemetery? I bet there are many dead people out there who thought they were in control and who would like to get back up so they could continue to be in control. If man is really in control, why does he not have any say-so in when he comes into this world and when he leaves? Or does he?

I remember reading in the Bible, in Genesis, how God said, "Let us make man in our image." I often wondered to whom the "us" referred. The Bible goes on to say that God made "them" male and female, in "our" image. Later on, in another chapter of Genesis, it says that God scooped up some dirt from the earth and "formed" man. What, I asked, happened to the male and female created back in the first chapter? That, I was told, was just the spirit. Everything is first made in the spirit, and the spirit takes on shape and form at another point. What begins in spirit, ends in spirit, I was taught. The form may change, but the spirit always remains.

Still, I had more questions: Why is everything born in spirit first? The answers: Spirit is the thing that is linked to God. The form may change, but the spirit never dies. It goes and comes in various ways at various times, but it remains forever attached to the creative source we know as God. It is therefore important to understand that even when you cannot see a thing, it exists in spirit. That when you do see it, you are only seeing shape and form. You are not seeing the real essence of it. You cannot see the spirit.

At various times along the journey of my life, I had read many books on the issue of spirituality and spiritual science. Most of the time, I read them when I was in trouble and looking for a way out of it. I had burned candles and said novenas. From my childhood, I remembered Grandma's soap and bathing in herbs. I knew a little about prayer circles and the laying on of hands. Most of what I learned, however, I had forgotten. I only vaguely remembered the things I had learned about African culture, specifically Yoruba culture, hanging out with Bunny as a child.

I remembered that I had been told many African women were midwives, healers, and dream visionaries—that the healing these women did was both physical and spiritual. The physical healing that they did was done most commonly with natural elements, particularly herbs. They often made people with physical ailments bathe in herbs or drink herbal solutions. African women, I had been taught, were among the greatest herbalists in the world. They were taught what herbs to plant or pick and how and when to do so, as well as the appropriate way to preserve them and use them to heal the body. These practices were transported to the Caribbean, to Latin America, and North America with the slaves. Throughout the American South, I had been told, these herbalists were called "root women." Although they had no degrees or formal credentials, they cared for children and adults, even their slave masters, with natural medicines based on African traditions. They were respected and relied upon for their knowledge and ability.

I remembered learning that these women also worked with forces that could not be seen, that they understood and respected all forms of "living" energy: fire, water, earth, and particularly plants and animals. Without knowledge of molecular theories or chemical compositions, they knew that all living forces received and transmitted energy. They called this energy—you guessed it: Spirit.

In most African communities, I was taught, women were regarded as the spiritual backbone of their clan, compound, community, or nation. They were seen as its strength and foundation.

Among the Yoruba, I was told, women were considered "dark," meaning they possessed mysterious and powerful forces. They engaged in many ceremonies, rituals, and initiations that strengthened their ability to see, hear, and communicate with the unseen forces of spirit. Yoruba women were seen as the bearers of mystery, the keepers of life, the mediums of all that comes forth. I was told that it was their wombs that made them so sacred and special because everything is born from the "darkness" of the womb—from that darkness, waiting to be filled, housed within a woman's body.

I remembered more: In the Caribbean, "obeah" women were the ones who communicated the secrets of nature. They could interpret the songs of the birds, the direction of the wind, and the way rocks fell to the ground. These secrets had been passed on to them from their foremothers, who got their information from hundreds of years of observation, practice, and success. Obeah women could forecast rain and other natural phenomena, and could treat all sorts of wounds and illness. They, too, knew which plants had a calming effect and which would ease pain. They knew which plants could be eaten directly from the branches and which ones could not be touched. They also knew which plants could be used to bathe in, and which ones made a good floor wash to create an energy of peace, love, or prosperity in the home. They understood that plants were God's gift to man and that, as living forces, plants gave off "vibrations." Obeah women respected plants and communicated with them, and the plants, in turn, worked for them. I had been told that women known as obeah women were still practicing in the Caribbean and many parts of the United States, following the traditions of their ancestors.

As an adult, the closest thing to African spiritualism I had come across was that of the Religious Scientists, but I had forgotten most of what I had read and known about them. I remembered, however, that Religious Scientists, like Africans, have a great respect and regard for the spiritual significance of women. They believe that everything is born in the feminine energy, which they call "Mother God." To them, this mother force, the feminine energy, is the creative, nurturing, teaching, loving force of God— the feeling nature of God. Thus, everything that exists or that is created has to emerge through the mother force. Yet, in order for anything to be born, it must first be established in thought, which is the masculine energy. In the metaphysical terminology of the Religious Scientists, all of this creation takes place in the "darkness" of the "womb," which cannot be seen. The womb represents the air we breathe, the atmosphere in which we live. Symbolically, our thoughts, our words, our creations, live in the womb of life until they take on shape and form and come forth into the physical realm where they can be seen, heard, and touched.

Then I made the connection: While African societies honored and respected African women as co-creators with God, European societies considered women as property to be conquered and controlled. While white women were protected and sheltered, African women throughout the Diaspora were whipped, abused, and often terrorized by white men. Slave women were often forced to fend for themselves and their families. They had to rely on their "mother wit," their intuition, to survive, and in many cases they survived because of their ability to "conjure" up an energy or power that could not be seen or logically understood. Enslaved and oppressed though they were, they nonetheless embodied a life force, an energy, a spirit, that both frightened and amazed their oppressors. That same force and energy is alive, but mostly dormant, in the female descendants of these women, who sometimes forget about their power because they cannot see it and are no longer taught how to call it up and use it to their own advantage.

If I did not think about it too hard, it made perfect sense. However, when I thought about it, I came up with all kinds of questions. And then, when I asked the questions, my brain could not figure out the answers. In the midst of it all, there were some things I just "knew." I don't know how I knew, but I did. Like the time I knew Charlie was coming back. Or when I knew someone was not telling me the truth, like when I knew Ernie was seeing other women. My brain might have told me one thing, but a part of me always knew the truth. My head may have wanted me to believe one thing, but my heart always let me know something else.

Why can't we live like that all the time? Why can't we stop thinking, stop controlling, and just know? Why is that such a hard thing to do? Why? Because the brain is masculine energy. It represents man, who, we are taught, is always "in control." The heart, on the other hand, is *feminine* energy. It represents woman— and everyone "knows" you cannot trust women!

I did not know what to believe, but I did not want to take any chances with my mother's life. Nett had gone into Brookdale Hospital on November ninth. Ivy spoke to me on April eleventh. I did as she instructed me to do on April twelfth. On April fifteenth, the doctors discovered that Nett had lupus. They could treat her with steroids, but the disease caused a degeneration of all vital organs. Fortunately, they said, it was not the strain of lupus that invaded the skin. Her problems were all internal.

They began treatment immediately. Nett improved. She had been in the bed so long, however, she had no muscle tone in her legs. The doctors said she would have to learn how to walk all over again. In the meantime, I rolled her up and down the halls in a wheelchair.

After a few weeks, they tried to remove the trachea tube from Nett's throat, but it had been in so long, her esophagus had collapsed. Two days after they removed it, Nett went into respiratory arrest again and the tube had to be replaced. She would have to live the rest of her life with that tube in her throat, the doctors said. We were not pleased, but we were willing to work with it. Eventually, she learned how to talk by covering the tube with her fingers.

Nett began to stabilize nicely. When it was time for her to think about going home, someone suggested a convalescent home.

I would not hear of it. Selma said she could not take care of her. Fine, I said, I'll do it. I'll find an apartment large enough for all of us. I'll take her, the machines, the nurse, the tubes—everything—home with me.

But first, I said, I have to get initiated.

ᐱᐧᐱᐧᐱ

I thought there would be some kind of training period for me to learn about the priesthood. There was not. The only thing I needed was the money. I gathered it from a variety of sources. My god-brother Olu, who was initiated at the same time I was, put most of it up for me.

The ceremony lasted seven days, during which I was washed with all types of solutions. I was prayed on, prayed over, and prayed for. My head was shaved. Parts of my body were cut and stuck. I spent some time between semiconsciousness and consciousness. There was a lot of talking and cooking, people coming and going, working very hard to make sure everything in the ceremony went just so. Other priests washed me, dressed me in white sheeting, and even walked me to the bathroom. They sacrificed animals on my behalf. There was much drumming and dancing. An *ita*, or reading of my life, was done. It lasted four-and-a-half hours. Many things were said to me and done to me that I did not understand.

At the end of the seven days, I was delivered back to my house, dressed in white, with a new name and seven pots of stuff called *orisa* to take care of. I had been assigned two godmothers, or spiritual teachers, who would guide and instruct me about my particular mission in the priesthood. Lolita was one, and a priestess named Mary was the other. Mary had held my hand for the entire seven days. It had been her presence that really made me feel everything would be fine.

I was given several restrictions: I could not look at myself in the mirror for the remainder of the year. I could not eat with a fork or sit at a table for ninety days. Everything I slept on, slept in, ate with, and wore had to be white. I could not go out after dark. I could not get wet by rain. I could not comb my hair. I could not be touched by anyone who was not a priest. Best of all, I could not ask any questions.

I was emotionally drained. I was totally broke. I had no job, no place to live, and an invalid, incontinent mother who was about to be released from the hospital.

But I was a priestess. Great! Absolutely great! The only thing I had to figure out was how the hell that was going to make my life any better.

THE
Journal

If you want the Lord to be your shepherd,
you must learn how to be a good sheep.
Good sheep do not have opinions
or give orders
or worry, whine, or complain.
Good sheep know how to "baa" and then surrender.
A really good sheep is always peaceful because it knows:
"I shall not want!"

CHAPTER 22

The Framing of the Truth

I had known him and seen him around in the community for several years. He was one of the older boys who dated one of my best girlfriends and dancing buddies in high school. He was at one time married to one of my college advisors. In fact, he had several wives at once. I knew his wife and his other "wives," the mothers of his "outside" children. His sister-in-law was a co-worker of mine. He had seven children by three different women, and he was in the midst of ending a fifteen-year-long relationship.

I was working at my alma mater. He was working with me to promote a benefit concert. We were talking, sharing our stories, spending a great deal of time together, and falling in love. It did not start out as a romantic affair. We simply had a great deal of respect for one another and for our work in the community. Adeyemi knew I was into a lot of spiritual stuff, so he often asked me for advice. As a budding young priest, I was eager to be of assistance.

I was just about at the end of my year of initiation. Nett was still living with me. I was emotionally fragile and sexually inactive.

The minute my children saw Nett, they all cried in unison. This was not the Nana they had known and loved all their lives. She was so thin, attached to so many machines, and, worst of all, she could not remember them. The steroids she was taking had affected her memory and her eyesight. There were times when she could not see at all, and when she could, she saw things that were not there. She was wheelchair-bound. She had to wear diapers and be spoon-fed food that had to be mashed to a pulp before she could swallow it. She could no longer play with the children, tell them funny stories, or put band-aids on their boo-boos. And she smelled funny.

We were all living in a three-bedroom apartment. Nett and her machines occupied one room. All three children occupied another. Because I had to sleep on white and could not be touched, I slept alone in another room. The home attendant slept on the sofa in the living room.

Due to the trachea tube in her throat, Nett could not speak very well, so I gave her a bell to ring when she wanted or needed anything. Unfortunately, the home attendant snored so loud she rarely heard Nett's ringing after she went to sleep. This meant that, all night long, I was up and down checking on Nett, suctioning her trachea tube so she could breathe, wheeling her back and forth to the bathroom, and swatting away the bugs, birds, and people Nett swore were invading her room.

The home attendant also liked to go to bed early, around seven or eight o'clock. Because the kitchen was connected to the living room, once she went to sleep, no one could turn on the kitchen light or go into the living room. This meant that the children and I were virtually confined to our bedrooms, even while it was still light outside, for fear of disturbing her. Three weeks of confinement and answering Nett's bell all night pushed me right over the edge. I had a terrible argument with the home attendant. She quit.

Melba, a friend of mine, was a home attendant. She happily took the job, glad to work with people she knew. I was glad to have someone in my house I knew.

Melba worked really well with Nett. She taught her how to chew again, how to stand up, and how to speak through the trachea tube. Things were going pretty well until the landlord, who lived on the first floor, began to complain about all the people coming and going in and out of the house. I explained to him that those people were generally only the visiting nurse, the oxygen supplier, the physical therapist, and my aunt—all of whom were coming as a matter of business. He said they were ruining the carpet and placing too much wear and tear on the stairs. I ignored him. It all came to a head one Saturday when I was trying to figure out how to wash Nett's hair.

Nett was sitting in her wheelchair. I was gathering the basins and towels and covering the floor with newspaper and plastic. All of a sudden, she started screaming and crying and cowering. It frightened the children so bad they started screaming too.

"What's wrong? What happened?" I asked her, panicking myself. The children were running around, bumping into each other as they crawled under the table to hide. I eventually got Nett to tell me what she was screaming about. She said that a goat was attacking her, that it was biting her. She wanted me to take it away.

"What goat? There is no goat," I explained calmly, trying to get her to settle down.

The children by then had realized it was just another one of Nana's hallucination episodes. "Yes, there is!" they said. "Please don't let him hurt her! Make it go away!"

We all tried to calm Nett down, but she was convinced the goat was gnawing away at her hands, feet, and face. Damon pretended to kill it. He attacked that beast and killed it, right in the middle of the living-room floor.

The landlord knocked at the door. He wanted to know what was going on. Did I know I was causing the chandeliers in his house to shake? he asked me. All I could do was say "sorry." But I could not explain what had just happened. Eventually, Nett went back to sleep.

Selma came by later to drop off some food. She bought two

chicken legs individually wrapped in aluminum foil, several single-service cans of vegetables, and two baking potatoes. I asked her what I was supposed to eat, or better yet, feed my children. She told me that was not her responsibility. Her responsibility was to contribute to her sister's well-being. I asked her if she knew how much rent I was paying in order to keep a roof over her sister's head? I asked her if she knew I was also paying the rent on her sister's apartment in the hope that she would one day be well enough to go back there? She told me that I had chosen to do it, that I did not have to do it. Anytime I was ready, she said, I could send Nett back to her own house. She left before it got too nasty.

Minutes after Selma left, Nett started screaming again. She was petrified with fear. This time it was birds. All her life, Nett had been deathly afraid of birds and feathers. Now she claimed there was a big black bird sitting right on the edge of her bed. She could not move. Gemmia broke down and cried. She simply could not understand what was happening to her Nana. Damon tried his best to kill the bird, but Nett wouldn't let up.

The landlord was screaming at me from downstairs to shut up the noise or he would put me out. Nett was screaming at the bird. I was screaming at the children to stop screaming. They were screaming at me to do something.

I did. I went into the bathroom, slammed the door, sat on the toilet seat, put my face in my hands, and cried.

Somebody once told me that there are thirty-nine toxic chemicals in a tear of sadness, while there are only two chemicals in a tear of joy. Tears of sadness are the tears that burn your eyes and sting your nose. They come forth in spurts as you try to figure out just what the hell is going on. Crying sad, toxic tears is a cleansing process. Crying cleanses the mind, body, and spirit of the toxic energy of negative thoughts and emotions.

Frustration, anger, and fear will make you cry. The trick is to cry with an *agenda*. When the tears start to flow in the midst of crisis, you must know what you are crying about so that you can clean up the problem. In the midst of the burning eyes, the stinging nostrils, and the awful pain that grips your body and makes you rock, you simply must take advantage of the opportunity to figure out what you are crying about.

There is a certain amount of responsibility that comes with being someone's child. If that parent has been there for you whenever you have been in need or trouble, you owe him or her a certain amount of love, loyalty, and respect. You remember what they have done for you, meant to you, and sacrificed for you. You look for the opportunity to return the favor because it makes you feel good to know that you can repay some of the goodness, kindness, and love with which you have been showered for so many years. Even more, it is your duty, it is your responsibility, to do for that person what they have done for you, and you attend to the task gladly.

The challenge arises when your duty and responsibility to your parent cuts off the stability and structure of your own life. How do you choose between taking care of your parent and taking care of yourself? How do you choose between protecting your parent and protecting your children? How do you stop living your life in order to provide a life of dignity and decency for the parent who took care of you and who now cannot take care of themselves? It is a mind-boggling situation. It is one that must be cleansed.

My basic frame of reference in life has long been rooted in African culture. Although there were many things I did not practice, there were certain things that were etched into the fibers of my being. One of these was the traditional African belief that children were responsible for and to their parents. Although Nett was not my birth mother, she was the closest thing I had to a mother and I loved her dearly. After losing Ruth Carlos, I could not imagine living without Nett. I had to save her, help her, take care of her any way I could.

It was this false sense of responsibility, however, that placed me in the middle of an emotional crisis. Nett's presence was destroying my children's sanity and wearing me out. I did not mind taking care of her, I simply was not equipped to handle the problems she had. I wanted to get on with my life. I wanted to pursue a relationship. I wanted to go back to school. I still wanted to figure out this priestess stuff. I could not do it that and fulfill my responsibility of taking care of Nett.

Like Selma had said, I had chosen this. No one had forced me to do it. Now that I was doing it, or trying to do it, did I have the right to change my mind? Then, if I did, what would that mean? What would people say? Most of all, would Nett ever forgive me if I deserted her in her time of need?

I was struggling to figure it all out. My tears were tears of conflict and struggle.

For some reason, we are taught to believe that struggle is noble. We think it will in some way bring us special rewards, or that God is pleased with us when we struggle. Many people, particularly Black women, struggle all of their lives. They have so much to do and say about the things they are struggling with, they hardly have any time to get things done.

Struggling people know how to struggle well. They know what to wear, where to go, and how to behave in ways that will undoubtedly create more struggle. Struggling people impose impossible restrictions, conditions, and expectations upon themselves because it is easier to struggle, accomplishing nothing, than it is to call forth and successfully use the creative force within. Struggling people love to sacrifice themselves, their families, and others in the name of their struggle. If you are not careful, they will sacrifice you too. However, God does not ask us to struggle. What God has told us is, *"Come unto me all ye that labor and I will give ye rest."* The reason we are reluctant to surrender the struggle is because we fear doing the wrong thing.

Forget Everything And Run. F-E-A-R. Fear. When we are in the grips of fear, we forget everything we know to be true and run away from what we think will happen. We forget the times and situations when, without our help or interference, things worked themselves out. We forget that we are, first and foremost, responsible to ourselves and to the lives that have been given us.

We forget that just as we have been protected and guided through difficult times, others will be protected and guided. We forget that it is not our responsibility to save anyone. Our responsibility is to do what we can, when we can, and to know when enough is enough. Fear of what will happen, of what we cannot see, what we do not know, and what others will say about us leads to the belief that we must struggle through our difficulties. Fear of death, of being alone, or of not being able to make it on our own keeps us locked into situations of mental, emotional, and physical struggle that can completely destroy our ability to create our own reality.

When we forget, we run. We run into, out of, away from, and around situations that, with a little faith, we can learn to understand and move beyond. Fear of what could happen, what might happen, and what "looks" like it is happening can push us to the depths of struggle. Then, only a good, long cry—one with a clear agenda—can cleanse us of our fear.

ΛΛΛ

Nett had protected me all my life. I was afraid that, without her, either Grandma would get me, my own bad habits would get me, or that I would fall so low I would never be able to get back up. Nett was the only person in my life who had accepted me exactly as I was—the good, the bad, and the ugly. She had always told me I was going to be somebody someday, and I wanted the opportunity to prove to her that she had been right. I myself had no idea who I was or what I was capable of doing, and I was afraid that, without Nett's love, support, and guidance, I would never figure it out.

I was afraid that Nett was going to die. Like Nancy and Ruth, she was going to die and leave me. I thought that if I loved her enough and took care of her, she would get well and things would go back to normal. I never once considered that Nett would have to want to stay alive herself. I forgot that even if she left her physical form she would always be with me in spirit. I had no idea that I had done all I could do, and that the time had come for me to make a decision: Do I give up my life struggling to keep Nett alive,

303

or do I let go and let her live or die according to her own choices?

I could not figure it out. There were too many toxins in my brain. The only thing I could do was cry.

It was one of the hardest decisions I had ever made in my life. One Monday morning, I informed everyone that I was sending Nett back to her apartment. On Wednesday morning, I packed up all her things, hired a private ambulance, and moved her home. She had a new home attendant, who was excellent with her. She worked with Nett twenty-four hours a day, six days a week. On her days off, the children and I stayed with Nett. We entertained her, took her out for walks, and generally tried to enjoy our time with her. A change of medication brought an abrupt halt to the hallucinations. Her vision was all but gone, so we bought her books on tape. The home attendant and physical therapist had her walking in less than a month. In what seemed like a very short while, Nett was up and around, talking, laughing, feeding herself, and moving rapidly toward recovery. I still could not shake the feeling that it was my sole responsibility to care for her, but I was confident that she was in good hands. So why was I still so unsettled?

I first noticed it a few days after my initiation into the priesthood: a surge of energy that frequently emanated at the base of my spine and rose up to my head. Whenever it happened, my thoughts would become crystal clear, as if they could speak to me. It seemed as if I could hear on a new level. I could not figure out what caused this energy to rise, but when it did, things happened that I could not explain. I still fell apart in moments of deep despair, but if I could make myself get calm and close my eyes, I could "see" what to do. When I allowed myself to see, things would pass before me as if I were watching them on a t.v. screen. What I saw and heard would then come to pass in a relatively short period of time. A matter of days.

Nowhere was this feeling more prevalent than in my dreams. There were certain dreams I would have repeatedly. Usually, they made no sense and were full of symbols, signs, colors, people I did not know and places I was unfamiliar with. I soon came to realize that if I had a dream three times, something significant would happen in my life that was somehow related to what I had seen in my dream. I don't know how I knew this, it just popped into my mind, but I knew it was real.

One dream sequence began on a Saturday night. In the first dream, the doorbell rang late at night. I went downstairs to open the door. When I looked through the peephole, I could not see anyone. As I turned to walk back upstairs, I heard the bell ring again. This time, without looking, I opened the door. A gust of cold air rushed past me, but there was no one at the door. I started back upstairs. As I reached the top stair, I looked up to find a tall, dark figure standing in front of me. The figure wore a heavy black cloak. I asked, "Who are you? What do you want?" The figure did not respond. As I peered closer, I noticed it had no face. It was as if the cloak were floating on its own. Suddenly, the figure turned, walked into my apartment, and disappeared from my sight. I ran in behind it, ordering whoever it was to leave. I could not find it anywhere. Frantically, I ran from room to room. Then I heard the door to my apartment slam shut. That is what jolted me awake.

On the second night, the dream began the same way. This time, I did not see the cloaked figure until I walked back into my apartment. It was standing in Damon's room—the same room Nett had slept in after she came home from the hospital. I ran toward the figure. As I reached it, it disappeared. I woke up frightened, jumped out of bed, and ran into Damon's room to see if he was alright. He was fine, sleeping quietly. But the dream had been so real.

I knew this was a significant dream, and the fact that my child was involved gave it even greater significance. As I thought about it, I realized that the figure I had seen in my dream was Death. At first, I thought it was a sign that something was about to happen to Nett. I thought Death was coming to claim her. I panicked, then decided I would be ready to accept that if it happened. I knew I had done all I could do for her. I would visit her one last time and steel myself for the blow.

Nett was fine that day. She was in a good mood. She was happy to see me, and she was getting around pretty good by herself. Still, every time I looked at her, I wanted to cry. I thought about the old saying, "The ill always get better before they die." Nett sensed that something was wrong. I told her I was tired. I asked her if I could lay down with her. We laid together on her bed until she went to sleep. I kissed her and left, thinking to myself that this was the last time I might see her alive.

All the way home, I kept thinking to myself, if Death is so smart, why was it looking for Nett at my house? Surely it would know where to find its victims. That's when it hit me. The dream was not about Nett. It was about Damon. Something was going to happen to my son! Instantly, I began to pray. I knew I had at least another night before the dream came true. I asked God to please reveal to me what the dream meant. I promised to pray and fast for three days, anything to save my son.

Thank goodness, the next day was election day and the children would be home from school. I would think of some excuse to keep Damon in the house all day. He could not leave my sight until I understood what the dream meant. That night, I had the same dream. In this episode, the cloaked figure was waiting for me when I got to the door. It walked through me, up the stairs, and into Damon's room. By the time I got to the door of the room, the figure was in the bed with Damon. I woke up screaming at 4:30 in the morning and refused to go back to sleep.

I sat in the kitchen rocking, praying, smoking, and trying to figure out what to do. I promised, begged, and, in every other way I knew, tried to cut a deal with God not to take my son. Pictures of his accidental death flooded my mind. First, he was shot. Then he was run over by a car, then a subway train. In the most frightening picture of all, he simply dropped dead in the street. What a shame! Such a young child! Why was God doing this to me? Maybe it was because I was practicing an African religion instead of worshipping Jesus. I promised to get rid of all of this African stuff, to throw everything in the garbage, if it would save my son. It was

6:17 when the telephone rang.

"Hello."

"Hello, Ronnie? This is Alberta. Your father is dead."

"What the hell are you talking about?"

"We don't know what happened. We were over my mother's house all night, and when we came home we found a note. When I went to ask him what was it all about, I realized he was dead."

"I'll be right there."

I was relieved and grief-stricken at the same time. My father had never been ill a day in his life. As a matter of fact, he had begun to study Yoga several years prior and had been living a pretty healthy, almost pious lifestyle. He had begun doing breathing exercises, meditating, and standing on his head. He loved to have deep philosophical conversations with me and anyone else who would listen. He did not eat meat. He spent at least three hours a day in silence, and he looked fifty at the age of sixty-four. He could not be dead.

Daddy was lying in the bed, covered up to his neck, with his hands folded across his chest. Alberta said he had washed all of his clothes and hung them up to dry. His papers were folded and neatly assembled on the dresser. He had cleaned the kitchen and dressed himself. He left a simple note:

Dear Ma and Bert:

I am sorry.

Love,

Horace

Next to the typewriter was a handwritten note:

Dear Ronnie:

371. 512. 274. 376.

I stood there staring at his body. He looked as if he was sleeping. I lifted the covers. Only when I saw the ring of urine making a circle around his body did I accept the fact that the man I knew as my father was no longer living.

Daddy's younger children were going crazy. They were screaming, crying, and running back and forth between the bedroom and the kitchen. Every few minutes, one of them would run into the room where Daddy lay, shake him, and beg him to get up. Then one of others would come in and drag that one out. Things would quiet down for a minute until somebody would have another screaming fit. I did not shed a tear. I watched what was going on and decided to call one of my college professors who was also a minister. He said he would be right over. In the meantime, the circus continued.

The word had spread throughout the block that Mr. Harris had died in the house. People started coming in to see for themselves. The neighbors came from his apartment building, the building next door, and all the houses in the block. The mailman came. The garbage man came. Someone told the owner of the corner grocery store, and he came too. They all crept up to the bedroom door, called his name several times, and walked away, shaking their heads, muttering their disbelief. Everyone commented that he did not look dead, but rather as if he were merely asleep. I wondered what kind of dead people they had seen in the past. To me, all dead people look as if they are asleep.

⩕⩓⩕

There comes a time when you must forgive. You must forgive yourself for all the things you have said and all the things you have not said. You must forgive yourself for what you have done and not done. You must forgive yourself for all that you have thought and wished for that would cause harm to someone else, even though at the time you believed it was their just rewards. There comes a moment when forgiveness is the only way to save your soul. You cannot feel sorry or have regrets. You must forgive. You cannot berate yourself or justify what you have thought, done, and said. You cannot ask for or expect another opportunity to get your thoughts and words in order. You must simply forgive. Right then, in that moment, you must forgive. If not, you will be locked into the pain of anger, resentment, and self-inflicted righteousness from which there is no escape.

The Creator brings each of us into the world as unique individuals. We come to this life to learn the lessons that will help us evolve spiritually, cleanse emotionally, and complete our own unique mission. Our mission takes us into the life paths of others just as it brings others into our own paths. Our lessons come through our experiences with those we meet along the way. There are instances when those experiences are dark and painful. Opportunities are presented to us to learn our most empowering and enlightening lessons. How we face, comprehend, and come through these experiences determines what we learn and whether or not we grow.

Very often, our parents teach us our most valuable lessons. As our first contacts with the world, they instruct, inspire, and determine how we evaluate, discern, and assimilate our experiences early in life. Our experiences with our parents determine our emotional foundations and mental constructs, which influence our perceptions throughout life. If our early experiences with our parents are negative, those experiences negatively influence how we see ourselves and our place in the world. It is most unfortunate that we do not realize we are learning from these negative experiences.

As we grow, we model. We model what our parents did, how they behaved toward us, what we believed about them, and how we felt toward them. If we are not careful, negative beliefs and ideas about our parents can color our entire outlook on life. The only way we can free ourselves from a such a mental prison is to forgive them and look for the lesson.

When Reverend White arrived, I asked him to pray with me for my father. He went into the bedroom, stood silently for a few moments, and then asked for a mirror. He placed the mirror beneath my father's nose. He, too, could not believe he was dead. He commented that not only did he not look dead, he did not feel dead.

We began to pray. Reverend White prayed for my father's soul to ascend. I prayed for the strength to forgive him. He prayed for a place to be made for him on the other side. I prayed for the courage to forgive him. He prayed for all of Daddy's relatives, friends, and loved ones to come forward and escort his soul into a better world. I told Daddy I forgave him. I said it over and over and over. I said it silently and aloud. I opened my eyes, looked my father's corpse in the face, and said something I had never said to him in his life: I told him I loved him. Only then did I cry for my father.

The reverend was sweating profusely. When he finished praying, he noticed that Daddy's skin was taking on an ashen tone, so he covered the body with a sheet and told us not to remove it until the van from the morgue arrived.

It took the morgue van thirteen hours to come for Daddy's body. During that time, Alberta and I had an almost violent argument. She wanted me to go home and get my children so that they could come and see their dead grandfather. I refused. She said I was stupid. I told her I thought I knew what was best for my children. She told me that if they could see him in life, they should see him in death. I told her that they had never seen anyone dead before, that they had just been through a great deal with Nett, and I did not want to upset them. I would tell them, talk to them, and get them ready for the funeral, I told her. Alberta told me she did not care anything about what they had been through with Nett. Nett was nothing to them, she said. This was their grandfather.

I felt the energy surge up my spine into my head. I told her she was nothing to me and could therefore not tell me anything about my children. Before she could get her mouth open to respond, the doorbell rang. It was Grandma. That shut everybody up.

I have always been told that there is no pain like the pain of a mother who has to bury her child. I guess Grandma had never heard that one. She burst into the room, demanding to know what was going on. We told the story again. She went into the bedroom, ripped the sheet off Daddy's body, and stared at him for a good minute. Then she covered him up and left the room. She never said a word. She never shed a tear.

"Was there insurance?" she asked.

"No."

"Horace was always so stupid! How are we suppose to bury him without insurance?" Alberta explained that we were going to check to see if the VA would give us anything.

"They are not going to give you *shit* to bury him. And he knew nobody had any money. We all live like niggers."

She went on to say that when she died, nobody was going to have to pass the hat for her. She had insurance, she said proudly, and had always had insurance, and did not need anybody to do a damn thing for her! How could a grown man be so stupid? How could Alberta have lived with such a stupid fool? How was she going to bury him?

Disgusted, I told them that I would pay for the funeral. Daddy had told everyone long ago that he wanted to be cremated. That was fine by me, and a lot more economical. I had some money saved, and I offered to give it to them to make up the difference of whatever was needed to get this over with. That shut everyone's mouth—for a minute.

The doorbell rang again. It was my brother Ray. Ray reminded us that Daddy wanted his ashes spread across the Chesapeake Bay, and that we would have to rent a boat to take the ashes there. I had no intentions of doing that, but he could pay to rent the boat if he wanted to. That started another argument. There was also a big argument about why Daddy left me a note and did not leave one for any of the other children.

The sparks really flew when, after all the back and forth over the arrangements, I announced that I could not go to the wake or the memorial. As a priestess, with four months to go before completing my initiatory year, I was not supposed to go to funerals or to the cemetery. With that, I was thrown out of the house and ordered by Grandma not to return.

There is nothing worse than a dysfunctional, fragmented family coming together for a funeral. It seems as if funerals are the only opportunity these families get to see how much food they can eat, how much liquor they can drink, and how much foolishness they can conjure up. My family was the absolute worse. Cousins, uncles, aunts, and family friends—all of them showed up at the wake as if by magic. They reminisced, swapped stories, and argued over the time and sequence of various events. And they did it all at the top of their lungs. Since no one I knew in my family had died since Aunt Nancy, I had no memory of how awful they could act and how much noise they could make. To make matters worse, everybody and their mama must have asked me why I was wearing white in the middle of the winter. By the end of the day, I had a monstrous headache.

Daddy was cremated on a beautiful day. The minister who delivered his eulogy was elegant and dignified. I remember him saying that because he did not know my father very well, he could not tell us what kind of man Daddy had been. Instead, he talked about the beauty of death. He reminded us that death simply meant our mission in this life was over. Death, he said, was an opportunity to evaluate ourselves and our lives. Speaking directly to the children of the deceased for a moment, he reminded us that Daddy would always be among us by virtue of his blood running in our veins and our love for him, which would remain in our hearts. However, he advised us not to lie to ourselves about him and not to hold any grudges against him either. Our duty, he said, was simply to love him in a way that would keep him safe in the life hereafter. He closed with the poem that was printed on the funeral program. As I listened to the words, I knew that while I still did not understand much of what my father did, I was no longer angry with him. It read:

> *In our deepest hour of need, the Creator does not ask us for credentials.*
>
> *He accepts us exactly as we are, knowing we are his erring children.*
>
> *He loves us and forgives us. Why can't we forgive ourselves?*

Adeyemi and I had gone beyond talking and were actively holding hands. Forget the part about not being touched by anyone—he was definitely touching me. He had decided his relationship with his wife was over and that it was time to move on. We worked through a lot of his fear and my anger together. By the time he was ready to find his own place, I was about to be evicted. It made sense for us to live together. It wasn't planned. It just made sense.

My children attended school quite a distance from the house, so I farmed them out to friends during the week. On the weekend, Adeyemi's children and my children were with us—ten children to feed and entertain. The fact that the weekdays were so quiet gave us the strength we needed for the weekend.

Adeyemi and I made a great team. We had worked on many projects together and always had great success. Where he was weak, I was strong. Where I was weak, he was strong. He was great at conceptualizing and organizing. I was great at planning out the details and finding the resources to get things done. He was great at long-term planning, while I was a more impulsive, on-the-spot person.

If we had not been in a sexual relationship, Adeyemi could have been my big brother. He let me know he was there to support and protect me. He could see the pitfalls I could not see. He was supportive and genuinely concerned about me and my children. He shared everything with me and I with him. More importantly, he was a peaceful man. He rarely if ever raised his voice. He never shouted, he rarely swore, and it took a great deal to really get him riled up. I had never experienced a man with such a sense of peaceful strength. Whenever I was in the midst of my drama about the children or money or work, he would simply look at me and say, "Relax." When I was upset with him and tried to press a point, very calmly he would look at me reassuringly and say, "Now, come on," and immediately I would cool out.

It was wonderful. Strange, but wonderful. Even so, we had our problems. Adeyemi, his wife, and their family were like an institution in the New York Pan-Africanist community. Everyone knew them, and everyone also knew that theirs was a polygamous relationship. But most folks were simply not willing to accept that he and his wife had separated, so they just did not take our relationship seriously. Whenever we went out, people would walk up to him, give him the greeting, and ask about his wife. When we were out in public with the children, he usually stayed far away from me until it was time to go. If we were ever in the same place as his wife, I almost felt like a leper. People would make a point of letting me know she was there or ask me if I had seen her.

Of course, I had ill feelings toward the woman. She had been with him for fifteen years, but they were separated, and now he was with me. Apparently, no one else saw it that way. Not even Adeyemi.

It is hard to have a relationship with a man when people do not take your relationship seriously, when you are walking in the shadow of another woman. It really wreaked havoc on my already low self-esteem. I wanted to be noticed. I wanted to be respected. I got the general feeling that I was merely being tolerated. As if everyone knew it would just be a matter of time before Adeyemi would leave me high and dry and go back to his wife.

We talked about it. He told me it would take time, that folks needed time to adjust, and that I need not concern myself with what other people said. He was happy with me and that was all I should care about. The words sounded great, but putting them into practice was a great deal more difficult.

To make matters worse, Adeyemi had a reputation for being a lady's man. He had a way with women, and he usually let them have their way with him. He had definitely been around the block a few times.

One night, the children and I had gone to New Jersey for an initiation ceremony and we were late returning. For some strange reason, at three o'clock in the morning, traffic on the Brooklyn Bridge was backed up bumper-to-bumper. As we crept along, we were able to see the source of the confusion: a car had broken down. The closer we got, the more familiar the car looked and the more I recognized the woman sitting in it. My suspicions were confirmed when Damon shouted, "Look Ma, there's Adeyemi!"

I looked and saw Adeyemi walking across the bridge with a gas can. As we approached, I honked my horn at him, letting him know that I knew, and pulled off. When he got home, he had the nerve to be upset that I had left him stranded on the bridge. I told him he should have been grateful I didn't run him down.

On another occasion, Adeyemi's son's mother—not his wife, but one of his other wives—asked him to escort her to an event. He agreed to do so, telling me that it was his duty to help his children's mothers whenever they needed him. I tried my best to understand, and I would have done quite well until he brought her home to our house to get dressed. Not only did she get dressed in our house, in our bedroom, she left her shoes next to his in front of our bed. This meant that to get into my bed I would have to climb over her shoes. Adeyemi did not see the significance of the act. I did, and I decided, right then and there, that it was time for me to move.

THE Journal

There are times when I speak and I have no idea
   what I am saying.
There are times when I write and I have no idea
   what the words mean.
There are times when I cry and I have no idea
   why I am crying.
There are times when I laugh and I have no idea
   what I am laughing about.
There are times, desperate moments, when I feel unloved
   and I have no idea who loves me.
There are times when I feel like I am searching,
   groping in the darkness,
   trying desperately to grab on, catch on, hang on—
   and I have no idea what I am searching or reaching for.
Could it be that I am searching for reasons to speak, to write,
   to laugh, to cry?
That I am searching for someone, besides me, to love me?
   I have no idea!

CHAPTER 23

The Fashioning
of Understanding

I had not seen him in at least ten years. I had lost track of him when he went to Africa the first time. He had been my guardian and godfather during my initiation year. He, too, was a priest in the Yoruba culture. He was the brother of my childhood best friend. When I heard his voice on the telephone, I burst into tears. Oluwo. He told me he was living in nearby New Jersey, and I should come right over. I was so eager to see him I went straight to the Port Authority Bus Terminal on a Saturday evening. That was a big mistake. When you are wearing white from head to toe in December, Port Authority is not the place to be. Every lost soul will recognize your light and try to get something from you. Some will want money, others will want to touch you. Some will point and stare at you, others will follow you around. I was met by a combination of all of the above, culminating with in one very drunk, very unkept man confronting me and asking, "What kind of Christian are you?" He was convinced that if I just prayed for him and held his hand for a moment, he could collect enough money to buy a bottle of wine. I gave him two dollars, and he eventually went away.

We had to catch up on ten years in four hours. Where he had been. Where I had been. What had happened to this one and that one. Most of all, we had to talk about my initiation and why I was not with my godmother Lolita anymore. Lolita and I were not on speaking terms. She had accused me of being disrespectful, and I had accused her of being paranoid and controlling. Oluwo and I made plans to stay in touch.

We did. Oluwo began to teach me the true meaning of being a priest. He never quite came out and told me what to do. He simply told me what he had done. My first order of business, he advised, was to read. I had to read every book I could find on being a priest, no matter what religion or what culture. Then he asked me to find the common theme in all of the teachings and figure out what each meant to me.

Priests, Oluwo told me, are the servants of God. I did not have a problem with that. They are the custodians of the cultures they represent. That did not seem too challenging. They are the spiritual mediums and teachers of non-priests. Hmmmmm, that could present some problems. Priests are the moral and ethical standard-bearers of their cultures. Now that could be a problem. The political, economic, social, and intimate lives of priests must be in compliance with the mandates of God and culture. I was in deep trouble!

Getting into the business of spirituality is no joke, no game, and no laughing matter. When you open your mouth and claim that you are a spiritual person, living a spiritual life, you had better be good and ready to walk your talk. Most of us are not ready. We have no idea what it is we are talking about. We think spirituality means having dreams, seeing visions, feeling things, and generally having weird things happen to you that cannot be explained any other way. We all know it has something to do with God—but exactly what, we have no idea. We certainly have no idea that it means changing the operating procedures of our most personal and intimate lives. If I had known that, do you think for one moment I would have gotten so deeply involved? Absolutely not!

Then, I had to take it one step further. I became a priest.

Not only was I supposed to surrender my life to God, God was expecting me to do it! Now that I think about it, that's probably why no one told me that surrendering your life to God was part and parcel of becoming a spiritual being.

When we talk about being spiritual, we are talking about surrendering our humanness, or that part of us which still has opinions, fears, doubts, guilt, shame, and, most of all, anger toward the people in our lives who have frightened us or made us feel guilty and ashamed. Becoming a spiritual being is a process of totally clearing out the mind and heart and replacing what *we think* with what *God knows*. It is accepting wholeheartedly that God know best and knows everything. God knows when we are truly making an earnest effort to bring ourselves into alignment with Her/His ways. God also knows when we are simply giving lip service. The way God knows is thus: when we are confronted with challenges or obstacles, do we revert back to our old way of doing things, or do we stand in the presence of the Almighty, have faith, and act accordingly? In the latter, we do not fear, doubt, or worry. We trust. At its most basic level, spirituality is about learning to trust in the divine order and divine wisdom of God. And that is a very tall order.

Most of us want to have things our way or the way we think they should be. We want to do the things that make us feel good, even if in the long run they are not good for us. We want people to be the way we want them to be because that makes us comfortable. We want things to be easy for us because most of us do not want to do the work. Well, it takes work to be a spiritual being. The work stems from the fact that if and when you really surrender your life to God, your life—as you know it—is bound to fall apart. It must be so. Your life must be torn down in order for you to rebuild it on a better foundation. When we start talking about getting or being spiritual and our life begins to look as if it is falling apart, we get scared. It looks like we are losing. We get busy, trying to hold on and make things work. We get real human. We whine and complain about how hard and unfair life is, how people are out to get us, how nothing ever goes the way we want it to go. We do not realize that it is our humanness that is not working, which is why we turned to spirituality in the first place.

Without a doubt, trusting God is something most humans have a problem with. We cannot believe that God, in all His/Her infinite wisdom and love, could possibly know better than we what is good for us. We think that we have to give God instructions and orders in order to make certain we get exactly what we ask for. I was once told a story about a woman who asked God for a bed to sleep in and a place to put her clothes. She got a five-by-ten-foot room. Then she realized that she could have asked for a mansion.

We limit God because we are afraid to trust. We limit God because we do not know how to completely surrender. We limit God because we have bought into all the stories we have been told about what we can and cannot do and can and cannot have. We limit God because we are impatient. We want it all right now. We limit God because we are human, locked into the limited consciousness of the human world. If and when we totally surrender our lives to God, God does some pretty amazing things in, as, and through us. The key is trust. The door is faith.

I was living with the kids in my own apartment, but I was still seeing Adeyemi. We were still doing community work together, going out socially together, shuttling children between our two houses, and virtually sharing every aspect of our lives and beds. I was still trying to fit in, to be accepted. I was still uncomfortable. He was still reassuring me that everything would be fine.

I decided it was time for me to go back to law school. I had no problems getting re-admitted. I would, however, have to work nights in order to go to school full-time during the day. I encouraged Adeyemi to go to school also. He was so intelligent and talented, but one of the things holding him back was his lack of credentials. He agreed, and we both started school. I was also getting a bit more curious about how to strengthen myself as a priest, a spiritual teacher and counselor, so I began to commune with other priests.

Your patterns do not change. They are the micro chips of who you are and how you operate. Your patterns motivate you. They let you know what is safe, what is comfortable, and what you can handle. We do not always recognize our patterns because it is so difficult for us to believe that we could cause our own pain. We do not recognize the habitual thoughts, consistent actions, and stagnant behaviors that repeatedly guide us to those places, people, and situations we want so much to avoid. Part of the challenge in recognizing the pattern is telling ourselves the truth when we see it.

When we first find ourselves in that place we do not wish to be in, we tell ourselves: this time will be different. It is like seeing a thing with webbed feet, feathers, and a beak coming toward us and convincing ourselves that it is not a duck. We hear it quacking and still we insist that it is not a duck. It is a midget moose, a deformed chicken, anything—but it is not a duck. For if we admit to seeing the duck, we also have to admit to taking, over and over again, the same road that leads to our painful fear of ducks.

What you do in the dark comes out in the light of your life. It is your pattern, your fiber. It comes out as the way you think and behave as well as in the conditions you must confront. The sexual abuse I experienced as a child showed up in my life as a misinterpretation of love, as sex performed in hiding and amidst scandal, and as an attraction to emotional abuse and emotionally unavailable men. Yet, each time the issue came up, it looked different to me. It was played out in different ways, with different faces and different names. That was the only way I could convince myself it was not a duck.

However, at the core, the pattern was set: I was convinced I was unlovable and unloved, that I had to compete for love, and that I always had to struggle to get it. It made me sick to my stomach to always know that the men I cared about did not have the time, inclination, or ability to return what I was giving them—but it was my pattern. It reinforced my core belief that something was wrong with me. I told myself it was the men. I came to realize it was me.

In any relationship, you are going to meet yourself. You will meet your fears, your secrets, your core issues in the manner in which people treat you. Since most of us have no idea about patterns and issues, we become convinced that the other person or people are treating us badly because something is wrong with them. We set up defense mechanisms. We judge people harshly. We try to find ways to avoid certain situations. Still, the problem always comes right back in our face to stare us down. The secret is that we forget. We forget those little hurts and pains we experienced as children. We forget the judgments we made. We forget the promises uttered aloud and silently. We tell ourselves that part of our lives is over. We convince ourselves it is forgotten. However, we may be able to get the memory of pain out of our brains, but until we heal it in our hearts, it will track us down and eventually catch us in a place we do not wish to be.

You can accept or reject the way you are treated by other people, but until you heal the wounds of your past you are going to bleed. The bleeding may be slow and laborious or it may be a gushing flow. You can bandage the bleeding with food, alcohol, drugs, cigarettes, and even sex, but eventually it will ooze through and stain your life. You must find the strength to open the wound, stick your hand inside, pull out the core of the pain—the memory—and make peace with it. You must learn from it. You must try to understand it, to get under the words and actions in order to stand in the truth. And the truth is this: People don't want to hurt you, they merely want to survive.

You must accept the lessons of patience, forgiveness, humility, strength, trust, or compassion, and you must put the painful issue to rest. If you attempt to avoid the pain by doing to others what you believe they have done to you, by resisting the urge to look inside yourself, or by making attempts to fix or change other people, it is inevitable: the duck will attack you and peck you to a slow and torturous death.

Once we have lived through a painful situation, we do not want to revisit it. We do not want to think about or experience the pain again. The first time was bad enough. Why would anyone in their right mind want to conjure up a distressing experience over and over again? The lesson is trust. You must trust yourself enough to feel bad and know you will survive. When we revisit old hurts and pains, the goal is not to stay there. The goal is to make peace and transcend. People who do not want to look at or discuss the past miss many opportunities to grow.

You do not look back to focus on what happened or how horrible it was, you look back to learn. Yes, it may sting a little, but if you look back with a consciousness of healing, you will learn what you need to know. If you look back with a consciousness of forgiveness, you will see what you need to see. If you look back with the expectation that whatever you find will make you a better person, you will grow, heal, forgive, and transcend. If you look back to blame or find fault, you will get stuck in a web of duck's feet.

Looking back to heal the past will not change the people or material conditions in your life. What it will do is bring you to an understanding that will help you to create more meaningful and rewarding relationships in the future. When you can get clear about your past experiences, you can move beyond them to have meaningful new experiences. When you heal your wounds and forgive those who were instrumental in your being wounded, you open a place in your heart for something new to come in. You erase the old tapes, dust off the micro-chip, and break up the pattern. No matter how difficult it may seem, no matter how painful you imagine it to be, cleaning up and clearing out the scars on your heart and in your mind is the only way to fly.

⋏⋎⋏⋎⋏

I told myself that Adeyemi and I had a good relationship. For the most part, we did. He never lied to me—he simply did not tell me the whole truth. He never abused me physically. He was extremely generous, supportive, and loving. He only had three or four outside affairs during our relationship. He involved me in everything he was doing—me, his children, and sometimes one or more of his ex-wives. He often bought me flowers and sent me lovely cards, and, I can honestly say, there was never a time that I needed him when he was not there.

323

He was there for me when my money ran out and I needed food or carfare. He was there for me when something or someone pissed me off and I was ready to explode. He was there for me when my son was stabbed, and again when he was shot. He was there when my father died and on both occasions when Nett went back into the hospital. When I celebrated my first-year anniversary as a priest, and my second year, and the third year, he was there, doing whatever needed to be done, saying exactly what I needed to hear.

There was one major problem in our relationship: there were so many people in Adeyemi's heart, head, and bed, there was no room for me. I knew from the bottom of my heart that he loved me—he simply had no place to put me or keep me in his crowded emotional life.

I really thought I could deal with it. I really thought he would change or, if he could not change himself, that I could "fix" him. I did my best to fix him. I was there with him when he bought his first suit with his very first credit card. I was there to help him decorate and furnish his very first solo apartment. I was there helping him cook and clean when the children came over. When he had a big project or event at work, I was there. When he needed help organizing, structuring, typing, or completing his school work—you guessed it, I was there. When he would get angry with his wife or ex-wife for something and vow to rebel in some way, I was there encouraging him to maintain a reasonable level of communication with them for the children's sake. If he wanted sex, even after one of his escapades with another woman, I was ready and willing to show him I was the one person he needed and wanted, even if he did not realize it. We shopped for food together. Sometimes we cleaned his house together. I thought that if I made myself absolutely indispensable to him, he would make room in his heart for me. I believed that if I became a part of every phase of his life, even those parts that made me totally crazy with insecurity, he would have no choice but to love me forever, maybe even marry me someday. His son got me straight and real clear about that idea.

Adeyemi's children were at my house one evening for some reason. One of his sons and I were talking. With absolutely no provocation on my part, the child looked at me and said, "My mother said Baba can't marry you because she and he are not divorced." Children can really put your foot in their mouths. That one statement told me everything I already knew, but was unable and unwilling to surrender: (1) Adeyemi was still emotionally attached to his 15-year relationship; (2) he had never fully committed to our relationship; (3) his children, or more importantly, his family took priority over our relationship; (4) Adeyemi's wife really did talk about me; and (5), worst of all, he would eventually leave me and go back to her.

Of course, somewhere in the back of my mind, I already knew all of these things, but I thought I could change him. I thought I could fix Adeyemi and the situation with quiet support and total tolerance. At that moment, however, I saw very clearly what was going on: It was a duck, but I had convinced myself it was a deformed chicken. I did not, could not, would not believe that God would send me such a loving, peaceful man and then take him away. What kind of God would do that?

All along, Oluwo had reminded me that I was a priest and Adeyemi was not. He had told me all along that there were levels and degrees of understanding I had and would gain that a non-priest could not be privy to. He had been extremely tolerant and patient with me. He never told me what to do or how to do anything about my relationship with Adeyemi, but, at that moment, I realized that whenever I mentioned Adeyemi's name, Oluwo had very little to say.

As a priest, he told me, it was required that I be the head of my household, meaning that my spiritual work and spiritual duties were to take precedence over everything and everyone over which I had charge. If there were rituals I needed to perform or ceremonies I needed to attend, my mate, and my dealings with my mate, were supposed to take a back seat. My home was a temple, Oluwo said, not a man's castle. When I realized this I realized that although Adeyemi supported me in any and everything I needed, whenever I needed to do it, never complaining about the days or nights I stayed away from home, or questioning the money I needed to spend when I needed to do something for my spiritual growth or priestly training—the simple fact remained that it would be almost impossible for him to totally be a part of my life if there remained a part about which he knew absolutely nothing. Furthermore, there were certain things that people simply cannot and must not do to priests, namely, lie to them or cheat on them. Priests must be trusted and respected for who and what they are. Above all, they must be viewed with a certain regard. Adeyemi did the best he could and still fell short.

I thought back on the first incident of intimacy between Adeyemi and me. It took place in a car. We had gone for a ride to the pier. We were sitting in the car, looking out at the water. He told me that this was the same pier to which he and one of his wives had come to scatter the ashes of their son who died at birth. He sounded so vulnerable and sincere. After a few moments of silence, he held my hand, looked at me, and quietly asked me if he could kiss me. I felt as if the sky had opened up and swallowed me whole. I held that one thought in my mind throughout our entire relationship. The gentle, loving, honest energy that flowed between us in that moment held me up in my deepest moments of despair. There were many other reasons that I cared about Adeyemi, but that one exchange was the most special. I felt loved and loveable for the first time in my life. I was no longer ugly, fat, or wrong. When Adeyemi put his hand on my face and gingerly drew me to him, I was convinced that I was really okay. I wanted to, needed to, hold on to that moment forever.

When you know something, you often think everyone else knows it too. I thought everyone else also knew that Adeyemi was going to leave me, but because I would not believe it, I did not want anyone else to believe it. I made up stories—actually they were lies—about how well our relationship was going. I told my friends about things he had done for me that I had actually done myself. I told them about the plans we were making, which we were not making. I told them little stories about funny, sexy episodes that had never occurred. I was determined to convince everyone that this was a match made in heaven, never revealing to anyone that I was living in hell. I was actually trying to convince myself that I was wrong. I wanted to be totally convinced that Adeyemi loved me and would not leave me. I spent so much time and energy worrying about him leaving, I missed out on much of the time he was there. Against my better judgment, I did what Adeyemi always told me to do when I got too uptight: "Relax." Against all the warnings I saw and all the voices I heard, against the never-ending restlessness in my spirit, I relaxed. I needed to believe him.

There is a time when we must withdraw and retreat to reflect and heal the mistakes of judgment and errors we have made in the past. It is a sacred time for us to sit in a sacred place and learn the lessons that will bring the sacrament into our hearts and minds so that they may be spiritualized. We do not want to feel this sacred aloneness because we are afraid it will hurt. But it does not really hurt.

In order to grow, in order to understand and get a clear picture of who we really are, we must allow ourselves the time—the sacred time—and space to transform. We must participate in the experience of surrendering everything in order to get more. Because we find it so difficult to face the truth, we must allow the truth to well up within us and fill the crevices of our minds. We must know, believe, and trust that whatever we are experiencing is only a prelude to the real story: the story of oneness with God. Only when we surrender to the void of transformation in the sacred solitude of internal peace will the truth of God be told to us.

Growing spirituality is like cultivating a farm. It requires attention, knowledge, and a great deal of care. The level of skill and degree of cultivation determines the quality of the crop. Our hearts and minds are fertile soil for the seeds of experiences, relationships, hopes, wishes, and dreams that are constantly being planted in them. These seeds grow into the crop of conditions and situations we experience. We must take the time to discover which will grow into weeds and which will develop into prize-winning roses. Fearing or fighting solitude gives the weeds the opportunity to strangle off the good crops. Constantly sifting through and turning over the conditions in which we live uproots the growing seedlings, barely giving them time to take root.

Spiritual cultivation requires that we get up early and be well-prepared to work long, hard hours. There will be times when we will have to swat away locusts and pick boll weevils off our crops. We must be willing to get our hands dirty in horse manure, to stain our good clothes with cow dung, and generally live in pretty unglamorous conditions for a while, trusting that, in the end, the profits we will receive from the crop will be worth it.

If we really want to grow mentally, emotionally, and spiritually, we need sacred time alone. We cannot avoid it. We must not be afraid of it. It is the only time we can feel free enough to take the lid off our minds to clean out the garbage in our thoughts. It is the time when we must drop our emotional baggage, open it up, sort through it, and discard what is weighing us down. We must take the steps to harmonize all the pain we have experienced. It is a time for us to take three long, slow, deep breaths as often and loudly as we need to in order to draw in new life and blow the waste out of our system.

When we are in our sacred solitude, that place of transformational aloneness, we can look up at the shining sun, knowing it is a place in the spirit. We can transcend into the universe, fly, and be free from all resentment. Solitude provides us with the opportunity to boost our egos with love, humility, new vision, and enthusiasm. It gives us the strength to realize that any problems or challenges we have and any that will come will only make us stronger and wiser.

Self-love is the key to universal wisdom and power. In our sacred solitude we enter the realm of the soul and bring forth the power. It is the same power existing at the center of the universe, and we are children of the universe. In our sacred aloneness, we can reach where no human has ever touched us: the place of Spirit. The temple of God.

Being in the Yoruba culture is not like being a member of a church in the Judeo–Christian sense. There are no churches, there are temples. Every priest's home is a temple. There is no specific order of services. Priests conduct ceremonies in their homes, sometimes in the basements of their homes, or wherever they reside. These ceremonies—the naming of children, cleansing rituals, initiations into the priesthood, and so forth—are generally attended by invitation only. There is no pope, no bishop nor minister. There are elder priests and junior priests, who are ranked according to the number of years they have served. There are priests called obas who have been trained to know all of the songs, rites, and ceremonies of the culture. The obas direct the ceremonies and rituals. There are also high priests, called babalawos or "fathers of mystery." They are superior to all priests. They are all men, and they are trained to understand the metaphysical order of the universe. They are the keepers and interpreters of the sacred "scriptures" of the Yoruba culture, which are called the Oracles of Ifa.

There is no missionary board, no deacons or deaconesses in the Yoruba culture. There is a choir, however. The priests and non-priests who attend the ceremonies are the choir. There are also musicians, mostly drummers, who are ranked according to the type of drum they play and the group with which they play. Among the choir, there are those who know all the songs and who sing superbly, but who are not priests. There are priests who cannot sing a lick. Then there are those who can sing who are priests, but who can only play one kind of drum—the unconsecrated drum—and there are those singing priests who play both consecrated and unconsecrated drums. This is important to know, because one of the most important aspects of the culture is the singing and drumming. Who the drummers and singers are, whether or not they can sing or play, can make or break your ceremonial efforts.

One of the most important ceremonies in the Yoruba culture is the initiation of a priest for it is the time when priests come together to perform the sacred rites of transforming a mere human into a spiritual being. During the initiations, every aspect of the culture comes into play: prayer, song, dance, ceremony, and intimate knowledge of herbs and other natural substances. The hierarchy of the priests also comes into play: what a priest can and cannot do is determined, for the most part, by his or her seniority and exposure to the ceremonies. Priests are also ranked according to their relationship to the host priest, or the godparent of the person being initiated. More often than not, priests are invited and ranked according to whether or not the initiate's godparents like you or know you.

Some priests are very well received, very well liked, and invited to almost everything that goes on in the community of Yoruba culture adherents. Others are not so well liked but show up anyway, and no one has the nerve to tell them to leave. Then there are those who are accepted, even though they are not liked, because they are good workers and eager learners. I was among that group.

One of the reasons I was not well liked early on in the Yoruba community was because those in the culture who were truly among the spiritually enlightened could see very clearly my confusion and emotional imbalance. The other reason was that I had the misfortune of being initiated by Latins. There is a definite distinction between the African American Yoruba and the Latin American ones, who practice what is called Santeria. The Latin community was the keeper of the Yoruba culture in the western hemisphere for many years. In Cuba, Santo Domingo, and Puerto Rico, many of the rites, rituals, and ceremonies of the Yoruba who were transported to the Caribbean and the Americas as slaves were successfully adapted to and camouflaged by Catholicism, the religion of their oppressors. The enslaved Yoruba found many similarities between the Catholic saints and their traditional deities or *orishas*. Many non-Africans, including native Caribbeans and Europeans of Spanish descent, became devout followers of Santeria, or *santeros*. As the practice evolved, it truly became a melting pot of cultures, religions, and spiritualities—African at its core, but a distinctly mixed bag of New World and Old World ways, based as much on necessity as remembrance.

When African Americans in North America got wind of the culture, they went to the santeros to get the teaching, training, and information they needed. Those who were initiated then began to practice and spread the culture in cities like New York, Detroit, Washington, D.C., and other places in the U.S. A few traveled to Africa, to the source. There they found marked differences between what the Latin Americans were doing and what was being done in Africa. As more and more African Americans were initiated, they pulled away from the Latin community and Santeria to establish practices of worship that more truly reflected the ancient African culture. Some in the Latin community welcomed the new information. Others felt it was not necessary, not true, and a sign of ingratitude and disrespect by the "Negroes."

In choosing to be initiated in the Latin community and practicing in the African American community, I was forced to revisit an old issue, namely, "Is there something wrong with me?" I choose to ignore the scorn and establish myself with the group in which I felt most comfortable. I worked hard to learn. I asked many questions and got a variety of answers, depending on whether I was talking to a male or female, an elder or a junior, or someone who had been initiated by a Latin American or an African American. I studied the cultural, historical, and philosophical constructs. I relied most heavily on my godfather's teaching. He was one of the only priests I knew who had been initiated in the African tradition, who had traveled to and studied in Africa, and who promoted the lifestyle of the Yoruba people rather than just the surface manifestations of the culture. His philosophy was "do it all the way or leave it alone." All the way meant the way you dress, the way you conduct your affairs, your views of life, and your approach to life—all had to reflect the philosophical ideology of the Yoruba or else you were making a mockery.

In my mind, that was too hard. It took too much work. Furthermore, it would require me to give up the "fun" parts of my life and the ability to do what I wanted, when I wanted. I wanted an easier approach. I wanted to listen to and hang out with people who didn't really care whether I evolved or not as long as I was a good worker at their ceremony. I chose confusion and strife over order and discipline. I chose to prove to the "in crowd" that there really wasn't anything wrong with me, that I was "just one of the guys."

There are times and moments, often when you may not be paying full attention, when someone will speak a word or a phrase and it will be exactly what you need or have been asking for. It can be a simple phrase or a sentence, but it will send an electric shock wave to your brain. A new flood of ideas and thoughts will bombard you. Things you never thought of, never even considered, will rush to the forefront of your mind. Other things that you did not understand, could not figure out, or almost gave up on ever knowing anything about will suddenly make perfect sense. The moment you receive this tidbit of information, you know it will change the entire course of your life. For me it was a very pointed, very direct statement, made by a perfect stranger. A priest.

⋏⋆⋏⋆⋏

There was once a very wealthy, very unhappy man. He had everything money could buy, plus a loving wife, beautiful and well-behaved children, and the respect of his friends and colleagues. Yet, he was miserable. The man began to search for the meaning of true happiness in life. He sought after the great religious leaders, asking each one, "What is the secret of happiness in life?" One told him he that if he gave away all of his money and lived a life of humility, he would find happiness, so the man literally went into the streets and gave away his fortune. He and his family took up residence in a small cabin. Still, he was not happy. Another religious leader told him that hard work was all he needed to find happiness, so the man hired himself out as a laborer, accepting no pay other than what was needed to buy food for himself and his family. Still, he was miserable.

The last religious leader he asked told him that the only man who knew the secret to happiness lived in the Himalayas, in the mountains way above the rest of the world. The leaders guaranteed the man that this wise sage could tell him the secret to

332

living a happy life, so the man worked day and night for a year to raise the money to take a trip to see the sage. He plowed fields, laid bricks, washed floors, and climbed and chopped trees until he finally had enough money for his transport and for the safekeeping of his family until he returned. He made the long, arduous trip by boat. When he reached land, it took him quite a while to find a guide to take him into the mountains. The trip took over two weeks. When he got to the base of the mountain, the guide set up camp and promised to wait for him to return. The man climbed for six days through woods and over rugged terrain. He fought off wild animals, lived off the land, and eventually made it to the top of the mountain where the sage lived in total isolation.

He cautiously approached the opening of the cave. He called out. No answer. He identified himself as a friend seeking the advice of a wise and powerful man. The sage responded and told him to enter. The old man was frighteningly frail. The hair on his head and face blended together across his shoulders, giving him an animalistic look. Animal skins hung all around the walls of the cave, and bones were neatly piled up against the wall. The sage sat on a worn mat, wrapped in the skin of an animal. The man approached. He explained his situation to the sage and told him how he had looked far and wide to discover the secret of happiness in life. He told him of the advice he had been given by great men of religion, how he had followed every word they had said, and how he still had not discovered the secret of happiness. After a brief but cleansing bout of crying, the man begged the sage to help him.

The sage agreed, but first they would have dinner, he said. It had been so long since he had shared the company of another human, he wanted to savor every moment. Ever so slowly, the sage prepared a soup of barks and berries. In silence, they watched the mixture simmer over an open fire. They drank from bowls made of hardened animal skins.

When they were done, the sage extended both hands to the man and looked him squarely in the eyes. He said, "My son, my friend, my brother, you have come to me to inquire of and find the secret of happiness in life. This is a very old problem among men. They search far and long, never realizing the secret is right before them. I, too, have searched and studied. I now give to you the fruits of my labor in the search for happiness."

The man took a deep, long breath, closing his eyes in order to capture every word. The sage said, "My son, my brother, my friend, there is only one secret to happiness. That is: Eat more bananas."

The man's eyes flew open as if he had been stuck with a hot prod. He was sure he had heard wrong. He told the sage he did not understand. He had given away his entire fortune, lived in squalor for years, subjected his family to horrendous conditions, all to find the secret of happiness. Now he was expected to believe that the secret to happiness lay in eating more bananas? He jumped to his feet and began to pace.

The sage watched him. After several moments, he said, "My son, my friend, my brother, the only thing I am trying to tell you is to keep it simple. The key to happiness in life is to keep it simple."

The man fell to his knees and cried.

I was at an initiation ceremony. All of the work had been done. The new initiate was sleeping peacefully. A group of elder priests were sitting around talking. Younger priests, like myself, were listening to their every word. That is how we got the majority of our information, by listening to what the elder priests talked about.

That afternoon, the elder priests were reminiscing about priests who had passed on, sharing stories about the things those who had come before us had said and done to establish African traditions in the community. Talk turned to one priest in particular. This priest had established the first Yoruba temple in New York and had initiated more than half the African American Yoruba priests in the country. She was Latin, but the majority of her work had been done with and for the African American community.

In the middle of a sentence, one priest, whom I had seen only a few times, suddenly turned and pointed at me. What she said sounded as if it came out of the blue.

"You don't know who you are! You have no idea who you are! You have never had role models, so you made yourself who you thought you should be. You think a lot, and that is your biggest block! Your biggest obstacle in life is your own head—not your mind—your head!"

"You must use your head to advance your life, not to hold yourself back. You must do a lot of transformational work on yourself. Go to the river and ask the ancestors to guide you. Let them be your role models. Study the great queens and learn the secrets of womanhood, the secrets of medicine, the secrets of life. You are a powerful woman who has allowed the darkness in your head to cloud your life. Stop putting yourself down! Stop disrespecting the sanctity of your head! Ask the spirit of your mother to help you. Let her guide you. You are destined to do a powerful work in this life."

With that said, she took a swig of Pepsi from a paper cup and was silent the rest of the afternoon.

THE Journal

Let there be light. Let there be an infusion of light into my heart and mind that I may know myself and my purpose. Let the light so fill me that I become one with the life source of the universe. Let the light so surround me that I may be eternally protected from all that is not for my highest and greatest good. Dear Mother–Father–God, let your light come forth and re-create the essence of my heart, mind, and soul. I want to be cleansed. I want to be strong. I want the power of the divine light to guide me and show me the way to that place of peace that is You.

Let there be light. Let the light cast out the darkness of fear, of doubt, of lack, of seeking and searching for that which is mine by divine right. Let the light reveal the secrets created in darkness, which continue to exist in the dark places of my heart and mind, creating more darkness, more pain, more fear, and more separation between my mind and the divinity that exists in my soul. Let the light spring forth easily and gently, lovingly and completely, that I may walk in the light forever.

Let there be a light of strength. Let there be a light of courage. Let there be a light of truth and understanding. Let the glorious light of mercy and grace cover and enshroud me with the goodness that is yours, Mother–Father–God. I am lost. I am lost and I am weary. I cry out to you because you promised me the light of protection. You promised me the light of truth. You promised me the light would find *me on the path and guide me home. You promised me that I shall not want, or need, or go without any good thing in Your name. You promised me, God, that you would be there when my earthly father and mother turned away from me. You promised to defend me in the face of my accusers. I am lost. I am fatherless. I am motherless. Where are You, God? Where is Your light?*

Let there be light, for I am worthy of salvation. I am worthy of love. I am worthy of the sacred gifts of the spirit. I no longer seek pleasure in the ways of the world. I seek only the light. I no longer seek the pleasures of flesh or food or drink. I seek only the light of salvation. I am Your child now, a child of God. I am asking for light. Dear God, put the right ideas in my mind and point my feet in the right direction. Make me worthy of wearing Your crown—the crown of glory, grace, honor, truth, peace, and light. As I speak and seek in the name of all that is good, may it be done unto me. In the name of my most honorable ancestors, who now sit at the feet of God, I give praise and thanksgiving. And so it is done.

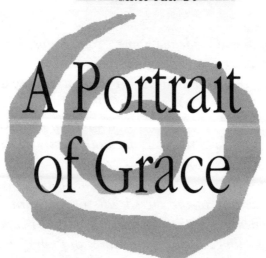

CHAPTER 24

A Portrait of Grace

"You have no idea who you are!"

I really thought I could handle it. I don't know where I got that idea from. Perhaps it was based on the number of times I had sworn to myself I would never go through it again, that I would never cry for another man. I honestly thought I could deal with it like a mature, responsible adult. I was wrong.

One evening, after Adeyemi had dropped his wife, then me, off at our respective apartments, I went back to his house to surprise him. We did that sometimes. I mean, after all, I had a key to his place, and he had a key to mine. He wasn't home. His children were asleep. I crawled into his bed to wait for him. An hour turned into two, then three, then five. By two o'clock in the morning, I was frantic. He must have crashed his car, I thought. He's laying dead somewhere. He must be. There was no other excuse for him leaving his children alone in the house.

"Stop dishonoring the sanctity of your head!"

I played back our earlier conversation in my mind. He had not said he was going out. As a matter of fact, he seemed pretty eager to get home. I refused to consider the fact that he was somewhere else with someone else. By five a.m., I had no other choice.

My mind conjured up sexually explicit visions of Adeyemi with every woman I knew, every woman he knew. I saw him in

338

places doing things that made me sick to my stomach. My mind raced and my heart pounded as I tried to figure out the who, where, and why of his actions. The why was the big question. Why would he do this? I thought he loved me. Why wasn't I enough for him? What did I fail to do? There were no answers, only more questions. Did this mean we were through? How could I take him back? Would he come back? What was I going to do?

I promised myself I would not cry. I lied. The tears began to flow from a place in me that was boundless. Hot, heavy, salty tears flowed from my feet, ankles, and knees. They flowed from my kidneys, my lungs, and my entire nervous system. I wanted to get up and leave. Maybe if I left, I thought, he would not know I was there, and we could act as if this had never happened. But I could not move. I cried from the marrow of my bones, from the tips of my breasts, from the hair follicles covering every inch of my body, and from the molecular structure of my DNA. I was still crying at six-forty-five when I heard his footsteps on the stairs.

Adeyemi tried to hide the shock of seeing me. I could feel his heart racing. My heart was still. I spoke in an almost inaudible whisper.

"Do you want to end our relationship?"

"No," he said.

"You know you cannot do this to me. I will not have it. You have twenty-four hours to decide what you are going to do. But you better know that I will not have this, not from you, not ever again in my life." With that, I stood up, excused myself, and walked out.

Once home, I took a shower, sent the children off to school, got dressed, and went to class. I was in my last year of law school. I had come too far, too long to give up. I made it through two hours of classes before I went into the bathroom and fell completely to pieces.

The moment I walked in the door to my apartment, the telephone rang.

"Where have you been?"

"I went to school."

"Why are you home so early?"

"Why are you calling me?"

"We need to talk."

"No, we don't need to talk. You need to die, and if you are not going to die, you really need to get your shit together. I will not have this!"

"I know. Let's talk."

"You cannot come into my house. I don't want you here."

"I'll pick you up when I get off."

"I have a meeting."

"Okay, so I'll take you to the meeting."

"I need to be there at seven."

"Okay, I'll pick you up."

"Fine."

"Hey, listen. Thanks. I know how hard this is for you."

Click.

Adeyemi picked me up as he had promised, but neither of us said a word the entire ride. When we got to the door of my destination, I told him to talk. It was not his intention to hurt me, he said. It was not his intention to do anything that would in any way make me sad or unhappy. He loved me. So why then, I asked, are you doing this? He did not know.

I knew he had a weakness for women, but this, I told him, was not about weakness. It was about him lying, sneaking around, and ripping my heart out. It was about the possibility of me catching a disease, about him taking a sacred part of our relationship and sharing it with the world. He told me that was not what he intended to do. He wasn't doing that, he swore. He asked me if I had any idea who he was with last night. No, I said, I did not. He told me he was with his wife. His children's mother. The woman with whom he had spent fifteen years of his life. My heart shattered into a thousand pieces.

"Was this the first time?" I asked.

"No."

"You had *that* woman in *this* car, riding with me. You dropped her off at *her* home, which was at one time *your* home.

You left me sitting in *this* car while you walked *her* and *your children* to the door. You pecked *her* on the cheek, *knowing* you had been sleeping with her, then left her waving good-bye to us, so you could go home to sleep with *me*?"

"You know," he said, "it's funny. She said the same thing. She said she used to be my wife, and now she is my girlfriend. You used to be my girlfriend, and now you are my wife..."

I cut him off. "I don't see it like that. I see you both as pigs, wallowing in mud together."

"Your own head is your biggest obstacle!"

I tried to figure out when I knew, because I did know. Women always know. We know it when they break their habitual patterns. We know it by the way they touch us. We know by the way they smell and feel. We know it by the way they perform in bed. A woman always knows when the man she loves is sleeping with another woman. I tried to figure out when I first knew, but I could not admit it to myself without admitting what a fool and a first-class jackass I had been. I could not admit it without accepting the fact that I had ignored my own inner promptings, my own head. If I told the truth to myself about what I knew, it meant that I had ignored the warning glances my godfather Oluwo had given me. It meant that I would have to admit I had heard the snide comments from friends. Worst of all, it meant that I would have to admit to myself that everyone knew I had been lying about our relationship all along. There was no way I could admit that to myself, so I decided I would "fix" it. I would find a way to fix this mess.

You are not ready for truth and understanding. You must pray for clarity and understanding. You must pray for the strength to forgive yourself. For nine days, pray for clarity, understanding, and truth. You are facing many problems because you are unable to face truth. You lie because you fear. If you accept and trust the Holy Spirit as your protection, you will have no cause to fear. You cannot rush the process. You must take time to develop a true understanding of yourself and all those with whom you come into contact.

The truth is that he loves you, but he loves her more. The truth is that he wants you, but he wants her more. The truth is that he needs you, but he needs her more. He is afraid of the responsibility of loving you. He needs the stability she represents in his life. Let him go and find out what he wants. He will never leave you in heart and mind. He will leave you and go to her. He will not stay with her, but he must go to her. He must correct his errors and heal his guilt.

Pray for him. Pray for his peace and enlightenment. You have done your work. The time is now to let go. Trust the Holy Spirit to show you the way. He will return to you, desperate and broken. Do not receive him. Receive the Holy Spirit instead.

⁂

I was trying to go to sleep, waiting for the telephone to ring, and trying to resist the urge to call him, all at the same time. I had not spoken to Adeyemi in twenty-four long, hard hours. I could not tell anyone what was going on without telling them the whole sordid story. I could not face that. I tried to figure out what I would say to people. If this thing continued, everybody would know. I wanted to pray, but I couldn't—I was too busy scheming, trying to concoct a plausible story, an explanation for what was going on. After all, I was a priest. People looked up to me. I had students. My students knew Adeyemi. What could I say to them if they knew that another woman had taken my man? Oh no, no, no. This would not do!

I wished for someone to talk to about the situation. I wished poor, sick Nett were in her right mind. She would know what I needed to do. I was completely on my own for the first time, and I was not faring too well. I needed help badly. I knew that I had been instructed in my meditation classes to let go, but that was spiritual stuff, I told myself—this was real life. If the spirits want me to let Adeyemi go, I reasoned, then let them produce another man to love me right now!

Two minutes later, I heard the key turn in the door. It was Adeyemi.

He didn't say a word. He came into my bedroom, took his clothes off, and slipped into the bed. I did not move. I did not speak. We laid there in total silence for at least an hour. Then he touched me, and my bone marrow started crying again.

I wasn't mad anymore. I wasn't confused. I was simply weak. I don't know if I wanted him or if I simply wanted to escape the pain of losing him. I was not a woman. I was not a priest. I was not an intelligent being, six months away from a law degree. I was a wounded soul, a broken spirit, laying in the arms of the only man who had made me feel as if life was worth living. I did not know who I was, I only knew I wanted to be with him. I wasn't thinking. I wasn't feeling. I was crying my heart out, and he was gently kissing away my tears.

I wanted to say it was sick but, at that moment, it was not. We were simply two human beings who had touched one another, who had made a marked improvement in the lives of one another, and who were on the way to healing issues that had plagued us both for most of our lives. Neither one of us had any idea that was what was going on, so—sick as it may have been—we made love.

⋏⋎⋏

Many people believe that once they develop basic spiritual understandings, they are set for life. Nothing could be further from the truth. There must be a constant, consistent, replenishing reinforcement of spiritual principles and practices. We must faithfully fill our minds with spiritual energy and information. Daily, sometimes several times a day, we must think about, read about, and listen to spiritually centered material. Such material will serve as the light that will cut through the darkness of our established thought and behavior patterns. Still, all the spiritual books and knowledge in the world will not help you if you do not put the principles into practice. If you do not put into practice the laws, principles, and mandates of the spiritual world, knowledge of them cannot help you.

True spiritual consciousness is an internal process that ultimately changes the way you think, feel, and behave. It is an "inside job," which manifests as a radical shift in your perception of the outside world. The goal of spirituality is thus to raise your consciousness, to elevate how you think and interpret what you experience. Consciousness, however, is not limited to thinking. It is the total or sum of all—the mind (our masculine nature), emotions (our feminine nature), and spirit (our divine nature)—all moving in alignment and complete harmony to produce knowing.

While spiritual consciousness does, at some level, affect the body, it does not begin with the physical world. You can be a vegetarian, but if you cannot forgive, you are not spiritually centered. You can read the Bible or any other holy book until you are blue in the face, but if you are still gossiping about and judging others, your mind has not been spiritualized. You can thank your god every day, fifty times a day, for the six-figure salary you earn. But if you are only working for the money and for what it can buy, you have not been spiritually empowered. You can pray, meditate, chant, and do yoga, but if your life remains hindered by toxic relationships, material lack, anger, fear, doubt, or guilt, you have not reached the core of your spiritual essence. If you believe that your husband, boyfriend, boss at work, parents, or friends "owe" you or should do for you, or that they can in any way stop or hinder your progress, you are existing squarely in the midst of your humanness.

A critical mistake we make in the development of our spiritual consciousness is talking about it and giving away our power too soon. Many times, the moment we have a spiritual revelation or experience, we run right out and tell everyone. We want everyone to know and be a part of our new-found "specialness." We believe it is our duty and responsibility to help, save, and enlighten everyone around us. We fail to understand, however, that as we are growing and learning spiritually, we need to build a reservoir of strength. If we speak too soon, or prematurely open our sacred experiences for public examination, we short-circuit the spiritual currents developing in our consciousness. In our spiritual quest, we must first work and evolve in secret.

For a baby learning to walk, making it across the room, half-running and half-falling, does not mean that the baby can stand on its own two feet. There will be many attempts, many days of trying and falling before the baby's legs are strong enough to support its weight, much less the weight of someone or something else. The baby must first be secure in his or her ability to put one foot in front of the other, balance the weight of its body, and move with ease toward wherever it chooses to go. Only then will the baby attempt to pick up a ball, a chair, the dog, or your good glassware, and bring it along on the journey. The same is true with our spiritual development.

It is our spiritual responsibility to serve and support one another. Sharing information is certainly one way of accomplishing this. However, we must first be secure and firm in what we know and must do. In order to develop a fuller understanding of their meaning, we must honor our sacred, spiritual moments by internalizing them. We must first be still before we spill or guts to the world.

Another principle we do not fully understand is that everything is not for everyone. We each have different lessons to learn, missions to complete, purposes to fulfill. Because something comes to you, works for you, or feels good to you does not mean it will have the same significance for or effect on someone else. Your blessings have your name on them. They are not one-size-fits-all. Your level and degree of understanding and comprehension determines how you will discern, assimilate, and utilize any spiritual information you receive. Where you are in your development may not match up with anyone else but you. Your demonstration of where you're at spiritually may not be applicable to anyone but you. Furthermore, demonstrations of spiritual phenomena such as dreams, visions, healings, and so forth are not the "real deal." They are merely manifestations of a deeper spiritual principle, evidence of a much deeper and far more intensive operation of spiritual law. When you expose your sacred information too early, to unenlightened people, without having gained a full understanding of the underlying principles involved, you do yourself a great disservice—bringing human behavior into the spiritual realm.

There are many cases in which we do not realize that our eagerness to share and demonstrate our spiritual prowess is a function of our ego. We want people to know how "special" we are. We want them to know, in some way, that God favors us. This is not always our conscious intent, but it is a function of our core issues. We want people to know what we know, what we can do, and how good we are at it. We want acceptance. We brag—in subtle, "spiritually correct" ways"—about what we have read, where we have been, and the feats we have accomplished through our newfound spiritual identity. We want approval. We begin to dress the part by hanging religious paraphernalia around our necks, carrying little bags and bottles of "stuff" that we whip out and offer to anyone at the slightest indication that somebody needs our "help." Without being prompted or invited to do so, we eagerly offer theories, advice, and information that we have read somewhere or maybe heard someone else speak about—even though we do not have a full understanding of what they mean or how they work. Then, if our offerings of spiritual assistance or self-declared expertise go unnoticed, we get angry, feel misjudged, and often feel disrespected. The ego tells us, "They think I am not good enough" or "They think I am wrong."

In the process of spiritual development, one must undergo various rites. These include spiritual initiations, which alter the molecular structure of your mind and influence the state of your consciousness. As we move into the Aquarian Age, the age of individual enlightenment that begins with the year 2000, spiritual rites and initiations will become a deeper, more internal process. They will be increasingly individualized according to each person's unique purpose and mission. Sometimes, as in the case of priests and ministers, the rites are administered by elders or masters. They are coupled with intensive study and training, by which one's level of understanding is tested through experience and practice.

These rites, of course, are culture-specific. The ancestral culture of your bloodline will influence the degree and nature of your initiation process. What you will do and how you will do it have already been determined by your choice of spiritual expression. If you are a woman, more specifically a Black woman, your spiritual rites will be determined by the bloodline you choose to participate in and experience.

Individual sacred initiations are the foundation of spiritual growth. They occur internally and result in the level of understanding called "knowing." This knowing may come as a result of prayer and meditation or through ceremonies performed on your behalf. It results in an immediate transformation of your perceptions and behavior. In some instances, it is accompanied by crying, shaking, or momentary paralysis, flashes of light, and sounds like music or voices. For others, there will be neither sound nor light, only the experience of deep realization or revelation of the truth of a matter. Without energy or effort on your part, this knowing will affect how you approach life from that minute forward. You will know to dress a certain way. You will know to eat or not eat certain foods. You will know the spiritual significance of certain oils, herbs, or information. You will have full confidence and faith in the knowledge that has been revealed to you. You will also know when to put it to use, and realize that whoever needs the information will be sent to you. As an initiate, however, you must resist the desire to run to the telephone to call your mother or girlfriend and tell them what has happened. You should sit on the information a while. Savor it. Honor it. And immediately put it into practice for your own benefit.

In the Yoruba culture, there are various levels of initiation which take place under the direction of elders. One of the most significant of these is the initiation into the priesthood. At that time, and in some cases before, a person's spiritual mission is revealed by the sacred oracles of Ifa in a process of divination. The oracles of Ifa, called *odu*, are ranked according to seniority. Each of the approximately 2,451 oracles carries a prophecy in the form of a legend that reveals exactly what you have come to the physical world to learn, un-learn, and master. Like I Corinthians 12:8-11, the odu reveal the spiritually potential gifts with which we are born. Some of us come into this world to counsel, others to teach. Some will heal, others will prophesize. One may be able to cast out darkness, while another will see visions. Some will write, some will minister to others. Still others are here to dance, sing, or make people laugh. One will have great business acumen. Another will care for the sick, the elderly, and the children. Some of us will do our work publicly with great fanfare, while others will go about it quietly, going totally unnoticed except by those whom they touch personally.

You may have one or more of these gifts. You may have all of them. Your spiritual gifts are determined by your purpose. Your purpose, which is reflected in all that you do, will unfold from within as a talent or inclination to do a certain thing. Your purpose gives your life meaning and is revealed as a function of your consciousness.

On the other hand, you may choose to reject your spiritual purpose. You may choose to live in doubt, fear, hate, anger, and human limitation, without ever realizing a day of fulfillment. Yet, you must realize that when you insist or persist in doing things to satisfy your physical senses and human mind, you fail to connect with your spiritual power. The choice is yours. Spirit will never supersede your conscious right to choose. It will, however, provide you with every opportunity to surrender and go within, to find your truth and evolve.

It is not easy to move beyond the seen and place your faith in the unseen. It is not easy to discern whether what you are seeing in your mind's eye, hearing in your mind's ear, or feeling in your heart is the voice of truth or some dark angel passing through your consciousness on his or her way to McDonald's for breakfast. It is not easy to move beyond the hangman's noose of family limitations and hereditary conditions. It is not easy, but it is absolutely necessary if you want to discover who you are.

348

Adeyemi moved into another apartment. We went back and forth for weeks, prolonging the inevitable. I wanted in and out. He wanted in and out. Neither of us could make a decision. For the first time in our three years together, we were arguing. Well, it wasn't really arguing. Usually, it was me screaming at him. He would listen and not respond.

One day, I got real dramatic and decided to try to kill myself again. I took a handful of pills and washed it down with a pint of rum. I had no intention of dying, I was simply trying to get his attention. I got it. He told me he could not take any more of my nonsense. We did not speak for several days.

In the meantime, the rest of my life was falling apart. I had a part-time job I rarely reported to. I was late with all of my final school assignments. I was behind in all of my bills and facing eviction again. In public, I put on a happy face and pretended to be the wonderful, marvelous person I thought I could never be without a man. I soon learned the hard way that when you live in a world of fantasy, your dishonesty eventually catches up with you.

⌁⌁⌁

You are creating much more pain for yourself than necessary. There is nothing in your life you will ever need that will not be provided in the divine time and manner. You must first build a solid foundation. You must build a place upon which to stand in your own mind. Begin there, begin by taking care of yourself, building your foundation, and preparing for your goodness."

Things are never as they seem. What seems as if it may be good may actually be detrimental. What appears to be heading toward causing you great harm may reveal itself to be good. Take the time to look, to notice whether your good is bad or your bad is good. If you do not look, you will not build. You will have nothing. To live in a state of nothingness causes pain. You are doing that to yourself. There is nothing further to say about him at this time.

⌁⌁⌁

349

To make matters worse, one of my initiates became critically ill right in the middle of my romantic crisis. As her spiritual teacher, it was my responsibility to perform certain ceremonies on her behalf. I did the best I could, but my own personal problems were taking up most of my attention. Luckily, when the student became somewhat disturbed because I did not visit her in the hospital, I had a viable excuse: as a priestess, it is taboo for me to enter a hospital unless it is necessary for my own or my family's well-being. Still, I was emotionally devastated and running out of lies. I could not tell anyone what was really the matter because of all the lies I had told before.

One Sunday afternoon, my student called me to ask if I had gotten in touch with an elder who was supposed to do certain things on her behalf. I had totally forgotten, a common human error. I, however, was not human, my ego told me. I was a super-being. I was never wrong. So, what did I do? I told her I had spoken to the person in question and that I would follow up on it, of course.

As soon as I hung up the telephone, I tried to get in touch with the elder. When I could not, I went to bed. Several days later, when my student called again, I lied and told her that everything had been taken care of.

Things got so bad, one day I got down on my knees and literally begged God not to take Adeyemi away from me. It was totally undignified. I was six years old again, promising to be good and do good, which included telling the truth. I promised to love, serve, and obey God with my every waking breath. I tried to cut all kinds of deals and cried profusely to demonstrate my desperation. I pleaded with God, swearing that if S/He would let me move to Adeyemi's house, I would never ask Her/Him for anything ever again. As always, God heard and answered me.

A few days later, my rent situation became critical. I talked to Adeyemi about it, and he agreed that the children and I could move in with him. He was on his way out of the country on a work assignment. He was to be away ten days. In his absence, I painted, polished, and cleaned. I turned a run-down apartment into a freshly painted and wallpapered run-down apartment. I was still determined to prove to him that I was everything he needed, that I could build a foundation for us.

The ten days took forever to pass. I busied myself with school work, looking for a position at a law firm, and taking the bar exam. I was about to become a lawyer, the first person in my entire family line to finish college or beyond, but that had absolutely no meaning to me. I was trying to save what I thought was my life line: my relationship with a man.

On the day Adeyemi was to return, I could not breathe. I had no idea what time he would be arriving. Every time the telephone rang, my heart stopped along with my breath. My mind would not stop racing. My mouth was dry. I ran from the window to the door, from the door to the telephone, waiting for his return. It was ten in the evening when I realized he was not coming home to me. He was going home to her. It was not until two a.m. that I forced myself to accept what was going on. But that's okay, I told myself. If he goes to her tonight, he will come to me tomorrow. However, the moment that thought materialized, my mind shot back with, "Is that what you want? Is that what you are willing to accept?" After two seconds of contemplation, I responded, weakly, "I have no choice."

ΛΛΛ

Goodness does not dry up. It cannot. Goodness is what God is made of. Goodness is what God made of you. Sudden events require decisions that can be turning points. Look at the pros and cons. Weigh and measure all situations. Nurture the ability to discern the true from the false. The truth will set you free. Act decisively and put it to practical use."

This is a period of growth. You will be restless and uneasy. The future is germinating now. Plan carefully. Reach reasoned conclusions. Use common sense. Know who you are and what you want. Do not lie. Control your emotions. Do not fear change. Fear will make you weak. Weakness brings poor health, disillusionment, loss of material goods, and spiritual separation.

Break out of stagnant situations. Investigate new opportunities.
Listen to your inner teacher. Awake to your inner awareness.

I knew I needed help in sorting out the mess I had made of my life. From the annals of my experiences, I remembered Mother Mary. I was sure she could pray me through this, so I called her. She told me to come right over. I had never seen her, but I remembered her beautiful prayer and how supported I had felt. Besides, she had told me exactly what to do. I needed her help badly now.

When she opened the door, I fought to stifle a scream. Her skin was black as coal. Her eyes shone piercing white through the black lenses of the sunglasses she wore. Her head was wrapped in what appeared to be a red bedsheet. The piles of cloth on her head matched the long red dress she was wearing. She reminded me of the "Mammy" characters I had seen on television. She even had on a red-and-white checkered apron. A cross at least twelve inches long hung around her neck from a thin piece of clothesline.

"Mother Mary?"

She never answered. She told me to step back from the door, walk back down the steps, and wait for her at the basement door. Then she slammed the door in my face. Stunned, I did as I was told. A voice in the back of my brain was laughing hysterically when the basement door flew open. Before I could say a word, Mother Mary threw a bucket of ice cold water in my face. I stood there, in shock, dripping wet from head to toe, shivering and trying to catch my breath.

"Come on in, sweetheart."

As I stepped through the doorway into the basement of Mother Mary's brownstone, I was muttering a silent prayer: "Dear God, when am I going to learn? When am I going to stop coming to these people? Please don't let her kill me down here!"

The basement resembled a church. There was a cross on every wall. An ancient piano, a stack of hymnals, and rows of chairs, set up auditorium-style, completed the decor. Mother Mary led me to a chair in a corner and told me to tell her my story. Shivering and soaking wet, I spilled my guts. No money. Trying to finish law school. Lost my love. Can't eat. Can't sleep. Mother sick. Losing my mind. I could feel Mother Mary's eyes piercing my skin as she stared at me, listening intently, fondling the cross around her neck.

When I had gotten it all out, I took a deep breath. After a moment of silence, Mother said, "The devil hates the cold, you know," and stood up and walked away.

"The devil likes Black people," she yelled out from another room. "He is particularly fond of Black women. You know why?"

"No, why?" I asked timidly.

"Because they are weak."

My political identity was immediately offended.

She continued: "They've been weak every since the old African mothers stopped teaching them about God and His medicine. They been weak ever since they started straightening their hair and putting on panty girdles. They weak 'cause they sleep in them big, fat, pink hair rollers. God can't talk through the hair rollers, you know."

I thought to myself, "Oh God, what am I doing in this basement with this crazy woman?"

Another moment of silence, then Mother's voice boomed out, "Come to me, sweetheart."

Obediently, I laid my wet coat on a chair and walked into the other room. It was a bathroom. Mother was standing beside a shower stall with a white plate in her hands. Quickly, I scanned the room. Glass-encased candles sat on shelves in every corner. To my left was a shelf with six or seven candles of different colors. A picture of Saint Michael was next to each one. Sweet-smelling smoke was swirling around behind Mother, making her seem like an apparition. On the wall, directly in front of me, above Mother's head, was a huge poster of the Virgin Mary, looking just like the vision I had seen so many years before. The Virgin was a beautiful Black woman.

Mother told me to kneel down. When I did, she placed the

plate on top of my head and started singing. She sang so loud and off-key, I felt embarrassed for her. Then she started praying, calling out the names of people I did not know. In the process, she called out the name "Horace Lester Harris," my father. Then she called "Sarah Jefferson," my mother. That wiped the embarrassed smirk right off my face. Then she started speaking in a language I could not understand. Somebody understood her, though, because they answered her. I heard two distinct voices: one male, one female, both loud. I closed my eyes, tight, and crouched down on the floor.

"Get in the tub," I heard Mother Mary say.

I opened my eyes and looked around. Who was she talking to?

"Get up and get in the tub!" she screamed. Scrambling to my feet, I half-stepped, half-fell into the shower stall.

"Put your hands on the wall!" She pulled a pair of scissors out of nowhere. "Spread your legs apart!"

I obeyed as she barked out her commands, all the while praying that she would not kill me. I felt her hands ripping at my clothes. One yank and my thirty-dollar sweater was gone. She pulled at me again. I heard more ripping, cutting, and tearing. My skirt fell off. Then my bra. She spun me around, cutting off my pantyhose and panties, almost knocking me down.

"Face the wall!" she commanded. "Don't look back! Don't ever look back!"

My toes gripped the tiles on the shower stall floor while my fingers gripped the tiles on the wall. The first blow came to the top of my head. Eggs. I closed my eyes again, almost crazy with fear.

Mother Mary began singing a strange-sounding song, again totally off-key, as she pelted me with eggs and washed my body with them, shells and all, from the top of my head, across my face, down my chest and torso, up and down the front and back of my legs. I could feel the shells piercing my skin. I tucked my lips in to avoid tasting the raw egg on my face.

Abruptly, she stopped. I heard her walk away, praying to herself. I couldn't open my eyes.

Without warning, she doused me with another bucket of

water and started scrubbing me again, this time with something pungent and fresh-smelling. She ordered me to open my eyes. I did. She handed me her tools. Lemons.

"Wash your face and your privates."

As I washed, she poured ice cold water over my head.

"Stomp on those clothes," she ordered, pointing to the pile of rags underneath my feet.

Shivering and scrubbing myself with lemon rinds, I stomped.

"Jump on those clothes! Stomp it out!"

I jumped harder and more frantically, up and down, still shivering and scrubbing.

"Tell him to get back!" She gave me a whack on the bottom with one of her huge hands.

"Tell him to leave you alone!"

I didn't know who "he" was, but I started screaming at him and yelling, "Leave me alone! Get away from me!"

I was stomping and screaming. Shivering and screaming. Scrubbing and screaming. Mother handed me more lemons. I was in a frenzy. Crying, screaming, scrubbing my legs, arms, and face. I lifted up my breasts and scrubbed under them. I opened my legs and scrubbed my vaginal area. I was screaming "Get back! Get away!" at the top of my lungs when I heard the calm, melodic, and soothing voice of the Mother Mary I had known years ago say, "Now don't hurt yourself, baby. It's gone."

I fell to my knees in a heap in the shower stall. This time, however, Mother was ready with another bucket of water. It was warm and sweet-smelling. Gently, humming a peaceful tune, she stroked my body to remove the egg shells and lemon rinds.

"You got a change of clothes?" she asked.

Of course not, I said to myself. I had no idea I was going to have my clothes doused or ripped off by a total stranger! Outwardly, I simply shook my head, indicating no. I was exhausted.

Mother walked away without a word, leaving me sitting on the floor of the shower stall. I heard her go upstairs and come back down.

"Put this on," she said, "but don't dry off your body." Then she left the room.

I got dressed. When I came out of the bathroom, Mother was sitting next to the piano. She stared at me. I was wearing a parrot-green, crocheted sweater and a red skirt that came four inches above my knee. My brown ankle boots were soaking wet from the first drowning, and they spurted water as I walked.

"Don't go feeling ashamed because your breasts hang! Any breast that has nursed three babies is suppose to hang," she said.

My mouth dropped open. How did she know I had three children?

"You look much better. You are such a beautiful woman. I don't know why you let people make you feel ugly."

I did not care how she knew. Somehow, I felt a hundred percent better. Lightheaded, but better.

Mother took my hands and prayed for me. She told me to go home and be good to myself. She told me not to worry about my man, just finish school and I would be fine. She told me God had given me special blessings—the problem was, I did not realize how specially blessed I was. Then she kissed me on my forehead, telling me that the work was free, but, when I could, I was to send two-hundred-and-fifty dollars to the post office box. I picked up my wet coat and purse and headed for the door.

"The church needs your support," she called out behind me as I walked away. "Eggs are the sacred forces of life. Lemons clean bitterness with bitterness. When in doubt, just get in the water. Water is the symbol of a mother's love. You know, my name is not really Mary, it's Carmen. People call me Mary because they say I have brought forth the God in them."

I told her thank you and left.

As I walked home, I remembered that the first step of my initiation into the priesthood was a bath. I realized I had just been initiated into something. What, I had no idea.

It was three days after my visit to Mother Mary's before I heard from Adeyemi. By that time I was numb. I could not bring myself to ask him where he was living. I knew, and he knew I knew. We had never brought our relationship to closure. He simply moved back home.

My student, out of the hospital, was doing much better and was still inquiring about the implement she was to receive from the elder. Once again, I had completely forgotten. Once again, I lied. I told her that I had given him the necessary money, but he had not gotten back to me. I promised her I would try to get in touch with him. I tried for days to reach him, but he never seemed to be home when I called.

Final exams and papers were piling up on me. I should have been studying for the bar. Instead, I was wasting away, smoking incessantly, and generally making myself crazy. Every other day or so, Adeyemi would come by, we would have sex, and he would go home. He never made me any promises. He never said anything. We just sort of settled into having an affair. I was now involved in a relationship with a married man.

I wish there were a nice way to say what I refused to admit to myself then. There is none: I used sex to get love. I wish I knew the therapeutic rationale that would explain away the need to engage in sexual activity to feel good. I do not know one. I must tell the truth as I know it and see it now: I used sex as a way to feel loved and feel good. I would not say I had a sexual addiction. However, I must admit, I had a terrible "jones" for the stuff.

But it did not begin or end with sex. I also used my talents, my money, my resources, and anything else I had to "buy" friendship. I would sew for my friends, help them out of all kinds of situations, do anything and everything I could to prove what a good friend I was. Then, when things went sour, when the relationship was over, I felt like crap. I felt used and manipulated. There were distinct instances when I knew the person I wanted to impress had little regard and sometimes great disdain for me. Yet, I would continue to make myself available to them, to stay at their beck and call, simply to keep them as my "friend." Why? Because

I just did not and could not believe people would like me for who I was, I settled for getting them to like me for what I did and could give to them. Sex was just one of these things.

Since most of my sexual activity took place in secret and hiding, the guilt was almost consuming. To soothe the pain, I would do it again. What a vicious cycle! On one hand, I hated when people asked me to do things, but I did not know how to say no. On the other hand, I did not want them to be mad at me or stop being my friend, so I "sold" myself to get their approval and acceptance.

There were two predominant character flaws with which I was challenged. One was waiting until the last minute to do something I did not want to do. The other was doing too many things at one time. The result was always a frantic, mad rush to get done the things I had committed myself to do. When the rush was over, I would vow never to do that again, to learn how to say no. Of course, I never did.

Increasingly, all of my frailties were very clearly being presented to me, but I had a very well-structured counter-argument and excuse for each of them. I was in serious denial. There were people I could blame, situations I could point to. It was not my fault. I was the "victim" of people and circumstances. I can honestly say that I was a neurotic bordering on psychotic. The need to be loved and wanted, the craving to be accepted, the fear of being alone, the inability to look at myself honestly, the habitual preoccupation with dishonesty, the reliance on making up stories and lies that would make me look good, the fear of being wrong or making a mistake, the inability to accept correction or criticism, the preference for living in a fantasy world where everything was just perfect—all of these character faults had more than damaged my self-esteem, they had dismantled my "self."

As a result, I would not take the time to look at myself because I believed that if I looked closely I would see that what Grandma and so many others close to me had said all along was true: "I ain't shit!" As a result, I could not admit my mistakes because I didn't want to believe what they had said—that "I was always doing something wrong." As a result, I would not admit that I had any weaknesses because, like everyone had said, "I was supposed to be like..."—you name it, somebody else, anybody else—and that somebody would never do the things I did. To top it all off, to make all my faults and shortcomings even more obvious, to prove how undeserving I really was—to myself if not to others— I had gone and become a priest, a missionary of God out to do God's work.

All I can say now is, "Thank Goodness!" If it had not been for my priesthood, I would have continued to self-destruct until I was totally gone, mentally and emotionally.

᠅᠅᠅

The letter came by certified mail. The return address was clearly marked "Federal Bureau of Investigation," and it was addressed to me. I read it ten times before I understood what it said. I was being investigated for fraud and forgery. I was to report to a Manhattan office of the FBI in two days.

I sat on the edge of the bed in total disbelief. I called my godfather. He told me to go and see what they wanted.

The two agents who questioned me were reasonably civil. They asked the general questions about my background, my health, and so forth. Then they lowered the boom. A report had been made on a missing Social Security check totalling fourteen hundred dollars. They showed me information indicating that I had signed and cashed the check. I did not deny it. I explained that the check belonged to my mother. I cashed the check when she was ill and in the hospital, I told them. Rather than put her in a nursing home, I used the money from the check to lease an apartment in which she lived with me for two months. Although Nett was ill, I told them, I had asked her permission to do what I had planned to do, and she had understood and approved because she did not want to go into a home.

This was information the agents did not have. They asked me if I could substantiate my claims with a lease and rent receipts and if there were any witnesses who could verify my story. I told them that I could and that there were. We set another appointment for one week later.

The moment I got home, I called Nett. I asked her why she had reported the check stolen when she knew I had used the money to get the apartment. She told me that Selma wanted her to repay the money she had spent on private-duty nurses before Nett's benefits had been approved. Selma was retired and needed the money, she said.

I was furious. I explained to Nett that if I were convicted of forgery, I would never be admitted to the bar in any state. After several seconds of silence, in a very flat tone, Nett said, "Blood is thicker than water." When I asked her what she meant, she repeated it. It was quite clear what she meant.

᛭᛭᛭

You have a special mission. You are to teach, heal, and save others from your greatest fears. First, you must heal yourself. You must be healed. It is a gentle, loving process that you make painful by resistance. Do not resist! You will do things no others have done.

This is a time of cleansing and spiritual purity. Be disciplined. Be obedient. You must see your face. You must accept it. Power is in the mind. Keep your head clear. Ask for strength and guidance in when to speak. Move slowly, carefully, and deliberately. Say very little. Lay down the past. When you leave the past, you will grow.

"Do not doubt. Do not fear. Do not lie. Those are your only obstacles.

᛭᛭᛭

I found the lease and the receipts indicating that I had paid eighteen hundred dollars to get into the apartment. I asked Adeyemi and Melba, who had been Nett's home attendant, to come with me to the FBI office for my second appointment.

This time, the two agents were ready to fight, but they wanted to circle their prey before the attack. So first they made what they thought I thought was small talk. They commented on how nice I looked, how well-dressed I was. Thank you, I said. They asked me if I had a car. I answered yes. They asked me if I liked school. Yes, again. They said they "guessed" I could buy a lot of school clothes with fourteen hundred dollars. I told them if I had that much money to spare I would put it into an account for my children.

Formalities aside, they moved in for the kill. Without batting an eye, I went to battle.

"How do you feel about ripping off a sick old woman?"

"Who, who are you talking about?"

"Did you give your boyfriend some of the money?"

"I told you I used the money to get an apartment."

"Did your boyfriend help you cash the check? You know, you don't have to take the fall alone. If he made you or forced you to do it in any way, and you help us get him, we can help you."

"Wait a minute! I don't think you understand. I was living in my mother's apartment. I had a key to her mailbox. I got all of her mail. I did not steal the check, I used the check on my mother's behalf."

"By the way, where is your mother?"

I blinked.

"She's home."

"No, I don't mean Mrs. Harris, I mean your *real* mother?"

I could feel myself turning green. The agents saw it and backed off right away, grinning with satisfaction at themselves. I was speechless. One of the agents told me they had been informed by "Mrs. Harris's sister" that I was a stepchild, that I had probably taken the money to use for school or for some kind of religious ritual. She also told them that Nett had never given me permission to use the check, that I had denied any knowledge of having cashed the check when she asked about it, and that she, as Mrs. Harris's next of kin, was entitled to the money for the care she had provided.

I was beyond speechless. I handed the agent the receipts and the lease. They asked me to sign my name on a sheet of paper several times and told me I was free to go.

From the look on my face, Melba and Adeyemi knew something God-awful had happened. It took me several minutes to get the words out of my mouth, "Nett told these people she was not my mother. She let her sister tell them that I stole the money to buy school clothes and pay for my initiation."

Melba said, "She told everybody she was not your mother, which is why she was so grateful to you for all you did for her. I thought you knew."

What comes after pain? It is not numbness because you can feel it. You can feel it running through your veins like blood. You can feel the ache of it in the hairs on your body. There must be a word to describe when devastation goes beyond pain. Whiplash? No, that doesn't fit. Thrombosis? No, that's not deadly enough. Death? No, you don't die. It is indescribable.

There is no word to adequately describe what you feel when the one person in the world you have trusted throws you to the dogs for fourteen hundred dollars. There is no phrase that can adequately convey what happens in your brain when the lie you have told yourself all of your life is revealed, in public, to two white FBI agents who do not know you from Eve. Neither Webster nor Roget can help you communicate what happens in your heart when you are rejected, abandoned, and betrayed for what amounts to less than two month's rent by the woman you told the world was your mother and best friend.

I prayed:

Heavenly Father, please take away the pain, the hurt, the disappointment. Help me to forgive and forget this. Do not let this destroy my mind. Dear God, if I could just understand this. Help me to understand.

I trust you, God. I trust You to work this out in Your own divine way according to Your divine will. I am praying for truth, clarity, and understanding. I will let go. I will let your will be done. God, all I wanted was a mother. I just wanted somebody to love me.

God, what am I going to do? What am I going to do now with everybody leaving me? I will trust you, God. I will trust in your loving kindness and your grace.

It had been coming for weeks. I had just kept hoping against hope. It was a Sunday morning when Adeyemi called to say he was coming to get his things. He brought his children and a stone face. He moved around silently as I sat on the bed, watching. His children were happy that their father was coming back home for good. My children were worried about me.

It took three trips. When the last load was packed, he sat down across from me.

"Well, this is it," I said.

"Yeah, I guess so. You're going to be fine, you know. Please don't do that. What are you crying for? You know this is like a habit for me—my children, my family. They are a like a habit. You always told me that I was a creature of habit, you know."

Silence.

"Let's do this knowing that if we are supposed to be together, we will be. Okay? Right now, I have to give back to my wife all the love lessons I learned with you. She stayed with me for fifteen years, now I have to show her that I have learned a lot."

Silence.

"I'll call you later in the week."

Without so much as a peck on the cheek, he was gone.

I prayed some more:

I shall not want. I shall not want. The Lord is my shepherd, I shall not want. He maketh me to lie down. I shall not want. I shall not cry. I shall not ache. I shall not want. The table

is being prepared for me. I am being led to the green pastures. I shall not want.

Dear God, you promised me I shall not want. Hold not Thy peace! Hold not Thy peace, for I am tired and weary. I shall not want! I shall not want!

⁘⁘⁘

Oluwo called to tell me about the confusion with the elder and my student. He had spoken to her, and she had told him about the situation. The elder had told him he had never spoken to me ,and I had never given him any money.

Had I given him the money, Oluwo asked.

"Well, I didn't put it in his hand... I left it for him."

Where had I taken the money?

I had to think quickly. I had not taken the money anywhere.

"Do not lie!"

I reached for my telephone book, turned to the "A" section, and read off an address.

"Well," he said, "it's the right address, but the wrong apartment."

I was dumb-struck. He instructed me to go to the right apartment, find the person I had given the money to, and get the matter cleared up as soon as possible. I stared at the telephone. I had told a blatant, outright lie, and it had turned out to be the truth.

What was I going to do? If I told the truth now, everybody would hate me. They would probably never speak to me again. And there I'd be, with No Nett, no Adeyemi, no godfather, no nobody. I had to think fast. Rocking and moaning, I chanted, "Save me, help me, save me, help me." Suddenly, I felt the power surge coming. It moved up my spine and erupted through my body. I heard myself saying things I had said, saw myself doing things I had done. Everything started coming together into one picture.

"Help me, please! Somebody, please help me!" I screamed.

I saw Adeyemi leaving. I saw my student's face. I saw Nett staring at me. I saw Wayne and Kirk and Charlie and Ernie. I saw my children crying. Everyone was pointing at me, laughing at me.

"God, what am I going to do? What do You want me to do?"

⋏⋏⋏

Let me digress for just a moment to say a word about prayer. It is nothing to play with. Prayer is the communication between you and your divine self, the energy of God that exists within you. When you pray earnestly, asking intensely for something, you will get it. You will get exactly what you asked for. It may not look the way you think it will look, but you will get it. You must be very careful and conscious about what you are praying for. You must also be very specific. This means that you must evaluate the entire situation and come up with the best possible outcome. If that is what you want, that is what you should ask for. If you do not know what you want, you would be better off not praying for anything other than divine will.

Prayer is very powerful. It transforms and creates energy. However, it creates and transforms according to universal law, not according to our selfish desires. We must therefore be extremely careful about praying for anything that will cause anyone else pain or distress. We must also be cautious about praying for things that we do not understand or do not have complete information about. Above all, we must be very conscious of the words we use, about how we structure our prayers. They can create the conditions of our lives.

I had been praying for understanding, clarity, and truth. Of course, because I was not clear, I did not mean for that to apply in every area. I was not telling the truth about Nett, and I needed to understand that. I was not telling the truth about my motives in anything I did, and I needed to get clear about that. I was lying to my student, who was a priest; to an elder, who was a priest; and to my godfather, another priest. That was too much divine energy misdirected at people with perfectly good intentions for me to get away with it.

I had prayed to move into Adeyemi's house, and that is exactly what happened: I moved in, he moved out. I had not been specific. I had been reading about and studying principles of truth and universal law, but I was unable to put them into practice because I was unwilling to let go of my old ways. I was asking for guidance and still "doing my thing." I was practicing my priesthood, but not living up to my spiritual responsibilities. I was a fragile, delicate human being, unwilling and unable to admit my faults or weaknesses. I was building upon a weak foundation while praying for strength. I had no idea that my prayers were being answered. I got exactly what I prayed for.

You cannot ask the ancestors, the Holy Spirit, or God to uphold you in your weaknesses. The universe simply does not operate like that. Your psycho-socio-history does not matter in the universal scheme of things. The universal life force, God, is concerned only with the evolution of humankind through love, harmony, balance, and peace. Every experience we have in life is an opportunity for us to gain a greater understanding of these principles through cooperative participation.

When you begin to dabble in the spiritual world, you are held responsible for the information you have. It becomes your duty to put into practice the things you learn. To do so, you must be willing to question every value you hold to be true. You must be willing to surrender everything you know in order to gain a broader and more inclusive interpretation. You must be ready and willing to surrender your head, your mind, your "thing," so that you can be filled with the Light. The Light will always cast out the darkness that shows up as conditions or situations in your life. It will always provide you with the opportunity to see the truth of them and be born again. In the Light.

When you are cleaning out your closet, you must create a mess before your can put things in order. You can do a thorough job or a halfway job. In order to do a thorough job, you have to take everything out of the closet, pile it up on the bed, the floors, and in any available chairs. Everything will look a mess until you are finished. You must, however, sift through the mess, piece by piece, to discover what is necessary and what you must discard. Depending on how much junk you have collected, it can be a long and tedious task. You can put on some music, take your time, and painstakingly move through the stuff. Or you can shift it around, haphazardly placing the same things in a different place.

Sometimes, in the midst of your cleaning and straightening up and organizing, someone might drop by unexpectedly. Because you do not want them to see your place in such disarray, you may close the door and pretend that the mess doesn't exist. You entertain the person, never once mentioning the pile of junk behind the closed door, hoping that they'll leave so you can get back to work. If you are not disciplined or committed to the task, you might be convinced to go with them out to the mall or to lunch. So you excuse yourself, go sift through the pile of junk in the other room for something to wear, and go out, leaving the mess laying in the middle of the floor.

While you are out ignoring your mess and having a good old time, you may eat too much or walk too long. When you finally get home, you're tired. You tell yourself you'll finish the closet some other time, but you take the new items you have bought, hang them up in the closet, shovel the rest of the junk in behind them, and shut the door. Or you might fold your old junk up neatly and put it right back in the closet in back of the new stuff.

The problem comes when you go back into the closet later to look for one of the new items, something you just bought, and you can't find it. You know you hung it in the closet, but there is so much junk in there you cannot find anything. You promise yourself that you will clean the closet out again one day, but you just don't have time to do it today. So you find something else to put on and close the closet door.

Prayer, earnest prayer, even when we do not understand the ramifications of it, is like cleaning out the closet. You may find yourself in the middle of chaos and disorganization as you're sorting through the mess, but you cannot let the momentary disarray distract you from the goal of cleaning and reorganizing. You must be disciplined. You must carefully sift through the clutter to find those things that no longer fit, that are out of style, that you do not like anymore. If you try to fix the things that are ripped or torn, alter the things that no longer fit, or hold on to what you do not need, prayer will create a condition in your life that provides you with the opportunity to either make a clean sweep or simply reorganize the same old junk. However, when you sincerely pray for spiritual growth and development, invoking the energy of your ancestors, angels, or the Holy Spirit, you must be ready to sift through your junk. When you see that something is broken, do not try to fix it. Do not allow yourself to be sidetracked. Affirm to yourself that you are willing to let it go and then stand firmly, praying for guidance. Eventually, the disorganization will be cleared away. Then, and only then, will you be able to find what you are looking for in the closet of your soul.

ᐱᐧᐱ

Can you imagine your entire life flashing before your face in a matter of minutes? Can you imagine coming face-to-face with yourself in a moment of desperation? Can you imagine having to make a decision when you cannot think? That is exactly where I found myself, sitting on the edge of the bed, knowing that I was being forced to save my own life.

I cried for help and it came. I do not know if it was a burst of light or a passing wind. I only know that some presence manifested in that room. I could see it, feel it, and hear it—not on the physical level, but somewhere in my mind. I want to say it was the presence of God, but I think that would be stretching it. Suffice it to say, the presence took over my being and spoke directly into my mind:

Be still! Be still! You want to be saved? You are saved! I will always save you. The question is, do you want to be saved in my eyes or in the eyes of people? It is your choice. I will save you, either way, because you are mine. You can go to the address your godfather gave you, make the appropriate inquiry, and it will all work out in your behalf. Or you can tell the truth, and things will work out in My behalf. I am leaving the choice up to you, but you must know, people cannot save you. They can help you destroy yourself, but they cannot save you. Whatever you choose, I will do. But if you make the wrong choice, you will lose something you cherish very much.

My heart sank. I thought to myself, "Adeyemi. I will lose Adeyemi!" There was an immediate response:

He is not yours to lose. He has never been yours. He is simply serving my purpose in the world. If you continue to immerse yourself in the eyes of people, you will lose your children. They, too, do not belong to you. They are Mine, in your care. They are watching you, learning from you. If you are lost, they will be lost. To save them, I will take them back. If you are not giving them what they have been sent to receive, they have no purpose, no reason to be here. The choice is yours.

As quickly as it came, it left. Afterwards, I felt so totally calm and peaceful. I knew immediately the choice I had to make. I had to keep it simple. I went to my desk and wrote my godfather a twelve-page letter. I explained exactly how the situation began: I had said yes when I should have said no. I was trying to prove what a good priest I was, but I was afraid to admit I had made a mistake. I admitted knowing that if I had explained the situation to him, he would have told me how to handle it. But I did not want him to know I had lied in the first place because I was afraid he would not love me anymore. I had risked my reputation, his reputation, and the foundation of trust in our relationship simply because I was afraid to admit I had made a mistake. I explained that I had not wanted anyone to know what was going on between Adeyemi and me because I thought others would think something was wrong with me. I admitted that I had lied because I was afraid what people would think about me if I, a priest, could not sustain a relationship. I did not make any excuses for myself. I simply asked him to forgive me. I wrote my student and explained the same thing to her, asking for forgiveness.

I sealed both of the letters, walked to the mailbox, and dropped them in. Then I went back home, took a long, hot bath, pulled the plug out of the telephone, and got into bed, which is where I stayed for sixteen days.

THE Journal

Something quite phenomenal is going on.
I'm not so sure what it is,
but quite frankly,
I don't care!
I simply know that,
whatever it is,
it will be great!
It has to do with change, healing, growth, and evolution.
And it has to do with women.
If I were pressed,
I would put it in words like these:
There are changes taking place in the hearts and minds of women
that are going to rock the world!
Women are changing their minds about who they are
and what their role will be in the world order.
Women are learning to be responsible for the healing of their
mental, emotional, and spiritual selves.
Women are learning to love themselves and each other.
Most of all, women are evolving to the point
where they are no longer willing to accept crap
from themselves or from anyone else!
I love it!
How, you ask, are they doing it?
Well, I can only tell you what I know:
Women are learning how to breathe.
They had forgotten how to breathe.

Now, they are breathing consciously.
They are breathing deeply.
Breath awakens the divinity resting at the core of our beings.
It brings light into the soul.
It lightens the mind, body, and spirit of women.
It brings light unto the world.
Women are learning how to lighten up.
Women are praying.
They know that prayer is the inner communication
between themselves and their Maker
which turns on the force—the power of the creative nature of life.
They are realizing that prayer can get into places they cannot.
Prayer can reveal what cannot be seen with the naked eye.
Women are learning that prayer is the best weapon one can use
when one is engaged in spiritual warfare.

Women are singing.
Somehow, they know that singing stimulates the forces of the Divine
and they are realizing that it is their responsibility to sing
to the glory of God.
Women are singing:
"Ain't Gonna Let Nobody Turn Me 'Round" because
"Momma Said There'd Be Days Like This."
Sometimes, they sing, "My Soul Looks Back and Wonders How I Got Over,"
but they know "There's Something Inside So Strong" and
they sing, "I Am Woman, Hear Me Roar!" and
"I'm Every Woman!" and
"Ain't No Stoppin' Us Now!" and
"Everything Must Change!"
They know "His Eye Is on the Sparrow" and
"I'm Gonna Pray Your Kingdom Down!"
'cause they know "You Got the Right One, Baby!"
Women are singing loud.
Women are singing joyfully.

Women are dancing.
Women are dancing playfully.
Women are dancing seriously.
When the pelvis of a woman swings in the movement of dance,
the energy she emits heals the world in which she lives.
Women are coming to understand that one of the major problems
in this country
and the world
is that it is being run by people who cannot dance,
who have no rhythm,
who are out of step.
These people are stepping on other people's toes.
Dancing women are women in rhythm,
women in time with the beat of life.
Women are beginning to boogie their way to peace and prosperity.
They are doing the Hustle,
Electric Sliding themselves out of darkness,
and waltzing into the light.
They are creating new steps and dancing to their own music.
Women are beginning to realize that their ultimate dancing partner
is the One Mind, One Spirit, One Power of Life called God.
It is a beautiful sight to behold:
Women—breathing, praying, singing, dancing, and living—
from that place of divinity that can change the world.

CHAPTER 25

A Masterpiece of Love

There is a thundering presence in silence. The presence of power. The presence of strength. The presence of peace. The presence of self. In silence, you can hear the orderly flow of your life. You can hear your breath leaving your body. You can hear the rhythmic beating of your heart as it sustains you, creating new waves of life in your being. In silence, you can hear your thoughts as they flow, creating new thoughts and bringing up and clearing out old ones. If you are very silent, your fears will present themselves. But silently, with strength and power, you can look them square in the face and dismantle them, piece by piece. New thoughts will overrun them, taking away your fears as you exhale and inhale new life, new thoughts, into being.

As the minutes remain silent extend themselves into hours, and as the hours of silence extend into days, you can become consciously aware of each of your thoughts. You can experience how soft and fragile they are, how quickly and easily they can be changed. You may wonder why you had never noticed before how easy it is to change a thought. Then you realize that you had never before taken the opportunity to become silent. Totally, absolutely, silent.

The children sat on the floor outside my door. Sometimes they would knock on it and call me. I would not answer them. They knew I was alive because I would come out of my room every now and then to go to the bathroom. When I did, they would run to greet me, grabbing and embracing me, and all start talking at once. I would give each one a kiss, then wave them away and go back into the silence of my bedroom.

The first three days were intense. I kept going over and over in my mind what had happened. There was so much I did not know. Where to begin? Everything kept running together—faces, words, situations. I found myself praying for all my thoughts to go away. On the fourth day, things slowed down quite a bit. The thoughts still came, but they came much more slowly and precisely, giving me an opportunity to interact with them.

After awhile, as each new thought presented itself, I would question it. Immediately, an answer would come to mind. If I was not sure about the answer, I would ask another question and it, too, would be answered. I also noticed that questions were being asked of me. I would take the time to think about each one—to contemplate each word, its meaning and placement—before eventually coming up with an answer. If my answer judged, blamed, or was in anyway noncommittal, instantly another question or explanation would present itself.

On the fifth or six night, I had a dream. In the dream, I was laying in my bed. A little man came into my room and sat down beside me. I say he was little because he was not a midget or dwarfed in any way. He was perfectly formed. But because I saw him as if I were viewing him from a distance, he appeared very small. Half of his body and his clothes were red, the other half was black. I sat up and looked at him. He was playing with the buttons and hem of his jacket. When he looked up at me, he smiled.

"Are you sure you are ready?" he asked.

"Ready for what?" I asked back.

"Ready to die."

I stared at him in disbelief. I could feel the fear gripping at my throat, the tears welling up in my eyes. He started laughing, pulled a cigar out of the inside of his jacket, and lit it. I don't know where the fire came from.

"I don't mean really die," he explained. "Well, I do mean really die, but what I really mean is, are you ready to die to all of the things that have brought you to this point? You have to be willing to die, you know. If you do not die, you will stay the same."

Instantly, I was relieved.

"Do you remember what happened to my brother Jesus? He was crucified. He died and he was born again. You are being crucified too, you know. All of the things that have kept you locked up, bound, and gagged will be lifted from you. You know, you're not a bad person. You are a sad person who has done bad things. The bad things you have done were not mean things. I mean, you didn't want to hurt anybody, you were simply sad—so you did things to make yourself happy."

He paused to puff on his cigar. He looked at me. "You don't understand, do you?"

I did understand. He had said in words what my thoughts in the silence had been moving toward all along.

"Do you know why you have gone through this and why you have to die?"

Before I could answer, he said, "Because you could. You could and you chose to. Don't you remember, a long time ago, when I came to you and told you never to tell a lie and to always smile before you speak?"

I scrunched up my face, trying to remember, but I didn't.

"I guess that mean lady, that ornery old grandmother of yours, helped you forget me when she heard you talking to me and told you to shut up. I fixed her good, though. I showed up in the bathroom one day and scared her half to death!"

He started laughing and puffed on his cigar some more.

"If you had listened to me then, you would have been fine. But you chose to forget. You chose to listen to other people. That has been your problem all along, you know. You listen too much to what other people say. You believe what they tell you, even when you know they are not telling you the truth. I tried to stop you, but you never listened to me."

"Who are you?" I finally got the nerve to ask.

He started laughing again.

"I am you best friend. I am your reflection. I am you. I am what you think, what you do, and what you want. But, enough about me. Here's what I want you to do. Are you going to listen this time?"

He laughed even harder. "What am I saying? Of course you are. You have no choice!"

His laughter and what he told me afterwards echoed in my mind long after I woke up:

"I am going to show you some things," he said. "I am going to send you to places and send you information to use along the way. Do not tell anyone what I say to you. Keep it to yourself until you know it is safe to talk about it. In the meantime, I want you to write down everything I tell you. I also want you to write down every thought, every word that comes into your mind, right now. Anything you write about other people, I want you to burn it. Anything you write about yourself, keep it tucked away in a nice, safe place. One day, you will have to read it over.

"There are circumstances or events in your memory that need to be neutralized and fixed. There may be a number of people you have to forgive—people who have hurt you. I want you to bless, forgive, and release them. You must also ask for forgiveness for yourself. Bless yourself and give yourself permission not to live in pain. Then you can and will begin to build and clear the way for a new life.

"Don't be afraid. You are going through a major transition. Do not panic, be nervous, or fearful. Do not talk to people who make you nervous, fearful, or undermine your confidence. Do not cling to things it is time to let go of. You are not a victim! Remember that. You are *not* a victim! If you think you are, people will treat you as such. You have been acting like a victim for so long, it has become a part of your permanent memory.

I will help you fix that. If ever you are in a situation where you feel like a victim, do this: get out! Run away fast! I will show you what to do.

"Be careful about talking. Do not subject your thoughts to negative people who will ridicule you. You think everyone is your friend. Everyone is not your friend. You talk to everyone. Why do you women like to talk so much? You must learn to keep your own counsel. When the time is ready, the right person will appear to whom you can ask all of your questions.

"Train your mind to concentrate on one thing at a time. Think about what is most important, decide what you want, and you will be shown what to do. Write down what you want, what you don't want, and what you are thankful for. Make a commitment to yourself to change.

"You *can* build a relationship, but you do not have to give up yourself to find love. You *are* love. You are *my* love. Celebrate your successes. A recovery is taking place. The seeds of success are being planted. Do not put too much pressure on yourself. Do not expect the worst—you have already gone through the worst. You will always get exactly what you expect. You will always see exactly what you are. If you do not like what you see, change it.

"I have to go now. You will remember this, and you will remember me. Do as I say, and you will be born again. Study hard. Be good at who you are."

He turned to leave.

"Oh, one more thing: people are going to attack you. People are going to ridicule you. People are going to say you are out of your mind. Remember, do not worry about what people say. If you know in your heart that you have done all you could, the best you could, with no intent to harm anyone, I will always protect you. I am here. Your mother is here. Carmen is here. There are many of us watching you and protecting you. We need you to do our work. Study yourself. Learn all you can about yourself. Tell your story in all that you do, and always remember to *keep it simple*. Tell the truth and keep it simple. Good day."

When he jumped off the bed, I woke up. The words he

spoke were hanging in the air like laundry left out to dry. I could see them and feel them. I went to my desk and, as I was told, feverishly wrote down everything he had said in my journal.

There are seven steps of creation that you must master in order to heal your reality. The first step is to bring forth the light. You cannot create or re-create your world without light—that is, the illumination of your consciousness. You must attain a truly enlightened idea of what you want your world to look like. Whether it is a new job, a new career, or a new relationship—your thinking about any situation must be enlightened above and beyond where you currently are. If you take the same ideas and behaviors into a new situation without the enlightenment of learning from past situations, you will reap the same results. If you are moving into a new situation, one about which you have little or no information, you must first bring the light to bear upon it, then hold your ideals high. Expect the best, and be prepared to receive it.

When God said, "Let there be light," S/He fully expected the light to appear. S/he did not doubt or worry. S/he did not wonder where the light would come from. S/he had an idea and S/he held to it. God had faith in Her/His ability. That is the second stage in any creation: faith. So much can be and has been said about faith, and yet we still experience a great deal of difficulty understanding and using its power. Let us begin with the concept that faith is not something you must acquire. Rather, it is something you already have. It is the nurturing and strengthening of your ideas, without ever allowing doubt or fear to enter your mind. Faith is power. It is the power that you are actively seeking, the expression of your ideas into action. Faith is what you have each time you exhale without questioning whether or not you will inhale. Faith is what you do when you lay down and close your eyes at night without ever wondering if your eyes will open in the morning. Faith allows you to walk down the street, drive your car, or take public transportation without concern about the law of gravity and how it keeps you firmly planted on the earth. Faith is knowing and then thinking, feeling, and behaving like you know.

The third step to creation is the proper use of the imagination. Your imagination is what you see in your mind's eye—that third eye you use to create images of that which you choose for your reality. Everything is created first in the imagination. In the invisible, intangible realm. That realm is the place of the substance of the universe, the place where all things are born. God is the substance of the universe. When you use your inner connection to God to create an image, the vibratory waves of that energy *must* manifest in physical form. Just like a baby in the womb—like life itself, which we cannot see but *know* exists—your imagination must be nurtured and fed without your ever once questioning whether or not it will emerge and be born. When you plant images in the womb of your mind, in your imagination, those images grow and bear fruit. Today, we call this process "visualization." The ancient mothers called it "getting in touch with God." Allowing the imagination to structure and create your world in the realm of substance ensures that your thoughts will result in live births.

Developing a disciplined will and a deep spiritual understanding are the next steps in the creation of a new reality. The will is the bridge to the future. It must be disciplined, meaning you cannot waver back and forth. It must be supported by a spiritual understanding of how creation works and what you are creating. For example, if you say you are going on a diet, you must manifest all the steps outlined thus far. You must have an idea of how much weight you want to lose, that is, how much Light you want to see. You must have faith in your ability to lose the weight (see the Light). You must see yourself as you want to be (use your imagination!), and you must take the necessary steps to get to that point by disciplining your will. You must come to understand your eating patterns and consciously eliminate those that you know are counter-productive. You must understand the purpose of food and learn what you need to sustain yourself. You must also understand that you cannot accomplish your goal of losing weight overnight. You must be very clear about why you want to lose the weight.

Once you make a disciplined commitment to your self and alter your diet with understanding, what you desire must manifest. Then, step by step, little by little, you will see the fruits of your labor. This same process holds true for creating work, meaningful relationships, or any other good thing we desire in life.

We must also master the art of discernment, of how to distinguish the truth from that which is not true. This is a difficult process since most of us are taught from a very early age to rely primarily on our physical senses. We generally place more stock in that which we can hear and see before we will give any credence to that which we know intuitively. Through discernment, you can train yourself to see beyond the physical to the deeper spiritual meaning of people, situations, and circumstances.

For example, say it is two days before pay day. You look in your wallet and it is bare. You have paid all of your bills and know that you have no cash left in the bank. Your first inclination is to say, "I'm broke. I have no money." That is *not* the truth! The truth is that you are only temporarily out of cash. You *know* that a check is being prepared for you. You *know* that you will have some money in a matter of hours, even if it is forty-eight hours away. Why then, do you use the creative powers of your thoughts and words to create a negative image? Why? Because you have not been taught to discern, to look beyond the physical.

Realization, the process of bringing one's thoughts and feelings into harmony, is the cornerstone of creation. You must know in your heart—in your feeling world—and support your knowing with thoughts that affirm. That which you *deserve* is yours!

Very often, we "think" we want something, but we believe or "feel" we will not get it. Once you realize that what you want already exists, that it is already yours, and that its creation began in your mind, you will achieve peace. This peace is called realization, the step before the actual manifestation of your desires. Once you have crystallized an idea with faith, imagination, will, and understanding, you can realize it as yours. You can then move on to the final step of creation: rest.

There comes a point when you have to release your ideas, when you have to rest and let the universe do its job. Once you have asked for something, once you have created it in the substance of your mind and given thanks for it, you can rest. There is nothing more for you to do. You have planted the seed. You must then relax and know that it will grow. You can continue to nurture the seed along with loving, supportive thoughts. You can think about how it will feel when you have reached your desired goal. You can get excited about what you will do. But you must never worry, doubt, or fear. If there is anything further for you to do, have faith that the Light will bring forth the information you need. If things start to look as if they are not going to go your way, use discernment. Search for and know the truth. Be flexible, but do not doubt. Just relax. And rest.

The act of creation is a sure and impersonal process. What you can see and feel will "become"—"be" being the act of existence, and "come" being the attraction of a force or object.

⋏⋎⋏

Each day, my thoughts became clearer. In the silence, I was busily writing down all of the information that was being presented in and to my mind.

I thought a lot about the men in my life. I realized that, like my father, the male partners I had chosen as an adult had all been emotionally unavailable to me. I began to see that, because of that, they could never give me what I wanted or needed. I also realized that I did not know how to ask for what I wanted or needed. In every relationship I had been in, I always wanted more from the man than he was able to give. Yet, I had allowed myself to settle for less, to settle for what each man gave, out of fear that no one else would want me. I felt like and believed I was a burden to them, so I was grateful for the crumbs of affection I received. I believed there was something wrong about me, and therefore I was eager to accept whatever and whoever came my way.

The truth was, I was very needy. I was looking for a foundation. I needed support and encouragement, the very things I

381

had missed in my upbringing. I created and learned to live in a fantasy world, where I could pretend everything was alright even as I was being mistreated and abused. I brought these childhood experiences into every relationship I had, with men and with women.

Like my Uncle Lee, the partners I chose were noncommunicative. They could not easily express their feelings, and when they did, they were dishonest about them. Like my brother Ray, my men were distant, verbally abusive, or noncommittal. There was always a wall between us that I never seemed able to penetrate. My perpetual "what's the matter?" was usually met with resistance and hostility. I was called a "nag," a "pain in the ass," and a "crazy bitch" in response to my attempts to "make things right." Because I was accustomed to verbal abuse, I accepted their labels and believed I was wrong to "bother" my mates.

Then again, I did not know how to communicate my feelings very well either. As a child, I had not been allowed to express myself or my feelings. I was punished and forced into silence. I was told what to do and reprimanded or brutalized when I did not follow directions. Consequently, I never learned the distinction between what was appropriate and inappropriate communication, either in terms of what I said or what was said to me.

To make matters worse, for many years I was dead from the waist up. The pain of not being loved, the belief that I was ugly, fat, and not worth shit was difficult for me to deal with, so I simply shut down. The only time my entire body came alive was during the sexual act. It was only then that I could feel loved, only then that I believed I was pleasing to another person. I had never experienced nurturing, supportive intimacy as a child. I therefore misinterpreted sexual activity for intimacy. I was fascinated with touching and with the effect it had on my emotions. I became preoccupied with attaining emotional security, with being close to someone, with feeling good and making someone else feel good, but all of these desires were couched in sexuality. Then, because I was told and believed that I was bad, I searched out and did bad things. From my very first experience, "doing it"—the sex act—was the ultimate bad thing. I could therefore rationalize to myself why I did it, not realizing that I was reinforcing something that was not true.

As I sifted and sorted through my experiences as the days passed by, I began to ask why certain things had happened in my life. Some answers came very quickly.

People come into your life for a reason or a season. Everyone comes into your life for a purpose. Your actions determine how that purpose plays out.

Ronald was there to nurture and support you. He made you feel as beautiful as the other girls. You chose to have sex with him out of anger and rebellion.

Tommy was just passing through. He could have helped you develop strength. You chose to give in. Your daughter had to be born. Her spirit chose you to set up precisely the lessons she would need to learn in her own lifetime.

Charlie was the manifestation of all your most negative thoughts and emotions. He did to you everything you were doing to yourself. He said to you your own secret thoughts and feelings. At any time, you could have put an end to that lesson by denying him access to you. You chose to stay.

Charles was simply a bad choice. Another act of anger and rebellion.

Ernie was your gift, your blessing, but you tried to make that relationship more than it was rather than just enjoying it for the moments you two shared. You lied to yourself about Ernie. He told you the truth, but you refused to hear it.

Adeyemi was your opportunity to make peace with your father. He did to you everything you saw your father do. You accepted it then, and you accept it now. In your mind, you had tried to make your father into something he was not. You tried to do the same thing with Adeyemi: to make him into something that he was not. You have had difficulty accepting the truth. You must do that before you can find true love with another person. You must learn to accept and love yourself.

I tried for days to answer the question, Who am I? I wanted, needed to know, but no ideas came to mind. I started writing down everything I knew about myself. What came most readily to mind was what I had done, not who I was. I started listing qualities next: the good ones on one side of the paper, the bad ones on the other. I ended up with two pages of bad stuff and four lines of good. That upset me to the point of tears. Why, I cried, couldn't I think anything good about me? What was the matter with me?

The answer came immediately, as before.

You have been damaged, and you live in pain. You draw into your consciousness the things you concentrate on. Your mind is the soil. Your thoughts are the seeds. If you continue to plant seeds of pain, you will remain damaged. Actually, your position is much better than you realize. You must release all negative energy, ideas, and thoughts. Once you learn that lesson, you will be free to move in any direction you choose. Right now, you must nurture yourself. Be good to yourself. You are in the final stages of transformation. There will be many reconciliations. You must be willing to revise your judgments. Think about your goals. All that you need will come. Love is the strongest force in the universe.

Of course, that revelation did not answer my question. But it gave me something to think about. It made me think about what I wanted in life, for myself and for my children, rather than about who I was.

♦·♦·♦

Piranhas are very vicious fish with voracious appetites. They travel in packs, capturing and devouring other fish and sea animals unfortunate enough to cross their paths. As an experiment, a scientist placed an adult piranha in a glass tank. He then poured hundreds of guppies into the tank with the piranha and allowed it to eat all the guppies it wanted. For days, the scientist supplied the piranha with a seemingly endless supply of guppies. One day, after the piranha had consumed all of the guppies from its last feeding frenzy, the scientist placed a clear glass plate across the middle of the tank. On one side was the piranha. On the other side, the scientist poured hundreds of guppies. The piranha, realizing it was dinner time again and seeing all those appetizers as usual, attempted to go after his meal. Each time he tried to get a guppy, he bumped his head on the glass plate. For several days, the piranha made futile attempt after futile attempt to catch even one of the little morsels—bumping, sometimes bashing his head over and over against the partition. After about ten days, the piranha stopped trying. The scientist then removed the glass divider from the tank. The guppies spilled over to the other side, swimming nonchalantly around the hungry piranha, who seemed oblivious to them. Six days passed, but the big fish made no attempts to capture or eat any of the guppies. Eventually, the piranha, a natural-born predator if ever there was one, died of starvation.

Life provides an unlimited supply of everything we need to survive. Nothing in the nature of life holds anything against or away from us. Often, we make attempts to get the things we want. If we are unsuccessful, we may try again and again with no success. Eventually, we come to the conclusion that something or someone can hold our good or goodness away from us. We figure that we have failed before and subsequently stop making any attempts to get what we want. As a result, we watch passively as our dreams and desires swim past and around us every moment of every day. Like the piranha who suffered repeated bumps on the head when it attempted to get at the guppies on the other side of the glass wall, we only remember those incidents in which we were unsuccessful in our attempts to capture our good. Eventually, we end up starving ourselves to death, depriving ourselves of the good that is all around us and ours for the taking.

Depending upon your conditioning in childhood, you may have a tendency to emphasize what you fear and do not want. You may focus on your failures or negative experiences. You may remember only the pain you have experienced in the past, refusing to understand the concepts of divine timing and divine order, which decree that there is a time and a place for everything. Still, no matter how much you might want something or do to get it, if the time for it is not right, you will not achieve your goals. When the universe does not allow your plan to unfold, it may not be a reflection of your worthiness to have. It may simply be an issue of timing or order. Then again, sometimes we ask for things we are not prepared to receive. We do not have our minds, lives, or spirits "in order" to receive them. Our foundations may not be solid, or we may not have received the necessary training, exposure, or expertise to accomplish and sustain our goals.

Another important factor to consider is clarity. You must be clear about what you want. All too often, we send out mixed signals: wanting one thing today and changing our minds about it tomorrow, saying we are ready for a thing one minute, and then expressing reservations about having it the next. Asking for something to manifest in our lives and then expressing doubt that it will happen. These are all examples of a lack of clarity. Clarity requires not only that you know what you want, but that you know why you want it, how you will use it, and what benefits you expect to derive from it.

You must believe with every fiber of your being that you are worthy of having that which you desire. Most of all, you must expect the highest and the best for yourself. The universe does not understand or respond to mediocrity. Ask for and expect the best. And be specific. Do not ask for "a little house in a quiet neighborhood somewhere"—that could mean a shack in the Appalachians! On the other hand, when you reject the something less than what you want that is presented to you because of your lack of clarity and specificity, the universe will respond to your ingratitude. You must *specify* your desires with clarity. In lieu of that, you must always ask that the greatest possible good in an area be brought into your experience. Without clarity and order, in cooperation with divine timing, you will continue to bump your head against the wall and wallow in disappointment.

I had been in my bedroom for fifteen days on the morning I first saw myself. I was on my way out of the bathroom when I had an urge to look in the mirror. For several minutes, I just stared at myself, looking directly into the reflection of my eyes. It was the first time in my life that I had ever really "looked" at myself. All my life, I had "seen" myself. I had stood before any number of mirrors brushing my hair, inspecting pimples, putting on make-up, and checking my teeth to make sure no fragments of meat were stuck between them. But I had never taken a long, hard look at myself. When I did, the energy of making direct eye contact with myself was incredible. I could feel it moving throughout my entire body. Again, I asked myself, Who am I? At first nothing came, so I asked again.

A voice answered. *"You are not ugly"*.

Who am I?

"You are not bad."

Who am I?

"You are...enough."

Who am I?

"You are good enough."

Who am I?

"You are goodness and growth."

Who am I?

"You are beauty and creativity."

Who am I?

"You are strength and power."

Who am I?

"You are divine light and love made manifest."

Who am I?

"You are...a child of God."

That is when I started to cry. I understood in that moment that there really was a God who loved me and accepted me. I knew from then on that I had to rediscover God.

I felt like a hermit coming out of a cave. Slowly, I immersed myself back into my life—talking to the children, going outside, tending to the house. I even plugged the telephone back in. I had not spoken to another living being in so long, I did not think I would know what to say. I was in a very delicate condition. For the first few days, the energy flowing through my body stayed strong. The voices inside of me guided me in what to do, every step of the way.

I had to decide what to do with my life. It was the day before Christmas. The children did not want to celebrate the holiday, but they did want me to cook, so I did. I made a big dinner and we all ate together.

I was eating when the thought first crossed my mind: *"Change your look. Let the outside reflect the inside."* I had never thought about it. I had not changed my hair or my style of dress for many years. I was reluctant to do anything because I did not know what would work. I decided to get my hair braided.

Tulani Jordan–Kinard is one of the kindest, most loving women I have ever met. For five days, she gently worked on my head, never knowing that all the while she was healing me. She took her time and handled my head with such tenderness, it felt as if she were praying over it. When she was done, I was a completely different person. That is why I now recommend to any woman: when you are in a state of healing, get your hair done. No matter what is going on in your life, if your hair looks good, you'll feel good.

I was shaping and building a new me. Actually, I was finding and discovering the real me, the me I had never known. I was thirty-three years old. I had three children. I had been married once and almost-married once. I had seen days of pain and anguish, joy and triumph. Yet, I had no idea who I was. Instead of being distressed about it, though, I decided to be excited about it. I mean, why not? I had nothing to lose.

I decided to go on a journey. A journey of self-discovery. My first stop was the bookstore. I figured any self-respecting bookstore would have lots of books on the subject. I stayed in the store for hours, scanning the shelves, thumbing through books and checking the bibliographies of the ones I liked. I spent a hundred bucks, but I wrote down the titles of at least five hundred dollars' worth of books that I wanted to check out later. I ran home to begin my journey.

Of all the books I purchased that day, the one that had the greatest effect on me was *The Dynamic Laws of Prayer* by Catherine Ponder. In her book, Ponder not only talks about prayer, she talks about the presence of God in our lives as the only force that matters. This was a totally new concept to me. I, like so many others, had been taught that God was far off and punitive. I had been taught that without Jesus I was doomed to hell. That we were all wretched sinners, born in sin and incapable of doing anything good on our own. That one book changed my entire understanding. From there I went to *Practicing the Presence* by Joel Goldsmith, and then on to *Great Women of Antiquity* by Ivan van Sertima. In each of these classic works, I found something new to be excited about. First God, then life, and then myself. I forgot that I was a law student preparing to take the bar exam and became engrossed in literature about spirituality and women. I spent every free moment I had searching to find the core, the truth of my being, of God, of the world.

I discovered that most of what I had been taught about being a woman had no basis in anything other than pain and anger. I came to understand that the women who had raised me were angry, and that their anger had caused them pain and the desire to inflict pain. My grandmother thought being a woman was bad. My Aunt Nancy thought being a woman meant you were less than a man. My "pretend mother," Nett, in her own quiet way, was a strong woman, but she had given her strength away. I had no idea what my real mother was like. It was then and there that I decided to find out.

I went back to school and to work and, within a matter of weeks, I was back in the swing of things. I began attending activities in the Yoruba community again. My fears over what people would think and say proved false. A few people had heard about what had happened. Most, I learned, had absolutely no idea, nor did they care what had gone on. When anyone asked me about it, I simply told them the truth.

I wish I could say that I did not see Adeyemi. I cannot. Slowly at first, then with more frequency, we began to speak to each other. Soon we became intimate again. This time, however, it was different. I was uncomfortable with all the sneaking around we had to do and he was too, but there was much unfinished business between us. I did not beat myself up about it. I stayed clear about what I was doing and never placed any undue demands on him for his time and attention. He, of course, never said or demanded anything.

One day, out of the clear blue, Alberta, Daddy's widow, called. She said she had found some papers, some old cards and letters, that had belonged to my father. She thought I might like to have them. When I went to inspect them, I found a letter from my mother's sister, my Aunt Alma. Alma's phone number and address were on the stationery. She lived in Washington, D.C.

I went home and sat staring at the telephone for hours. What would I say? How would I explain who I was? A voice from inside me provided the answer: *She is your mother's sister, she will know who you are.* After a moment of silent prayer, I called. A very soft, fragile voice answered the telephone.

"Alma? I hope I am not disturbing you, but this is Ronnie, Sarah's daughter."

Silence.

"Hello? Alma? Are you there?"

All of a sudden it sounded as if a dam had broken on the other end of the line. The voice boomed back.

"Thank you, Jesus! Thank you, Jesus! Thank You! Thank You! Thank You! Oh, I have waited so long! Thank you, Jesus! My baby sister has waited so long! How are you, baby? How are you? Thank you, Jesus!"

Aunt Alma carried on like that, crying and shouting for joy and Jesus, for about three minutes. I couldn't get a word in edgewise. Every time she thanked Jesus, she would ask me something else.

"Where are you?! Thank you, Jesus! Where have you been? I've been looking for you for years! Nobody knew, nobody knew! I prayed and prayed and asked God before he closed my eyes for the last time to let me see my baby sister's babies. Where is your brother? Thank you, Jesus!"

We stayed on the telephone for three hours. I told her where I was, where Ray was, how I was, how he was, and everything else she asked me between shouts and thank-you-Jesuses. I told her I was in law school. That made her cry. She told me my mother had been very smart too. She would have been very proud of me, Aunt Alma said. I told her I would try to get down to Washington to see her as soon as I could.

When I hung up, I knew the piece of me I had been looking for all my life was about to fall into place. I had to find the money to make the trip to D.C.. I just had to!

When I spoke to Adeyemi the next day, he told me he was going to Washington the following weekend for a conference. He was driving down alone. I asked him if I could ride with him and told him why. He said it was fine with him.

When I got to the door of my Aunt Alma's apartment building, my hands were shaking and my knees were trembling so bad, I had to talk myself into a state of calm before I could ring the bell. She was waiting for me in the hallway by the time I got to the top of the stairs. For a full minute, we just stared at each other. Seeing my mother's sister was like seeing an older version of myself. She was somewhat shorter than me, actually she was very petite, but for the first time in my life, I saw someone, another woman, who looked like me. And she was absolutely gorgeous!

I don't know who cried first, but we both stood in that hallway crying our hearts out. And this was even before we embraced one another! When she touched me I fell apart, but not like before. This time, I was overcome with joy.

She had fixed some tea, cornbread, and collard greens. She explained that she did not eat meat because of her heart and blood pressure. She said she was sure I would like tea because my mother had loved tea. Until that day, I had hated tea. We chatted for awhile, talking about minor things, before we got down to the real business at hand:

"Tell me about my mother."

Aunt Alma left me sitting in the kitchen sipping tea while she went into her bedroom and pulled out an old photo album. She placed the album before me on the kitchen table, opened it, and gave me life.

The book was filled with family pictures dating back to the 1800s. In it, I met my maternal great-grandmother. A pure Black African, Aunt Alma said. I also met my maternal grandmother, a Black sharecropper from Virginia who married a man who was part Indian and part African. Finally, I met my mother, Sarah Jefferson.

She looked just like the woman I had seen many times in my dreams. For the first time, I knew she was real. She was a tall, thin woman with large breasts. Her face was my face. She had thick shoulder-length hair, which she wore pinned in a bun on the top of her head. She had long, graceful fingers and legs. The closer I looked, the more I realized that my oldest daughter Gemmia looked just like her. I devoured page after page of pictures of her—in cars, on the beach, in the street, with Aunt Alma and her two other older sisters, with my father, carrying me. On one page, there were two pictures, side by side: one of her when she was pregnant with me and another of her holding me as a baby and kissing my face.

Of course, you know what I did when I saw that, right? I cried. Like a baby. Aunt Alma poured me some more tea, and then she told me the whole story.

My mother, she said, was a stubborn, hard-headed, strong-willed child who was always getting whipped by their daddy. According to Aunt Alma, her sister Sarah had a spirit about her that made her special, but "she just wouldn't listen to nobody." She went to work when she was sixteen years old, following behind some boy—a man, really. He was in his twenties and married, but my mother swore she loved him. She got a job as a porter and servant for the Pennsylvania Railroad. She hated that job, but she held on to it for almost fifteen years. That was how she met Nancy and Dora, Aunt Alma told me. They all worked together cleaning the cars of the trains and babysitting the white passengers' children.

Being told that Aunt Nancy was not really related to me, that she was only my mother's "play sister" and not really my blood aunt took me a minute to digest. Still, I was only a little bit stunned. So much had happened. I had been told about and had found out about so many lies and stories with regard to my family, I had learned not to be surprised by anything.

Anyway, Aunt Alma continued, my mother worked the run from Virginia to Philadelphia and then to New York City and back. On the weekends, she and Nancy and Dora would sleep over in New York and party.

"Your mother loved to party," Aunt Alma said. "She was a great dancer and loved to hang out in the clubs and bars in the Big Apple, they called it. That's how she met your father. He was a gambling man."

"One thing Sarah always told me was that she wanted a pretty man to make her babies. Whenever she had a new beau, she would call me up and say, 'It ain't him. He ain't pretty enough!' Your Daddy was *just* pretty enough."

"Nancy got married first and left the job, then Dora, but your father would just not marry your mother. So Sarah would work all week, and then spend the weekend partying with Horace."

"Anyway, she took ill and had to stay in New York for awhile. She had no place to stay, so your father took her to his mother's house. They thought it would only be a few days or so, but she didn't get any better. I told her it was her drinking. She was a heavy drinker and smoker. I had a great suspicion that your Daddy's mother was putting something in her food, but nobody dared to say a word to either one of them about it."

"Sarah had been off work so long, they fired her, even though she was only five years away from her pension. I guess she hated that job so much, getting sick was the only way she knew to get out of it. She had no sick benefits, but they gave her a little pension money and just fired her. It didn't matter because she couldn't go back to work pregnant. She was pregnant with your brother."

When my brother Ray was born, Aunt Alma told me, the doctors discovered that my mother had breast cancer and leukemia. They were treating her for the leukemia, but they wanted to remove her breasts. My mother loved her breasts, Alma said. They were big and they stood up, and she was very proud of them. So she told the doctors to go to hell. They were not chopping her breasts off like some chunks of bad meat at the butcher shop.

Aunt Alma got quiet for a minute. She reached for my hand and squeezed it tight before she went on. "By then, she was drinking real heavy. If the truth be told, Ronnie, your mother was really an alcoholic, but nobody never said nothing to her because she would get mad and want to fight if they did."

Aunt Alma's face lightened a little bit, then darkened. When she started speaking again, her tone was hushed. "Your mother was a fighter. She needed to be, living in the house with your grandmother while your father was out gambling. He used to beat her, too you know. She would get drunk and he would beat her. And his mother never said a word. Sarah would call me up afterwards to come over and dress her wounds. That mother of his would hiss and complain, but she never helped my sister. Not one bit."

When my mother told Aunt Alma she was pregnant again, Aunt Alma said she begged her not to have another baby. She thought it would be too much for Sarah, what with her sickness and all. Besides that, Aunt Alma told me, just as if she was talking to her sister again, Baby Ray wasn't quite two years old yet.

Aunt Alma said she begged my mother to leave my father, but she told her no, she wouldn't. She loved him, she said.

"When your mother loved a man, she loved him forever. You couldn't tell her anything about him, and the man could do no wrong."

"By the time you were born, she was confined to the bed. It

was a miracle that you were born normal. They tested you in the hospital for days and couldn't find anything wrong with you."

"I knew you were going to be fine once I heard you were born in the taxi," Aunt Alma said, smiling at me. "You were so eager to get here and get away from the liquor in your mama's system, I knew you were here to stay."

I thought, that probably explained why I've never been much of a drinker and don't drink at all as an adult: my mother kept me drunk when she was pregnant with me.

"Anyway, Sarah could barely walk. She kept you in a dresser drawer right by the side of her bed, but there were days when she could not even pick you up, she was so weak. But one day, to everyone's surprise, she got up and started walking around as if she were fine. She did her hair, painted her nails, and started cooking and cleaning up around the house. She didn't touch a drop of liquor, but she still smoked."

"She told everybody that she had something else to do before she died. She had promised God that if he let her do it, she would never touch another drop of whiskey. What she had to do was get pregnant again. Lord! It almost killed her. By the time the baby was born, she couldn't even move."

"It was another miracle baby. She didn't even bring the child home, poor thing. She gave it right away to Dora and her husband."

That was my "cousin," Junior, I thought, remembering back to the day when Ray had broken the news to me about Junior being our brother and all. Once again, I was finding out just how little I had been told of the truth.

"That was sometime in December or January," Aunt Alma continued. "By then, Sarah's breasts were oozing and the smell was so bad you could hardly stand to be in the same room with her. Your grandmother complained about it all the time. Your Daddy begged her to go to the hospital. She refused. She said she wanted to stay home long enough to give your brother a birthday party."

I remembered from my dream that Sarah's birthday was March the seventh. Ray's was March the thirty-first.

"She didn't make the party. On March twentieth, your Daddy took her to the hospital. Her breasts were removed on the twenty-second, and she died on the twenty-sixth."

I had just turned two years old, I thought.

"Your father didn't have no insurance and no money. He never asked anyone for help. When I got to the cemetery and saw that your mother was being buried in a pauper's grave with five other people—complete strangers—I fainted dead away."

"That was when the mess really started. Your mother had a lot of Social Security money that you and Ray were entitled to. Everyone knew that whoever took you two would get the money. Sarah and Nancy had always played pretend-sisters, and your mother made Nancy promise that if anything ever happened to her, she would take you two babies."

"Your Daddy wouldn't hear nothin' of that. He said he and his mother would work it out to keep you. He would not even entertain the idea of you all living with any of your aunts. I lost track of you for awhile after Sarah died, and it was not until you moved to Nancy's that I even knew where you were. But for some reason, Nancy was not too keen on y'all seeing us, either."

Closing the photo album carefully, Aunt Alma said she had only met my father's new wife Nett once or twice, but she seemed very nice. She told me she knew about the lies everyone had told me about my mother and how everybody had wanted us for the money. She also knew that no one had ever told us about our younger brother.

I felt relieved and crazed at the same time. Finally, everything made sense, but it didn't make sense. Why the lies? Why had my father been so abusive to my mother? At last I understood my seeming tolerance for abuse myself. At last I understood my unexplainable addiction to men. I still didn't understand my grandmother's disdain for me, but I did understand the reasons behind some of it. She did not like my mother, so it was no surprise that she would not like me. Yet, she liked my brother. That part still confused me.

Aunt Alma must have sensed my distress and confusion

because she took me by the hand and said, "Your mother was a beautiful woman. She was strong, powerful, and smart as a whip. She was also blessed. She had the gift of sight. She could 'see' things, and she could speak them out. It made people kind of afraid of her. Her weakness was men. Men made her drink herself to death, made her abuse herself. Women did not like your mother because she spoke her mind and took all the men."

"There are a lot of things about your mother that you would do good to follow, but don't ever give your life over for no man. Love God, and He will bring you the right man, honey. He brought me one when I was seventy-six years old."

I stopped sulking long enough to raise my eyebrows at what Aunt Alma had said.

"That's right! *I* am a newlywed! Only been married fourteen months. He's old, he's bald, he's got a bad heart, but he keeps me warm at night and does everything in his power to keep me happy."

As I was getting ready to go, Aunt Alma hugged me and told me, "Ronnie, if I never see you again, remember this one thing: Your mother loved you. She loved you, and I love you. You are a miracle. You came into this world to do a good work."

I promised Aunt Alma I would call her in a week or so. She was moving into her new husband's house and would have the new phone number given out on the old number. I also promised to get in touch with my Aunt Lizzie who, Aunt Alma told me, lived in Brooklyn, just seven blocks away from my house. She gave me several pictures of my mother and some of my parents together. I kissed her and left.

I tried to get in touch with Aunt Alma for two weeks after I got back to New York. When I repeatedly did not get an answer, I called Aunt Lizzie. She was glad to hear from me but not excited like Aunt Alma had been. Aunt Lizzie told me she had just buried her sister. Aunt Alma had died the week before, just ten days after my visit.

THE

Journal

I'm gonna get me some tonight!
When I think about it, I get chills.
I can't wait!
All my hairs are standing on end.
Oh, Joy! Oh, Rapture!
I'm gonna get me some tonight!
I've got to be cool.
Can't be too anxious.
I don't want anything to go wrong
Let me think about something else.
I can't!
I can't think about anything else!
I'm too excited!
Be still, my panting heart!

Wait a minute!
I don't have anything to be ashamed of!
I want everybody to know.
I want to shout, "Hey, you! Guess what?
I'm gonna get me some tonight!"
I feels good just to think about it.
I can remember just how it feels.
It's warm.
No, it's cold.
It slips. It slides.
Ooooh, I can't take it!

When I close my eyes and think about it,
I get goose bumps.
My nipples get hard.
My brain gets muddled.
Everything inside of me starts shaking and quivering.
I can't wait any longer.
I feel like I am losing my mind!
I'm actually going crazy
Oh, Lordy! Lordy! Lordy!
I'm gonna get me some tonight!

Hägen Daazs!
What a way to go!

CHAPTER 26

An Exhibit of Peace

A female child needs a mother. She needs a mother to teach her about the intricacies of womanhood. That mother must be a friend, a confidant, a disciplinarian, and a role model. She must nurture, teach, support, push, hold back, and know when to let go. I never had a mother. I tried to make Nett my mother. She had most of the qualifications, but in a crunch, she simply didn't make the grade.

The mother is the lifeline of the female. The mother's energy determines how the female child develops, how she looks at herself, and what she will do with her own children. You cannot replace a mother. There is a part of you that will always yearn to know, to have the connection to her. I slept around, ate too much, and chain-smoked because I was not connected to mine. Once the connection was made, however, I was able to move to the next level of development.

I never knew that all those years I had been mad at my mother. How can a woman be mad at her mother, you ask? You cannot allow yourself to explore the true depths and feelings of such an awful emotion. It's too horrible, too painful, to contemplate.

So what did I do when I realized what I was feeling? I shut down. I shut down the part of my womanhood that was connected to motherhood, mothering, and being a mother. I made up new rules and guidelines for myself. I also made up all kinds of excuses.

The truth of the matter was that I was pissed off that my mother had died and left me. I was even more outraged that she had left me to be raised by my grandmother. Then, once I discovered the truth about my mother's relationship with my father, I was furious that she would allow herself to be so consumed by him that it killed her and I was left alone. One day, I got so mad at my mother that I taped her picture to my bathroom mirror and cursed her out, but good. I called her every name in the book. I told her what I really felt about what she had done. About her dying and leaving me, and about what had happened to me as a result.

When I finished my tirade, I cried for hours. Then I whimpered for at least two days. And then I felt better.

In a spiritual seminar I once attended, I learned a concept that has helped me a great deal: we choose our parents. We choose them because they can provide us with the exact circumstances and situations we need to learn our own special spiritual lessons and complete our unique spiritual mission. When I first heard this, it sounded totally insane to me. Why would I choose a mother who would die and an emotionally distant father? Were they all that was available at the time? No. I had to look for the lessons. I had to discover what it was that I had learned as a result of my experiences with my parents.

After a silent moment of contemplation and soul searching, I realized that I had learned how to forgive, how not to judge, and how to take care of myself. I had also learned the value of freedom and how much most people take it for granted. In order for my spirit to be at peace, I had to learn to forgive my parents. I had to accept the fact that if they had known better they would have done better. Nothing else made sense to me.

All of us are here on this earthly plane trying to survive. We each do the best we can with the circumstances of our lives and core issues, given the lessons we must learn. Parents are no different. They too are simply hurt little children who grow up to be hurt adults, who in turn hurt their own children. I wanted to blame my parents for all the pain they had caused me, but that was too painful. It took me a long time and a lot of internal struggle to understand that the blood of my parents, which ran through my veins, was a living energy that sustained me.

Eventually, I came to realize that whatever I felt about my parents would dictate how I treated myself. It was an inescapable fact: If I wanted to survive, I had to let go of any negativity I felt about my parents. It was easy to forgive my mother. She had died when I was very young. It was not so simple with my father.

I was at a friend's house one Saturday afternoon watching television while she went out. There was a movie on about a little boy who had been molested by a Catholic priest. In one scene, the little boy was in the bathroom when his father came in behind him suddenly. The child went berserk. He had flashbacks of the face and hands of his attacker, the priest, and went wild. The father was confused and upset. He could not figure out what had happened to his son, so he grabbed the boy and began to shake and chastise him for his behavior. All of a sudden, as I sat watching that scene, my entire body began to tremble. I was remembering my own molestation, when I was raped by my Uncle Lee. Waves of despair ripped through my body, causing me to double over in pain. But it was not a physical pain. It was the pain of trauma.

At first, I did not realize what was happening to me. I thought I had healed that memory. I was pretty sure I had forgiven Uncle Lee. I found out differently that afternoon. Something happened to me when I saw the father in that movie shake his son. Immediately, I began to wail and cry like a baby. There is no way I can adequately describe what I experienced next. It felt so strange. It was almost as if I was outside of my body. I could hear and see myself wailing and carrying on like crazy. I tried to shut my own mouth. I began to call out for my father, begging him to save me, to help me, to protect me.

My inner voice spoke to me again:
Let it out and let it go. You have held on for too long. You have only scratched the surface. You have not reached the core.

There are levels and degrees of pain, of suffering, and of healing you have yet to experience. Some levels are quite simple to heal. Others take much more time and work. You have done well on your own. Now it is time to forgive and move to the next level. Forgive your father for not being there. Forgive him for his inability to love and protect you the way you wanted him to. Forgive him for being who he was because he had pain in his heart too. Once you forgive him, the healing can proceed. A new scar will form, and the pain will subside. It will co-exist peacefully with you until it is time to go to the next level.

Healing is a miracle from God. It is a miracle about which you must learn and know more. Right now, forgive, surrender, and let go.

All those years of working to forgive Uncle Lee and it was my father whom I had blamed and not forgiven for the pain Uncle Lee had caused me. The pain of that thought was so unbearable I fell to my knees and began to scream out loud, "I forgive you, Daddy. I forgive you. Please, let me go!"

I stayed on my knees for at least an hour. When I was finally able to raise myself off the floor, the movie was over. I remember looking at the clock, trying to figure out how I was going to get home to the children. It was ten minutes after four on a Saturday afternoon, the same day of the week and just about the same time of day that Uncle Lee had violated my life, some twenty years earlier.

The next day, Sunday, I went to the bookstore and found a book called *The Course in Miracles*. It literally saved my life.

ᐯᐧᐯᐧᐯ

All each of us really wants in life is to be happy. We want to feel good about getting up in the morning. We want to feel good about whatever it is we do and how we do it. We want to feel happy about the way we look and how people respond to us. We want happiness, but we need love. Every living being needs to be loved and nurtured and supported and encouraged—not because of what they do, but simply because they are. Love makes us feel worthy. When we feel worthy, we are happy. In a state of happiness, we find the necessary courage and motivation to make valuable contributions to our growth and to the growth of everything and everyone around us.

One of the things that keeps us from being happy is our belief that we are separated from God. We think there is something we must be or do to attain god-like qualities. In order to find out what those qualities are, we are taught that we must behave a certain way. Actually, behavior has nothing to do with what is going on in our hearts, and it is within our hearts that God resides. We do not have to seek God. We are God, each one of us, expressing God in a unique and divine way.

According to *The Course in Miracles*, God is all there is. God made everything. Therefore, God is everything. When we forget that, we start seeing things with jaundiced eyes—criticizing, judging, and fearing. What we have not been taught is that the further we think we are away from God, the less likely we are to act like God. As a result, thousands of years of indoctrination that we are unworthy and unfit to know God has caused us to develop very ungodly behaviors and attitudes.

Further complicating the matter is the proliferation of male images of God. In the Judeo–Christian belief system, the Christ, the disciples, and almost all of the holy people mentioned in the Bible are males. The first woman we meet in Christian lore and training is a defiant old apple-eater named Eve, who, we are taught, defied God and caused so much pain and destruction to mankind. Consequently, we women are taught to be ashamed of that part of our nature which questions and explores. We are taught about all the ills women create for mankind and the problems we create for ourselves. God, we are taught, doesn't create problems. How then are we women to accept ourselves as divine creations of God when we are taught that we are wicked troublemakers? These stories and many others foster women's belief, in particular, that they are separate from the source of all good, from God. In the telling of the story, however, the men overlook one very important point: If women are so evil and unworthy, why did God turn to the body of woman to bring forth His only begotten son? Men, in all their innocence and greatness, could not do for God what a woman could do.

As Black women living in a white male-dominated society, it is sometimes difficult to determine what will make us happy. It is difficult to determine what happiness looks like, period. This difficulty and lack of clarity leads to the chaos, confusion, and strife identified as "Black women's issues." These issues must not be attacked. They must be healed.

America will not, cannot, heal its wounds until the African American woman's wounds are healed. The wounds of slavery, racial violence, segregation, poverty, and contemptuous disregard for life. Of children killing each other. Of men killing and abusing women and warring with one another. Of starvation, homelessness, disease, and despair in every corner of the world—not one of these wounds will be healed until the Black woman in the United States is healed, or rather, heals herself.

The Black woman is the lowest common denominator in the American work force. She does the drudge work. She is the cook, the nanny, the nurse, the teacher, the secretary, the telephone operator, the cleaning woman, and the receptionist. It is she who makes sure things are ready and able to run smoothly. It is her shoulders upon which other workers—white men, white women, black men, and others—stand as they move up the career ladder. It is the failure to address the Black woman's issues that creates the work other people are paid far more than she to do.

The Black woman is also the primary nurturing source of both the Black and white communities in this country. If all Black women were to stay home for just one day, how many systems of survival could not or would not function? If she were to pull her presence and her dollars from the economic structure, what would happen? It is quite possible and highly probable that everything and everyone across the nation would feel the blow and recognize her power.

If we understand that people create the energy of the environment, and if we would consider that the energy at the top and in the forefront is merely a reflection of the energy at the bottom and in the background, then we can catch a glimpse of the power Black women have. But it is we Black women who are not fully aware of our power. Look at the quality of life that a large number of us accept: Living and raising our children in poverty and in shelters. Living in abusive relationships. Living in anger, confusion, and disillusionment. Slaving away in work places that do not honor or respect us or our abilities. Dying disproportionately of breast cancer, uterine cancer, strokes, heart attacks, and AIDS. However, the ills of Black women manifest as problematic conditions in every facet of U.S. society.

The African American woman must be healed if this nation—indeed, the world—is to survive. How do we do that? Begin within.

We Black women have to stop looking outside of ourselves for validation, authorization, or qualification. We have to learn to love ourselves, to value ourselves, and accept ourselves for who and what we are. We have to relinquish our attachment to decadent and immoral attitudes and values and embrace the divinity of the Creator within each of us. We have to stop dressing up the outside, embellishing the physical body, and begin addressing the inside— the mental, emotional, and spiritual bodies. We have to stop kicking and complaining about our wounds while relinquishing responsibility for our own healing to others. We have to take responsibility for each and every thing that happens to us and in our lives. We must look at ourselves, individually and collectively, to determine what we must do, how we must do it, and how what we are doing or not doing keeps us from getting the things we want.

We have to stop holding our men responsible for our happiness. We must discover the things that make us happy, do them fearlessly, and set a new standard by which our men must treat us. We must know, believe, and have faith in the fact that we are the captains of our ships—our bodies, minds, and lives. Consequently, we must master our own fates. We can no longer afford to shift the blame to our men or to society for our broken hearts, shattered minds, unhealthy bodies, bad feet, or thinning nerves. We must honestly examine and correct what we ourselves are doing to contribute to our condition.

Black women in America have a rich and valid history, one that demonstrates our ability to "make it" against all odds. All we need to ask ourselves is this: Are we Black women today following the examples of our female ancestors, of our grandmothers and great-grandmothers? In many ways, many of these women were real clear about who they were and what they had to do. Some of them were so in tune with the Creator that they used that divine spark within themselves to accomplish seemingly impossible tasks. We have a connection to those women. They are in our blood. The circle has not been broken. It cannot be destroyed. The memory of their faith, courage, and strength is buried in our subconscious minds.

We Black women must make for ourselves the time and space we need to investigate and explore the world within us. What is inside us is our source of power. We must teach ourselves the things we need to know that we have never been taught, and we need to remember those things we have forgotten. In order to do this, we must use different language and terms to describe and define ourselves and communicate with one another. We do not want to continue to use the language and terms that have been used for centuries to dismiss and denigrate our culture and our very beings. We need to redefine and redescribe our experiences, practices, and beliefs in the context of the experiences and traditions of our ancestors. We must, however, expand our traditional African concepts, ideologies, and understandings to make them conducive to the constructs and realities of our modern-day psyches. This means we must expand our concept of family beyond the walls of our own individual living quarters and our concept of community beyond political boundaries. We must see wealth as something beyond the acquisition of money, material possessions, or good credit. Our ideals about womanhood should extend beyond diatribes about sexual righteousness. We Black women want to define for ourselves what our happiness looks like, and we want to set the standards by which we can achieve it.

Until we heal our wounds, we will not find happiness. Until we find happiness, we will not have peace. Until we have peace, the world will remain at war.

Aunt Alma stayed alive just long enough to give me the information I needed to advance my healing to the next level. That information connected a piece of my soul to my brain, my brain to my heart, and my heart to the universe. I had a mother. A spiritual woman, a third-generation African. A working woman. She was feisty and stubborn and she hit the bottle a little too hard sometimes. She was a "party girl" who lost herself in a romantic fantasy. But none of that mattered because she had also lent her body to God to bring me into the world. She was the body who made it possible for me to have a body. And knowledge about my mother brought me a feeling of connection and completion that I had never known. So many things began to make sense to me as a result.

The one thing I understood totally was that part of my mission in life was to break the mold, to stop the pattern and take my matriarchal line in another direction. I was up to me to recognize clearly the issues, learn from the poor choices each of us—my maternal ancestors and I—had made, and move myself and my daughters to another level of existence. My ancestors were depending on me. I accepted the mantle and took the responsibility very seriously.

I completed law school. Adeyemi came to my graduation, as did several members of Ernie's family, several of my close sister-friends, and a few priests from the Yoruba community who had stood by me and supported me through thick and thin. Again, other than my children, none of my "blood" relatives attended, but I forgave them.

I had been offered a job with the public defender's office in Philadelphia, but I was not sure about taking it. It would mean that I would have to leave New York. I had never lived anywhere else. The prospect was frightening. On the night before I had to give a response to the offer, I got down on my knees and prayed:

"God, I want a house. I want a house where I can raise my children and live in peace. It doesn't have to be a big house, but it should have lots of sun and be situated in a quiet, peaceful neighborhood where I can feel safe leaving my children. If you want me to take this job, God, give me a house. If it is Your will and desire for me to leave New York and build a new life in another place, then You must show me by giving me a house. I know it is done, and I give thanks and praise."

That was at ten-thirty on a Wednesday night.

At seven-forty-five Thursday morning, the telephone rang.

"Hello. You don't know me, but I am a friend of Sandy's. You two went to law school together."

"Yes..."

"Well, she told me that you were thinking about moving down here and I was just calling to tell you that I have a house to rent if you are interested."

"Hello!"

I did not take the time to question, worry, or wonder. When things fall into place like that, it just has to be divine order working on your behalf. I went to see the house and took the job on Friday. We were all packed by Sunday.

I arrived in Philadelphia in advance of the kids and the furniture at 2 o'clock that Monday morning. I had two suitcases of clothing and a bag of law books. A friend had advised me to stay at the Divine Tracey Hotel, an institution built by Father Divine. She told me it was cheap, clean, and safe. I went directly there, only to discover that I could not get a room because I was wearing pants. Father Divine had taught his followers that women could not wear pants, make-up, or nail polish, nor were they allowed to mingle with the men. I begged the woman at the desk to let me go into the bathroom, and I put on a skirt. She told me I could not even walk through the building in pants.

I hailed a cab. The driver suggested the Benjamin Franklin Hotel. It was a real whorehouse of a dump, but they had a room and they didn't care what I was wearing. The room was the size of a modest walk-in closet.

I had been in bed for five minutes when I heard a knock at the door.

"Yes?"

"Twenty bucks for a full lay, fifteen for a blow job."

"Well, that sounds very reasonable, but I have nowhere for you to lay and nothing for you to blow. Thank you, anyway."

I had two hours before it was time for me to report to work. I was about to become a lawyer.

The minute I walked into the office and sat down, I could feel the old familiar fears and feelings of intimidation rising up my spine. These people seemed pretty smart, I thought to myself. Not only that, they looked pretty wealthy. I spent two weeks in training with a group of new hires. When the training was over, I concluded that most of them were damn smart and the rest were pretty well-off. I felt dumb and out of place, not because I could not do what they did, but because I knew I did not want to be there. Deep in my heart, I knew I did not want to be a lawyer either. But I went to work anyway.

There was only one other Black woman in my trainee group, and she and I decided to hang out and study for the bar together. Shortly after making her acquaintance, I began to notice small things about my new friend, like the way she was always late, always needing to borrow money, and always making excuses for the various bumps and bruises that showed up on various parts of her body. I soon discovered that she was living in an abusive relationship and that she had a rip-roaring cocaine addiction to boot.

The word started spreading around the office really fast that "we" were trouble. One of the brothers in our group tried to pull my coat about her, but it sounded as if he was giving me the "good-girl, bad-girl" rap, so I cut him off at the knees. I tried to talk to my sister-friend myself. She was not ready to listen. One day, I was called into the head defender's office "for a chat," he said. He was thoroughly patronizing. I was much too good an attorney to start out like this, he told me. I needed to be more selective in picking my friends. If I needed help or counseling I should let somebody know. He was on a roll, and I stopped him in the middle of it.

"Wait a minute! Are you talking to me or to her?"

"Well, you're her friend, aren't you? Why would you be hanging out with her if you didn't have similar problems?"

I explained to him that just like all Black people didn't really look alike, we didn't all do the same things. *She* was beyond hope. *I* could be saved. My sister-friend was fired soon after that.

I was still going back and forth with Adeyemi. I had moved to a new city where the only people I knew were in jail (they were my clients). I was trying to furnish a four-bedroom house and studying for the bar exam. I was completely frazzled. And broke.

I woke up one morning realizing I didn't have a dime to my name and no where near the money I needed to put some gas in the car to get to work. Frantically, I searched all my purses and pockets. I looked underneath the sofa cushions and in the corners of all the rooms. I came up with thirty-seven cents. I was walking around the house feeling very sorry for myself, whining and crying, trying to figure out what I was doing in this half-dead city and how I was going to get to work with no gas and thirty-seven cents, when I heard the knock at the door.

It was a neighbor. The mailman had dropped my mail in her box because he didn't know me yet, she said. She was on her way out and hoped she had not disturbed me.

For a moment, I just stood there staring blankly at the three envelopes she handed me. My first three pieces of mail in my new home. A welcome letter from the gas company. An invitation to buy new storm windows and doors. A card from a good sister-friend back in Brooklyn. I ripped open the card from my friend first. A twenty-dollar bill fell out. The card said, "If I know you, you are broke and trying to figure out where to get the money to go to work. Save yourself and myself a lot of time and worry. Love ya, Bisi."

"Thank You, God!" I shouted. "Another ram in the bush!"

No matter what problem we are faced with, there is always an answer. Our problems are actually opportunities for us to grow, exercise faith, and find new horizons. Whether we realize, recognize, accept, or understand it, our problems are the result of our not facing some truth about ourselves, our habits, or how we allow other people to influence our lives. Problems thrust us into the darkness. What we must do is call forth the light. We can struggle with our problems, curse our situations, tell ourselves there is something or someone else to blame, but hidden in every apparently bad situation is a truth we need to realize. When we find it, all the other pieces will fall into place. The truth is, problems arise to let us know it is time for us to move beyond the limitations of our minds and emotions to a place of Light where we can develop the understanding we need to dismantle the cause of the problems.

We cannot aspire beyond who we think we are. We can educate ourselves, dress up real pretty, make sure we smell good and talk good, but who we think we are is the determining factor in what we will achieve in this world. How we feel about ourselves is called self-esteem. But before we can have esteem, we must first have a self. We must know our selves, inside and out, and be committed to the goals we have set. We must each know what our self is capable of doing and willing to do. We must then trust our self and learn to rely on it, knowing that, in a crunch, it will be there for us. If we cannot do that, our best-laid plans will fall to pieces every time.

The self represents who you are at the very core of your being. The self is the Spirit. In order to draw on the power of Spirit, you must maintain constant, conscious contact with your self. You must align both head and heart in order for the self to function at full capacity. You must get still, go within, and check up on your self frequently. You must make sure you know what you are doing and how you feel about what is happening around and within you. If you do not, you may get caught in the trap of doing and not feeling, thinking and not feeling, or, worst of all, not feeling anything at all.

I wore crystals around my neck, herbs in my belly button, oils on my forehead and behind my ears, and bells on my waist and ankles—and I still failed the bar exam by three points. I was devastated. I stayed home from work for three days, crying and trying to convince myself that I really was stupid and never would amount to anything. Then someone told me that Richard Nixon failed the bar twice before he passed it. That didn't make me feel a whole lot better, but it did give me something to work with. Working for a public agency also helped because it meant I could practice law without being barred.

I continued to work and study. More importantly, I resumed my "self search." I was really into it—reading and buying books, attending workshops and lectures and seminars, and generally finding out the good and not-so-good things about me. My readings and other sources led me to the conclusion that I had not passed the bar for two reasons: First, I did not think I could pass it because I didn't think I was smart enough. Second, I did not really want to be a lawyer. Pursuing a law career was for me a way of seeking power. I had been disempowered all of my life and I wanted power. Everyone respected lawyers, I figured. The only people considered more powerful than lawyers were doctors. Plus, I was still playing the old tapes from my childhood—all the stuff Grandma told me would surface whenever I was in a crunch. I had to find a way to heal that, to clear it out.

I called Grandma. I had not spoken to her since Daddy died, when she physically attacked me and pushed me out of his house. She was the same, wanting to know if I was still giving my money to that no-good man I had, if I had given the children the dresses she had sent them six years ago or thrown them in the garbage, when was I going to stop lying about being some damned lawyer, and where was my brother. In the midst of her inquisition, I was hit with an inspiration: ask her about your father's side of the family. That really set her off. What was I digging up that old shit for, she wanted to know. Why did I need to know whose father was who? Nobody had any money for me, she snorted indignantly, and "you sure ain't going to load your kids off on nobody."

Gently, I persisted. I kept prying until I got her to give up the names of three generations of ancestors in her line and two from my grandfather's line. I promised to call her again soon and send her some money. I lied about calling, but I sent her fifty dollars.

Acceptance was the key, I figured. I had to accept that my grandmother was a tortured soul because she chose to be that way. Case closed.

I took the bar again and failed by one point. This time, I did not fall apart afterwards. I realized there was something else for me to do. I prayed and meditated. I did not get a response about that, but I did discover it was time for me to let Adeyemi go.

After his graduation, Adeyemi had taken a very good-paying job in upstate New York. We were still seeing each other on and off. He was really trying to make a go of his marriage, but I knew we had a weakness for each other and I had been playing it to the hilt. However, I was at the point where I knew I wanted and needed more. Most of all, all the sneaking around and lying we had been doing about what we were doing was starting to wear me down. Not to mention the fact that it was in total conflict with my own spiritual work and development. Since my reconciliation with my godfather, I had made a commitment to live the mandates of my priesthood. As a result, I became increasingly uncomfortable with the nature of my relationship with Adeyemi. I knew he wasn't comfortable with it. Because I still loved him, I wanted him to be happy. I decided to love him enough to let him go. He was eager to make the transition.

I was enjoying a new phase of my life called celibacy. I had never lived more than nine months without being sexually active since I was fourteen years old. I began to explore what was going on in my body. When I felt the need for sex, I would allow my mind to explore the parts of my body that were responding. This exploration took me into the exploration of my chakras, those points of power in our bodies that respond to sound, light, and vibration. Without a long explanation here, I will say two things about chakras. One: What Europeans called chakras, our ancestors called *aché*, which means "power" or "truth." There are seven aché centers in our bodies, which correspond to our seven most basic life issues. The development and energy of these seven points determine how we approach life and respond to life's situations. Two: What we sometimes think is the need for sex, food, drugs, or activity in our lives is actually our inner response to an energy imbalance in one of our aché points. If we make an effort to understand how aché functions, we will learn more about how we ourselves function.

A friend of mine encouraged me to challenge the bar and make them find and give up the one point I needed, but by then it simply wasn't important to me anymore. I had decided I wanted to be a writer.

At first, I held on to my job at the public defender's office. My supervisor was willing to keep me on, and I was afraid to leave. You do not live eleven years on welfare, work your way off of it and up to making fifty grand a year with full medical and dental benefits, just to walk away and become a writer. I was also doing private spiritual consultations on the side, which generated some income but certainly nowhere near a fifty-thousand-dollar salary. Still, that little voice in the back of my head kept saying, over and over: *"Leave this place. Trust in the Light."*

I kept telling the voice, "Shut your mouth, I have to eat!"

᎙᎒᎙᎒᎙

I needed help. I was stressed out. The political climate at my office was getting more and more intense. I went for an astrology consultation. Astrology, the science that reveals the placement of the planets at the time of our birth, is one of the most revealing spiritual sciences known to humankind. The study of astrology dates back to the ancient African civilizations. However, it is not enough to know what sign you are born under, you must know what cosmic energies influence and impact you. Astrology reveals that type of information. It provides important guidance for understanding and confronting the most basic and vital issues of life. Each of the twelve astrological "houses" addresses a specific life issue everyone must face. The placement of the planets in a house at the time of your birth reveals your strengths and weaknesses in confronting those issues.

The astrologer I chose to see was also a Yoruba priest. He spent over three hours with me, breaking down and explaining the components of my astrological chart. I was born under the sign of Virgo, he told me, the sign of the mother, the hand of God. My moon was in Scorpio, the sign of the healer. My rising sign was Capricorn, the teacher and keeper of information. He told me that, based on my astrological chart, it was my destiny to learn about life through my relationships.

"You must learn to change the part of yourself that has been mortally wounded," he said. "Learn to let go of losses. Never let challenges get the best of you. Learn how to enjoy your life."

I asked him what my life's mission was, my purpose.

"You must study religion, metaphysics...things of the higher mind. You have come to life to teach and heal. Everything you need will be provided for you. God has a plan for your life. What else do you need to know?"

I had heard it all before. I knew every single word he was going to say to me before it came out of his mouth. Still, it made me feel better to hear someone else say it.

"Relax," he said. "In the right time and in the right way, you will be shown exactly what to do."

I knew that too.

I eventually did challenge the bar and they did find the one point. I never told anyone. I kept it to myself. I continued to work at the public defender's office while I was trying to figure out what to do and how to do it. One day I was pushed to make a decision.

I had been assigned to interview a client who was preparing for trial. He was accused of gouging out his brother-in-law's eye. The police found him with the eye in his hand, but they forgot to read him his rights when they arrested him. I was assigned to the case. With a little legal fancy footwork, a motion here and there, the man was about to be set free—with *my* help. I felt awful about it. It became crystal clear to me right then that the legal system was not about right and wrong. It was about following procedure and having a good lawyer.

I went back to the firm to submit the paperwork for the case. When I got to the door of my office, I noticed something strange.

It was two o'clock in the afternoon on a sunny day, but inside my office it was pitch black. I tried to turn the lights on. Nothing happened. I asked my secretary why my office had no lights. She walked to the door with me, flipped the switch, and said, "These lights work. What's wrong with them?"

A light came on in my head. The voice in my head said, *"Get out of this place. Trust in the Light!"*

I made my decision. I left and never returned.

᠅᠅᠅

In order for Black women to heal ourselves, there are four distinct things we must do. First, we must establish an individual relationship with God, Allah, the Creator, Yahweh—whatever we choose to call that energy. We must develop that relationship after our own independent investigation of truth. We cannot get to God based on something someone else has told us. We must each explore, examine, and discern the truth of the Creator within our own being. We cannot make God what we want Him or Her to be. We must know who or what God is for us and then live that truth as the guiding force and principle of our lives.

Second, we must learn how to develop and maintain a healthy, respectful, and loving relationship with our parents and ancestors. We must learn how to honor and respect the fact that, were it not for them, despite their human faults and failings, we would not be who we are today. Their blood runs through our veins. When we are ignorant of or at odds with our parents and ancestors, we cut off a vital piece of ourselves. Regardless of who they were, what they did or did not do in their lives, or what they did or did not do to or for us, we must learn to honor their energy within us.

Third, we must develop a relationship with our own heads. We must learn to trust and honor, as well as listen to and follow, the voice of our own spirits. We each have a divine mission and purpose, individual lessons to learn, a unique path to follow, and specific tasks to accomplish. Our spirit—our head, our inner voice—knows exactly what it is that we must do. Until we learn to follow that spirit, we cannot claim to be responsible for our lives or for the healing thereof.

Fourth, we must develop a healthy relationship with our clans—that is, the clan of Black women, the clan of Black people, and the clan of humanity. In that order. We cannot commit harm against a member of any of the clans to which we belong and not expect to experience repercussions. We cannot harbor ill thoughts or feelings toward or speak ill of a member of the clan, and expect not to be affected. In the universal scheme of things, there is only One Mind, One Heart, One Life. Whatever one part of the life does, all other parts of the life are affected.

We Black women must heal ourselves so the world can be healed. We must empower ourselves so the individuals of the world can collectively be empowered. We must nurture and love ourselves because love heals all wounds. Love is the driving force of the universe. It is all there is. The only thing that exists outside of love is fear.

You may ask: Am I singling out Black women and forgetting about all other women? Absolutely not! Like draws like. I am a member, first of all, of the clan of Black women. I must therefore concern myself with Black women first. Being a Black woman, however, a descendant of the primal mother, all other women are my daughters. As Black women heal, the daughters must heal, for a daughter is only a reflection of the mother. At this time, we must ask our daughters to give us the time, space, and the opportunity to heal. Remember, the fruit does not fall far from the tree.

You might also ask: Am I saying that the healing and

empowerment of Black women means the disempowerment of Black men? No. We need our men. We love our men. However, our men cannot be whole until we are whole. We are their mothers, wives, sisters, co-workers, the ones who raise them, cook for them, share with them, and bear their seed. What Black women need right now is for our men to assist us, support us, and give us time.

We want them to stop being suspicious of us and afraid of us. We want them to stop abusing us. We want Black men to recognize our weaknesses without blaming us. We want them to forgive us. We want them to respect us while they assist and support us in respecting and forgiving ourselves. We want them to talk to us and allow us to talk to them. We want them to protect us, provide for us, and give us the time and space we need to heal.

When we Black women stand up for ourselves and tell other Black women to stand up with us, we do not want our men to feel left out. We want them to applaud us, celebrate us, and share the victories of healing with us. When we slip, we want them to pick us up. When we fall, we want them to carry us. When we get weary and do not know what to do, we want them to take up the slack. Most of all, when the darkness of life falls around us, we want Black men to cry with us and share in the knowledge that the dawn is about to come.

Our men must be taught how to do these things. Some things they must learn on their own. Other things we will have to teach them. We cannot teach our men until we are fully confident in our ability to do what we need to do for ourselves.

Love and trust God, Black woman. Forgive yourself and everyone else. Trust your head. Respect nature and divine law. Know your purpose. Purify your intent. Make peace your priority. Let the healing begin.

ᐱᐧᐱᐧᐱ

I was writing, getting a few articles published here and there, and spending most of my time doing spiritual consultations. Every now and then, someone would ask me to do a workshop. I had attended so many, it was easy for me to develop my own using information specific to women and Black women in particular. My big break came when I wrote Susan Taylor, the editor-in-chief at Essence magazine, and she responded with interest in publishing my story. After that, things seemed to skyrocket. I began publishing and distributing my own newsletter focusing on Black women's spiritual issues. I was holding classes, teaching and training others about Yoruba culture and spirituality. I had my challenges, but for the most part things were going pretty well.

Still, whenever my bank account would get low, I would panic. I would start doubting and questioning God about whether I was doing the right thing. During one period, I was absolutely, completely, out of cash, with no prospects in sight. I couldn't pay my bills. The kids needed everything. My food supply was low. Even the cat was beginning to look worried. He would follow me around the house as if I had something to eat hidden away somewhere. One day, I was looking at him and he cocked his head to the side and licked his whiskers as if to say, "Look, I know you are undergoing a career change, but I really do need some Tender Vittles!" I stroked him and told him not to worry. But I did.

Your learning never stops. I don't care how much you know or what you have learned, every day you are provided with the opportunity to learn something new about yourself. The one thing I wish someone had told me as a child was how divine and unique I am. I never heard it when I was young, so it was difficult for me to accept and understand as an adult. As a result, when good things happened to me and for me in my life, I thought it was the exception rather than the rule. I did not know that goodness and divinity go hand in hand. If I had been taught that during my early years, I would not have experienced so much down-time as I grew and matured.

People seem to think that the higher up you go, in your career ladder or anything else, the more you know. This is true in one sense—you do develop a deeper understanding of certain things as you move to the top of your field—however, you also learn new things about those things you already know about. I had chosen the spiritual path. My job, my calling, my profession, was to learn about faith. I thought I had it down pat, but I was mistaken.

᭡᭡᭡

I got up early one morning specifically to worry. I was praying hard, asking God to send me a sign that I had not quit my job in vain, and that S/He had simply been off on vacation somewhere and hadn't known that my children, the cat, and I were about to starve to death.

The radio was on. The morning deejay was interviewing Barry White, the singer. I was coming down the stairs, praying and pleading for a sign. As I reached the bottom of the stairs, I heard Barry White, in his deep, resonant voice, say: "You gotta have faith! You've got to be willing to take the ups and the downs. You've got to be willing to do it for free. You cannot do it just for the money. If you have faith and determination, along with the ability, you will make it! You've *got* to make it!"

I lifted my eyes to the ceiling and said, "Thank You, God! Thank You for that sign!"

I was fine until the mail came.

Every bill I owed came in the mail that day. Bills are what I call "faith shakers." The sight of all those beautiful, multicolored envelopes shook my faith that day like they had so many times before. I was afraid to look. I was afraid not to look. I thumbed through the mail looking for a sign of something that contained any kind of currency. In my search, I came across a small envelope addressed to "Dear Occupant." I figured that this could not be anyone who wanted money, so I opened it.

On the inside of that envelope was a small pamphlet. Inside that pamphlet was a poem that has been my guiding light and source of inspiration ever since. I share it with you now and encourage you to use it as I have on your own journey to healing, the undertaking of which I leave you to attend to now:

When you come to the end of all the light that you know
And you are about to step off into the darkness,
Faith is knowing that one of two things will happen:
There will be something solid in the darkness
For you to stand on,
Or you will be taught how to fly!

—Poem by Etty Hillason

Four years and four books later, I encourage you to join me in flight. Have faith, and I'll see *you* among the stars!

Also by Iyanla Vanzant

Tapping the Power Within:
A Path to Self-Empowerment for Black Women

423

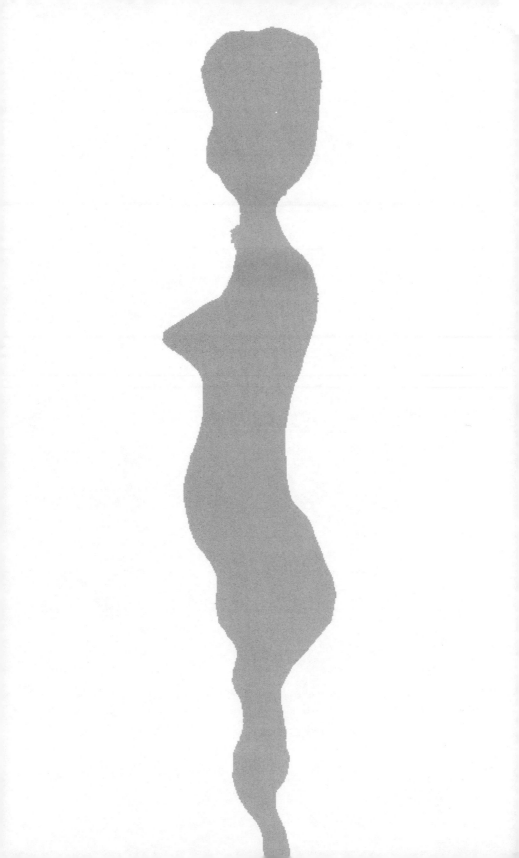

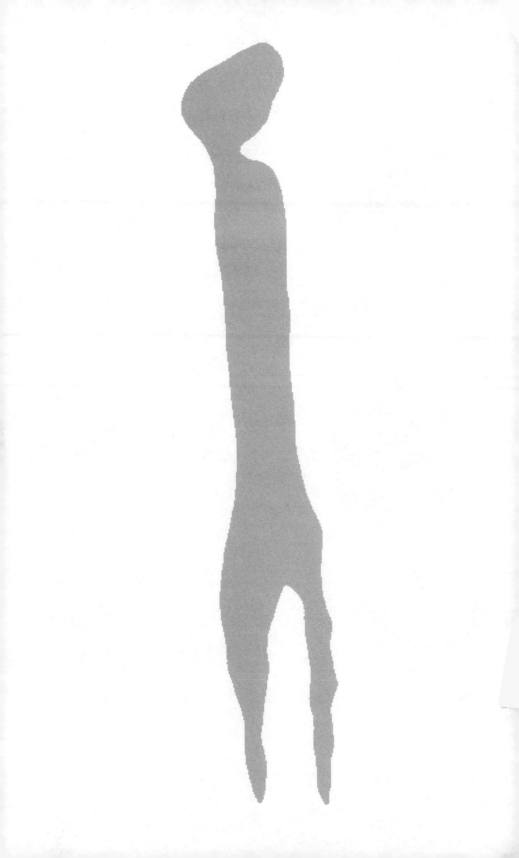

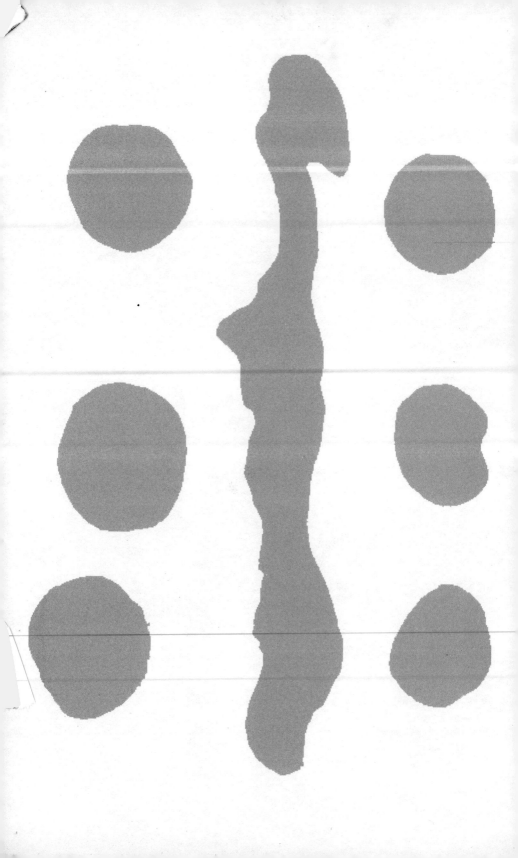